A History of Trinity Fields

A Sporting Oasis

Graham R Jackson

ISBN 978-1-9196172-0-6

Printed in Great Britain by
Aquatint-CHP Ltd
Units 3&4 Elm Grove Industrial Estate
Elm Grove
Wimbledon
London SW19 4HE

www.aquatint.co.uk

About the Author

Graham R Jackson was born in Balham in 1952 and was educated firstly at Swaffield Primary School (subsequently attended by boxing legend Frank Bruno) and secondly at Sir Walter St John's Grammar School Battersea between 1963 and 1970 and currently lives in Sutton. A former President of the Sir Walter St John's Old Boys Association (Sinjuns), he served as a trustee on the Trinity Fields Trust from 1997 until 2014.

With an involvement in cricket administration at both club and league level since 1974, he has been a cricket umpire for over fifty years and a member of the Surrey Championship Umpires Panel since its inception. He was one of the first recipients in 2009 of an OSCA award from Surrey County Cricket Club for services to Leagues & Boards. He also stands with well-known wandering sides including the Free Foresters and the Cricket Society. In 2019 he officiated in the National Final of the Cricketer Trophy. Currently Chairman of the Ground & Facilities Sub Committee on the Surrey Championship, in 2020 he was made an Honorary Vice President of the Club Cricket Conference for his contribution to amateur cricket.

A History of Trinity Fields

Contents

Foreword by Amol Rajan

Foreword

I can remember as if it were yesterday the moment that Graham 'Jacko' Jackson said, in the cramped living room of my house on Lessingham Avenue in Tooting, that he would personally stump up £20 of the £40 required for me to attend a cricket course at Chestnut Grove School in Balham. If I close my eyes now, I really can see the moment that Jacko took out a £20 note, and put it on the table between him and my dad, adding that Sinjuns was serious about developing young talent, and they thought I had something about me.

The rest, as they say, is history.

Graham- as I shall call him henceforth, despite the universal and affectionate appeal of his nickname, 'Jacko' - changed my life. Besotted with leg-spin, he propelled me on a path that would lead to a lifelong obsession. I won Player of the Course. I joined the Sinjuns colts and would play every summer Saturday and Sunday for the next seven years. This is all, of course, a polite way of saying that Graham influenced my childhood. I was wholly determined to play for England, an ambition that my parents discouraged with increasing severity as my fatal lack of talent became ever clearer. But for those long and glorious summer days at this remarkable sports ground, I will forever be in Graham's debt.

Which is what made reading this book, and writing this Foreword, such an honour. I found the pages that follow to be riveting. They are full of vital, intricate details showing the depth of Graham's scholarship and research. They added huge depth and understanding to the sports field that I have such sepia-tinged memories of. And in two important ways, these pages really surprised me too.

First, the sheer interconnectedness of the ground and the area around it captivated me. For instance, I discovered that it was the expansion of Clapham Junction which indirectly aroused the School's interest in this particular patch of earth. Graham writes that in the final quarter of the nineteenth century, that station a few miles away, which would become one of Europe's busiest terminals, was expanding so fast that the South Western Railway Company purchased land that was then formerly part of Battersea Grammar School. This pressure on space forced both schools to look for a playing field. Thus, were two of my childhood obsessions, railways and cricket, connected, where I spent so much time as a child, the playing field and Clapham Junction station.

The second revelation, or rather set of revelations, concerns the sheer number of frankly fascinating characters who have 'graced' this Field. Please forgive the pun: I am ashamed to say that in all my years playing at Sinjuns, I had no idea, until reading this book, that none other than W. G. Grace had played there. If I also told you that, based on his deep research, Graham raises the fact that George Lohmann, the bowler with the lowest average of any Test player with more than fifteen wickets, also certainly played there. Again, I had no idea. There are countless other dazzling characters who appear in the pages that follow, but I won't give them away.

Such revelations mean this book makes a very significant contribution to our understanding of South London. Graham has shown that cricket cannot be fully understood unless set within the historic context and social whirl of the times in which it is played. It follows that his book is as much a social history as a sporting one, and all the better for that.

Being of a different generation to Graham, I am not an Old Sinjun in the sense that he is; though the school I went to, Graveney, does have its roots in the school founded by Sir Walter St John. But I am very much an Old Sinjun in a prouder sense: someone with a deep attachment to this sacred patch, and a romantic yet firm belief that it deserves to be protected and treasured. Only by understanding its history can we recognise its true value. And anyone who wants to do that now owes, as I have long owed, a tremendous debt to Graham 'Jacko' Jackson.

Amol Rajan

May 2021

Research & Discovery

There are known knowns. There are things we know that we know. We also know there are known unknowns. That is to say, there are some things we do not know. But there are also unknown unknowns. There are things we don't know we don't know. It is the latter category that tends to be the difficult ones.

Donald Rumsfeld (1932 -2021)

In some respect this account of the History of Trinity Fields was started almost by accident. When I was asked by the Trinity Fields Trust to come up with a few 'bullet points' on the Field's history for display on the walls inside the Burntwood Lane pavilion, the latent desire to learn more about its past took over. That was over three years ago. I am not a historian, politician or academic, for that matter, but what follows is more of an overview, giving an interesting and fascinating insight into local social history and the influence that individuals and amateur clubs have had along the way with Trinity Fields as the centre of my research. What is clear now, beyond expectations, is the leading role that the Field played in the early years of amateur sport in providing a background from which many clubs have gone on to grace on a wider stage, and others which, sadly, did not! Having attended Sir Walter St John's Grammar School between 1963 and 1970 and subsequently with the Old Sinjuns Sports Club, I had the opportunity to play at the Field. I was not known as 'Teflon', with my loose impersonation of a goalkeeper for nothing, although I would like to think my cricket umpiring was a little better! In a sense this account is in many ways an equivalent comparison to the television series, *Who Do You Think You Are?* as it goes back to what is regarded as the birth of the ground as a playing field and prior to that how and why it was created as a field in the first place. However, some findings by careful research of back issues of various newspapers reveal some facts in direct contradiction to previously accepted knowns. As I soon discovered also, there is a lot of factoid on the internet. It is not designed necessarily to deceive, but at the time it was regarded as a genuine attempt to report the facts as they were perceived. My intention is to put the record straight where I can, and where not, to suggest a reasonable interpretation of events.

Without the Field, of course, none of the following would have been possible. For the purposes of this book and the recent history of the immediate area, references in this document to the *Surrey Tavern* refer to the building on the corner of Bellevue Road and Trinity Road immediately opposite the Field. This establishment was synonymous with the Field in its early days but it was eventually a casualty of changing social trends and habits which continue until today with the ongoing closure of public houses. It has survived since by reinventing itself on at least two separate occasions. Additionally, because the main entrance to the premises has also changed, so has the address, from 226 Trinity Road to 35 Bellevue Road. It is currently home to 'Brinkley's Kitchen', which is certainly an improvement on the pub that it was, when it closed its doors in 2005, and describes itself today as being situated on Wandsworth Common as 'a large contemporary restaurant'. The conversion has been sympathetically carried out, with the high ceilings of the original Victorian pub still apparent. However, it is not a place where you would routinely entertain visiting cricket or even football sides after a match, which the former pub had done in times gone by. Today the area around Bellevue Road on the edge of Wandsworth Common is far more 'gentrified' than it was but it still retains an almost village atmosphere if walking up Bellevue Road from Wandsworth Common station to give a flavour of the area before the start of the twentieth century.

A History of Trinity Fields

From a sport perspective this book started off essentially to explore the cricketing history of the Field which was well known, and to a degree it remains so, but it soon became evident that in its early days the Field played host to a number of well- known football and rugby clubs which, for them, was their 'home' ground, which have helped shape the future of both sports and arguably have had far more influence over the future of amateur sport as we know it today. The Field has a truly remarkable past which should be celebrated. I have also touched upon other sports which at various times also participated in the Field's rich history of amateur sport. So, like thousands before and after me, mostly with a minimum of sporting ability, we have enjoyed the use of a playing field which has slowly given up its secrets. The eight acres in question, today situated firmly within the London Borough of Wandsworth in South West London, was not always regarded as an urban ground as at the start it was situated in open countryside until the suburban sprawl of an expanding London engulfed the area. However, Wandsworth Common nearby gives a clue as to how it has managed to survive as a playing field when many other areas intended for the same purpose have perished.

In much the same way as the *Surrey Tavern*, neither Sir Walter St John's Grammar School nor Battersea Grammar School exist today, although both buildings are still used for educational purposes by other institutions. Both schools fell victim to the state reorganisation of education prompted in part by the decrease in population within Inner London and the move at the time against selective education. It is not the intention of this account to discuss the rights or wrongs of those decisions, which were taken almost in the spirit of the way that Beeching had dealt with the railways during the 1960s. However, it is important to add that none of the Field's post Great War history would have been the same without Sir Walter St John founding of a School back in 1700. Although this date is accepted as the year of the school's establishment, Sir Walter St John had succeeded to the baronetcy and estates as long ago as 1656, and there is good reason to believe that the existence of the original schoolhouse that was to become Sir Walter St John's School originates approximately from this time for the 'Education of Twenty Free Scholars in Battersea'. During his life he divided most of his time between the family's country seat at Lydiard House near Swindon - he was, for a time, MP for Wootton Bassett & Wiltshire - and his manor house at Battersea. He died in 1708 at the age of 86. From 1918 until 1992 the Field was owned by the Sir Walter St John's Schools Trust. Indeed, and owing to some tenuous school related connections, it was wholly appropriate that when the opportunity arose to purchase the Field, it was taken, and that it become an important part of the school life. In May 1909, for instance, Old Sinjuns arranged a cycle run to the Kent village of Farnborough 'leaving the corner of Trinity Road and Burntwood Lane at 3.15pm'. This was an interesting coincidence, as the members involved in this event probably watched the cricket being played on the Field before the start of their cycle run, and would have certainly not imagined at the time that the Schools' Trust would effectively purchase it less than nine years later. After 1992 when both schools had closed, the Trust transformed itself into an Educational Charity bearing a similar name, but with no ongoing connection to the schools as we shall learn later. This account proves that, however much we think of history being consistent and unchanging over the years, it is far more dynamic than we think!

Prior to the school's ownership, it was the Heathfield Cricket Club which played an important part in the ground's consolidation and development as a playing field from its earlier days until 1924, and the club's sustained presence was important for the continuity of the Field. At the turn of the century the club was renamed to incorporate the lawn tennis section and shortly afterwards renamed again having introduced bowls to the Field. In 1904, it again renamed itself from the unwieldy 'Heathfield Cricket, Lawn Tennis & Bowling Club', to become, simply, 'The Heathfield club'. Chronologically, I will try my best to reflect that distinction in the account that follows.

Although, the involvement of the Heathfield club in the Field's history was known, together with the terms of the original covenant in 1852, and its purchase by the Schools Trust in 1918, very little else was known about the identity and involvement of the football and rugby clubs that used the Field during the winter. The problem is that when it comes to history, there is so much of it, and by definition it grows larger day by day.

Whilst no history about a playing field can ignore the sport played on it, if there is a bias towards any sport, it is cricket, but only because it is the one sport that has probably been played constantly at the Field throughout virtually every summer during almost a hundred and fifty years of its history - and that includes two world wars. There have also been considerably more international cricketers who have played at the Field than both international football and rugby footballers combined. Although I have managed to retrieve many more results than I thought possible from various sources, including newspaper archives, I have been economical with providing specific results season upon season for two reasons. Firstly, to do so would convert this account into a rather tedious and mundane document and secondly because, despite considerable research, it is quite clear that in many cases results, particularly on the cricket side, have gone unreported and have disappeared forever into the mists of time. To provide incomplete sets of results for individual seasons would damage the integrity of any list. I have also concentrated, in general in the Appendices on matches played at the Field.

History has been unkind to all sorts of famous sporting venues. Various grounds have succumbed to all sorts of misfortunes over the years. Some have fallen prey to property developers as towns and cities expanded, as witnessed by the demolition of the Central Ground at Priory Meadow, once the grand home of cricket in Hastings, to make way for a shopping centre in 1994. Other disasters include the sudden disappearance of part of the outfield (probably owing to limestone workings underneath) which did for the Dudley Cricket Ground on one morning in 1985. On the football side, White Hart Lane (Tottenham Hotspur), Upton Park (West Ham United) and Highbury (Arsenal) are more recent casualties, although in these cases this has been more driven by the financial considerations of running professional sport rather than just playing amateur sport for fun. In addition, far more grounds have just simply closed owing to the cost of upkeep and maintenance owing to the declining numbers of players participating in classical recreational sport, and the bewildering number of gyms or sports centres that are available all year long which have further diluted the need to support summer or winter sports in recent years. History has little respect for age or tradition. It is only very occasionally that a cricket ground is revived, such as Sheffield Park was in 2009. This historic ground is owned by the National Trust and home to the Armadillos Cricket Club, but, even then, it would be hard to imagine the touring Australians playing there again to a crowd estimated at 25,000 as happened in 1896.

The Field has had various owners and users over the years. Based partly on forgotten minute books and documents, found almost accidentally in a store cupboard at Heathfield Bowls Club, combined with other documentary evidence at the time, I have been able to bring back to life a far more comprehensive account of the Heathfield club which for the first fifty years of its existence, with cricket to the fore, was one of the leading and most influential cricket clubs in London. This information has also assisted in understanding the Field's history also as well. What we know now is how the club was involved in the 'Golden Age of Cricket' and how amateur sport was far better followed in those days, and its subsequent decline. This should not be taken, in any way, as a slight against the two 'Old Boys' clubs when club cricket was effectively reintroduced to the Field after a gap of almost twenty-five years after the end of the second world war. it is just that by then, given the social changes that had occurred, that spectator attendance of amateur cricket had largely disappeared. Another club central to the Field's story is Clapham Rovers, but more of that later. By reference principally to archival material in the London Metropolitan Archives, it is also a story of how rivalry between two 'sister' schools literally and physically divided the Field, and how eventually that situation, largely out of necessity, was reconciled. Suffice to say, there is often more politics in sport than politics! So, in this account, to avoid confusion, the former Old Grammarians pavilion and clubroom is referred to as the 'Burntwood Lane pavilion', even though, paradoxically, apart from walking the length of the Field from Trinity Road, the only entrance to it today is from a short flight of concrete steps in Beechcroft Road!

It should be said that the chapters involving the Heathfield club and the purchase of the Field by the schools' chronologically overlap. This is deliberate, because for six years both coexisted in an uneasy alliance on which to play their cricket until the Heathfield club's lease ran out in 1924. Also separated in this account under the 'Football Years' are the clubs that used the Field predominantly during the winter before and during the Heathfield club's tenure. However, it is the cricket club's name that has left its mark. The ground was commonly referred to as 'Heathfield' or as on some maps at the time, 'Heathfield club'. What, perhaps, is surprising is that the name stuck around for so long afterwards, even on maps, when the Heathfield club had clearly left the Field years earlier. In 1935, for instance, a report of a football match between Sir Walter St John's School and St Marks and St Johns College (Marjons) states that 'good football was served up at Heathfield' even though the club in question had vacated the ground more than ten years previously. A 1932 map actually identified the Field as the 'London Public Schools Sports Ground' and whilst both were indeed effectively public schools at the time, it was only ever owned at that stage by the Sir Walter St John's Schools Trust, and not generally by any other school or organisation. Years later the Field was referred to generally in Old Sinjuns Cricket Club fixture cards as 'Heathfield, Sir Walter St John's Playing Field' which can be said to have been a compromise, but inside the fixture card all home matches were referred to as 'Heathfield' and that was even the case in 2006 when the first, and perhaps possibly the last, fixture card of the newly merged SinjunGrammarians Cricket Club was printed before all fixtures went 'on line'. After that and until 2009, in Surrey Championship Yearbooks, it strangely morphed into 'Heathfields' until being replaced by 'Trinity Fields', in 2010. Although the name disappeared for a few years, in 2020, remarkably, it resurfaced on 'Play-Cricket' in relation to being the location for 3rd XI and 4th XI fixtures. Whilst the address of Trinity Fields for 1st XI and 2nd XI matches is 209 Trinity Road SW17 7HW, 'Heathfields' (at the other end of the Field) is 238 Beechcroft Road SW17 7DP (although, if satellite maps are to be believed, it should today really be 242 Beechcroft Road). Uniquely, having two addresses and postcodes for the same field bears testament to the time of its division between 1925 and 1949. The fact is that some visiting sides, when the Heathfield Club were tenants, tended to identify the Beechcroft Road end as 'Upper Tooting' and even today some sides turn up at the wrong end of the Field to play cricket or football as they have done so for more than a century! During the intervening period after its purchase, presumably in remembrance of Samuel Cresswell, the term 'The Cresswell Ground' must have been used in council circles, as it is stated in brackets after 'Sir Walter St. John's Playing Field' in an agreement with ILEA in 1966. This was obviously an acknowledgement to the man who not only was the driving force in securing the Field for the schools, but also did so much for the local community in Wandsworth. Initially, Battersea Grammar School called the Field 'Heathfield' but with their school having been relocated, the Old Grammarians just called the Field 'Burntwood Lane'. It will be interesting to see that when the Trinity Fields Trust lease runs out in 2067 whether anyone will remember the name of the of the Trust that acquired the Field in 1918, and indeed also the Heathfield club that played there at that time. For a ground that started off without a name to have so many over the years (and more) is something of an achievement!

The fact is, Trinity Fields is a true survivor. It has escaped some very real and varied threats to its existence especially in the early years, when the Field passed from one owner to another, each with their own agenda. It is also a testament, particularly from the time of Samuel Cresswell, whose legacy lived on well after his passing, to ensure that the sporting opportunities presented by the Field were carefully preserved, protected and nurtured for the use and benefit of others in the years to come. Something which is as relevant today as it was then.

A Field with no Name (1852-1882)

You have to know the past to understand the present.

Carl Sagan (1934-96)

Early Days

Early accounts of the Field's location within the manor of Wandsworth are enshrined in history. Before the Conquest of 1066, it is likely that firstly Edward the Confessor and then Harold II appear to have been landlords. In 1086, Wandsworth Common is referred to in the Domesday Book as the common land of the Manor of Battersea and Wandsworth and perhaps unsurprisingly, as Battersea West Heath and Wandsworth East Heath with the Field in the latter. Sometime later, ownership of this area passed to Westminster Abbey. This ended with the Dissolution of the Monasteries in 1540 when the lands reverted to the Crown. In 1627, Sir Oliver St John (a cousin of Sir Walter St John) whose ancestors had come over with the Conqueror, bought the manor of Wandsworth and Battersea from the Crown for £4,050. Upon his death, the estate passed to Sir Walter St John's cousin William Villiers, but essentially remained in the St John family until 1763, when in order to settle debts, it was sold and bought in Trust for John Viscount Spencer. Although nowadays the present Earl Spencer as 'Lord of the Manor' has only nominal powers – he is only responsible for authorising and appointing the Vicar of Battersea – in those days, and for at least a further hundred years after he acquired Wandsworth Common, he imposed, it could be said, an almost feudal grip on the area for his own benefit.

Originally the area known as Wandsworth Common was far larger than it is today and consisted of heathland, gorse bushes and scrub interspersed with the occasional isolated manor house, villa, or farm, with views towards and in some cases across the Thames to the north. It was essentially open countryside, and by all accounts it was a windswept and 'wild' place extending from East Hill in the north, and southwards to and beyond Burntwood Lane and Bellevue Road, which runs west to east across the Common. Although Burntwood Lane predates the Field by more than a century, as it is mentioned on a John Rocque map of 1746, it was not until 1832 that maps begin to show the Field in essentially its present form shortly after Burntwood Lane, which links Wandsworth Common with Garratt Lane, had been consolidated into a proper, and using the word loosely, 'thoroughfare', between the latter and, via Nightingale Lane, effectively linking it with Clapham Common. At that stage the Field was still essentially part of Wandsworth Common. Some reports of Burntwood Lane describe it as a 'drove' road used principally for the movement of cattle and sheep between Wandsworth Common and Garratt Green. On the other sides, the Field was delineated by what is now Trinity Road and Beechcroft Road, the latter hardly not much more than a track, and in its early days to the south, separated by fields from Wandsworth Lodge.

Wandsworth Common itself however was regarded less favourably than Clapham Common and between 1794 and 1866 there were no fewer than fifty-three enclosures depriving it of around 50% of its original area. For a brief period from 1839, Wandsworth Common was managed on a similar basis to Clapham Common with five lessees, including Henry McKellar at Wandsworth Lodge, nearby. However, these arrangements were terminated in 1851 and by the mid-1860s the improvements made during that time were no longer evident. A combination of enclosures and excessive gravel digging had drastically reduced the Common's size and the quality of the surviving land, which was often waterlogged during the winter. The Common by then, as a result, was little used for grazing. All but one of the public footpaths had been stopped up and an area formerly used as a cricket ground (not the Field it seems) had become useless. On the southern edge, and technically beyond the Common was Wandsworth Lodge, which had been home to Henry McKellar since around 1836. The main access to this building was directly off Trinity Road in the vicinity of where Crockerton Road is today. It was a large estate with Wandsworth Lodge as its centrepiece, a luxurious residence with extensive grounds, lawns, outdoor pool, a fountain and a driveway, with the estate itself consisting principally of fields and orchards. Its area was expanded over time (sometimes allegedly without proper authority) by enclosing sections of the Common into the estate. McKellar claimed that his 'enclosures' as they were called, were necessary because gypsies on the Common endangered his property but according to an opponent 'he rather encouraged these encampments by giving the gypsies beer, and then made it an excuse for his enclosures.' By the time of McKellar's death in 1862, the Wandsworth Lodge Estate extended to around 143 acres, straddling the parish boundaries of Wandsworth and Streatham. Indeed, the old parish boundary effectively ran along the route of the dividing garden fence between Crockerton Road and, for the most part, Brenda Road as it is today.

During this time Henry McKellar had also been steadily and assiduously increasing his influence by enclosing an area between 1848 and 1856 that became known as 'McKellar's Triangle' which was neatly bounded by what is now Bellevue Road, Trinity Road and St. James Drive. However, during this period, McKellar had turned his attention to another 'piece of land' he wished to enclose, which was the Field itself. At the time, although Burntwood Lane and Trinity Road effectively limited its extent, it was still open common but on 20 September 1852 it was conveyed to him by Earl Spencer for the sum of £180 subject to the following covenants that;

i) *The said land should be forthwith enclosed and be used as arable pasture or market garden only, and that*

ii) *In the meantime, no building whatsoever shall be erected or built on the said premises by Henry McKellar his heirs or assigns to use the land otherwise.*

If buildings were erected without such licence or permission, a right of re-entry was given to Earl Spencer. These covenants made between Earl Spencer and Henry McKellar at that time, have since formed the cornerstone for maintaining the status of ground over the generations. From now on, in this document, the 'ground' will be generally referred to as the 'Field' to reflect the fact that from 1852 it was now enclosed, and by doing so, its status had changed from common land to 'field' forever. It is only speculation as to why Earl Spencer imposed a covenant on the Field. However, with McKellar's unreliable record of not entirely keeping his promises on land that he had unilaterally enclosed, perhaps Spencer had grown wary of the way the Common had been managed and maintained over the last few years by his lessees, or maybe he used the sale to supplement his income, or to preserve the area in an acceptable condition to demonstrate that he did care in some way about the wellbeing of the Common. Whilst we shall never know, as users of the Field, we can only be grateful that the 1852 covenant has been the foundation to its survival and that sometime later the phrase 'arable pasture or market garden' enabled it to became the sports field that it is today. After its enclosure, the Field would have invariably been, in some way, fenced off and cleared of gorse and scrub, but one thing was now clear- it would now be distinctly different to the Common nearby. Effectively, it would become Henry McKellar's paddock or perhaps his back garden!

A Field with no Name (1852-1882)

By consulting an 1864 map it is easier to understand exactly why Henry McKellar purchased the 'piece of land'. Perhaps he was influenced by having already enclosed the land to the south from where Brodrick Road is now situated down towards Wandsworth Lodge on the westside of Trinity Road, although, apart from the Field, this particular area was actually strictly outside the demise of Wandsworth Common. More likely he was eager to prevent the owners of Burntwood Lodge or Burntwood Grange on the other side of Burntwood Lane encroaching on what he regarded to be his domain. At the time, trees were beginning to be introduced onto the Common and the area from Wandsworth Lodge up to and including the Field would be tree lined around its whole perimeter with Trinity Road to the east, Burntwood Lane to the north and Beechcroft Road to the west and, of course, Wandsworth Lodge to the south. This all made for an agreeable environment in which Wandsworth Lodge was situated. However, it was perhaps fortunate for the Field that McKellar's priorities appeared to lay elsewhere.

Henry McKellar was most likely of Scottish descent and seemingly quite an entrepreneur in his time. He was the son of Duncan McKellar who ran his own tailoring business in Old Burlington Street nearby to Bond Street in London. In 1827 in India, he married Ann Gibson (nee Moir) who was born in Madras in 1801 probably also of Scottish extraction, and had lost her previous husband George Thomas Gibson in Calcutta in 1826. Ann's father-in-law Robert Gibson who had died four years previously, was born in Slains, Aberdeenshire. As was often the custom in those days George Thomas Gibson and his wife Ann had a daughter who was also, rather confusingly, named Ann. She was to return with McKellar to Wandsworth Lodge having been adopted by Henry McKellar at the age of five after his marriage to Ann in 1827. The records are incomplete, but suggest that George Thomas Gibson had been married to Margaret Moir, who was probably either Ann's elder sister (or even mother!), before her death in 1813 and his marriage to Ann in 1816. It would seem that there had been a connection between Henry McKellar and Ann's previous husband because, at least initially, McKellar carried on with his father's tailoring business but by the time of his own death in 1862, one of his interests was with tailors Gibson & Co. However, McKellar was first and foremost a businessman in his own right involved in local projects as well as other interests further afield although not always did his involvement bring the dividends it might have done.

In 1845, McKellar became involved in the project to erect the original Chelsea Bridge. For various reasons construction of the bridge was delayed. Initially called the Victoria Bridge it did not open until 1858. However, concerns were soon raised about its safety and the tolls imposed to cross the bridge were unpopular. By 1861, the bridge had been strengthened but with concerns by the government that it did not want to risk a potential collapse to be associated with the monarch, the name of the bridge was changed to Chelsea Bridge. Another project McKellar was involved with by 1860 was The Westminster Chambers Co, which was a building in Victoria Street. However, despite these projects it appears that Henry McKellar's main interest was to be involved with mining in North Wales, so it is quite likely that he spent much of his time there. One of these interests was the Sygun Copper Mine. This was a serious business. In 1836 the annual production of ore from the mine was valued at £2,800. In 1840, David White Griffith, the owner of the whole Sygun Estate which accounted for over 1,300 acres (just over 2 square miles) of land, situated near Beddgelert, had raised a loan of £3,000 from Lord Redesdale, a liberal peer and parliamentarian on the security of the land and a further £1,000 from Charles Wing, who was then joint lessee of the Sygun Copper Mine. In 1841, always the opportunist, McKellar bought out his partner, Charles Wing, and became manager of the mine taking over the £1,000 loan from Charles Wing and advancing it with a further £250 loan from his own money. By 1848, Griffith owed McKellar £1,890, so in 1849, McKellar took over all the profits from the Estate, with which he paid the interest due to Lord Redesdale each year, adding any or keeping the balance remaining. Griffith was loath to lose his property but in 1853 he was forced to make a deed of conveyance for the whole of the Sygun Estate to Henry McKellar, subject to the existing first mortgage, for a purchase price of £2,403, the sum by which Griffith was now indebted to him. McKellar continued to pay interest to Lord Redesdale until 1859, but in 1860, McKellar's brother redeemed the mortgage for him. Looking at records it would appear that the buildings at Sygun Fawr urgently needed repairing and extending, but perhaps Henry McKellar's local interests in London had left him vulnerable. Could this have been a reason for his brother paying off his debt, and in so doing, securing the mine for the family? However, in 1861 with McKellar apparently living at 'Sygun Fawr' farm, he was made High Sheriff of Caernarvonshire; not bad for someone that was also listed as a member of the Upper Tooting gentry at that time! When McKellar died at Wandsworth Lodge a year later, around two to three thousand tons of ore had already been extracted from the mine. He left the entire estate to his wife Ann who inherited around £60,000, a fortune in those days, and worth over £7 million in today's money.

In 1863, when the Wandsworth Lodge Estate was put up for sale, it was divided into nineteen lots of which one was the house itself, and another would have been the Field. However, interestingly only six lots were originally sold at auction with the others being left unsold. It was recorded in *The Times*, in terms of acreage that, only 59 of the original 143 acres were sold at that stage. Further adjacent lots it appears were sold privately and indeed development of the surrounding area was rapid, enabling Ann McKellar to downsize to Richmond Lodge, a more modest property in Telford Avenue, Streatham Hill, to live out her days in comfortable retirement. However, she kept the Sygun Estate in North Wales and perhaps also the Field. The mine in particular would have been quite an undertaking for a woman to administer, and it must be assumed that she would have maintained a staff to carry on locally working the ore. She retained the Sygun Estate until her death in 1886 at the age of 85. Ann's daughter, Ann Gibson, by her mother's first marriage to George Thomas Gibson had sadly died in 1875, and as Ann McKellar's marriage to Henry McKellar, had apparently not produced any heirs, she willed the Sygun Estate to her son in law, Samuel Wix, who was already at an advanced age of 71. However, was this the same Samuel Wix who had sent a letter of support on the death of his father, Charles, to the Vicar of Battersea in 1845, who was by default in those days, also the headmaster of the Sir Walter St. John's School, with the following directions? *'It is the wish of my late Father's Exors that the annual Income arising from this sum should be applied towards the clothing and fitting out of such poor boys as may from time to time be apprenticed from the Battersea School out of the Fund bequeathed and in accordance with the provisions contained in the Will of the late Sir Walter and that the application of such income be in every respect under the control of the same parties as for the time being may have the management and control of the Funds bequeathed by the late Sir Walter St John.'* This was known by the School as 'The Wix Benefaction'.

It seems quite plausible that although Ann McKellar had little use for the Field after her retirement it perhaps remained unsold within her ownership because without being able to be developed, it was regarded more as a liability than an asset - a problem that would surface from time to time during the course of the Field's history. Assuming Samuel Wix did inherit the Field at the time of her death, although there is no actual specific mention of it in Ann McKellar's will, he lived some way distant in Tonbridge and it would have been unrealistic for him to keep the Field anyway, even if it was in his power to do so. In 1889 he started selling off the farms and the mine he had inherited on the Sygun Estate in Wales, a good source of income for a man of his age. Samuel Wix died in 1898. Described as a solicitor during his working life, his four sons survived him. His eldest son Arthur McKellar Wix emigrated to New Zealand where he married and briefly between 1873 and 1875 played 'first - class' cricket for Nelson in the formative years of their involvement in cricket. Some years later, with his wife, Arthur McKellar Wix returned to Britain and died in the Holloway Sanitorium, Virginia Water in

1918. However, it was his three younger brothers that had inherited Samuel Wix's fortune in 1898, worth over £25 million in today's money.

The story about the Sygun mine does not quite end there. Copper mining continued and by 1898, the Elmore brothers Frank and Stanley who by then owned the mine with their father, invented the 'Flotation Process' by which, using oil and water to extract minerals, increased the rate at which copper could be extracted from the ore. This hastened the end, and the mine was shut down in 1903 when further working of the veins became unprofitable. Some eighty years later, in 1983 the entrance to the mine was reopened and restoration work began in earnest in 1986. Hundreds of tons of rubble were removed and access was improved. Today the mine is a leading attraction and has since been further upgraded. It is a winner of the Prince of Wales award for tourism, and today is one of the 'Wonders of Wales'.

Common or Not?

When the Wandsworth Lodge estate was split up in 1863, the lands that Henry McKellar had enclosed in the vicinity of Brodrick Road and the McKellar's Triangle were acquired either by the National Freehold Land Society or the British Land Company to form a new estate. Although some were a little larger to enhance the local district, the plots were generally quite small and were only as big as was required to give the new owners the right to vote.

The speed and scale of these developments for building on what was previously common land, alarmed local people who were galvanised into action. As one of the campaigners, John Buckmaster, later put it referring to the Common that, 'land-grabbers and jerry-builders would soon have joined hands on the last square foot of turf'. Initially, neither a petition to Earl Spencer in 1863 nor appeals to the Metropolitan Board of Works in 1868 were successful; indeed, the latter organisation indicated that if it took over the Common it would sell more of it for building in order to defray the cost of keeping it in its present form! In 1869, Buckmaster led about two thousand people in breaking down fences on part of the Common where Chivalry Road now stands. His contribution to saving the Common is remembered today in an adjacent road bearing his name. A committee was formed to contest Earl Spencer's claim to absolute ownership of the Common. Meetings about Wandsworth Common were held locally and as far afield as the Mansion House in London. Eventually, perhaps influenced by negotiations over Wimbledon Common, which also fell within Earl Spencer's jurisdiction, he agreed to a meeting with two members of the committee. At that meeting he apparently thought his income from the Common amounted to around £500 a year and that he was entitled to the annual receipt of that sum if he parted with his rights. The committee maintained it should be less than this, as the Common was wanted for public purposes, and eventually an annual annuity of £250, was agreed with the understanding that Earl Spencer be allowed to reserve for himself the area known as the 'Black Sea' (modern day Spencer Park) which included a lake which was subsequently filled in. The result was that The Wandsworth Common Act passed through Parliament in July 1871 with only minor amendments. Eight conservators were elected, three nominated by official bodies and five by the ratepayers, which safeguarded the area of Common not yet enclosed for future generations. However, the damage was already done. Apart from part of an area originally leased to the Royal Patriotic Building which was returned to the Common in 1913 as the 'Wandsworth Common Extension', eventually providing much needed sports facilities, other enclosures such as the rather confusingly named Allfarthing Piece which had been enclosed around a century earlier were never returned to the Common but were not fully developed until almost thirty years after the Act became law. Known as the 'Toast Rack' because of its grid like structure, one of its residents was David Lloyd George (until 1907), later Prime Minister between 1916 and 1922. In 1887 the freehold of Wandsworth Common was transferred to the Metropolitan Board of Works, the same organisation that had almost twenty years earlier regarded the Common as a liability, and only less than two years later, under the local government reorganisation, Wandsworth was transferred from Surrey, and incorporated into the new London County Council. Although the Common itself was protected, this paved the way for the general expansion of London going forward.

As for the Field, technically, it was not subjected to its protection, because of the original 1852 covenant and so the Act was not crucial to the Field's survival. A map attached to the Act shows areas in green, yellow and red. The green area effectively showed the protected areas of the common for public use. The red areas shown had already been enclosed and either were already built upon, or if not, although still open countryside, had been leased for development. The Field fell into neither as it was shaded in yellow. Together with two other areas they were no longer common land but had been enclosed and were now in private hands and as such were not freely available to the public. Of these three areas, the Field is the only area whose status has essentially remained unchanged, although now used, of course for sport. Of the other two, one area was in front of what is now Wandsworth Prison sandwiched between Heathfield Road and Trinity Road. This land had been acquired by the Justices of Surrey in 1861, presumably to provide a 'buffer zone' between the Prison and what is now Trinity Road. By 1970 owing to the dualling of Trinity Road and the loss of common land to do so, and then owned by the Home Office, it was transferred, apart from other minor areas, to Wandsworth Common as compensation. It is used as a nursery and claims to be 'London's biggest plant nursery in a garden centre'. Apparently, various attempts to build on this area have since been rebuffed. The other area of about twelve acres in total, was land obtained by the railway immediately north east and adjacent to Wandsworth Common station which had been bought from Spencer in 1854. This was originally used by the railway to dig gravel and ballast. Although after the construction of Wandsworth Common station, most of the area had become surplus to the railway's requirements, apart from the goods yard, it had been 'bought by adjoining owners to prevent it being built upon'. However once local solicitor and conservationist James Anderson Rose had died in 1890, the land came onto the open market and by 1894 it had been acquired by builder-developer Alfred Boon. This meant that the area was eventually lost entirely and most was given over to housing, with a small area immediately next to the station eventually being used for commercial purposes.

However, the Field's position opened up the question as to whether it was situated in the Wandsworth Common district or Upper Tooting district of London and this has been a source of some debate and confusion ever since. Before it was enclosed in 1852 by McKellar it was undoubtedly part of Wandsworth Common. In 1857 when London was first subdivided into postal districts the Field fell, just, into the Southern district of London with Upper Tooting, whilst Wandsworth fell into the Southern Western district of London; indeed, it is likely that the original boundary between these two areas ran approximately down Burntwood Lane much as the current postal district boundary does today. In 1868 when the Southern postal district was abolished, the Field fell comfortably into the South Western postal district of London. Given that the land on the other side of Burntwood Lane is undoubtedly Wandsworth Common, the issue was finally resolved in 1917 when the postal districts of London were numbered. The Field was allocated to SW17 which is in the postal district of Tooting, whilst the other side of Burntwood Lane was allocated to SW18, the postal district of Wandsworth! However, whilst any postcode is apparently by definition not an absolute indicator of an area in which any land is situated, the debate continued. So, actually, although some stalwarts would insist that the field is located on Wandsworth Common as indeed it originally was before McKellar bought it, as far as the postman is concerned, technically, it is located in Upper Tooting! Additionally, over the years both the district and the name of the Field itself would be open to further controversy and debate.

As mentioned earlier, it is quite possible that given his public-spirited gesture to the School in 1845, that perhaps Samuel Wix decided in 1886 to hand the Field back to Spencer from whence it had come. Alternatively, perhaps on Ann McKellar's death, the Field could have reverted to Spencer anyway. However, by March 1887, reflecting the anxiety over the future of the Field by the Conservators, the *Wandsworth & Putney Observer* reported *'Having ascertained from an examination of the Court Rolls that Lord Spencer, as Lord of the Manor, has a right to veto over the erection of buildings on the portion of land formerly part of the Common at the corner of Burntwood Lane and Trinity Road, the Conservators took steps for the acquisition of his lordship's right. They have not, at present been successful in this respect, but the ratepayers will be glad to learn that his lordship, as at present advised, has no intention of permitting the erection of buildings there'*. By then, of course the Field had already been a sports ground for around ten years as we shall learn later.

On 30 December 1890, it was Earl Spencer who conveyed the Field to the London County Council in consideration of a sum of 5/- and a covenant by which the Council would observe the conditions by which Henry McKellar had accepted the purchase in 1852. The Council, presumably backed by the former Conservators at the time, stated that it would 'throw' the Field into Wandsworth Common when in control, something that the Wandsworth Common Preservation Society had suggested the year before when the manorial rights had lapsed to the Council. This appeared to have never happened, perhaps because the Field had been previously enclosed and effectively excluded from the Wandsworth Common Act of 1871, and that to do so would have needed a further Act of Parliament for the purpose. Although today, as previously noted, Lord Spencer's rights as 'Lord of the Manor' are nominal, there have been recent incidents where he has chosen to remind various organisations of the original intention of the land he had formerly gifted, particularly if a change of use from a charitable to a commercial use of such land was contemplated. As regards to the Field, by 1887, it appeared that Spencer had already acquiesced to its use for sport and the rights to adjudicate on these matters (since 1889) were vested with the Council, so when the time came the Council would use its discretion as to the erection of changing facilities and other temporary structures on the Field to improve its lot for amateur sport.

In an interesting twist, the Wandsworth Common Conservators, to an extent, got their wish to a degree, albeit almost a hundred years later! In September 1986 the *London Gazette* gave notice that Wandsworth Borough Council 'in pursuance of its powers under section 277 of the Town and Country Planning Act 1971' had extended the Wandsworth Common Conservation Area to include the then 'Sir Walter St John's Playing Fields and pavilions'.

Perhaps the answer about the status of the Field came in 1898. It was then, in an acknowledgement that the Field was to be treated separately to the Common, that the London County Council sold it through auction to John Mills Thorne. The *South London Press* observed at the time that *'another greensward had been snatched from the 'octopus' grip of the enterprising builder'*. Perhaps they should have added the London County Council to that list, who obviously found the expense of maintaining the ground prohibitive, but fortunately, although John Mills Thorne had interests in developments elsewhere, his interests regarding the Field were benign. From then on, the Field has remained in private hands.

The Scope & Burntwood Lodge

Returning to Wandsworth Common, other enclosures had for some time been gradually diminishing the area of the Common. The construction of the railways in 1836 and then again between 1854 and 1862 had effectively separated the Common into three parts. Additionally, and also rather strangely, an area of about two acres of Common adjacent to Lyford Road was enclosed for the Craig Telescope which was supported by Earl Spencer. On it was built apparently, the largest refracting telescope in the world from which, it was said, it was possible to read a quarter-inch letter at a distance of half a mile! The fact was that during its lifetime it was beset by problems and doubts about its performance were raised. The erection of the telescope would have been clearly visible from the Field which McKellar had purchased about the same time as its construction. Given that the land was open heathland the contraption was even visible, apparently, to passing passengers on the railway. The telescope remained operational in one form or another from 1852 until 1855 by which time the project had effectively been abandoned owing to the telescope's poor performance and subsequently it was dismantled owing to a combination of Craig's personal problems and bankruptcy. A plethora of famous people at that time, apparently, had an interest in the project; these even included the celebrated engineer Isambard Kingdom Brunel. Strangely, the telescope cut an odd sight. It was shaped like an elongated cigar hung from a tower and the telescope itself was run on a circular azimuth trackway around the tower, but exposed to the elements. The completed telescope weighed 220 tons! Whilst it was suggested the tower and possibly astronomer's accommodation was built with bricks from the nearby Frying Pan Brickworks, other reports suggested it might have been constructed partially with bricks left over from what is now Wandsworth Prison which had been constructed on the periphery of the Common in 1851. Furthermore, when the central tower was demolished some years later, the surviving distinctive red bricks, it was alleged, were incorporated into helping to build part of the *Surrey Tavern* the pub and coaching inn on the corner of Bellevue Road and Trinity Road which opened its doors in 1865. However, this claim is unlikely because if there were red bricks, it is not immediately apparent from a cursory inspection of the elevations how or where the bricks were incorporated into the building. Demolition of the telescope tower was apparently not completed until around 1870. Today the demarcation visible on the Trinity Road flank of the building, although coincidently built of bricks which are redder in colour from the rest, is part of a far more modern improvement carried out sympathetically to extend the upper floors within the last twenty years.

Intriguingly, when the former owner of the Field John Mills Thorne died in 1913 in Burntwood Lodge, mention was made in its sale prospectus (and of the adjacent property of Collamore which he also owned) as to its prominent position looking towards Wimbledon, which was true, but also to the allegation that *'in front of Burntwood Lodge'*, sometime earlier, was the site of Ross's Telescope *'previous to its being sent to Ireland'*. No mention of Craig here, and indeed to remember the fiasco of his telescope would have surely detracted from any sale rather than added to its value. Was this simply just part of a sales pitch-a myth to claim some sort of credit for something that had gone so badly wrong sixty years earlier, or might it really be that parts of the Ross Telescope had been constructed in front of Burntwood Lodge to ensure its viability before shipping to Ireland? This seems hardly likely. What we do know is that on his estate at Birr Castle in County Offaly in 1845, William Parsons as the 3rd Earl of Rosse had constructed the largest telescope of its time. This had a six-foot mirror and would hold that title until 1917. It is known in 1852, Craig's Telescope's site had been visited by Rosse, who gave suggestions to Craig about correcting its optics. So, when the telescope on Wandsworth Common was eventually abandoned, what happened next? Accounts suggest that by the time the fencing to the compound was removed by around 1874 no remnants of the telescope, or buildings remained. A *Time Team* survey of the area in 2003 largely corroborates this and tends to support the idea that the telescope tower was carefully removed rather than simply and crudely demolished as very little evidence – including that of any foundations were found. Maybe the bricks were required for a nearby building elsewhere after all. It seems as various eye witness reports suggested at the time, that all 220 tons of the telescope itself was cut up for scrap or, in an early example of recycling, ended up as horseshoes! In this sense the Craig Telescope could be considered as a folly. Perhaps Earl Spencer had generously donated the land on which the Craig Telescope was built to, in some way, rival Rosse's Telescope in Ireland? The fact is we shall never know, and we shall also never know what really happened to the demolished bricks that were so carefully removed. The two acres of land which included the redundant telescope was returned to the Common when it was included in the 1871 Act. It seems that whoever demolished the buildings and tower associated with the telescope was however determined to do a good job.

The taming of Wandsworth Common

Whilst the Wandsworth Common Act had saved the Common from certain oblivion, the nature of what was left was changing. In 1872, Earl Spencer permitted the founders of the Spencer Cricket Club to 'drain and enclose by posts and chains a portion of Wandsworth Common'. Whist the club would only remain there for around five or six years' the ground was thought to be adjacent to *The Hope* close to Wandsworth Common station. The ground's construction, whilst retaining the land as Common, was to set a precedent for clearing areas of gorse bush and scrub for sport and recreation -and it has to be said for cricket in particular. In early 1877 a further cricket ground was proposed for the same transformation, or spoliation, as opponents of the scheme called it. This time the area was nearest to Bolingbroke Grove and also running parallel with the railway. The area proposed for the actual cricket ground was to be on the common opposite Mr Du Buisson's residence. Under an influential body of residents, the Conservators, subject to certain conditions, granted the use of this portion of Wandsworth Common, which was to be levelled and kept in order at the expense of a newly formed club. The club would be known as the Wandsworth Cricket Club which, as a newspaper article boldly pronounced *'is intended shall rank as the leading club in the neighbourhood'*. Their headquarters were based at the *Freemasons Hotel* on the northernmost extent of Wandsworth Common. This must have been met by some disquiet by both Spencer and other clubs at the time, such as Heathfield, who having only been recently established would have seen this as an intrusion. In order to allay fears that the proposal was by some regarded, effectively, as a private cricket ground on Common land, it was stated that the Wandsworth Club did not intend to monopolise the ground, but that they should have common usage with any other recognised clubs whom the Conservators may deem of sufficient standing in either Wandsworth or Battersea. The club had sufficient financial backing for levelling works and by March 1877 the construction of the ground on the Common had been placed in the hands of a local contractor and was already proceeding. From the playing perspective the whole project was doomed to failure and was a good illustration of a club trying to run before it could walk. In the two fixtures arranged with the Battersea club, an established club with a reputation for turning out strong sides, the Wandsworth Club were soundly beaten in the return match by more than two hundred runs. Unbelievably, worse was to follow, when Kingston Cricket Club scored a massive 285 and bowled Wandsworth out for only 11!! So, in that respect, the secret was out as the Club was of insufficient strength to cause much of a threat to anyone in club cricket circles.

Although the Wandsworth Cricket Club played on and indeed may have survived the Great War, it was never able to regularly call upon real quality players to turn out for them. As a result, it never really challenged the Spencer or Heathfield clubs nearby, but together with the Spencer cricket ground just up the road, it had changed the aspect of Wandsworth Common forever from a place where walking and rambling amongst attractive heathland was enjoyed, to a place for sport and recreation. Today although the formal cricket pitches are long gone, the area is still occasionally used for organised football, and up until the 1960s, speaking from personal experience, the local council was not adverse in cutting a pitch on the common for casual cricket matches. On long, hot summer days, in a reminder of times gone by, the area adjacent to Bellevue Road is a popular location for sunbathing, picnicking or just enjoying the delights of Wandsworth Common after a day's work.

We know that when Wandsworth Lodge was sold in 1863 the land to the north, being Brodrick Road and Wandle Road, was also sold for development. It should be noted that subsequently, apart from the Field, and despite the estate's sale, Wandsworth Lodge itself remained intact. However, as the eight acres of the Field could not be developed and probably remained in Ann McKellar's hands, this would explain why only the intervening area between the Lodge and Field was subsequently developed before Wandsworth Lodge was sold on again. The buyer of Wandsworth Lodge in 1863 could possibly have been Richard Henry Wyatt, Clerk of the Peace for the County of Surrey from 1871. His name is mentioned in the prosecution of two of his servants for petty theft at Wandsworth Lodge. They were both sentenced to two months of hard labour about the same time that the Lodge was sold again in 1877, this time to the de Selincourt family. An 1878 map shows Wandsworth Lodge as a private residence and the Field, although unmarked as to its purpose, was obviously distinct from the Common. However, by 1894, although a map shows the Field as a 'Cricket Ground', already having two pavilions and a shed, or possibly a stable for a horse, Wandsworth Lodge had disappeared, sold for development and demolished around ten years previously. The de Selincourt family perhaps, were better known through the marriage of Dorothy (always known as Daphne) de Selincourt to the author A.A. Milne. Their son Christopher Robin Milne is of course well known for his fictional adventures in the Winnie the Pooh books. The literary connection runs through the family as Hugh de Selincourt, the youngest brother of eleven siblings, was born at Wandsworth Lodge in 1878, and was the author of the celebrated 1924 book, *The Cricket Match* which is a timeless tale of village cricket.

'Lot 2'

Sport was becoming a popular pastime. *Wisden* records that as early as 1700, Clapham Common had been used for cricket. Although it was not until 1828 that cricket was officially recorded on Wandsworth Common it should be remembered that a Wandsworth XI actually defeated a side representing the MCC on that occasion and were praised for their "science and thorough knowledge of the game", so its actual origins on Wandsworth Common probably went back some years previously. In 1855, remarkably, a cricket match had actually been convened on top of the frozen ornamental lake known as the Black Sea on the northern side of the Common – although perhaps comparisons with the annual cricket match played on a similar surface in St. Moritz, Switzerland, ends there! However, in much the same way as today, there was a chronic shortage of grounds on which to play cricket. Battersea Park, was a hotbed for sport as in 1864 it had hosted the first ever football match played under the rules of the recently formed Football Association. Today cricket and football are still played in Battersea Park but being a public ground, it is very much given over to casual use by various clubs. In 1865 an open letter to the editor of the *South London Press* by H. Dann recorded that several suitable places to play cricket were 'swarmed' and that in Battersea Park, thirty applications had been made for only six spaces on its match ground. The letter went on to appeal to any philanthropists to came forward who were willing to offer a suitable ground on which to play cricket having 'good railway connections'. Would this appeal, however, had some resonance with the Field? Perhaps not at the time, given that the current Wandsworth Common railway station would not open in its current position until 1869. Indeed, one of the first mentions of the Field as distinct from Wandsworth Lodge was as a result of a Bay Horse which disappeared 'on the night of 28 December 1869 from a field opposite the Surrey Tavern'. To give an idea of its importance a reward was offered for information leading to its recovery which amounted to around £600 in today's money, but probably worth it, particularly if the horse was employed to pull a carriage. We do not know whether the appeal for the horse's return was successful, but what we do know is that the Field was still described as 'a field'. However, a few years later, matters were about to change.

When Wandsworth Lodge was put on the market in 1877, the Field was simultaneously offered under the same advertisement. Described as 'Lot 2', it was offered *on a short agreement with a proviso for re-entry if the land be required for building purposes'*. There was no suggestion at the time that the Field was anything other than 'Open Space'. So, did the new landlord at the *Surrey Tavern*, John Bonner, act as a catalyst for the Field's conversion to sport by taking up the 'short agreement'? This seems quite possible, as he would have seen this as an ideal opportunity to further his business with the view to providing changing facilities before and refreshment after matches. The pub was also a focal point for the auctions of local property. Quite apart from the sport, in 1886 the Field was also subject to a series of spring meetings in connection with 'Fox terrier rabbit coursing!', more commonly known today as hare coursing. Apparently, the events were attended by large crowds so the *Sporting Life* claimed. The final meeting was *'brought to a satisfactory conclusion... in the cricket field adjoining the Surrey Tavern Hotel'*, by which time the season for coursing was almost over and in any event the organisers had run out of rabbits! Obviously, the reception prior to these meetings, and probably after, was in John Bonner's Tavern. It may seem strange that a 'country pursuit' should take place at the Field at all, but, of course in those days, it was just open countryside! The reference to the *Surrey Tavern Hotel* is also interesting. As a coaching inn it obviously had accommodation and this is confirmed by the early advertisements for the Tavern although confusion still reigned (as with the Field) as regards to where it actually was. George Ferris the first landlord had done nothing to help things when in 1867 he advertised the pub as a *'Wonderful Discovery on Wandsworth Common'* only then to say in the same advert that the address was *'Trinity Road Tooting (on the borders of Wandsworth Common)'*, which was perhaps a better description of the area. The pub, the advert said, also included 'Stabling Accommodation'- in the event that you could find the pub with your horse, that is. After only two and a half years George Ferris had moved on, so the pub's life was off to an uncertain start; perhaps not everyone had 'discovered' the pub after all. However, during John Bonner's tenure, calling the premises the *Surrey Hotel* rather than a Tavern, was probably John Bonner's idea of upgrading the attractiveness of his pub next to Wandsworth Common. So apart from running the *Surrey Tavern / Hotel* did John Bonner enjoy his sport? If we take a cricket match at the field on 18 September 1889 and accept that the scorecard spelling of his name is incorrect (given as 'Bonnor'), then although 56 years old by then, he participated in a match for a Mr Lett's XI against the Royal Courts of Justice. Perhaps the latter were of a certain vintage, because despite batting with fourteen they were dismissed for a paltry 38. In reply with John Bonner making five, his team ran out comfortable winners. Also, one of the umpires was Martin and given this was the surname of the groundsman at the Field at the time, perhaps he umpired the match as well!

John Bonner was not a local man, being born in Queenborough, Kent in 1833. It seems that he ran the *Surrey Tavern* with his family for over twenty years before returning to the Isle of Sheppey. When he died at Sheerness in 1903, he was described as being 'of the Goat Hotel', so it seemed that working in the wine licensed trade remained with him throughout his working life. Bonner has not been forgotten, because in a nod to the past, a recently built block of apartments adjacent to where the *Surrey Tavern* stands today, is called the 'Bonner Building'.

As regards to the Field, its days as 'Open Space' and pasture land were over, but confusion still remained as to where the location of the Field really was. On 5 January 1878, Clapham Rovers took on the Gipsies in a rugby match. However, even the club were of the same confusion as George Ferris had been some years earlier, when they described the Field as their *'new private ground at Wandsworth – so called, but which is in reality much more adjacent to Tooting'*. The match was played in a 'regular Scotch mist'. A reporter, from *The Referee*, noted on that day that having *'...wended our dreary way from Waterloo to Wandsworth.'* that the *'scene of the action was about three miles off in the direction of Tooting, where after much suffering from the effects of misty rain which only a true born Highlander can thoroughly appreciate, we landed in an obscure field'*. In truth the clue lies that he had travelled from Waterloo and would have landed up at Wandsworth Town station, whilst had he travelled from Victoria, he could have got off at Wandsworth Common station and at least largely saved his walk through the mist and drizzle! Neither side could achieve a breakthrough in a match where both sides obviously lost their way. The contest finished, unusually for a rugby match, with neither side scoring. However, such reports of the Field's location have conspired to shield its true location until this day.

The mention above of Clapham Rovers is significant. For many years, football historians have debated exactly where the club played on Wandsworth Common. However, from examination of local newspaper reports and maps there is no doubt. Clapham Rovers played at the Field! In the winter it was more commonly known as the *Rovers Ground*, but this never appeared on local maps. As there were no changing facilities on the Field at the start, both the football and the cricket clubs would change in the *Surrey Tavern*. Indeed, changing facilities on the Field did not arrive until probably the early 1890s after the London County Council assumed control. An 1896 map shows it as a Cricket Ground and by then there were actually two sets of changing facilities on the Field! Later maps refer to it as the Heathfield ground after the cricket club that was the principal user during the summer months as we shall see later. The only thing that perhaps is debatable is whether Clapham Rovers survived long enough as a club to enjoy those new changing facilities.

Start of Play

It is now accepted that 1877 was probably the start of sport on the Field. When the Heathfield Cricket Club arrived in 1883 it was said in their centenary brochure that the club 'were fortunate in being able to rent a pitch', which gives a clue to the fact that the field was already in high demand, as indeed was the whole of Wandsworth Common for cricket and sport. It is not certain which club or clubs were already playing at the Field. However, Brunswick Cricket Club may have been one, because they refer to a 'private pitch' in occasional reports for playing some matches on Wandsworth Common but this is really just speculation. However, in the same centenary brochure although the Heathfield club refers to the Field as 'Bonners Field' it was a term never used by the club in press reports with 'Wandsworth Common' preferred. 'Bonners Field' was probably used on a colloquial basis because of the involvement of John Bonner as we have seen.

However, another side that may have used 'Bonners Field' for their matches at that time was the Church Institute club. Formed in 1868, it was the educational, social and sporting arm of the Anglican Church of St Mary Magdalene which is located immediately opposite the Field in Trinity

Road. As both the Institute's and Heathfield's fixture lists appeared in the 1890 *Cricket* newspaper it can be deduced that the Beechcroft Road end of the ground was called 'Upper Tooting' by Heathfield whilst the main pitch adjoining Trinity Road was known as 'Wandsworth Common'. The Church Institute Cricket Club preferred to call the Wandsworth Common end 'Bonner's Field Heathfield Pitch' and the 'Upper Tooting' end by elimination, just Bonner's Field. This has led to some confusion over the years, but given that when the bowls section of the Heathfield club at the Beechcroft Road end started, it was often referred to as being in Upper Tooting being easily accessible via an entrance in Burntwood Lane, which although nowadays no longer exists, is still marked by the cobbled remains and dropped kerb in the pavement. However, the fact that the Church Institute Cricket Club promoted temperance as one of their objects, this was probably one of the reasons why they opted to change in their own headquarters in Wiseton Road. Amongst the Church institute's players was one of cricket's all-time greats, George Lohmann, who is remembered as the bowler who still holds the lowest bowling average for a player taking over fifteen Test wickets. He was the second of three cricketing brothers and in only 18 Tests he took a remarkable 112 wickets at an average of 10.75. He was also a useful lower order batsman. His career was cut short by tuberculosis. In 1897 he emigrated to South Africa for health reasons and although he returned as assistant manager of the second South African touring side in 1901, he died shortly after his return there at the young age of 36. There is speculation that he played at the Field before he was even a teenager, as between 1876 and 1878 he won awards for his batting and bowling with the Church Institute club. It is therefore just conceivable that he played there in the last of those years mentioned. Before becoming a professional player with Surrey, he switched his allegiance to the Alma Cricket Club. The debate about him ever playing at the Field was eventually settled in 1889 by a reference to another match played at the Field. In that year, on 22 April, as a pre-season friendly, *Cricket* records a match between 'Beaumont's (Surrey) Eleven and Eighteen of Wandsworth & District'. Many of these local matches were played by the first-class counties to help, foster and promote cricket within the county. The scorecard (no bowling figures recorded) shows that the local side had little talent as they were dismissed for only 52 (only seventeen names are recorded on the scorecard rather than eighteen!). By close of play Beaumont's Surrey Eleven had amassed 107-2. Lohmann's contribution in the match appears to have been rather limited, although he was credited with a catch in the Wandsworth innings. He was due to bat at six, so never got as far as the crease. As regards to the team only surnames are recorded. Why do we think this really was the great man himself? Later that season, Lohmann played in a similar local match at Richmond and took a hatful of wickets! He was not averse to turning up on these occasions even though he had received his first England cap in 1886. Three other members of the eleven representing Surrey on that day at the Field were Beaumont himself, plus Bowley and Brockwell. All played for Surrey that season and were essentially team mates of Lohmann. His younger brother, Joshua, ten years junior than George, played against the Heathfield Cricket Club for the Surrey Club & Ground side in 1896, but only went as far as playing Minor County cricket at Shropshire. His older brother Stewart Lohmann became a professional cricketer in Georgetown (British Guiana) and in Philadelphia.

Much has changed since those days. 1889 was actually the year when Wandsworth was transferred from Surrey to London. Richmond would follow in 1965 as part of the reorganisation which helped create the Greater London Authority. However as far as cricket administration is concerned, London has never existed as a county in its own right. Because the London Borough of Richmond is the only authority that straddles the Thames, the whole of the borough for cricket purposes including that part south of the Thames is regarded, curiously, as being part of Middlesex. So, Richmond being in Middlesex? That would never have been envisaged back in 1889!

3

The Football Years (1877-1914)

There are people on the pitch...They think it's all over. It is now!

Kenneth Wolstenholme (1920-2002)

Up for the Cup - Clapham Rovers

In many ways a forgotten club, founded probably, although accounts differ, in 1869, Clapham Rovers started life on Clapham Common and were a hybrid club that played both Rugby and Football invariably using a similar pool of players to do so. To support its credentials the club, amongst others, was instrumental in the official founding of Rugby Union in 1871. Indeed, as a rugby club, their best years were from 1870 until 1881, during which time the club played 151 matches, winning 80, drawing 41 and losing 30. Although the Rovers were good at rugby, several more players would go on to represent their country at international level at football and Reginald Birkett would have the honour of playing both codes on the international stage. Another, Norman Bailey was probably the football star. His England career lasted almost ten years (from 1878 until 1887) and he gained nineteen caps, fifteen of those as skipper. From 1872 the club used a ground in Bedford Hill Balham probably, on what today are the northernmost fringes of Tooting Bec Common. However, in April 1877 it was reported that Clapham Rovers had lost their ground as it was required for 'other purposes'. From there, some accounts suggest that Clapham Rovers moved to Wandsworth Common using *The Hope* as their base, but if they did, any stay there was brief. These must have been anxious times but it is likely that John Bonner the landlord at the *Surrey Tavern* would have relished the opportunity of having one of the leading amateur clubs playing at the Field, even if it was under a short agreement as detailed in *The Times* advertisement.

On 13 October 1877 the club played its first match at their 'new playing field, not far from Wandsworth Common Station'. By all accounts, their luck was in. Favourable reports matched their good fortune as the Field was thrown open to sport. Clapham Rovers were already known as a top amateur side, and the club were able to rent the Field whilst using the *Surrey Tavern* as a base and as a changing and social facility after matches. Even today it is not hard to imagine the players changing in some of the recesses behind curtains before matches prior to heading across Trinity Road onto the ground to play their sport. Moreover, as the Field was enclosed, it was regarded more as a private facility distinct from the Common. Inevitably, it was not uncommon for the club to play matches of football and rugby on the same day, and sometimes both at the Field. The first match against Marlborough Nomads, was played under the rugby code and was won by a goal and a try to nothing. Describing the Field as *'large, and will undoubtedly prove dry, even throughout a wet season'*, the accounts suggested that its position on high ground would be of benefit, but, in reality, there was no guarantee that it would remain dry through any prolonged period of unsettled weather, as generations of players since would acknowledge! On the same day in October, the football section of the club was taking on The Wanderers at the Kennington Oval winning by 3-1. Indeed because of the club's heavy involvement with the FA Cup, where most of the later rounds of matches were held, their visits to the Field during the first few seasons were less frequent than the rugby section, although this could have been due to the patchy reporting of results at that time. For the time being however, the rugby section of the club would generally hold sway at the Field. On 2 October 1878, however, a Wednesday match with the Casuals was scheduled at the Field and although sadly the result was not reported, there probably was a tenuous link between the Casuals side and the apparent foundation of that club itself in 1883. it is interesting to think that perhaps by the time the Casuals first official match took place at the Field they were perhaps not unfamiliar with the place. Clapham Rovers would obviously enjoy their new home, and would use the *Surrey Tavern* or as it was later called, the *Surrey Hotel* as their headquarters and the Field itself regularly for around another eighteen years. It would also be used for some quite high-profile rugby matches as in February 1879, it staged the first-round matches of the Inter-Hospital Cup between King's College and London and also between St Bart's. and Charing Cross. In the following month the Field staged the Surrey v Middlesex rugby match with many notable players on display.

Regarding football, in recognition of their reputation on 4 November 1878 the two strongest amateur sides in London, Clapham Rovers and The Wanderers met in one of the very first floodlit matches at the Kennington Oval. It was almost a demonstration event to judge the suitability of the new technology available, and followed a previous match staged at Bramall Lane Sheffield a few weeks earlier which had been regarded as an outright success. The authorities had anticipated a huge crowd to watch the match, but in the event, only around 4,000 supporters did so, which was regarded as a disappointment at the time. Every preparation had been made. A military band had been engaged and four 'electric' lights had been set up to illuminate each corner of the ground. The result apparently was almost surreal, with shadows cast over the pitch from the movement of players and the ball sometimes disappearing into the gloom above the scope of the floodlights making it difficult to play with any certainty. *The Sportsman* observed that *'unless some considerable improvement is made in the arrangements for lighting, football under such influence will be more of a burlesque than real sport'*. The match finished in a 2-2 draw, but although floodlighting at grounds had got off to an uncertain start, it is today, of course, an essential part in the staging of all evening sport quite apart from football.

In 1871 the Football Association Cup had been inaugurated. In those days amateur football clubs still ruled the roost and Clapham Rovers entered the very first FA Cup competition when the total entry was only fifteen clubs. One of their players Jarvis Kenrick was credited with the very first goal in FA Cup history when he scored early in the match against Upton Park in a 3-0 victory at West Ham Park. A plaque on the Old Rectory, Caterham where his father was rector commemorates Kendrick's feat. He also enjoyed cricket and made a single first-class appearance for Surrey in 1876, and, in later life was Honorary Secretary of the Croquet Association from 1904 until 1909. He lived until the age of 96. In the following round however, the club were defeated at home 1-0 by The Wanderers who were the eventual winners of the first competition and who were to prove tough opponents in the decade ahead. In the 1873/74 season the club were actually semi-finalists, but although they invariably progressed beyond the first round, further success eluded them. By 1878 Clapham Rovers as a leading amateur club were rewarded with a match against the mighty Glasgow Rangers played at the Kennington Oval which they lost 3-1. The breakthrough came later that season, however, when during only their second full season at the Field they progressed to the Final at the Kennington Oval only to be beaten 1-0 by Old Etonians. In that match the Rovers fielded the youngest player to take part in an FA Cup Final, James Prinsep at 17 years and 245 days. Additionally, just a week later, Prinsep made his England debut in an international match against Scotland, his only cap, again as the youngest player to do so. Both records were to stand the test of time. The former was not beaten until 2004 and the latter only a year earlier, when Wayne Rooney made his England debut against Australia. By 1880 Prinsep was playing for his Old Boys school side, Old Carthusians, so did not play for Clapham Rovers in the FA Cup Final side. However, the following year, he was an FA Cup winner with Old Carthusians (like the Rovers their only FA Cup Final win), and actually played against the Rovers when in the fifth round, Old Carthusians beat them 3-1 after extra time. Prinsep was a keen sportsman also playing a good standard of cricket with the Free Foresters. Born in India, he spent most of his adult life serving as a professional soldier in Egypt, and was involved in the failed attempt to save General Gordon in Khartoum. Remarkably, whilst a soldier he received two separate Royal Humane Society Awards for helping to save a soldier and subsequently a Sudanese sailor from drowning in the Nile. Unfortunately, at the young age of 34, whilst on holiday in Scotland, he succumbed to pneumonia as a result of catching a cold after playing golf.

From being runners up, it was the FA Cup Competition of 1879/80 that was to make history for Clapham Rovers. With 54 entries this meant that the competition had grown considerably since the early days and more rounds had to be arranged. Although the record shows that the first-round match with Romford was a home tie, with the Field perhaps was being used for rugby, the Rovers travelled to the Essex club to play the fixture. Despite this, the Rovers ran out 7-0 winners. Playing 'away' having been drawn at 'home' happened on several occasions in the next few years, suggesting that the rugby section still had first preference at the Field and were unwilling, perhaps, to postpone a pre-arranged fixture. The second-round fixture was the only match played at the Field during their run to the Final, and this resulted in a comfortable victory by 4-1 against South Norwood. Indeed, the goal conceded in this match proved to be the only one scored against the Rovers in the entire FA Cup competition that season. The matches in the later stages of the competition including the Final were again played at the Kennington Oval, nowadays more well known as the home of Surrey County Cricket Club. It was there that the Rovers went on to play The Pilgrims in the third round and then Hendon in the fourth round. The crucial match was to come in the fifth round when the Rovers exacted revenge over the Cup holders Old Etonians 1-0, the side that had defeated them in the Final in the previous season by the same score. Whilst on 27 March 1880, Oxford University were busy beating Nottingham Forest (who had received a bye in the fifth round), in the Semi Final, Clapham Rovers remarkably drew a bye themselves in the Semi Final for the second season running! So it was, on 10 April 1880, that the club found themselves in the Final pitched against Oxford University at the Kennington Oval. With both Varsity clubs difficult to beat, whether at home or away, this would present a serious challenge. Although from reports Clapham Rovers had the better of the first half it was not until late in the match with just six minutes play left that the Rovers broke the deadlock. The winner was scored by Welshman, Clopton Lloyd-Jones who at 21 years and 150 days was the youngest FA Cup Final scorer up to that time. There were understandably great celebrations amongst the crowd reported to be 6,000 strong. It was a remarkable achievement for Clapham Rovers, and it could truly be said that the Field was the home of the 1880 FA Cup Winners! However, like their opponents in the Final, Oxford University, neither club would appear in a FA Cup Final again.

Invariably, and for many years, traditionally, the FA Cup Final would signal the end of the football season, but remarkably there would be one more match for the club. Clapham Rovers were invited to take part in a charity match for Mrs Dick, the mother of the late Secretary of the Scottish Football Association at what is now known as Hampden Park Glasgow against Queens Park the Scottish Cup winners. The Rovers, although having not played for five weeks, generously took up the challenge. A report tells of a very large crowd at the match, won by Queens Park by 3-2.

Clapham Rovers commenced a robust defence as FA Cup holders. On 13 November 1880, they started with a 15-0 victory at the Field against a hapless Finchley side. Up until that stage, only the Wanderers with their 16-0 demolition of Farningham in 1874 had won by a higher margin in the competition. However, the strength of the northern professional sides was beginning to show. As if to emphasise the increasing gulf, on 7 February 1881, Clapham Rovers were beaten at the Kennington Oval by Blackburn Rovers by the margin of 7-1. Although a report emphasised that

Clapham Rovers were fielding a weakened side, it should be noted that Blackburn Rovers would go onto win the FA Cup five times between 1884 and 1891. The Rovers were then beaten again at the Oval by Queens Park Glasgow by 1-0, presumably returning the favour for the Rovers visit to Scotland earlier in the year. A further reverse was suffered away to Nottingham Forest by 3-0, but this match was attended by a huge crowd which could have even been larger than those at the Cup Final itself. All these matches were played in their capacity as Cup Holders which they were until 19 March 1881 when they were beaten in the fifth round by the Old Carthusians who would be the eventual Cup Winners that season.

Apart from the football and rugby, the Rovers held their annual athletics meeting usually on the first Saturday in May at the Field. This was a continuation of the meetings they had previous organised since their inception at Broomwood, Clapham Common, courtesy of Sir Charles Stewart Forbes, and were a highlight of their year. After their FA Cup success these meetings became far more popular for athletes and supporters alike. This was an 'open' event insofar that those registering to take place had to be in turn a member of any recognised amateur football, cricket, rowing or athletic clubs including universities. Many different races were contested. The numbers competing in the events were considerable, and the club threw its entire weight and reputation behind the meeting. On most of these annual occasions, either the band of the Coldstream Guards or the Grenadier Guards would entertain the crowd during the intervals between racing. Some serious silverware would exchange hands for the winners. From the start of their tenure at the Field these meetings continued until 1887. In 1888 the event was held in July at the South London Harriers Ground at Balham where entry to the races was restricted rather than being open to allcomers. By 1889 the event had moved to Stamford Bridge and was attended in that year by 1,500 spectators, encouraged no doubt by free entry to watch what had effectively now become more of an internal club event.

Decline and Fall

In the next few years, Clapham Rovers did not progress beyond the fifth round of the FA Cup. In 1885/86 season the club were disqualified by the Football Association who were not willing to extend the 31 December deadline for their away match at South Reading. Early elimination from the London Challenge Cup meant that during the second half of the season they played more matches at the Field. By then the northern professional sides were taking over the honours in the FA Cup and would retain a virtual monopoly over winning the competition for almost the next fifty years. In succeeding years, with entries to the FA Cup increasing year on year, qualifying rounds were introduced on a regional basis and of course nowadays although that system still prevails, it is not until the professional sides enter the competition that the FA Cup starts in earnest.

Clapham Rovers continued to play both amateur football and rugby at the Field and together with other clubs, would effectively groundshare with them from time to time as we shall see later. Occasionally rugby matches would also be played at Stamford Bridge. At times the club might raise an additional football or rugby side on a Saturday presumably dependent on availability. In 1885 the Field staged a Surrey v Kent rugby match and would stage Surrey Trials rugby matches from time to time. However, although normal attendances at the Field would not often attract more than a thousand spectators perhaps on a good day, mention should be made of a match on Monday 27 December 1886. Perhaps to fulfil a promise that the club made to Hull Rugby Club when they played at the Field in 1883, the Rovers made the long journey up north. The instructions for getting there were interesting *'Train 5pm from Kings Cross on Sunday via Leeds'*. However, there is no record at what time or day they got back from the match! Nevertheless, although being well beaten by 8pts to nil, the match was played in front of 10,000 spectators! The club would keep their rugby connection with Hull, playing them again at the Queens Club on another visit that club made to the capital and the Rovers in future years would not only head north on tour occasionally, but also undertake a Christmas Tour to Devon and Cornwall. The club would also play the Harlequins and London Welsh from time to time, little realising that both clubs would have a part to play in the Field's history in the future.

On the Association front (so called in those days to distinguish between football and the rugby codes of play), in December 1886 after a 1-1 draw at the Field in the London Senior Cup with the Casuals, the record showed that the Rovers scratched the replay, but there was a further match played between the two sides at the Casuals' new ground at the Upper Tooting Cricket Club only two weeks later, which the Rovers lost by 9-1! The season would also mark the last in which the club would enter the FA Cup and, having been bundled out in the first round by Old Brightonians by 6-0, Clapham Rovers withdrew from all cup competitions for the next four seasons, only re-entering the London Senior Cup in 1891. For the Clapham Rovers, at least, the romance of the FA Cup was sadly over.

All indications were that the club was certainly not short of support. The Annual General Meeting in September 1893 at Westminster Town Hall was full and the *Sporting Life* reported that *'towards the close it was standing room only.'* And that *'The grounds, as usual, will be at Wandsworth Common'* (in other words the Field). In addition to the London Senior Cup, the club entered the inaugural season of the FA Amateur Cup and survived the regionalised qualifying rounds. When the draw was made for the final stages of that competition, Clapham Rovers unluckily were drawn away to play on 3 February 1894 at Bishop Auckland who would prove, in the years to come, to be one of the leading northern amateur sides in the country. However, the club declined the long trip to County Durham and pulled out of the competition, and took their frustrations out on Old Westminsters with a 7-2 victory at the Field instead. In London, the Field was identified as a marker point on the route of the South of Thames Junior Cross-Country Championships and in both 1893 and 1894, thousands of spectators lined the route to watch around 150 runners complete two laps of the course, around eight miles in all, commencing at the *East Hill Hotel*. It was quite an event but unfortunately for Clapham Rovers their race was almost run.

Reports strangely do not give much of a clue as to what went so badly wrong so quickly. Even as late as 27 January 1894 a reporter observed that there were good crowds at the Field, and as there was a rugby match being played there at the same time as a football match you could, according to the report, *'pay your money and had your choice!'* It appeared, also judging by reports in the newspapers, that the club could still turn out at least one or sometimes two teams of rugby and football every Saturday potentially involving around fifty playing members. However, despite the encouraging attendance at the AGM the previous September, there were signs that all was not well. By now, however, it is quite possible that the whole club were changing at *The Hope* rather than *The Surrey Tavern*; certainly, the football club were. Whether the use of the Field under the auspices of the London County Council who had owned the ground since 1890 had placed more stringent conditions upon the Field's use, we shall never know. It is even conceivable that by then the rugby club may have been changing at the 'Heathfield' pavilion on the Field by then, but the club did not tour at Christmas in 1893. Early in 1894 Clapham Rovers indicated that it would not stage another spring Athletics Meeting at Stamford Bridge which had hitherto been an essential part of their season. Given this was a scaled down event by now anyway, and the 1893 event had been poorly supported, perhaps, this was not a surprise. There was no hiding the fact that the 1893/94 season had been a wretched season for the club. The rugby side failed to score in eleven out of eighteen matches reported. It was just that their overall playing standard by then was not very good. Significantly there was no mention of a September AGM.

The rugby club had not started the 1894/95 season when at short notice they cancelled their first match against London Scottish on 29 September through the lack of players. The collapse of the rugby section of Clapham Rovers was nevertheless a shock and it was reported in newspapers from as far afield as Exeter to Nuneaton and probably beyond. Those involved in the rugby world however were not unduly surprised. The club's weakness and lack of leadership were given as the basis for their demise. Additionally, far too often they would scratch matches or turn up short and perhaps the club was getting a reputation for doing so, or both. All of this would have sapped moral. Ironically and coincidental to the collapse, was the news that London Welsh rugby club had also folded. The story of that club's successful revival is mentioned later in this book, but both failures spelt the slow decline of 'hybrid clubs'. Since the advent of rugby in 1871 both codes of playing a game with a 'football' had coexisted side by side. Indeed, early rugby matches were played with a similar ball, but because a rugby ball needed to be carried, it is likely that its unique shape evolved to make it easier to do so. As rugby and football slowly diverged as the decades went on, players made a definitive choice as to where their loyalties would be for playing their winter sport, either with the Rugby code or the Association code. Today, although less so, 'hybrid clubs' still exists but perhaps not truly in the conventional sense. Most Universities provide a much wider "multi-sport" set up to cater for their students. Some Old Boys sides provide football and rugby together with cricket for the former pupils of their school mostly adopting an 'open' policy towards membership. Other clubs, such as Battersea Ironsides nearby do so as well. However, examples of players combining both rugby and football for their winter sports are vanishing rapidly.

The Rovers Return

Almost immediately after the collapse of the rugby section in October 1894 there was an attempt by some of the membership to revive its fortunes. It was announced that the club would now simply be called 'The Rovers' and they would continue to play at the Field for almost the next five years. The new club, or a 'phoenix' club as some would say, would open their account against 'Clapham Park A' on 27 October at the Field. There is no actual report of the result of the match, or even if it was actually played. The local press still referred to the 'phoenix' rugby club as 'Clapham Rovers' which just added to the confusion. It would have been a struggle because along the way the new club would have had to recruit additional members as it was a shortage of players that had led to its downfall in the first place. When in the following season 'The Rovers' were on the wrong end of 37-0 drubbing at the hands of Brighton at Preston Park in February 1896, it must have seemed that the whole venture could have been in jeopardy. However, matters gradually improved and by the 1897/98 season the impartial observer could have been led into thinking that the good days were back, as around a thousand came to watch The Rovers beat Olney by 8-6. Other visitors to the Field in that season included Saracens and the Wasps, the latter being defeated by 8-0. During the close season the club changed its name again, and would now be known as the 'London Rovers'. Perhaps this is ironic, as when Clapham Rovers were originally formed it was claimed that they were the first club to use the term 'Rovers' as an integral part of their name, but by now so many football clubs had followed their lead that it was hard to distinguish between one 'Rovers' and another. it was important to qualify geographically the area in which the club was situated – although by then London, of course, was a city rather than a town. However, the 1898/99 season would prove to be their last. Changes were afoot at the Field as the ownership passed into John Mills Thorne's hands and the Heathfield Cricket Club, who were now looking for a more reliable winter partner. Although that might have spelt an end of the rugby, but interestingly in early 1899 there are reports of a 'Ye Olde Clapham Rovers' Angling Club' operating out of *The Windmill* in Clapham Park Road. Is it really possible that this club which organised excursions to various places in Southern England, had some connection with the defunct rugby club? Perhaps some of the former players of the club had retired and simply 'Gone Fishing!'

However, the football club did carry on, but although it retained the Clapham Rovers name it would literally distance itself from the rugby club. Initially it would use the Field as its home, but by the 1895/96 season it had moved away and taken up residence at Crystal Palace in the shadow of the magnificent structure by the same name, built for the Great Exhibition of 1851. The club's opening match there on 28 December 1895, brought an encouraging 5-1 win against Old Carthusians and two other matches against Old Foresters and the Casuals were also staged there in their inaugural season. In the following season further matches, amongst others, were staged in the qualifying rounds of the FA Amateur Cup, but after beating Old Harrovians 6-0 the club were eliminated in the next round by Old Wilsonians, 5-0. How a club in turmoil could be granted use of such a magnificent home on which to play football is unsure. It may have been through their contacts at the London FA which were still quite strong. The Crystal Palace ground had taken over from the Oval as the venue for the FA Cup Final in 1895 and would continue to host the FA Cup there until 1914. The ground would have been a good base from which to properly relaunch the football club. There were two pitches there, named North and South, and possibly the former was used for the Cup Final. It was quite an imposing stadium, and Clapham Rovers would stay there for three seasons in all, bolstered strangely by most of the Old Wilsonians side who after their defeat of the club in the previous season probably fancied playing at the Crystal Palace as their new home club! It is not known what caused Clapham Rovers to move on, but certainly a 10-1 defeat at the hands of Marlow at the Palace would not have helped, nor, perhaps, indifferent attendances and the expense of hiring the ground. From the 1898/99 season, the club would have to rely on the generosity of other clubs to entertain them. Although they were still playing a decent standard of amateur football, there was apparently a real concern that the club would have to disband completely as results and the quality of the opposition continued to slide. However, in 1900, in conjunction with the Old Westminsters, the club embarked on an Easter Tour to the Netherlands, and slowly, to a degree, things started to improve. Back home between 1902 and 1904 intriguingly they found a home for a couple of seasons at least in Burntwood Lane Wandsworth Common, not far from the Field's location – perhaps at the ground used by Old Leysians. Brixton Wanderers Cricket Club's ground at East Dulwich (1909/10 season) was also another temporary home. By the 1912/13 season they were playing, according to reports, in the vicinity of Kent House, which for those unfamiliar with the name, is a railway station between Penge East and Beckenham Junction. Nevertheless, the Clapham Rovers by virtue of their past exploits in the FA Cup still enjoyed playing a reasonable standard of amateur friendly football even if their exploits in the 1880 FA Cup, occasionally mentioned by the press, were now more of a liability than an asset. The club travelled considerable distances to do so-including visits in no particular order to Tunbridge Wells, Marlow, despite their embarrassment at the Palace, Eastbourne (on the Saffrons), Dover, St. Albans, and remarkably on more than one occasion away to Ipswich Town for an annual Boxing Day match. However, despite their illustrious past, and a flirtation with league football, they had really just become another amateur football club playing friendly matches by the time the Great War was approaching. In October 1912, in an AFA Senior Cup First Round match, they were rather unceremoniously dumped out of the competition by the Old Boys of Battersea Grammar School, Old Grammarians by 3-1. Although the football club had survived the trauma of 1894, if anything, the reminders of their past glory days invariably became more of a curse than an asset as the years went on, and the magic of another cup run, even at amateur status, was, it seems, well beyond them.

On 17 February 1914 Clapham Rovers, held its supposed forty fifth annual dinner at the *Hotel Cecil*, which, given its apparent dissolution and reincarnation in 1894, and the fact that only the football club had survived, was open to debate. It proudly boasted that owing to its position, originally, as a 'hybrid' club, the Rovers contained together more international players in both codes than any other club. The article admitted that the club had gone through some difficult times but by inviting so many former players from both codes to a reunion, the Rovers were obviously determined to enjoy themselves and remember the good times once again. The Dinner was principally given over to speeches from mostly past players which were of 'an historical and reminiscent character.' From the lengthy article in the *Westminster Gazette*, it almost sounded more like a wake than a celebration! The club were still playing in the spring of 1914, and intended to play on, but in September 1914 the club announced that they were cancelling all their fixtures for the forthcoming season owing to the War. Unfortunately, of course, as with so many other clubs, they would be one of the casualties.

Today, Clapham Rovers FA Cup triumph has been relegated to the subject of a pub quiz question. 'Name the five sides who have won the FA Cup whose name begins with a C'? Chelsea, Charlton Athletic, Coventry and Cardiff City are names that the enthusiast would probably remember, but Clapham Rovers less so. However, that was not quite the end as in 1996 a team operating under the name of Clapham Rovers surfaced. Whilst, of course, there was no connection between the two clubs, apart from the name, the new club today currently plays in the Southern Sunday Football League. On 23 May 2015, Clapham Rovers met the Wanderers (who had re-formed in 2009) in a charity match at the Mayfield Stadium, Thornton Heath wearing the same Cerise and French Grey kit as their predecessors. For a match involving two sides who had 'won' the FA Cup six times between them, although Clapham Rovers only 'won' the FA Cup once, a totally underwhelming crowd of about forty watched the Rovers beat the Wanderers 4-2 by virtue of two late goals. Hardly a return of the good old days but hope springs eternal so they say!

A Casual start

Officially formed in 1883, the Casuals football club can track its origins back to the Field. Although the Casuals restricted their membership, initially, to the old boys of Charterhouse, Eton and Westminster this condition of membership was soon extended to include other private schools and universities. The origins of the name 'Casuals' is uncertain and indeed there were tenuous links to a forerunner side by the same name. It is claimed that the club used the *Surrey Tavern* as their headquarters, and also as changing facilities for their matches on the Field, but this is probably unlikely as it had been occupied since 1877 by Clapham Rovers for that purpose. Although it is known on odd occasions that the Casuals did change at the *Surrey Tavern*, this was invariably more the exception than the rule, depending on the use of Field on Saturdays. It is more likely that the club's base was at *The Hope* virtually adjacent to Wandsworth Common station. This is borne out by the memoirs of Frederick Wall who we shall discuss later, but he noted that *'The Casuals used to dress at a tavern and had to run 300 yards across the Common to their field'*, or perhaps to be more precise, up Bellevue Road with the common on the right-hand side and then onto the Field. The reference to 'their field' is interesting. Frederick Wall played for another local side known as the Rangers and this would imply that the Rangers might probably only have used the Field on occasions for their football and perhaps Wandsworth Common itself for other home matches. There is evidence also that he refereed an odd match from time to time at the Field and also occasionally played cricket there.

The Football Years (1877-1914)

The Casuals stay at the Field was quite short; in fact, only three seasons in total. After several away matches, the Casuals first home match was on 8 November 1883 against St Thomas' Hospital which resulted in defeat by 3-2. Only eight matches appear to have been played at the Field out of a total of 28 matches that season, with a 2-2 draw against Guy's Hospital being the only home match not lost. The tendency for the club to play most of their matches away from home was to continue throughout their early years. Although the initial season had been difficult, the club had survived.

In the following season (1884/85) the Casuals entered the FA Cup for the first time. The layout of the Field was probably similar to today and perhaps being in some sort of unofficial ground-sharing arrangement with the Clapham Rovers and possibly others, different pitches may have been used at the Field by different clubs on an *ad hoc* basis, probably managed, of course, by John Bonner at the *Surrey Tavern*. Invariably perhaps the main pitch, as today, runs parallel with Burntwood Lane and at times the Trinity Road end was referred to as the 'Hotel' end after the *Surrey Tavern / Hotel* opposite and the other end as the 'far end' or sometimes the 'top end'. This must have confused a reporter of the *Berkshire Chronicle* into thinking there was a pronounced slope on the pitch, which is hardly the case, as in the FA Cup first round match on 8 November 1884, which had been switched to the Field from South Reading, the account noted *'… having lost the toss, Johnson the captain, drew up his men with the wind, sun and hill against them…'*. The Casuals were strong favourites to win the match but the visitors ran out victors by 4-1. The Casuals report was very much shorter, as the club owed their defeat *'in no slight measure to so many of their best men playing for their old schools in the Cup.'* Maybe, but the uncomfortable fact was that the Casuals, remarkably, were destined never to get beyond the first round of the FA Cup in their history! On the adjacent pitch, with the wind also being a factor, Clapham Rovers played out a 3-3 draw with Hendon in the same competition. Save for the Kennington Oval, might this be the only occasion in history that two FA Cup ties were played simultaneously on the same ground on the same day? Returning to South Reading, having been formed in 1878, the side were well known for their distinctive black shirts and white shorts with the former rather curiously emblazoned with a white Maltese Cross. The 'Southerners' as they were known proved that their victory over the Casuals was no fluke. However, like a shooting star, the club shone brightly for a short time, before disbanding in 1891. During that time, arguably, they were the best team in Reading but beyond that Reading Football Club became the leading team in the town. And the rest, as they say, is history.

In the London Senior Cup, the Casuals fared a little better, defeating Argus 2-0 in the first round but then going out to Upton Park by the same score in the second. All the other matches were friendlies and again most of the matches were away. Of the thirteen home matches they eventually broke their duck at the Field with a 2-0 win against Guy's Hospital on 18 December and repeated another home win against the same side, 5-3 later in the season. There were other wins at the Field against East Sheen and also Oxford University 2-1. The club were also beginning to travel quite extensively to play away matches, on tour at Derby County, Blackburn Olympic, Nottingham Forest and Bolton Wanderers. The first of these matches was won by 2-1, but a match against Bolton Wanderers found the home side too strong, as the club went down by a score of 12-1. Again, the season was mediocre, but overall an improvement on their first.

During their final season (1885/86) at the Field, the Casuals famously defeated Tottenham Hotspur in a London Senior Cup 2nd Round match 8-0. Tottenham Hotspurs' history recalls *'The result was to be expected…… They [the Casuals] fielded a side that in later years-after the advent of professionalism – would have done duty for an England amateur international side. Better equipped in skill, and overwhelming in physique, they overshadowed the young, by no means tall and still rather raw, Spurs side.'* The club's run in the London Senior Cup did not last and they went out in the following round to Old St Marks. By now the club was beginning to get more coverage in the Press. On tour the Casuals added amongst others Burnley and Aston Villa to their list, which resulted in a draw 2-2 against the former and a notable 4-3 win against the latter. They suffered a heavy defeat away to Swifts in the FA Cup first round again.

From the 1886/87 season, the Casuals would spend their next four seasons at the Upper Tooting Cricket Club in Beechcroft Road before moving away from the area, rather strangely returning there for a single match with Old Brightonians in 1892. One of the reasons for playing at Upper Tooting was probably because there were changing facilities on the ground itself. The club obviously liked their creature comforts! The Casuals would return to play Clapham Rovers from time to time, but at the Field where they used to call 'home', they would now be the visitors. It was perhaps no surprise with his increasing involvement in football administration, that Frederick Wall was often appointed to referee the Casuals matches at the Upper Tooting Cricket Club. He also ran the line in important matches at the Oval in the days when linesmen were known as umpires.

In subsequent years, the Casuals won the London Charity Cup in 1890/91 by beating Old Carthusians 5-2 in the final (after a replay) and were successful in that Cup on several occasions during the 1900s. Ironically, apart from sharing the London Senior Cup with Old Westminsters they were destined, despite finishing runners up no less than five times, never to win the trophy outright. They did, however, win the AFA Senior Cup three times. The Casuals played their last FA Cup match in the 1893/94 season as professionalism made it far more difficult for the amateur clubs to compete. In the same season they also entered the Amateur Cup and went out in the semi-final, ironically, to Old Carthusians, former FA Cup Winners and one of the schools that supplied Old Boys to their ranks in their inaugural season. The club continued to play friendlies until the 1905/06 season when they were one of the founding clubs of the Isthmian League. They were runners up of the Isthmian League in 1913/14 and again in 1935/36. In the latter season they won the FA Amateur Cup beating Wycombe Wanderers on the way to the Final where they beat Ilford in a replay. This was the highlight of their later years and the club thereafter went into a sharp decline, performing only moderately in the Isthmian League. Their reserve team also struggled.

The Casuals played their final match on 6 May 1939 defeating Wimbledon 4-3 to at least go out on a winning note. A merger with the Corinthian football club which had openly been discussed for a couple of years finally came to fruition and the merged club played just one match before the Second World War. In a sense the amalgamation was inevitable with their more illustrious partners who continued to play friendlies right until the end and arguably were a match for many of the professional clubs in their halcyon days, but they too were struggling to be fully competitive by then. Despite Casuals involvement in the Isthmian League, both clubs shared the same amateur ethos. Today as Corinthian Casuals the club play at the King George's Field in Tolworth in Tier 7 of the football league pyramid.

In summary it seems that during their relatively short stay at the Field a majority of their matches were away and that the more high-profile matches were played on neutral venues such as the Oval. As mentioned previously, upon looking at the records, even after entering the Isthmian League, a vast number of friendlies were played away from home. It was not until football resumed after the Great War that a more balanced look to their fixture list became apparent. So, it could be almost said that in the early days the Casuals were, in effect, a wandering side that played a few home matches along the way. Although the 'gate' at the Field was never recorded or even estimated, it is interesting to imagine spectators heading up from Wandsworth Common station on match days in the early afternoon. Little did the Casuals know it at the time, but the year of their founding 1883, marked the last occasion that an English amateur club won the FA Cup and since then no amateur club (save the Scottish side Queens Park in 1884 and 1885) has even reached the Final. Although in many ways they were similar to Clapham Rovers in their ethos and approach to football, the Casuals willingness to embrace amateur league football stood them in good stead. As a club they were survivors, and although they did not kick a ball in anger between April 1914 and September 1919, they lived to fight another day as we know.

Which Rangers?

Much as Clapham Rovers is a forgotten side, so too are the Rangers Football Club. The club was founded shortly after Clapham Rovers and this was, maybe, the reason that they were generically named as such. As Clapham Rovers, the club started life on Clapham Common but circumstances generally associated with overcrowding dictated they should move, and the club rented a field behind Philip Cazenove's house in Chatham Road Battersea. Coincidentally, Cazenove was the first Chairman of the Sir Walter St John's School Trust between 1874 and 1879 and also a School Governor. It was here, more than likely, that the school originally organised its annual sports day. He conducted a bible-class in his dining room. When Cazenove died in 1881 it is likely, within a year or so, in order for the land to be developed, that the Rangers had to seek a further ground on which to play their football. Before that, during the 1880/81 season, the Rangers were involved in an unlikely FA Cup run. In the first round the Wanderers (previous Cup Winners) surprisingly scratched to them and in the second round the club received a bye! In the third round the Rangers were drawn against the Royal Engineers, Cup winners in 1875. The match was played at the Kennington Oval, so this really was indeed the club's own 'Cup Final'. The Royal Engineers won easily 6-0. In Frederick Wall's book he remembers that he prepared for the match by having a good rump steak for lunch and that in those days what players ate before matches as an amateur was less important *'for football was then just a game'*. So perhaps this was one of the many reasons why professional football took the lead as the years went on!

The move away from Chatham Road presented problems, and with so many clubs appending 'Rangers' to their names trying to discover the truth is not easy, but what follows is probably an accurate course of events. Firstly, changing accommodation had to be found and when no suitable inn or pub could be located, the club went 'cap in hand' to the Wandsworth Common Church Institute who welcomed them on the condition that all the Rangers should become members of the Institute enjoying its advantages but sharing their responsibilities. The Church Institute's base was in Wiseton Road and, like the Rangers, they would, perhaps, from time to time, use the Field to play their football. For the Rangers, changing at the Church Institute seemed quite a good idea, but in 1884 their loyalty was tested. The Church Institute also had a reasonable rugby side and had entered a competition for the Jersey Football Trophy reaching the Final where their opponents were to be the Richmond Church Institute. Richmond was a rugby stronghold and news came through that some of their players qualified for their counterparts. Their rivals at Wiseton Road anticipated defeat, but the Secretary of the club asked for help from the Rangers requesting 'three fast men'. In the event, two of the Rangers fastest forwards volunteered and, although usually goalkeeper for the Rangers, Frederick Wall also volunteered. Much to their surprise the Wandsworth side won and Frederick Wall kept his medal to remind himself of the occasion he played rugby rather than football! Perhaps inspired by the Rangers, the Church Institute had their own football side. Known as 'The Stutes' they played local football usually on Wandsworth Common. In recent times with the Church Institute now effectively defunct, the site was sold to developers and in 2017 Charles Baker Place, a development of nine houses, was completed.

As for the Rangers, their stay at the Church Institute was short lived because according to Frederick Wall again *'The Rangers became quite a good club and it was advisable to hire another field. This was near to Wandsworth Common adjoining the ground of The Casuals, and adjacent to the county gaol.'* The reference to Wandsworth Common was misleading but in those days most of the surrounding area was open countryside and the Upper Tooting Cricket Club, where the Casuals played would abut open land. The reference to the ground being adjacent to the county gaol is also somewhat ambiguous, but although it is true that it looked like a gaol, this was in fact the County Lunatic Asylum! Sadly, inmates inside that institution would have probably spent longer there than most of the prisoners at what is now Wandsworth Prison about a mile to the north in Heathfield Road.

In December 1885, in conjunction with the Heathfield Cricket Club, the Rangers organised the first in perhaps what they thought might be a series of smoking concerts at the East Hill Hotel Wandsworth. The initial evening was a success apparently both vocally and numerically. The local press declared that *'The success achieved by the Heathfield cum Rangers in the field bids fair'*. During the evening a Mr Strong, probably a Rangers man, talked 'in well-chosen terms' about the efforts to amalgamate the Heathfield and Rangers clubs. The speech was well received and the *South London Press* implied that an amalgamation was almost a done deal. However, it was not to be. Further smoking concerts went ahead without the Rangers. The connection between the two clubs was probably because some players were members of both clubs. One of them, T.J. Faulkner, went on to play cricket with the Heathfield Cricket Club for the best part of twenty-five years. However, with the cricket club still trying to establish itself, a pragmatic approach was likely to have been taken, and given that the Clapham Rovers were the established club at the Field by then, the talks of an amalgamation came to nothing. Perhaps the Rangers already knew of the Casuals intention to vacate the Field at the end of the season, negating their dash from *The Hope* to play their football? During the 1880s the Field was a hive of activity on Saturdays conceivably containing up to two football pitches and possibly two rugby pitches. Maybe the joint smoking concert was an attempt by the Rangers to gain a stronger foothold at the Field in place of the Casuals at the end of that season.

The Rangers were to break any association they had with the Field soon afterwards, choosing to use a ground adjoining the Upper Tooting Cricket Club, now the Casuals new home. They could not have been there for long. In his book Frederick Wall states that the club then had to move again, *'and make way for the house builders'*. On the face of it, this statement seems contrary, but the key to this lies in part to the piecemeal construction of Beechcroft Road. By 1886, new housing had already replaced what used to be Wandsworth Lodge and only a short time afterwards Beechcroft Road was extended to accommodate more housing. This would have reduced the size of the cricket ground which, although not fatal to the existence of the Upper Tooting Cricket Club at the time, meant, with less outfield available during the winter, that a reorganisation of that ground for hockey and football purposes was probably required. The extension of Beechcroft Road would have similarly affected the adjoining field where perhaps the Rangers played. Later maps show a lodge on the lower corner of that field and it is likely that the land had been taken into the grounds of Park Hill, the house nearby adjoining the lodge. Either way, the Rangers were to lose out, and moved to the Hasking's Sports Ground in Balham. The final part of Beechcroft Road down the hill from Glenburnie Road to Upper Tooting Road was not installed, probably, until the start of the twentieth century.

The other interesting feature of the Rangers club was that the side consisted of men largely connected with St Marks Training College in Chelsea; indeed, Frederick Wall studied there. There is evidence that both St Mark's Training College in Chelsea and St Johns College in Battersea, both founded as teacher training colleges, had significant footballing traditions certainly going back to the early 1870s. Indeed, the Old Boys side of St Marks were strong enough to participate in senior London competitions, as their defeat of the Casuals demonstrated. On at least one occasion they entered the FA Cup itself. St Johns College competed in the Clapham League alongside Wimbledon Old Centrals at the turn of the century. Predictably, when playing Old St John's, Old St Mark's would have the better of the exchanges. Graduates of St Mark's College were also involved in the foundation of the Hotspur Club and another in the establishment of senior amateur leagues in London in the first decade of the 1900s. St John's College had definite links with Sir Walter St John's School in Battersea and indeed was the first teacher training institute in the country having been founded around 1840. Several teachers over the years taught at the Sir Walter St John's School which effectively backed onto St John's College. When in 1923, St John's College amalgamated with St Mark's College in Chelsea, the site of the former was demolished to make way for a new estate with the exception of the original manor house, Old Battersea House which, following a determined campaign by the Headmaster of Sir Walter St John's School, J.G. Taylor, himself a former graduate of St John's College, saved the house from destruction. It still stands today having been completed originally in 1699, by Sir Walter St John, and reputedly designed by Sir Christopher Wren and is a Grade II listed building. It was eventually bought by Malcolm Forbes, editor of the *Forbes Magazine* and the house was visited by U.S. President, Ronald Reagan, Elizabeth Taylor, and Prime Minister Margaret Thatcher amongst others during his time as owner. Although Forbes moved out in 2011 and the considerable collection of artefacts in the house were sold at auction, it still remains in private hands today, having been seized from Russian Sergei Pugachev otherwise known as 'Putin's banker' in 2014. Indeed, from time to time in later years, both Sir Walter St John's School in Battersea High Street and Battersea Grammar School, used to interact with the college known as 'Marjons' in occasional sports events (including chess!) and cultural matters. In 1973, the college moved away from Chelsea, in what seemed a rather radical relocation to Plymouth. In 2013 it attained full university status and is now known as Plymouth Marjon University continuing to offer sporting and cultural courses similar to and in addition to those originally offered at Chelsea.

Frederick Wall was born in Battersea in 1858 and served for almost forty years as Secretary of the Football Association, presiding over enormous changes in that organisation both nationally and internationally, as the professional game took over from the amateur. In 1930 he was one of the first to receive a knighthood for his services to football. He was also awarded a gold medal for his work by the United States Football Association and presided over many Cup Finals and the opening of Dulwich Hamlet's new stadium in 1931. In later life, he was also a director at Arsenal from 1934-38. In his book, *50 Years of Football 1884-1934* he rather wistfully recalls in childhood *'the lavender fields...... market gardens with chestnut and yew trees on the landscape'* although he omits to mention, according to the *South London Press,* that Battersea was at one stage famous for producing the finest asparagus. Things have changed, of course, as Lavender Hill is nothing like that today.

The Westminster Connection

The departure of the Casuals and to a lesser degree the Rangers at the end of the 1885/86 season gave other clubs the opportunity to use the Field as their home ground. One of these sides was the Westminster Football Club. However, if we think of Clapham Rovers and the Rangers as forgotten clubs, actually less is known about Westminster! Remarkably they would play at the Field from the autumn of 1886 until perhaps as late as the spring of 1898, although there is a suggestion that in the final few years, they may have taken up residence at a ground next to the former Spencer CC ground between Lyford and Ellerton Roads prior to that club's move to Fieldview. Possibly established as early as 1864, around the birth of the modern game, the club appears to have previously used a ground in the Dulwich area adjacent to the *Grove Tavern* to enjoy their football. Westminster were, initially, to replace the Rangers in using the Church Institute as a changing facility from the 1886/87 season. The club, rather loftily, referred to the Field as their 'private ground on Wandsworth Common'.

So just what were the Westminster club doing playing in South London, considering where their roots were situated? It is unfortunate that they existed under the shadow of two other famous footballing sides, Old Westminsters and Westminster School itself, who were both at the forefront of amateur football. Both used Vincent Square as their base and attracted good crowds and the latter would invariably play most, if not all, of their matches at home. Upon visiting Vincent Square today, the problem the Westminster club faced as outsiders can well be understood. It is an oasis of calm in the metropolis, situated within the confines of the London 'congestion zone', and within sight of 'Big Ben'. Many buildings surrounding Vincent Square are invariably as old as the ground itself. Travelling by car today to play a midweek match at the ground would be quite an expensive exercise. However, in those days with space at a premium, despite having the Duke of Westminster as their patron, Westminster were just a regular football club, and the prospect of finding and funding a suitable ground within the locality would probably have been beyond them. However, with the Field having a direct link by train from Victoria to Wandsworth Common, this would have been an attraction and the most convenient option outside the area of Westminster itself.

Old Westminsters, known as 'The Pinks' because of their distinctive football shirts, were frequent visitors to the Field. From time to time the Old Westminsters club would play the Westminster club, but given the other commitments they had on the same day, they would invariably only send a Reserve side at best to play them. On one occasion on 15 January 1887, Old Westminsters actually hired the Field for a London Senior Cup Match against the Hotspur. A report on the match tells us that a crowd of five hundred spectators witnessed the club defeat their rivals by 2-0.

Returning to the Westminster club, they were able from the 1888/89 season and the following three or four seasons to use the *Surrey Tavern* itself to change for matches. By then, although not playing the highest standard of football, they were nevertheless running three sides. One of the problems was that few of their matches were regularly advertised and even fewer results were reported. On 2 November 1889, Westminster FC played the Wimbledon Old Centrals in one of the very first matches that the latter club played on Wimbledon Common in their inaugural season. The notification of this match was not advertised, unlike two other matches the Westminster club were playing on the same day. The result of the match went largely unrecorded, with one exception. The *Surrey Independent & Mid Surrey Gazette* reported that the Old Centrals won 1-0, but against which one of Westminster Football Club's three sides?

Like many other sides, the Westminster club enjoyed its smoking concerts. Such forms of entertainment have long died out, but these functions involved an audience of men only, who would smoke and speak of politics, whilst listening to live music and singing. On one occasion held at the club's headquarters at the *Fleury's Hotel*, Artillery Row on 25 January 1892, a Monday evening, the entertainment did not start until 9.00pm and because of the number attending, and entertainment provided, so the report goes, 'Encores were prohibited'. However, the event confirmed the connection with Westminster School as the Old Westminsters were represented by the Moon brothers. Other football clubs attending included St Andrews and Excelsior, both Westminster based clubs. Looking at team sheets there were also a few players from the Heathfield Cricket Club that would keep themselves fit with the Westminster club during the winter.

The one thing that the Westminster Football Club did, however, was to introduce league football to the Field. In 1892 the club entered the newly formed South London League. Although records are incomplete the club did sufficiently well for five members of the club to be selected to play for the South London League at the Field against the Woolwich League on 9 March 1893 with the match ending in a 2-2 draw. The following season was a disappointment as the league expanded. The 1st XI finished bottom of Division One and the 2nd XI fared little better in Division Two finishing in penultimate position. The club then apparently withdrew from league football for the next couple of seasons.

In December 1894, the Westminster club finally got a chance to play Old Westminsters at Vincent Square. The report stated that 'the residents' as they were called were 'strongly represented'. The report observed that the Old Westminsters 'were not fully represented in their front rank', but in truth it was the defence that went missing. The result was a triumph for Westminster Football Club as they ran out 5-0 winners. The same month saw an interesting appeal made by the club to the London Football Association about a match played with Unity. The club claimed that a major factor in their defeat had been the similarity of club colours. The referee however was of the opinion that it had made 'no difference as regards to knowing the men' and so the appeal was dismissed!

For the 1896/97 season, the club made another attempt to play league football with the 1st XI entering the West London League and finishing mid table. The 2nd XI bravely entered the South London League Division One and unsurprisingly finished in penultimate position, after the bottom side had withdrawn in mid- season. In a match on 7 November 1896 between the Westminster Football Club and East Sheen a reporter observed *On that part of Wandsworth Common which is separated from the public portion by a fence…..The ground was in an awful state and the mud prevented anything like good playing.*' Not perhaps for the first time has the Field been criticised for its drainage. East Sheen duly won 4-1.

Whilst the Westminster club had reverted to changing again at the Church Institute from 1892, by the start of the 1895/96 season with the Clapham Rovers Football Club having moved away, it is quite possible that for the next three seasons they may have changed in the Heathfield Cricket Club's pavilion at the Field. It is likely by now that the Heathfield club had obtained a licence and the need to patronise the *Surrey Tavern* had passed. Assuming the club were still at the Field, the 1897/98 season, was to be Westminster's last in the vicinity. Only the 1st XI entered the West London League and struggled to finish sixth out of eight. However, the uncertainty over the future of the Field which cumulated with John Mills Thorne purchasing it during the latter part of 1898, could not have come at a worse time for the club as they had entered, ambitiously, Division One of the Southern Suburban League for the 1898/99 season. Perhaps as the sale of the ground was imminent, the London County Council could not guarantee the use of the field during the winter, so the club moved away to a ground at Denmark Hill. Predictably, later that season on 10 April 1899, the club suffered a humiliating 14-0 defeat at Deptford playing three men short, and finished rock-bottom of the league. It appears this was the end of their league aspirations and maybe ultimately the club itself. In September 1900 a new club under the same name was formed and certainly from the 1901/02 season they moved north of the river nearer to the place which bore their name. Thereafter the local papers concentrated more on Chelsea, Fulham and Queens Park Rangers as the leading sides in the area, and at some stage the new Westminster side would also fall by the wayside.

Before moving on it is worth also remembering Morton Rangers. Like Westminster and Rangers, they were also one of four clubs (Clapham Rovers being the other) out of the original fifty-two, that helped form the London Football Association in 1882 and were able to a greater or lesser extent to call the Field their own. Indeed, such was the quality of the football played at the Field that at least a dozen more of the original founder clubs of the London Football Association would play at the Field as visitors. Morton Rangers moved to the Field from Shepherds Bush at the start of the 1883/84 season, at about the same time that the Casuals were forming their own club. They probably shared changing facilities at the *Surrey Tavern* with Clapham Rovers. In the 1881/82 season, they had entered the FA Cup going out in the first round to Old Foresters by 3-0. Thereafter it would appear they must have thought that the competition was not for them, as there are no further records of them taking part. Perhaps the one notable football match that Morton Rangers played involved a 4-0 drubbing at Luton Town on Easter Monday in 1885! Thereafter, the club went into decline. They were perhaps better known for their Tuesday evening runs from the *Surrey Tavern* that was open to anyone, come rain or (moon)shine, over a course of about four miles. Remarkably, these events commenced in the pitch black at around 9pm returning to the *Surrey Tavern* afterwards to take on some refreshment and presumably to undo all the good work running around in the dark had done! Again, it was a club that was struggling to turn out sides, and it seems they eventually folded by the end of the 1887/88 season if not before. Perhaps, by then, they were just running on empty.

Once Morton Rangers had gone, other clubs would fill the void without suggesting anything more than a temporary involvement. It is quite possible that although Clapham Rovers were still constant occupants at that time, the use of the Field was quite dynamic, and would have required a good degree of coordination for the organisers, whether that be the London County Council by then, or not. Of course, you also took your chance with the weather as on a good day the Field would be described as 'magnificent', but on a poor day, with the wind blowing the rain, as dire! One thing is quite likely. When in 1890, the London County Council assumed control of the Field from Earl Spencer, John Bonner at the *Surrey Tavern / Hotel* would have invariably lost overall control of the sports clubs that used it.

Wandsworth Woes

When Clapham Rovers Football Club effectively vacated the Field in 1895, it seemed that the winter months were a little quieter for the next couple of years. One club to play at the Field from that date was the Clapham Lacrosse Club who carried on doing so until the spring of 1899. By then, with the Field now in the hands of John Mills Thorne, and with the Heathfield Cricket Club effectively maintaining the field all year long, things were changing.

For the 1899/1900 season Wandsworth FC played at the Field. Seemingly a club on the way up, they had won the South Western Cup in 1894/95, and retained the cup in the following season. However, it was not all plain sailing. On 2 January 1897 they played the Thames Ironworkers FC – later to be known as West Ham United - away in the London Senior Cup and were losing 7-0 when the match was abandoned ten minutes from time owing to fog. The match was ordered to be replayed a week later, but the Ironworkers still won 3-1. In 1897/98 Wandsworth FC had entered the newly formed Southern Suburban League as a founder member, Dulwich Hamlet were also one of their number, and they were eager it seemed to up their game.

The move to the Field from their rather humble surroundings in Franche Court Road, Summerstown was to prove controversial. On 23 September 1899, the club kicked off at the Field against Sheppey United having vacated their Summerstown ground only the week previously. The altercation had stemmed from the mismanagement of finances and perhaps players, with an implied admission that the club had probably overpaid on expenses during the previous season, during a period when many clubs were still keen to keep the distinction between an amateur or a professional club. There was a boycott organised by a number of disgruntled supporters when the move was announced and wholesale changes to the playing membership were made. A former player, Fred Spackman, one of their better-known footballers, who would go on to represent Great Britain as an amateur at the 1900 Paris Olympics where Association Soccer was a demonstration sport-a competition that Great Britain would win, reportedly said of the dispute that he 'would never kick another ball for Wandsworth again'. He would remain an amateur footballer at Fulham for some years, although, by now, that club was regarded effectively as a professional outfit. After football, Fred Spackman went on to work as a journalist in the Great War and a proof reader for *The Times* newspaper, dying in Bromley in 1942.

The main reasons for moving, despite the additional expense, were apparently the larger fan base that the Field would offer which the club hoped would attract larger attendances and a superior playing surface. Initially, the club made a promising start, and were pleased with a gate of £13 (suggesting a crowd of perhaps around 750 spectators) from their match on 7 October 1899, but it was clear that matters had not been fully resolved. Three weeks later the club progressed as far as the third qualifying round of the FA Cup before being overwhelmed 7-1 at the Field by Queens Park Rangers who demonstrated the widening gap between the amateur and the professional game. Thereafter, the seasons fortunes declined somewhat and in March 1900, less than six months after making their debut the Heathfield Cricket Club closed the Field to football to concentrate preparing the turf for the forthcoming cricket season. The Wandsworth club were never destined to return. At the start of the 1900/01 season, again with an extensive change of playing members, the club transferred to the London League Division One and although threatened with dissolution owing to financial and playing irregularities were now playing at a new ground in Earlsfield. It is no secret that the season was a catastrophe for the club, as they finished bottom of the league, having lost all but one of their twenty league matches, remarkably scoring only 4 goals and conceding 115 in the process. Their reserve side fared little better. Some weeks it was a real struggle turning a team out at all, and players would also turn up late for matches! By the end of the 1900/01 season it appears, the 'Spiders' as Wandsworth FC were known, were in discussions regarding returning to the Field for the following season, and there was speculation that the Heathfield club would look favourably upon their request over and above the discussions being held with a rugby club. However, given the football club's troubles, the Heathfield club were no doubt wary of granting Wandsworth another chance at the Field, and instead chose the rugby option. Perhaps the Heathfield club had learnt from their experience. It was probably a classic case of false economics, prevalent to this day, of renting a ground to a football club during the winter and then paying much more than the rent for spring renovations. This, and the fact that the Heathfield club must have regarded a rugby club as a far better and reliable proposition, given the increased interest in rugby at that time. It was probably reasoned also that rugby would help raise the profile of the Field as a sporting venue and promote the growing influence of the game within South London and bring in larger crowds as well. Wandsworth's troubles continued. After that, another attempt to regroup was made at a new ground near Wimbledon Park station and subsequently at yet another ground in the Earlsfield area again for the 1902/03 season. In September 1903, the *South London Press* posed the question *'Is Wandsworth Defunct?'*, as Clapham Football Club had moved into their Earlsfield ground at the start of that season. The answer would appear to have been in the affirmative, and we must assume that the club had disbanded during the summer. It was a sad end for a football club that had promised so much only a few years previously. What happened at Wandsworth FC unfortunately is not unique, and owing to poor or dysfunctional management, a club is ultimately at the mercy of its stakeholders or benefactors irrespective of whether results on the field are successful or not. On a larger stage, ask Bury FC.

The Wandsworth name as a sports club brand appears to be blighted. A football club by the same name reappeared in the 1960s but like their cricket counterparts who compete in the Surrey Cricket League from time to time, neither football nor cricket clubs that exist today show any signs of permanence.

The Harlequins Arrive

Ongoing discussions that the Heathfield club were having with a rugby club were unveiled at their AGM on 12 September 1901, when Harlequin FC (colloquially known as 'Harlequins' or just 'Quins') confirmed that they had secured the use of 'the enclosure at one time the ground of the Clapham Rovers' as their new home. Rugby rather than Association rules would now prevail at the Field and teams of fifteen playing with a rugby ball would replace teams of eleven playing with a football. In a sense this was nothing new given the ground's dual use as a rugby and football field through most of its previous twenty-five year's history. Harlequins were a well-known club when they arrived at the Field, and played a good standard of rugby. This was to be one of the finest eras in their history before they departed for Twickenham in 1909. Rugby would continue to be the dominant winter sport at the Field until the Great War. Remarkably this was Harlequins' fourteenth ground since their foundation in 1866, and because the club was founded before the official establishment of rugby football as a separate and distinct sport from football, Harlequins are still known today, officially, as a football club! The club were on the move again after effectively wandering the previous season, and only having spent one season the year before that, at the Polo Grounds in Wimbledon Park. Designed by Capability Brown for Lord Spencer in the 1760s, this must have been quite a pleasant location for a pitch just north of the lake, but by the time of the move to the Field, the club were facing a crisis as this coincided with the Boer War, and the club was struggling for membership as a result. Funds were so depleted that there was a real threat that the club would have to disband. However, convinced that the move would be a success, and perhaps inspired by Wandsworth FC's gate money receipts, admission to the Heathfield cricket ground (rather confusingly initially described by the Harlequins as 'Heathfield Park' in the South London Press) was fixed at 6d for the matches while season tickets were 7s 6d. The gamble to move to the Field however was a success. If confirmation was needed as to the suitability of their new home, over 400 spectators attended the opening match at the Field for a 2nd XV match with Rosslyn Park on 28 September 1901, and over the next eight years crowds would be considerably larger than elsewhere they had played. If previous spectators of the football at the Field had been confused by the colours of the Casuals' shirts of exotic chocolate and pink or those of the Clapham Rovers, they would have certainly been bemused by the Harlequins' colours of magenta, chocolate brown, French grey, and light blue quarters which was to become, if not already, the world's most famous trademark rugby shirt.

The Heathfield club agreed terms with the Harlequins of an annual rent not exceeding £35 for the winter season. It could be at this stage that the Field had been invariably reconfigured to suit the high standard of rugby the Harlequins would be playing, given that rugby pitches are generally larger than football pitches. There is also good evidence to suggest, with the Harlequins charging an admission fee to matches, that a more secure and sturdy chain link fence to Burntwood Lane and Trinity Road was introduced at this stage. For Harlequins, money was still tight, however, and a proposal to bring Oxford University to the Field for a first home match (the club had always played them away since 1876) was finally shelved as the club was not in a position to offer the University a fixed guarantee to do so. Unfortunately, few pictures seem to survive of the club's time at the Field, but a sketch in The Daily Graphic relating to a match with Richmond on 3 October 1903 (which the club lost 6-3) clearly shows the Heathfield pavilion in the background and a crowd lining the pitch –

no stands in those days, suggesting that the pitch was aligned parallel to Burntwood Lane and that the Field perhaps accommodated one full size rugby pitch in winter at that time. It should be remembered that by then the Heathfield club had installed a bowls green and tennis courts on the periphery adjacent to Beechcroft Road.

The first senior match at the Field was against Richmond on 5 October 1901. It was not a particularly good start for the club as they lost 12-5 but after that the club's form improved as the season progressed. Their first win at 'home' was against St. Bartholomew's Hospital (8-0) and other notable wins at the Field were recorded against Rosslyn Park (21-6) and Old Alleynians (13-0). The match against Oxford University mentioned earlier was duly played away again losing 27-3, but it was notable for the debut of A.D. (Adrian) Stoop who scored the only try. Stoop's involvement with the club would not only transform their fortunes, but also the game of rugby itself. In all he was to gain fifteen caps for England and play 182 matches for Harlequins up until 1939. And to think that the Field witnessed many of those earlier performances!

It was not all rugby however, because on New Year's Day 1902 a football match was staged between the South London Boys and the Rest of London Boys, (perhaps the rugby pitch was converted for the purpose, or the Field had an adjoining football pitch by then) in conjunction with both the Harlequins and the Heathfield club. The report says that *A capital gate assembled, the majority of whom were juveniles'*. The match was won by the latter by 2-1. In a repeat of the 1879 rugby match staged by Clapham Rovers, another match that caught the eye as Harlequins showcased their new ground was a rugby match between Surrey and Middlesex. Those were the days when county rugby was taken more seriously. So, on 5 November 1902, in front of a crowd of around 1,000 spectators, this match took place at the Field. It was interesting to note that no fewer than seven of the players were already internationals and Adrian Stoop, who played for Middlesex would soon be. In a close contest Middlesex got home by 11-10. The Harlequins also hosted several Surrey trial matches at the Field over the next few years, in much the same way that Clapham Rovers had done before them.

The following season 1902/03 seems to have been extremely wet and only nineteen matches were played whilst fourteen were cancelled. There were wins at the Field against Oxford University and St Bartholomew's Hospital in successive weeks and later in the season a scoreless draw was recorded against Blackheath- an unusual occurrence in rugby matches. Because the Field was under water on 28 February the match with Richmond was moved to their second ground and after half time moved onto the main ground which had been occupied earlier by the London Scottish and London Irish match. There cannot be very many matches in any sport where a match had started on one pitch and finished on another, but the Harlequins came away victorious by 26-0. Whilst it was true that the season was wet, with too many matches abandoned at the Field as a result, an attempt was made to thoroughly drain the lower pitch used by the Harlequins 'at a big cost' to the Heathfield club. Sadly, this made little difference to matches called off in the following season, and the situation only marginally improved after that.

In 1903/04, a good number of matches were again cancelled (probably again by weather). Notable victories included a 14-8 success against London Irish at the Field and a first victory at Blackheath by 16-10. An end of season tour was arranged and matches at Plymouth and Redruth were organised.

1904/05 saw the first appearance at the Field by another future international player H.J.H. (Herbert) Sibree, but it was not enough to see the Harlequins slip to a 15-3 defeat at the hands of Old Merchant Taylors'. The start of the season also saw the controversial defection of Ted Dillon to Blackheath. Already a rugby international, he is perhaps best remembered as a leading first-class cricketer who led Kent to three county championships in 1909, 1910 and 1913, and as a result is the only Kent captain to have led the county to the Championship more than once. Although, again, a number of matches were cancelled, it was a poor season with only six victories to show for the club's efforts. By the start of the following season at the AGM, the club was showing a serious financial deficit, but enough was raised to keep the club afloat. It was at this meeting that the club's fortunes were about to turn. A youthful Adrian Stoop was elected Secretary as well as vice-captain, and the following season was more successful and, mercifully drier. The club was beginning to travel further from home, but notable wins at the Field included those against United Services Portsmouth (16-6) and Old Alleynians (42-5), whilst on the debit side the club lost to Old Merchistonians (from Scotland) (21-0) and Northampton (18-3), but away from home the club beat both the Universities.

At the AGM before the start of the 1906/07 season, Adrian Stoop proposed that the rules should be amended to show that the Club now played in white shorts ('knickerbockers' as they were known in those days) as opposed to dark blue shorts, which it seems had been the case for several years previously. The club were obviously attracting significant crowds to matches at the Field, and the Heathfield club wanted to purchase an automatic checking turnstile out of the gate money for use at the Field- perhaps they had a share in the take by then as well! The Harlequins made a better showing in the season, recording wins at the Field, amongst others, against Richmond (35-9) and Cambridge University (11-0). Oxford University were also scheduled visitors but the Field was unfit again. In an echo of the 1902/03 season, the match was switched thanks to the generosity of Richmond and London Scottish to their second pitch. As it turned out, two thirds of the gate preferred to watch the club beat Oxford University narrowly by 9-8. However, for all the efforts of the Heathfield club, the poor drainage at the Field was a continuing problem. In one fixture against Devonport Albion, it was reported that the pitch was like a *'quagmire with pools of water evident'*. Having travelled all the way from the west country and despite the difficult conditions which were hardly fit for play, the visiting side were anxious to do so, and the match went ahead with the visitors winning 6-0.

The 1907/08 season proved to be one of the most successful yet. Richmond were 'put to the sword' by 42-0 at the Field and so were visitors, Bath (49-8). Other victories included Old Alleynians (32-3), London Irish (31-0) and Blackheath (11-0). Old Merchant Taylors', in front of a home crowd of over 3,000 spectators, together with Rosslyn Park were beaten both home and away. At the end of the season, just to demonstrate how influential Harlequins were as a side it was reported that 'two new English internationals had played for the club during the season alongside eight other capped winners who had appeared before'. The club was obviously riding high, and was fast becoming a 'conveyor belt' for international players.

1908/09 would prove to be Harlequins final season at the Field. The RFU had been looking for tenants to occupy a new 17,000 capacity stadium at Twickenham. Stoop engineered the change by suggesting that Harlequins effectively ground share with the RFU. His name, on behalf of the club, would be one of the signatories to the lease. Apart from a sticky patch of form in autumn, after overwhelming Old Merchant Taylors' 53-5 in the opening match at the Field, the rest of the season was a runaway success. Although both 'Varsity' matches were lost at the Field to Cambridge and then Oxford University, they were watched by around 3,000 and 5,000 spectators respectively. Surbiton were demolished at the Field by 74-3 – a record score, but perhaps the best result of the season was the 20-13 victory at Leicester. Harlequins' stay at the Field was rounded off on 20 February with an 11-0 victory against Richmond. By now the Harlequins had truly established themselves as one of the most influential clubs in the country-a position they still hold today.

Apart from Stoop, the Harlequin's team now included other quality players such as John Birkett and Ronald Poulton, who both went on to skipper the English rugby side. The latter, a friend of Stoop's, described as the 'Archetypal Harlequin' was a gifted player and made his debut for the club in its last year at the Field. He used to travel up from Balliol College Oxford where he was studying, to play for the Harlequins. In 1912 Poulton moved to Reading to join his uncle at the Huntley & Palmer biscuit company. After his uncle died the following year, he inherited a fortune on the condition that he changed his surname to Palmer, presumably to maintain the official link with the company. This he did by Royal Licence in 1914, although it is said that he never used even the hyphenated name of Poulton-Palmer. Upon duly inheriting he is reportedly quoted as saying 'What troubles me is the responsibility of how to use the money for the best'. In the last international match before the Great War in 1914 Poulton scored four tries in a 39-13 rout of Scotland which was only matched, when Chris Ashton equalled that record for individual tries in an international in 2011. Five English players in that side lost their lives during the Great War. Poulton was one of them.

As for Stoop, he was awarded the Military Cross during the Great War, and went on to become President of the Harlequins from 1920 until 1949 and of the RFU in 1932-33. He was a friend of Douglas Bader and was responsible for teaching him the 'art of golf without using legs'. He was credited with revolutionising back play and introducing the concept of Scrum Half and Outside Half. He died aged 74 in 1957. As a tribute to the man who was absolutely inspirational and crucial to the development of rugby and to the Harlequins, their current home ground, the Twickenham Stoop lies literally within sight of Twickenham itself.

London Welsh Take Over

In the close season of 1909, with Harlequins' departure to Twickenham another rugby club, London Welsh RFC, were quick to see the advantages of using the Field, being close to many other first-class rugby clubs. In many ways their situation was remarkably similar to the Harlequins. Coincidentally, this was also their fourteenth move since their foundation, but in contrast to the Harlequins they arrived at the Field having played all their early rugby since 1892 north of the river with their immediate former home ground situated at the Memorial Athletic Ground in West Ham which was the former home of West Ham United before their move to Upton Park in 1904. This move was subsequently superseded by West Ham's later move to the London Stadium in 2016. The Heathfield club would have been eager to replace the Harlequins and would have seen this as a good opportunity to have a partner at the Field in the winter helping to pay rent towards their own lease.

On 18 September 1909 at 3.30pm, London Welsh, in front of no fewer than 4,000 spectators (similar crowds would be present at the Blackheath and Neath matches later in the season) kicked off a new chapter in their club's history which resulted in a 6-3 win over Glamorgan. It was a grand affair with no fewer than six international players being involved in the match. Officials from the Welsh Rugby Union who had come up to witness the facilities that the Field had to offer were entertained that evening at the *Holborn Restaurant* in London. The atmosphere at the Field apparently had a beneficial effect, and indeed in the opening season, the Welsh were to defeat clubs such as Bristol, Richmond, Rosslyn Park and most notably the Welsh champions, Neath by 8-6. An advertisement for the impending match against Richmond displayed the admission prices at '6d; Boys at 3d; Ladies free with the Stand and seats at 6d extra'. In other words, for a comfortable vantage point it would cost the equivalent of 1/- (or 5p in today's money), so perhaps on a good day the gate money may have approached as much as £100 or around £10,000 in today's money - not an insignificant amount in those days. Although all matches were effectively friendlies (league and cup competitions came much later) they were still fiercely competitive. After a drawn match with Blackheath at the Field, a *'couple of well- dressed young men darted from the crowd on the touchline'* to remonstrate against the decisions of the referee, a Mr. Williams, in his officiating of the match. Fortunately, the players quickly surrounded the referee, and a potentially ugly situation was averted, but it just illustrated the passions that spectators good or bad had for the game just as much as the players. During the season the Welsh also set foot on foreign soil for the first time. Their opposition were the Paris based Sporting Club Universitaire de France who they comfortably beat 19-0, but their other trips away from home were less successful. In front of a 10,000 crowd at Newport on Christmas Eve the Welsh lost 9-0 and worst was to follow at Cardiff Arms Park where only 5,000 spectators witnessed Cardiff's victory over the Welsh by 23-0. Hop Maddocks their captain and Welsh International was recalled to play for Wales for the match with France. The record shows that he scored two fine tries - and was promptly rewarded for his efforts by never being selected again! The weather that winter was 'vile' and several matches were lost to the weather. On one Saturday the Field was 'frost-bound, and on the next it was under water! The Easter Tour took the Welsh west, and matches were played at Stroud, Cinderford and Bath, but only Stroud were beaten. Nevertheless, the initial season at the Field had gone well.

The 1910-11 was a mediocre season, but useful wins were recorded over Bath, Blackheath and Cheltenham at the Field whilst a crowd of 3,000 cheered on the Welsh against Oxford University, although the students held on to record an 8-3 victory. The Welsh again won in Paris, but their only other notable wins away from home came at Richmond and their Celtic cousins, London Irish. The Easter tour was rather bad tempered. At Redruth the referee was frequently required to caution hot-headed players on both sides, whist at Torquay one player who remained incognito was sent off as the home side won 12-11. The Bristol match on tour ended in an 8-8 draw.

In 1911 the Field came on to the market and notwithstanding a difficult financial position the Welsh were quick to see the advantage of owning the ground on which they already played. The cost of the freehold was £3,800 but with other incidentals including a new grandstand and drainage the overall cost was around £5,000. On 2 June 1911 the Field was duly conveyed by John Mills Thorne to the London Welsh Athletic Club. By a further agreement in 1912, London Welsh got their grandstand by way of a licence through the Council even though a stand had been temporarily erected previously during the winter!

At the start of the 1911-12 season, the London Welsh used their new ownership of the ground to organise practice at the Field after cricket matches with the rugby players using the *Surrey Hotel* as a changing facility. However, despite optimism at the start of the new campaign, the club endured a poor season, in fact the worst since the start of the century. Their biggest defeat was suffered at the Field when Cambridge University were victors by 44-5. There were also heavy defeats at Newport and Guy's Hospital. Pontypool made their first visit to the ground and squeezed a 12-10 victory and won the return match in Wales by 14-0 on an Easter tour where the Welsh lost all three matches. There were however a few good wins at the Field. Ealing, winners of the Middlesex Cup later in the season, were demolished by 31-0, and another was the 26-0 defeat of Upper Clapton aided by two rugby playing Reverends, Williams and Lewis, who were responsible for most of the scoring. The Welsh also beat the touring Maoris although for most pundits the 13-0 victory came as no surprise. In truth, London Welsh was rebuilding the side but reports expressed surprise that a team with such talent could not quite reach its full potential and had lost matches they really should have won. Divine intervention had certainly deserted them! While there were reports that the Welsh were experimenting with a new formation and this was debated openly in the press, it did not improve their fortunes.

When the 1912-13 season arrived, the season started brightly and finished strongly but a poor middle season ensured that progress was limited. Tours at Christmas and Easter did not improve matters as all matches were lost! Apart from the matches with London Irish, the best result at the Field was the 34-3 hammering of Ealing (again), although the Welsh came desperately close to beating Bedford losing by a single point. Away from home there were wins at Blackheath and Rosslyn Park and the club did the double (home and away) over Catford Bridge.

1913-14 started encouragingly, but more than ninety players turned out for the first team. The London Welsh confirmed their new groundshare agreement with another exiled club, London Irish and details of the latter's involvement at the Field are covered later. The only upshot of this arrangement was that the Field would provide a 1st XV rugby match at the Field on every Saturday of the season. Additionally, to confirm their close working relationship with London Irish, the two clubs combined at the Field as the 'London Celts' in a match with Middlesex, which the combined side won narrowly by 3-0. However, as the season wore on, apart from good wins at the Field against Bedford (avenged in the return match on the last day of the season on 18 April 1914) and away at Coventry, the rest of the season saw the club if anything going backwards. There was also another dismal Christmas tour to Wales. In fact, during London Welsh's time at the Field the club failed to win a single rugby match on Welsh soil!

By the end of the season, with the storm clouds gathering over Europe, they were also doing so over the Field, in what turned out to be the London Welsh's final match there against Rosslyn Park on 14 March before the outbreak on the Great War in August 1914. In an earlier report, the *Sporting Life* had said of the rugby *'Wandsworth Common can be a bleak kind of place even when the sun is shining…. If you choose your day carefully, you can be as finely frozen as you could be on your way to the North Pole. The spectators well deserve to be described as enthusiasts. It was a day not fit for a dog'*. On the day in question, high winds (described as a hurricane in some reports) aided by driving rain, swept across South London and drove the players off after fifteen minutes of the second half, to the shelter of the pavilion and the match was abandoned without a point being scored. One of the soggy players was Gwilym Lloyd George, playing his first and last match of the season.

Although a further return match was planned with the London Irish for the following weekend, which was to coincide with the last match of the season at the Field, in a supreme irony, the match was called off on the day before, owing to the ground being unfit for play. An abject attempt at an apology was issued in the Monday edition of *The Sportsman* to spectators who had obviously turned up expecting play, only to find the Field closed. Little did the London Welsh realise, in another twist of fate, that the abandoned match against Rosslyn Park from the previous weekend, would, sadly, prove to be the very last competitive match of club rugby that the Field would ever stage again in its history to this day.

Regarding the timber grandstand which was erected and then taken down for the cricket during summer, it was surplus to requirements and the cost of storing it was prohibitive. The interesting fact was that the Heathfield club claimed that the timber was their property. This might have been the case if the timber had been bought before the purchase of the Field in 1911 by the London Welsh, although the licence for a grandstand was not officially granted until 1912. The Heathfield club claimed that the London Welsh had sold the timber stored for the grandstand in late 1915 without consulting them. Perhaps unsurprisingly, London Welsh's account of this is somewhat different. In the club's book *Dragon in Exile* the club's side of the story suggests that apart from the freehold (in 1911) the overall cost to the club at that time was estimated at £5,000 to include, amongst other items 'a new grandstand'. Perhaps the club's unilateral decision to pocket the money for the timber was all wrapped up with unpaid rental at the Field. Whatever the case, this did not improve or disguise the rather difficult relationship that the Heathfield club had with the London Welsh. The matter was put into the hands of the solicitors and the dispute rumbled on during the

War. Even at the time when the Field was sold in 1918, the dispute appeared to have still not been fully resolved! Perhaps the whole affair stemmed from London Welsh's purchase of the Field which effectively reversed the role of landlord and tenant in 1911.

The appraisal of London Welsh's final season at the Field was accurately summarised in *The Sportsman*. It confirmed that the club could rarely field the same team twice in what had been an average season. Interestingly the report continued that now they had acquired their own ground, the club had plans to erect a covered stand and pavilion at the Field. Quite how these plans would have compromised the cricket, or the groundshare arrangements with the London Irish, or indeed whether the council would have permitted a permanent stand, we shall never know.

The purchase of the Field in 1918 by the Sir Walter St John's Schools Trust, had left the London Welsh homeless when the players came back after the Great War. Col. J.C. Jenkins having returned from active service in France was so incensed to find that his co-trustees had sold the freehold without his prior permission that he severed all connections with the club he had served admirably as an international player and administrator. The Welsh finally found a base for 1919 when they secured the tenancy at the London County Athletic Ground in Burbage Road better known subsequently as the Herne Hill Cycle Track. The Field ranks as third behind Old Deer Park and Herne Hill for the number of matches played at home by the club, which numbered 73 in all with 40 wins, 28 losses and the balance drawn including, one presumes, the abandoned fixture with Rosslyn Park.

Whilst playing amongst the top sides in the country, since London Welsh RFC left the Field, their fortunes have been somewhat chequered. As early as 1930 the club won the Middlesex Sevens tournament and during the 1960s and 1970s featured regularly as Champions in a variety of Merit Table Rugby matches. However, in 2009 the club went into administration but were bought from the receivers. From 2012 until 2015 they played at the Kassam Stadium, home of Oxford United FC, before returning to Old Deer Park where the club had played since 1957. At the end of 2016 the club were liquidated, and early in 2017 season they were removed from the RFU Championship and had their results expunged. The club were amalgamated into their former amateur set up, previously known as the London Welsh Druids. They are currently working their way back up the rugby pyramid. Whilst the signs are promising, and although the club has provided so many Welsh international players such as John Dawes, J.P.R. Williams, Gerald and Mervyn Davies, Gavin Henson and Tom Shanklin, whether or not the club will ever return to top flight rugby again remains to be seen – but there are reasons to be optimistic about their future.

Although the original London Welsh rugby club was founded in 1885, it was then disbanded in 1894. The following year on 27 March 1895 the London Welsh soccer club which was already establishing itself within the London Area, consisted of ninety members all of whom were exclusively Welsh. They decided to set up a rugby section. Although the newly formed rugby club had 'nothing to do with the late London Welsh RFC' it contained several members who had been prominent in the previous defunct club. Matters came to a head in July 1898, when the financial losses sustained by London Welsh FC were entirely down to the rugby section and the two parts of the club decided to go their own way. Shortly afterwards, however, the tide began to turn when the Welsh Rugby Union gave official recognition to London Welsh RFC by making a grant of £50 to club funds. From that time onwards the rugby club quickly outgrew the reputation of their soccer counterparts. By coincidence or design, in 1911, the year that London Welsh bought the Field, the club modified their membership qualifications. Players had to be Welshmen, or of Welsh descent or to have played for a Welsh club. The requirements proved controversial and hardliners complained that these regulations were open to abuse as non-Welshmen have qualified for the club simply by appearing for a minor Welsh club in a single match. Nevertheless, these regulations were still in force some seventy-five years later when their Centenary book was written.

Regarding the football club they maintained their amateur status and obviously a lower profile compared with their rugby counterparts. Did they still have any connection with their rugby cousins? In November 1915 according to the Heathfield club's minutes *'Permission was given (for) the London Welsh to use the area between the Bowling Green and the cricket square for football for junior boys only.'* Certainly, the request would not have come from the rugby club who would have asserted their rights as owners to do so as they still owned the Field! In 1921 the football club were elected to the Southern Olympian League until that league merged with the Old Boys League in 2002. Today you do not need to be Welsh to play for them- indeed membership is open to all. Coincidentally both Sinjuns Grammarians FC and London Welsh FC both play together from time to time, and in their latest league encounter at the Field, in the Intermediate South Division of the Amateur Football Combination in December 2019 the former ran out winners by 3-2.

The Luck of the Irish

The 'Exile' sides added an interesting dimension to club rugby. These matches were well supported and were often billed as 'club internationals' and, apart from the London Welsh, involved the London Scottish, the London Irish, and to a lesser degree, generally playing these clubs' second fifteens, the London French. The latter club perhaps did not survive for long. A reference to them can be found in the *Sporting Life* from 30 September 1911 seeking further fixtures to add to their list. The current London French RFC claim to have been founded in 1959 and currently play at the Barn Elms Sports Trust ground, but like their predecessors retain a low profile.

The Irish played a decent standard of rugby and after their match at the Field on 2 November 1912, which the Welsh won comfortably by 22-3, both clubs staged a joint smoking concert held at the *White Horse* in Holborn. The closeness of the clubs was soon to become apparent, and as the saying goes 'There is no smoke without fire'. By arrangement with the London Welsh the London Irish subsequently played three matches at the Field, one against the Royal Engineers on 23 November 1912 and another against United Services both ending in victories. The other match, curiously, was against the London Welsh's second fifteen on 21 December 1912, whilst the Welsh's first fifteen were playing away at Cheltenham. The relative comparison in the strength of depth of the two sides was apparent when the London Welsh ran out comfortable winners of this encounter by 20-5. The Welsh cobbled together a side included some interesting characters to make up the numbers, amongst them being the old Welsh International J.C. Jenkins, H. Rhys the English Wrestling Champion, and Gwilym Lloyd George, who was the younger son of David Lloyd George, the future Prime Minister, and was currently at that time a member of the Eastbourne College XV.

The operation of a limited groundshare arrangement continued Into the following season which would prove to be the last before the Great War. It was agreed that the London Irish would use the Field for their 1st XV matches when the Welsh were playing away. The London Irish were obviously interested by the prospect of attracting larger crowds and having the use of the Field, with Wandsworth Common station, which was only seven minutes by train from Victoria, nearby. This would also suit the Welsh as well with the increased number of paying spectators to watch a first-class match being played at the Field every Saturday, and all the benefits that would entail. The London Irish would retain their Perry Hill ground at Catford for any 2nd XV and junior fixtures.

The London Irish enjoyed their time at the Field so it appears. Inevitably on 11 October 1913, the London Irish had a regular fixture with the London Welsh in a match between the 'landlords' and 'tenants'. Against all predictions, the Irish prevailed by 8-5. Including the two matches against the London Welsh, the London Irish would play thirteen home matches in their two seasons at the Field, winning ten of them. Apart from their triumph over the Welsh, they scored notable victories at the Field against Bedford and London Scottish.

With the Great War intervening and London Welsh's disposal of the Field in 1918, we were never to learn if or how this unique relationship between the two 'exile' clubs would have developed. Today unlike their Celtic cousins, the London Irish continue to play in England's Rugby Union Premiership Division. In the 2020/21 season, they relocated from the Madejski Stadium in Reading where they had been based for the past twenty years, to the new Brentford Community Stadium in West London which they share with Brentford FC.

4

The Heathfield Era (1883 – 1924)

Cricket to us was more than play. It was a worship in the summer sun.

Edmund Blunden (1896-1974)

The origins of the Heathfield Cricket Club

The origins of the Heathfield Cricket Club are uncertain. Whilst the club claims it was established in 1875, there is clear evidence according to press reports, that a club by the same name of 'Heathfield' were playing on Wandsworth Common as far back as 1867. The first known scorecard which appeared in *The Sportsman* regarding a match with the Stella Cricket Club played on 25 May that year, was won overwhelmingly by Heathfield by a margin of 133 runs and 4 wickets on the first innings. Other reported matches included wins against Waifs & Strays, St. Mary's, North Brixton and a draw against a Mr Fairweather's XI with only one defeat against East Sheen. Results of other matches, assuming there were others, went unreported. The following season, Heathfield's name appeared twice on Stockwell Park CC's fixture list supposedly playing both matches at Wandsworth, and whilst other fixtures were against teams such as Craig's Court and Surrey Wanderers which became established fixtures for at least the next three years, some sides were played twice on a 'return' basis. Indeed, it seems that a fixture with St. Mary's was one of the original regular fixtures as apart from playing them in 1867, a further result was posted in 1869. All these early matches suggested that Heathfield were running just the one eleven, and although few matches were reported, it is possible that the club was playing on a regular basis. After 1870 however, the cricket reports disappear.

Despite mention of a couple of scheduled matches with Surrey Wanderers in 1871, it was not until 1876 when just a year after their foundation the press reports start once more when it was recorded that the club played the Heron Cricket Club at Wandsworth Common winning by 18 runs (89-71). Interestingly, although perhaps not surprisingly, not one of the players in that match had featured in the 'Heathfield' matches prior to its 'foundation' in 1875. The six-year gap in the cricket reports is puzzling and it suggests that the matches played before 1875 referred, perhaps, to a forerunner of the club. It was also not uncommon in those days for two clubs to be known by the same name, even playing cricket at the same time, on adjacent grounds! It is also complicated further because the *South London Press* refers to an interview with a Mr Arthur Martyn in 1899, a well-known local politician. In that article it refers to him as being *'one of South London's best-known cricketers in the early 1870s, his name being associated with the Surrey and Heathfield Clubs'*. Despite extensive research, no reference can be found in local press reports of the two matches played in 1875 against St Mary's and Bolingbroke Park, mentioned in the Heathfield Club's centenary booklet and that perhaps there were other matches played with less positive results. The information is likely to have been extracted from a long-lost minute book detailing the club's beginnings. However, it is quite possible that Heathfield adopted the name from the defunct club, and looking at the reports that have survived from the early years it can be seen that both 'Heathfield' clubs played similar opposition. All early home fixtures may have well been played at the same original Heathfield ground on Wandsworth Common located on what now is bounded by Windmill Road, Trinity Road and Wandsworth Common West Side and the flank wall to the gardens of 1 Heathfield Cottages. By the turn of the century, it was quite clear from their Annual General Meetings, that the Heathfield club clearly regarded themselves as being established in 1875, and this matches with their final year's entry in the Club Cricket Conference Yearbook of 1924. The suggested row between various players at the Clarence Club which led to the foundation of the club, may well have taken place, but the reasons for the altercation which led to various players of that club forming their own separate and independent club might not have been as straightforward as thought. If there were any vestiges left of the original Heathfield club (if it still existed), any additional influx of new players would have certainly propelled the 1875 club onto the club cricket stage.

The Heathfield Cricket Club claims that their first match was against a side from St. Mary Magdalene Church which stands opposite the Field, but this is hardly credible, because it would be a further eight years before the Heathfield Cricket Club would take up residence there, and it was more likely that the match had been played at the very other end of the Common, a mile north of where the church is situated. More likely, given that the pre 1875 club would had played St. Mary's at the original Heathfield Ground, fixtures of that club suggested that their home ground was probably in Pimlico! Nevertheless, in their opening match in 1875, Heathfield scored 47 and the opposition only 17. In 1875, St. Mary Magdalene Church was only a temporary structure anyway - little more than a tin shed. It was not until 1888 that a new church was built there which still stands today. The top of the west front of the church incorporates a double arched and gabled bellcote and this would come into its own on Sunday evenings during the cricket season when the single bell would be rung, almost plaintively, to summon the congregation to church. Judging by the response, certainly by the 1980s, you would not get trampled in the rush to attend the service! This act of campanology invariably coincided with the commencement of the final hour of play at 6.30pm (all timed matches in those days on Sundays), and often by then a good idea as to the eventual outcome of the match would be known. 'For whom the bell tolls' it could well be said! Hopes were raised of tracing the link claimed by the Heathfield club, when a St Mary Magdalene Cricket Club was noted to have won the verbosely named South London Auxiliary SS Union Association Cricket League in 1914, but that side was connected with the Southwark area.

As the position of the original Heathfield ground is now known, the club's description that it was located 'on a scrubby piece of land' between 'East Hill and the Railway', is a little misleading. At that time the actual area was open countryside or in fact heathland as the name suggests fringed with gorse bushes, but it was a favourite spot for cricket matches, and since it was known as 'Heathfield', it is certain that the cricket club (both versions) adopted the name. However, Wandsworth Common being remarkably accessible by rail and with the fares low, it was increasingly used by members of the public and not exclusively by the club itself. A picture of the cricket ground, probably taken around 1900, after the club had left shows perhaps, that the public almost took too much interest in the cricket and indeed in the winter the football pitch would be temporarily roped off presumably to prevent crowds from encroaching onto the pitch. In 1879, the Conservators planted forty-one sycamores at the boundary of the Common between the Heathfield Cricket Club's adopted ground and Mr. Leach's land who resided in Heathfield Cottages. By 1880, although some matches were still played on this original ground, others took place on that part of Wandsworth Common near to the old goods station, then known as Bolingbroke Common, and also possibly on the ground used by Wandsworth Cricket Club, or on part of the Common facing Bellevue Road approximately opposite to the *Hope Tavern* and known as the Spencer Ground after the Club which originally occupied it. However, the problems on the original Heathfield ground were mounting. In April 1880 an article in the *Wandsworth & Battersea District Times* complained that '*while I and a few friends were enjoying a game of cricket on the Heathfield ground last Saturday afternoon we were requested by the common keeper to remove to some other part of the common. On demanding to know the reason, he handed to me a note which ran as follows – "Mrs Nixon is annoyed by the cricketers playing too near* to her house and garden and wished them to be removed immediately". The article continued, and referring to the Wandsworth Common Act, bitterly complained "how is it then that one resident has it in his or her power to peremptorily order us to be removed? We used to play at cricket on the Heathfield ground long before this good lady took up her abode in its vicinity....' It may have been this incident amongst others and perhaps the overcrowding of what is a reasonably modest area that persuaded the Heathfield Cricket Club to move away. If Mrs Nixon was concerned about the cricketers and potentially balls hitting her house or being hit over her wall into her garden, the photograph mentioned previously suggests by 1900 a steel mesh perimeter fence had been constructed to supplement her garden wall to make that task more difficult! Another example of these type of disputes occurred in 1882 at no other place but the Oval which was adjudicated upon at Lambeth Police Court. During a club match a ball had been hit through an adjacent owner's window who had then refused to give the ball back. In those days, new balls cost the equivalent of around 25p (about £30 in today's money) and the club sued the owner for its return. The court found against the defendant on the basis that it had no powers to stop such an action. 'Whilst the game was so much in vogue'. The court apparently suggested that nets might be put up to prevent such future occurrences, but the defendant was ordered upon payment of 5p (around £6 in today's money) by the complainant (the club) to give back the cricket ball. Whether that sum was ever paid by the club to get their ball back we do not know, but if they did it presumably went towards the replacement of the window! It is fair to say that such disputes are still as commonplace today as they were almost a hundred and fifty years ago! One big hit can cause all sorts of problems! Also owing to overuse and drainage issues a couple of years previously, Clapham Common was described as being in a 'disgraceful state' with writers to the South London Press casting doubt as to its suitability for staging cricket matches during the coming summer and suggesting that areas of the Common should be re-turfed for that purpose. Invariably, cricket did take place as scheduled, of course, but all this would have added to the general long-term viability of playing organised or even impromptu club cricket on open public commons. Wandsworth Common included, demand had more than reached its capacity. After the Heathfield Cricket Club left their original ground, it is quite possible that cricket matches continued there until the Great War in one form or another, but if they did, it would never have had the advantages that a private ground would bring.

From 1881, the Heathfield Cricket Club, as confirmed by a scorecard of a match with Waverley CC, were forced to rent a pitch and play the majority of their matches at the Half Moon Cricket Ground in Putney. Although this ground had been established since at least 1854 when, in its early days, the ground extended as far as the River Thames itself, it too was also becoming overcrowded partly through encroaching development, so that the Heathfield Cricket Club had to look again for another home. Eventually with what was left of the ground, the Half Moon would become the venue for several years of the Wasps Rugby Club who between 1891 and 1895 actually shared the ground with Fulham FC. The Half Moon pub still exists today in Lower Richmond Road behind the boathouse used for the University Boat Race on the Thames. It claims to have hosted live entertainment every night since 1963, save for a period more recently of three and a half years, when a burst water main flooded the place. Some of the biggest names in pop music have played there including the Rolling Stones, The Who and Van Morrison. Kate Bush's first public performance, apparently, was also at the Half Moon pub. Other acts include the comedians Billy Connolly, Jack Whitehall, Josh Widdicombe and Katherine Ryan. In fact, the list of well-known bands, comedians and entertainers performing there is almost endless, but, the original cricket ground is long gone.

However, despite the difficulties at the Half Moon ground at Putney, the club did not rest on their laurels. They played some matches away from home. In the year that was to become famous for the establishment of the 'Ashes' in cricket's history, an early scorecard shows the club playing on 10

June 1882 at the Aeolian Club in Dulwich resulting in a win by twenty runs. This was a good result against an established club. The club also enjoyed a day trip to the seaside town of Bexhill in a sequence of matches that were an annual event through the 1880s. It has been playfully suggested that the Heathfield Cricket Club used a stagecoach to get there, but, of course, it was the railways which had dissected Wandsworth Common some thirty years previously that would have transported the team there and back and indeed probably more quickly than by taking the car to Bexhill today! Heathfield Cricket Club were obviously an enterprising, enthusiastic and well organised group of players with the will to succeed.

Players or Gentlemen?

So, what of the Clarence club who apparently played an unintentional part in Heathfield Cricket Club's foundation? The problem, is, which Clarence? Different versions of the name abound. Firstly, the Royal Clarence Cricket Club dated from around 1828 and was named after the Duke of Clarence who became King William IV in 1830. Before becoming King, he resided at Clarence Lodge, in Roehampton. For a time, the cricket club was quite powerful even representing Surrey at one stage, and in 1833, according to the Court Journal organised a ball and supper evening at Molesey Park. However, this was a high point for the club which soon went into decline and by the time King William IV had died in 1837 it had apparently disbanded. Despite this, as a favourite name for minor royals, all manner of pubs and cricket clubs seemed to be named 'Clarence'. There was a Surrey Clarence, a Putney Clarence, a Vauxhall Clarence, a Croydon Clarence for instance and touring sides from the north such as Stockton Clarence and Leeds Clarence and many more!

However, although it is suggested that the Clarence club itself could have been linked to a pub in the 1870s, and although many clubs would invariably have their Annual General Meetings in a pub, tavern or ale house at that time, there is little tangible evidence specifically to link the club to Battersea as suggested by Heathfield's centenary booklet at all. There were two Battersea pubs within about a mile of each other, one called the *Clarence* and the other, the *Clarence Tavern*. Both were built around the same time. It would have been even confusing to the local pub crawlers of Battersea! Indeed, with the loosely royal connections, there were invariably as many 'Clarence' pubs as there were cricket clubs! However, even if we accept the notion that the club was attached to a pub, what about the row over the awarding of a cricket ball to the winners of matches played, which prompted some players to accuse others of unmitigated professionalism and led to the split? A certain amount of speculation here, but perhaps another reason was that some of the players may have actually been directly sponsored by a patron! Just like the Heathfield Cricket Club, the Clarence Cricket Club entered local cup competitions. *Cricket* tells us that the club was *'formed from the staff of cabinet and furniture makers Maple & Co'* which claimed to be the largest company of its type in the world. Although this possibly was the case, it is evident that with Sir John Blundell Maple being a keen club player in Surrey, he took the Clarence club on under his patronship, after the company expanded, some years after its foundation. The Clarence club was not only a cricket club, because the football section of the club entered the FA Cup in the 1880/81 season - although they were convincingly beaten by Marlow 6-0 in the first round. Indeed, several clubs at the time were effectively known to be company sides, so club sponsorship goes back much further than we might have imagined. Whatever the case, in 1881, Sir John Blundell Maple moved to Childwickbury Manor just outside St Albans. The Clarence Cricket Club continued to be a leading cricket club and won the Associated Cricket Challenge Cup three seasons in succession with the last of these finals against Tottenham House in 1886, possibly played at the Field. Perhaps the cricketers who had left the club some ten years earlier to form the Heathfield Cricket Club could have felt alienated because, not working for the company, they did not receive the same benefits financially from its patron. It should also be said that a number of matches at that time were openly arranged on betting who might win the contest.

Then perhaps an equally unlikely twist occurred at St. Albans itself. Clarence Park we are told, was almost certainly named after the Duke of Clarence (or Duke of Clarence and Avondale to give him his full title) in his short-lived tenure of the post from 1890 until 1892, but is this strictly true? Despite being private land, with, remarkably, Earl Spencer having been one of its previous owners, in the 1870s it was used occasionally by Hertfordshire County Cricket Club. However, in 1893, Sir John Blundell Maple having at some time acquired the land that was to become Clarence Park itself (all 25 acres of it), generously donated it to the citizens of St. Albans. Given the unfortunate death of the Duke of Clarence a year earlier, the citizens of St. Albans had to make do with the Duke of Cambridge (not the present incumbent of course!) to open the Park. For Maple's act of generosity, he was the first person to be granted the freedom of the city of St. Albans. Furthermore, the first football match played at Clarence Park on 22 September 1894 resulted in a 1-1 draw, and this was played between St. Albans Football Club and the Clarence Football Club *'whose members were employed by Sir John's London based furniture store, Maples.'* Regarding cricket, the present St. Albans club dates from 1898 when the Clarence cricket club renamed itself St Albans Town CC and began to hire pitches in Clarence Park for the purpose, and does so today. So, perhaps the suggestion of naming Clarence Park, actually came from Sir John Blundell Maple himself? After all, it would have been a happy coincidence given his patronage of the Clarence club with the loose royal connection, and a good way of continuing to use the name for his business interests. It was no coincidence, therefore, that the Clarence club were involved in the opening stages of Clarence Park!

Sir John Blundell Maple was MP for Dulwich from 1887 until his death in 1903 by which time he had amassed an enormous fortune of £2,153,000 (over £260 million in today's money). Apart from the company business, he was a successful racehorse owner, also running a stud close to his home near St. Albans. Although the Clarence club was subsumed by the St Albans clubs, there is evidence that the company continued to support the Clarence club after his death and that the Clarence club brand itself was revived and moved to a new home at Mill Hill, continuing maybe up until almost the Great War. It was certainly one of the longest sponsorships in club history. Although inevitably declining with the changing times, the furniture business subsequently became part of the Allied Maples Group Ltd which in 1997 went into administration only to be taken over by Allders who in turn closed its doors in 2012.

Linking back to the early days of the Heathfield Cricket Club who apparently regarded themselves as 'true amateurs', it would seem that those ideals would soon be challenged. For instance, in 1877 the Battersea club advertised a benefit match in favour of their 'courteous and painstaking club professional' who was effectively their bowling coach. There is certainly an indication that Heathfield Cricket Club followed this example some years later, as the club's playing standards improved, and indeed introduced admission charges to the Field which were to become an important source of club income. So, who were the Gentlemen and who were the Players?

Heathfield and the Golden Age of cricket

The Heathfield Cricket Club, being fortunate to rent a pitch at the Field in 1883, was to cement its position in club cricket. It proved to be a game changer literally, and transformed the club from being a semi-wandering cricket club to a club with a settled home. The name of Heathfield, although it referred to another area of Wandsworth Common on which the club had originally played their cricket, as we know, quickly became synonymous with the Field which they were to grace for another forty-one years. In their first season the club entered a cup competition organised by the rather grandly named London & Suburban Cricket Association. This separated the thirty-one London clubs entering into two sections. Fifteen clubs competed in the South of Thames Section (the only other club recognisable today being Alleyns) and Heathfield were drawn against Balham. There was also a considerable number of conditions attached to the competition. No professional players, which included groundsmen, were allowed to compete in the competition. Given that the Heathfield Cricket Club had been formed less than ten years previously with lofty ideals of maintaining their amateur status, it has to be assumed that the club supported this stance. The start time for the matches was to be 3.00pm. However, given that daylight saving was not introduced into this country until 1916, it is hard to see how matches could be completed before darkness arrived, and how a knock out competition could be arranged when only 'time' matches were played. The answer was that if the side batting second had not exceeded the side batting first's total, but still had wickets at close of play to fall this, for the purposes of the competition would be deemed a draw, and the match was to be replayed on another date. The only proviso was that if both sides had completed their first innings before 'time', and the match had progressed further by close of play without a further conclusion having being attained, then the winner would be decided on the side that had scored the most runs in their first innings-again standard practice in those days for single day matches. The final of this competition would be a two-day affair, both days starting at 11.00am and be played on the same principle, but of course with cricket still being essentially a two innings game if a further conclusion could not be reached then that result on the first innings would stand! For the record Heathfield lost their first-round match with Balham by just seven runs (79-72) so their involvement in the competition was soon over.

To a cricket player, nowadays, the regulations regarding the result would sound odd if not confusing. However, the law in those days deemed that a cricket match was a two innings per side affair. With poorer pitches, scores were lower and duration of a team's innings much shorter; indeed 'sub 100 scores' were quite commonplace for both sides. However, the players (and presumably the spectators) obviously wanted their money's worth, and on having both completed their first innings (or not) sides would normally bat on until 'time', or indeed go in again and bat until the agreed close of play or until both sides had completed two innings whichever was the shorter. Declarations were not allowed under cricket law until 1889, but by then the majority of unfinished matches (two innings per side) were still decided on the first innings. There was none of this "over limit" nonsense or T20 stuff which would take around another hundred years or more to catch on fully in club cricket, by which members or supporters would turn up towards the close of play only to find that the match had finished an hour or so earlier! Remarkably, in cricket law, the concept of a two innings match per side endured for some time although it was evident as years went on that clubs would agree effectively a 'one innings' match if they felt it suited their purposes. With improved pitches the concept of batting on after effectively winning a match on the first innings gradually disappeared. Interestingly the current laws still make provision for a one day, two innings per side match with the follow- on option set at 75 runs or more on the first innings! That type of match today is effectively redundant. On rare occasions, in an echo of times gone by, the importance of a first innings lead is recognised as witnessed in the Final of the 2020 Bob Willis Trophy, for although that match was drawn, Essex prevailed over Somerset to win the Trophy on the basis of scoring most runs in the first innings.

In their first season at the Field in 1883, the Heathfield Cricket Club also used their settled status to run at least two elevens and also remarkably an occasional third eleven. One such example was a double fixture against Champion Hill CC on 19 May, which was one of their first matches at the Field, with a return fixture in August. No doubt, the Field's proximity to Wandsworth Common station was a help in attracting players. In October the club staged a 'ballad' concert at Bolingbroke Hall on Battersea Rise to celebrate the close of the season. It was reported that *'The hall was filled by a fashionable audience and the concert altogether was a great success'*. For the following few years these gatherings would actually take place at Wandsworth Town Hall. After years of effectively wandering, Heathfield as a cricket club had certainly arrived.

By the following season of 1884, the club were playing Spencer CC, with Heathfield generally having the better of the earlier exchanges between the two clubs. The Honourable Artillery Company (HAC) were also added to their list of fixtures at their ground in London. In 1885 the club were confident enough to publish their full fixture list in *Cricket* a highly influential weekly newspaper promoting cricket not only in this country, but around the world. Some of Heathfield's scorecards and results were also included. With a season running from April 18 until September 19 no fewer than sixty-three matches were scheduled, a considerable number of fixtures given that only Saturdays were permitted for club cricket in those days. At the close of the season the 1st XI record was played 24, won 8, drawn 11 and lost 5, whilst the 2nd XI played 29, won 15, drawn 5 and lost 9.

The next few seasons were generally successful. In 1888, East Molesey were put to the sword and A.F.W. Humm scored what may have been the first century for the club in the drawn match with Honor Oak. By 1889 the Field was good enough to be used for local representative matches, and to underline how far the club had come, Heathfield's match on May 2 at the Oval to play the Surrey Colts was listed by *Cricket* as one of the Principal Fixtures for 1889-an honour indeed. Unfortunately, as there was no after match report it had to be assumed that it was rained off, given that the Surrey Club & Ground's two-day match at Lord's starting on the same day was also abandoned, owing to two days of rain. Sadly, this appears to have been the only opportunity the club ever had to play at the Oval during its lifetime, as the year previously the Surrey County Cricket Club had restricted the use of the Oval for regular club matches. Heathfield also arranged series of single matches played over three consecutive evenings against the Private Banks, Bank of England and the Post Office.

The club obviously continued to enjoy their concerts and dances because the latter became known locally as the 'Heathfield Cinderellas' and in November 1890 it was announced in the local press that these dances would resume at *Stanley Hall* in Clapham Junction on 2 and 16 January 1891. Presiding over these was G. Ashley Hyem who was not only a leading Heathfield Cricket Club member but also President of the Bolingbroke Tradesman's Club. Both the Heathfield Cricket Club during its stay at the Field and the latter organisation through annual fetes, staunchly supported Bolingbroke Hospital through fundraising events. In the years before the National Health Service, voluntary and charitable contributions amounted to an important source of revenue for the hospital which had been founded by the Vicar of Battersea, the Rev. Canon John Erskine Clarke in 1876, and who was also to become the first President of the Sir Walter St John's School Old Boys Association (Old Sinjuns) in 1898. A good example of this enduring support occurred on 12 September 1906 when in aid of Bolingbroke Hospital, the Balham & Tooting Traders' Association held their third annual sports day at the Field. Events such as the 100 yards, half-mile cycle, 300 yards flat and a two-miles walking Handicap races were staged for competitors from as far afield as Reading. The crowd watching these events was about 3,000 strong. Although the hospital as such is now closed, the Bolingbroke Medical Centre continues to function from the same site.

Given initially that the Clapham Rovers, and the Heathfield Cricket Club would have to make do with changing facilities in the *Surrey Tavern*, conditions were improving and by 1894 maps show the existence of not one but two pavilions on the Field. The smaller pavilion was used exclusively by the ladies and additionally to the pavilions a shed or possibly a stable for a horse? Although the main pavilion looked imposing, the changing room accommodation was apparently very limited. Additionally, it seems pretty certain that shortly after the pavilion was constructed the premises were licensed, bringing in valuable revenue for the club and effectively severing the link with the *Surrey Tavern* across the road. In 1896, as an example of the Heathfield Cricket Club's increasing profile and influence, the club staged a 'Festival Dinner' at the *Holborn Restaurant* in London which included a seven-course dinner! The venue was regarded as one of London's finest and frequented by several leading cricket clubs at the time for their Annual Dinners. It was there that the British Chess Federation was founded in 1904. Additionally, during the 1908 Olympics, its vast dining room hosted banquets for participating athletes. The *Holborn Restaurant* eventually closed its doors in 1954 and was converted into offices, which in turn were eventually replaced by a modern glass-fronted office block incorporating a Sainsbury's supermarket!

The reason for the club's growing reputation and sustainability was, invariably, down to two outstanding players who although principally bowlers, at club level, were also useful all-rounders. Throughout the 1890s, S.J. ('Sammy') Bowles played occasionally for Surrey II (best bowling 7-43 against Kent II in 1893) and he is mentioned regularly in club cricket reports. He was a young player who had grown in stature as part of the Heathfield's policy to promote youth. Charles Mills would join the club towards the end of the century to make the Heathfield Cricket Club one of the leading sides in London. His had a remarkable career as a player with the club spanning almost twenty years and we shall explore his contribution later.

In 1890 only a year after the unfortunate abandonment of the 1889 match at the Oval, the club finally got its chance to show what it could do when they entertained a Surrey Club & Ground side at the Field. The result was a calamity. Perhaps after having dismissed the Club & Ground side for just 71, complacency set in, but in reply the batting imploded and the club were dismissed for a meagre 17, possibly their lowest ever total and even that total included five extras! Paradoxically, in this first match, Charles Mills played for the Club & Ground side, but he obviously liked the ground and in later years would become a cornerstone for Heathfield's success. However, for the time being, this defeat was a setback and the Club & Ground side were not to return until 1895. This time Heathfield were better prepared and having batted first won a close contest by eight runs. The results of these matches are recorded elsewhere and ran almost unbroken until the outbreak of the Great War in 1914. At the AGM in 1898, the Heathfield Cricket Club reported that the 1897 season was one of the most successful with 51 matches played, resulting in 20 victories and only 10 defeats. The club was in a strong financial position and were about to enter, arguably, the most distinguished decade in their history.

Back at the Field, a change was coming which would again put the Field back into private hands. Hitherto various other clubs had also used the Field for cricket, including occasionally the London County Council themselves, who, of course, owned the Field during most of the 1890s. In early 1897 rumours were circulating about the club's future at the Field. This forced a denial by the Heathfield Cricket Club that their position was in peril. It took a further year for matters to come to a head. As we know, in 1898, London County Council, put the Field up for sale at auction subject to the same restrictive covenant against the erection of any building on the ground which McKellar had accepted in 1852. Although the Heathfield Cricket Club made a bold attempt to acquire the freehold, they were outbid by John Mills Thorne (some versions of his name use 'Mith' as his middle name, to avoid confusion with his father). Although already in his early seventies, John Mills Thorne was described as *'a gentleman who favours sport and pastimes'*. Ironically, in a situation which Henry McKellar had skilfully opposed, the Field was now to be effectively controlled by the owner of a property on the other side of Burntwood Lane. John Mills Thorne had purchased Burntwood Lodge in 1880. It was a building of some substance. When it had been previously sold in 1867 it comprised of *'six bedchambers and dressing rooms, three servants rooms, bath room, drawing room, conservatory with adjoining smoking room, dining room and morning room, all opening onto the grounds by French Windows plus water-closets, kitchen, servants hall, the usual domestic offices, stabling for six horses and rooms over for coachman, lofts, greenhouse, melon and cucumber houses, summerhouse, gardens and a 'paddock', altogether about five acres'*. An impressive building indeed. Perhaps his reasons for buying the Field were more altruistic than commercially driven in order to keep Burntwood Lodge surrounded by an oasis of countryside, but he was also known to be a developer as well and had connections with the Upper Tooting Cricket Club in nearby Beechcroft Road, who were potential rivals. John Mills Thorne, whose father had moved from Sherborne Dorset in 1841 upon acquisition of the Nine Elms Brewery, was in all probability the joint owner of the Brewery at the time of the Field's purchase with his older brother Benjamin Thorne as a result of their father's death in 1865. As Thorne Brothers Ltd, they controlled fifty-two tied houses mainly in South West London. Regarding his credentials or motives for purchasing the field, it is interesting that he had stood for election as one of the five ratepayer members of the Wandsworth Common Conservators in March 1887. Whether he was successful at that election or not, is unknown, but in any event any appointment would have been short lived as it was overtaken later that year by the Metropolitan Board of Works Act 1887 which transferred responsibility of Wandsworth Common to the council. However, intriguingly one of his sons, F.G. Thorne played for Upper Tooting CC. This club were as influential as the Heathfield Cricket Club, having been founded earlier and were also one of the few to publish its 1866 results in the 1867 edition of *Wisden*, playing sides such as Richmond, Streatham, Free Foresters, Uxbridge and Banstead -all clubs that we would recognise today. Their hockey section also had an influence in the formulating of the laws of that game. With their ground in Beechcroft Road nearby, it is perhaps surprising that despite being of equal standing, there is no evidence that the two clubs ever played each other. John Mills Thorne was to keep the Field for almost another thirteen years. He died at Burntwood Lodge in June 1913 at the age of 87.

The Heathfield Cricket Club faced some difficult decisions. In November 1898, as negotiations presumably continued with John Mills Thorne, Burntwood Wanderers signalled the approval of their secretary's arrangements to secure a new match ground on part of the Field belonging 'to the Heathfield cricket club'. In the meantime, it seems, an ultimatum had been given to the Heathfield Cricket Club to take on the use of the Field for the whole year or not at all. The pressure was on. Faced with this situation the club agreed terms, including a higher rental cost, with John Mills Thorne the following month, and by May 1899 the agreement had been ratified. Despite the Heathfield Cricket Club's healthy finances being tested, the club also took the decision based on a new twenty-one-year lease they had negotiated, to radically upgrade the Field and its activities. This bold move effectively relaunched the club and the benefits of doing so were quickly apparent. Six double tennis courts were laid out and fifty tennis members were elected to the club. The pavilion was substantially extended and improved so as to include the luxury of a shower-bath, plus an additional area to be utilised for refreshments for club members and opponents, whilst ordinary members (effectively those paying to watch matches) would be catered for by means of a large tent situated on the periphery of the Field close to the entrance in Trinity Road. This process of upgrading happened over a period of about five years as in 1904 it was reported that the pavilions had been repainted and that a 'new wooden bowling-screen', presumably what we know today as a sightscreen had been purchased, which was an improvement on the canvas screens that were erected on match days and which are evident in some early photographs. Owing to Heathfield's intention to run four cricket sides on Saturdays to give younger players an opportunity, Burntwood Wanderers lost their intended share of the Field but were permitted by the Heathfield Cricket Club to use the new practice pitches that were now provided. Ornamental railings were erected around the ground outside the existing hedge which was retained so as to keep the ground's setting quite rural, but private and secure. Although both the railings and the hedge have since disappeared, the former was subsequently replaced with a more robust and functional structure aimed more at keeping balls inside the ground rather than out. Levelling the Field where necessary was carried out, and at the Beechcroft Road end of the ground with the tennis courts having been placed 100 yards from the cricket pitches, it was thought that they would not unduly interfere with play. A bowling green was also planned and constructed. The club also employed a new groundsman for the purpose. He was E. Collett (later mentioned favourably by W.G. Grace) of whom a report said 'comes from the *Parks* at Oxford with the highest credentials'. Their trust in his appointment and his experience of preparing pitches at 'first-class' level was well founded as in the four seasons that followed the reputation of the Field in having one of the best surfaces on which to play club cricket was recognised. Instead of squeezing three matches on the Field at any one time, it was decided to restrict the cricket to two matches, the only exception being when special matches, such as visits from the Surrey Club & Ground or London County teams were staged, which demanded a greater area of the outfield to be used, to accommodate the increased number of spectators attending. Indeed, it would appear that the use of the central part of the Field was given over to playing cricket and it is quite possible that during the winter some of this area may have been given over to playing either rugby or football to be renovated before the cricket season began. On 12 July 1900 the club staged its first Garden Party attended by some 600 guests and friends and a cricket week was introduced together with the club's own brand of al fresco concerts. Fortunately, the club reported that they had only marginally been affected by players being summoned to the front in South Africa as part of the ongoing conflict in the Boer War.

In retrospect, and as a result of the purchase of the Field by John Mills Thorne, it could be argued that the Field had engineered a lucky escape. Although he was involved in other developments, there was no real evidence that he had bought the Field with the idea of building on it if he could break the covenant, as might have been the case with other bidders. Ultimately, however, the full implications of the Heathfield Cricket Club failing in their bid to buy the ground there and then, would become apparent in the future. It would also be a turning point in the destiny of the club. To balance the books, they would be obliged to take on tenants during the winter, and the whole profile of the club, with the introduction of tennis courts and subsequently a bowls green, would broaden the basis of the club for sport on the Field going forward.

At the club's Annual Dinner at the *Holborn Restaurant* in 1899, and now renamed as the Heathfield Cricket and Lawn Tennis Club, a presentation of a gold watch was made to T.J. Faulkner for recognition of his twenty-one years' association with the cricket club and on his retirement as club captain. The Hon A.C. Ponsonby, a Vice President of the club also noted at the gathering that, for the first time, the fair sex would be admitted to the club as a result of the opening of the lawn tennis section. Given that this change happened some years before women were granted the vote, it did not immediately meet with the universal approval of all the members.

With their dances and dinners, the Heathfield Cricket Club were also quite keen in enjoying themselves, but at the same time supporting charitable events. One such example was on the occasion of entertaining Dan Leno's XI. Born George Wild Galvin in 1860, Dan Leno was a leading comedian and stage actor of the Victorian and early Edwardian era famous for performing in music halls. He took the stage name of Leno from his step-father. In terms of his popularity and public profile he was 'huge'. He appeared for sixteen consecutive years at *Drury Lane Theatre* and became by most accounts one of the highest paid pantomime artists and comedians in the world. He started accompanying his parents onto the stage when he was a child and as a youth and soon became the star of his family's act. Indeed, in 1880 he won the clog dancing world championship at the *Princess's Music Hall* in Leeds (a bit like *Riverdance* with clogs on!). Leno's biographer stated that '*I could honestly say that I never saw him absolutely at rest*', but like the genius he was, in later life, he became increasingly eccentric.

From 1898 until 1903 Leno formed a cricket side. They played a series of cricket matches with sides who were willing to put up with their comedic mayhem and took their brand of entertainment to the Oval where in 1902, around 24,000 spectators enjoyed watching the spectacle complete with the Surrey eleven wearing top hats whilst fielding. On one occasion, the Heathfield Cricket Club agreed to be part of the fun. On Wednesday 4 July 1900, a crowd of no fewer than 7,000 people poured in through the gates leading to the '*well-kept field of the Heathfield Cricket Club*', possibly swelled by this also being Independence Day in the USA, such was Dan Leno's popularity in America. However, it was probably the largest attendance of any event in the Field's history. Described as a 'Carnival' this was really an outdoor pantomime with cricket as a sub-plot in aid of the Bolingbroke Free Accident Ward. In reality, with little attention paid to the accuracy of the score, most matches were never concluded. Leno's bat was apparently hollow so that when he hit the ball in the middle it would become wedged there! As for the match in question, with the Heathfield Cricket Club being '*paralysed with mirth*' the match report stated that "*no serious batting was indulged in*". Various competitions were organised. The Carter House Cadet Corps gave a display and various cycles and cars were decorated. Mr Taylor took first prize for his decorated tricycle (with Nordenfeldt gun). Mounted horsemen and decorated carts and carriages also competed for prizes- the winner of the latter contained Henry VIII accompanied by three ladies in fancy dress. 'Nurse Biglake' won the prize for the Best Dressed Nurse!! Apart from the 'gate' impromptu collections made inside the Field continued to swell the coffers. Photographs at the time bear witness to the huge numbers of spectators and also a few watching, presumably for free, from the common opposite the ground beyond Burntwood Lane. In the match, Leno's side, more commonly known as the "Dainties" were mostly dressed as policemen. Although sadly lost, the event was recorded as part of a two-minute film called *Dan Leno's Cricket Match*. In a speech at the end of the day, Leno expressed delight at being able to support such a well-respected local charity and declared that the match would be finished next year!

Dan Leno supported a variety of good causes which included the well-known entertainment charity, the Grand Order of Water Rats and served as its leader, the King Rat in 1891, 1892 and 1897. However, by 1902 illness had begun to take hold and the organisers suppressed the news at the Oval match mentioned earlier, fearing that his non-appearance on the day would affect the gate. One of his troop impersonated him so that some of the crowd never realised he was missing on the day! As his health declined, the 1903 event at the Oval was attended by only a third of the crowd from the year previously. His behaviour became increasingly erratic, possibly brought on by heavy drinking, which sadly led to a mental breakdown and insanity; he was committed to an asylum twice. He did however make an uncertain limited comeback in the following summer, and intriguingly the *London Daily News* reported on 14 September 1904 that today '*for the benefit of the Bolingbroke Hospital*', Dan Leno would captain the Heathfield Bowls side against a London County Bowling Club side led by none other than W.G. Grace! The fete was to start at 2.30pm and that there would be many other attractions on offer, perhaps on a similar basis to the 1900 extravaganza. Just what the famous cricketer might have made of Dan Leno's antics we will never know, as the event appears to have gone unreported. Apparently, checking another source, it rained all day and it is suspected that the event was abandoned. Sadly, this probably would have been Dan Leno's last scheduled appearance on a sports ground as less than seven weeks later, he passed away at the comparatively young age of 43. Thousands turned out to witness his funeral cortege thread its way through Balham. His death made national and international headlines. It was a fitting climax and celebration of his life by the many he had so royally entertained and helped through his career. He is buried in Lambeth Cemetery, Tooting. In recent years there has been a revival of interest in Dan Leno. He is one of the few people to have more than one place named after him. In 1898, Leno was involved in a consortium which constructed the *Granville Theatre* which was demolished in 1971, in what is now *Fulham Broadway*. Dan Leno Walk nearby recognises his contribution to establishing that theatre. Additionally, Dan Leno's association with Lambeth is recognised by the Dan Leno Gardens which is specifically laid out for people with disabilities. Gyles Brandreth produced a biography of Leno in 1977 and a recent stage production remembering his life called *The Royal Jester* has received critical acclaim. Additionally, a modern-day tribute to remember the life of Dan Leno entitled *Naturally Insane* is planned to do justice to his lost talent.

By 1900 apart from the Surrey Club & Ground fixture, the Heathfield Cricket Club were playing sides such as Sutton, Banstead, East Molesey, Addiscombe and Mitcham all of which are still with us today. Beddington were also another side played from time to time. Most were afternoon starts at 2.30pm but a few were all day affairs such as the matches with the Club & Ground side, Mitcham and East Molesey, and as time went on more matches were enjoyed under the longer format. The Field also became a very popular rendezvous on Saturday afternoons. Although tennis as we know was introduced in 1899, initially, both the tennis and bowls sections were not taken very seriously, as the grass courts, which were sometimes used as part of the cricket outfield, were not exactly of championship quality. Nevertheless, the tennis section recorded a victory over the nearby Magdalen club by 8 matches to 3 and membership of the new bowls section continued to flourish, proving the investment of £300 to lay down the bowls green had been a sound investment. The improvements carried out to the Field in the spring of 1901 were much praised by the local press, who reported that although a large portion of the ground had been raised and levelled the result was that the *'enclosure may now rank as one of the finest in London'*. The improved facilities and favourable reports would also have a positive effect as the standard of cricket at the Field would testify.

By the start of the summer season of 1901, the overall club membership was approaching 300, and was said to be one of the largest in South London. It was reported that *'New match wickets [pitches actually] have been laid down for the cricket section, additional courts for the tennis section and a new bowling green for the bowls section'* had been completed. Four elevens were playing Saturday cricket. The cricket week was a success including an excellent win against Banstead on the Tuesday. The Hon A.C. Ponsonby, presented the club with a complete set of acetylene gas fittings so all members could enjoy the luxury of gas illumination in all the rooms of the pavilion – a great improvement on the old-fashioned oil lamps. Buoyed perhaps by the success of the Harlequins after their introduction of an admission charge upon their arrival at the Field in September 1901, a charge of 3d was levied to 'see decent local cricket on a weekend afternoon' (Saturday only of course) was introduced in 1902 in tandem with many other metropolitan clubs at the time.

Undoubtedly, what propelled the Heathfield club into the limelight were the matches they played against London County Cricket Club and their connections with W.G. Grace. Between 1900 and 1904 London County, although actually not officially part of the County Championship, was considered to be a first-class county. So much has been written about 'the grand old man of cricket' that it would be impossible to repeat all his performances and records here. Born in Downend, Bristol in 1848 and playing his first-class matches with Gloucestershire, until transferring to the London County side in 1900, there is no other player who has ever enjoyed such unquestioned supremacy on the cricket field in their time. He is described as being a tall, imposing but rather cumbersome figure (literally larger than life) and of course was famous for his beard, but appearances were deceptive as he possessed great strength and power and was no slouch in the field. What makes Grace unique is that he achieved iconic status in his own lifetime and more than any other cricketer helped shape the sport for future generations to come. In later years Bradman would come close to assuming the same reputation in Australia. Grace was a major draw to any cricket ground on which he played, bringing the game to the people. Although there has been a dispute over the years as to the total aggregate of runs he actually scored on the account of what constituted a first-class match it is today widely accepted that between 1865, when he made his first-class debut at the age of sixteen, until the end of his first-class career in 1908 at the age of almost sixty, he made a total of 54,211 first-class runs at an average of 39.45 (including 126 centuries) and took, which is often overlooked, 2,808 wickets at an average of 18.16 per wicket. Whist it could be said that his average of just under forty is not exceptional in today's cricket, it has to be taken in the context that pitches in those days were nowhere near as good as they are today. His involvement in minor matches, (which included the Heathfield matches) yielded a further 45,283 runs and a further 4,578 wickets which brought the figures to a grand total of 99,494 runs and 7,386 wickets, and 1,532 catches (first class 876: minor 656.). In some quarters it is suggested that by adding matches that apparently escaped unrecorded, he actually did make the magical overall figure of one hundred thousand runs. Although never a professional as such, stories about his status as an amateur player, his excessive expenses, and the will to win at all costs abound, and on some occasions, he would travel first class to cricket matches while the professionals would have to make do with second class travel. No wonder that he was regarded as a Shamateur! However, to Heathfield's credit, given that he played against the club several times, he managed just the one century. What is perhaps also forgotten was that, apart from cricket, he founded the English Bowling Association at the South London Bowling Club, in Lyford Road, in Wandsworth and was a leading player in that sport. Being so close to the Field, one could almost imagine him playing a few early morning ends on the green at Lyford Road and then heading up to the Field for a full day of cricket afterwards. However, on occasions, he combined both sports when playing cricket at the Field also availing himself of Heathfield's bowling green!

The historic match in question, when Grace scored a century, took place at the Field on Tuesday 29 July 1902 during Heathfield's cricket week. The London County Cricket Club brought a very strong side to the field including W.L. Murdoch often regarded as the 'Australian Grace' who had skippered the Australian side and indeed led the Australians in the first Test match between England and Australia which subsequently gave its name to the 'Ashes'. Grace scored a magnificent unbeaten 137, but however, when on five, as the *South London Press* reported, he gave a chance to slip, but *'...the Heathfield members and spectators no doubt were sincerely pleased to observe that it was unaccepted because everyone wanted to see the veteran bat and their best wishes were gratified'*. In the whole scheme of things when time had been called and a draw had resulted, it was of no consequence, but to drop any batsman at slip when he had only made five, particularly a batsman of the calibre of Grace (even though he was 54 years old by then) is more than unfortunate. They say 'Dropped catches lose matches' but one thing is certain, they do not win matches! Grace however was generous with his praise for the pitch afterwards in saying that he *'would like to put this pitch in my cricket bag and take it away with me'*, and suggested possibly a two-day match next summer which the Heathfield President, G. Ashley Hyem on behalf of the club, readily accepted, although it appeared this offer never came to fruition. The *South London Press* continued that *'The Heathfield wickets {pitches} are renowned for their trueness and accuracy and to Collett in whose care they are entrusted (and who by the way takes his benefit next Monday in the Ashford game at Wandsworth) is to be warmly congratulated upon having his work so critically examined and praised by the greatest cricketer of this or any age'.* History does not record what the great man's opinion of the pitch might have been had he been dismissed for five! Would future generations have been aware that Grace had actually played at the Field or would that just have been a story lost in time? For years there used to be a trophy in the Sinjuns Clubroom with the original cricket ball and a plain wooden cup in which the ball rested plus, apparently, a scorecard which confirmed that a former pupil of Sir Walter St John's School, possibly W. Paice (who also played in the 1902 match) had actually bowled out Grace in another of these matches. Remarkably, after years of assuming it had been lost this artefact was found lying forgotten on a shelf in the Sinjuns Clubroom, but the scoresheet which apparently accompanied it as proof is no longer with it. Nevertheless, it is a tangible example of past cricket matches at the Field which we know Grace visited on several occasions. During his time playing for the London County Cricket Club, Grace moved to Sydenham to be close to the Crystal Palace ground. Adapting a well-known phrase at the time, a member of the public knocked at the door of W.G.'s house and enquired *'Is Dr Grace in?'*. The reply came back quickly *'Of course he's in; he's batting at Heathfield today!'*.

However, Grace did not have it all his own way. Being interviewed by *Cricket* in 'Chats on the Cricket Field' three years later, Heathfield player Charles Mills remembered what happened in the second encounter with London County Cricket Club in 1902, played at Crystal Palace on 30 August. *'I was playing for them (Heathfield) in 1902 against London County and Grace was in the team against us. I had always been very anxious to bowl at him and I can tell you I was delighted when after he had made eight runs he hit me to mid-on but did not get hold of the ball well and was caught'* by W. Paice. *'That was an enjoyable day for me, for I went in first and made 116 putting on 223 for the first wicket with T.T. Brewer'.* There cannot have been many players in the world who could reasonably claim to have scored a century against the side Grace was captaining and then dismiss the Grand Old Man in the same match. For the record, Heathfield got the better end of the draw with London County being 148-4 at the close in reply to Heathfield's 281-2 (dec). This latter encounter described by Charles Mills (although not all the results of the matches were reported), was probably the closest the Heathfield club got to defeating the London County Cricket side, and in 1904 with Grace and Murdoch again batting in tandem at the Field, although both were dismissed cheaply, the London County side ran out comfortable victors. With Grace in 1902 being only three seasons out of Test cricket, this was the last season in which he made over 1,000 runs in first-class cricket and whilst in minor cricket, he scored no fewer than 91 centuries overall, despite his failure in the return fixture with the Heathfield club at Crystal Palace, he still made 1,200 runs in that season for London County at an average of exactly 100. There is a curious misprint in the newspaper report of the match at the Field as it refers to a W.T. Murdoch rather than W.L. Murdoch. Analysis of Grace's handwriting demonstrates that he wrote his 'Ls' with a flourish and this could have confused matters. From his handwriting his 'Ts' were quite different in format. So, assuming that Heathfield posted the report in the *South London Press* it seems quite likely that they were copying the scorebook whose batting order was possibly scripted by Grace himself.

After the match Heathfield continued their cricket week. On the following day (Wednesday evening) The *South London Press* again reported that *'The Heathfield Club held an al fresco entertainment, the pavilion being decorated with fairy lights and bunting of gay colour. Unfortunately, the weather was unpropitious and drove the fair sex inside the pavilion, but the concert proved a brilliant success....'* The club could therefore count themselves lucky that the match with the London County Cricket side had been played the day before.

The Dinner in 1902 was held at the *Criterion Restaurant*, Piccadilly Circus. Although apparently it was reported that Dr W. G. Grace was going to attend, there is no mention of him attending on the evening in question. Originally opened in 1873, the *Criterion* is in the top ten of the most historic and oldest restaurants in the world still trading today.

Returning to the Charles Mills interview in *Cricket*, he gave an interesting insight into the life of a leading cricket player in those times. Although often referred to in press cuttings as South African this is not so, but perhaps this was because he represented South Africa in one Test Match in 1891. Apparently, he was self-taught. *'I never learned to play. I simply picked it up when I was a boy at Dulwich and would play for any club that asked me'*. Although he studied to be an artist, he liked the outdoor life and trialled for Surrey who could see his potential. In 1887 and 1888 he played occasional first-class cricket with the county. Besides playing he had wide experience as a coach in South Africa, America and Scotland. He came over with the first South African tourists in 1894 and although there were no Tests in that series, he, by then, had identified himself with South African cricket for some years. At the end of the 1889 season, he went to South Africa "as a speculation" where he played for the Kimberley Club. He made an immediate impression, as in his first match he made 297 against The Arabs (which, for some time, was the highest score made in Africa) and by all accounts should have made a triple century having being caught at cover point off a very loose ball. For the next four years he played his winter cricket in Cape Town. He also went to coach in Philadelphia revealing that 'Americans are exceedingly good cricketers'. In his first match for the Philadelphia club, he took 5-19 against the Germantown Zingari. In Scotland, he coached at Kilmarnock and remembered starting a match at six and drawing stumps at nine when it was still quite light enough to play cricket. In England he had coached at Tichborne Park in Hampshire (the ground still exists) and also coached at Haileybury, Bradfield College and Mill Hill School. In 1904 perhaps, unusually, with his first-class matches behind him, he became an umpire in Minor County matches. Perhaps significantly he played with George Lohmann both at Surrey and also in South Africa. Could it have been that Lohmann, who had played at the Field previously, recommended the Heathfield Cricket Club to Mills as a good place for him to play his club cricket? The fact was, however, that he indeed did play his club cricket at Heathfield as his principal club, and was one of the reasons for their continuing success. He was a genuine all-rounder and perhaps, although records are incomplete, could well have taken around a thousand wickets during his club career, which spanned almost twenty years at the Heathfield club.

By the start of the twentieth century Mills was not the only decent player at the time with the Heathfield Cricket Club. Thomas Brewer, who played for the club for many years, got his chance to play first-class cricket for the London County Cricket Club in 1903 and, played for the Gentlemen of England against Surrey CCC at the Oval. This latter match took place between 24-26 April 1905 and also marked Jack Hobbs's first-class debut. Later, in 1909, Brewer played Minor County cricket for Cheshire. Percy Francis also played for the Heathfield club in 1903 heading up the batting averages. He played a total of three first-class matches between 1901 and 1902 for Worcestershire and later played for Suffolk. Also, in 1903, two players in Heathfield's 3rd XI side attracted some attention and amusement in the *South London Press*, as their surnames were Codd and Herring! Were either involved in the 'Catch of the day?'

Returning to Grace, his involvement with the Field was not at an end. In 1905 the relatively new bowls section of the Heathfield club had performed well in the Jaques Trophy run by the London & Southern Counties Bowling Association, beating Spencer Bowls club 27-11 on the way to the final before losing to Balham Bowls Club at the Bromley club. The bowls club also decided to run matches to coincide with the cricket week. It also marked the final match between the London County Cricket side and the Heathfield club. On the day of the match in question the bowls club lined up a match with the London County Bowls club. This was, it seems, not a coincidence. Having scored 43 out of an impressive 313 by London County, Grace apparently turned his attention to the bowls green as he is recorded as having played his part in that match as well!! In the end the Heathfield club drew the cricket match and the bowls match finished in a tie. So, honours were even on both counts. In 1906, Grace skippered the London County Bowling Club in another match at the Field which the Heathfield Bowls Club won by a single point by 40-39. Not that Grace would have necessarily been concerned, as only around three weeks earlier he had signed a contract with the Crystal Palace Company (who were the holding company for the London County Club) to not only be the Secretary and Manager of the Cricket Club but also of the Bowls Club as well, with the princely annual salary of £600 (worth almost £75,000 in today's money), this despite the loss of London County Club's first-class status. Needless to say, despite the defeat on the green at the Field, the Doctor took his revenge the following season when the Heathfield Bowls club visited Crystal Palace. It is entirely possible drawing on reports, that he visited the Field on as many occasions to play bowls rather than cricket!

There is one other player apart from Grace, who we should take seriously during this period, none other than Jack Hobbs, who was starting out on his first-class career. He played at the Field with the Club & Ground side in both 1903 and 1904 whilst qualifying for Surrey. Born into poverty in 1882 in Cambridge, he was an absolute legend in his lifetime in this country, and second only to W.G. Grace in terms of influence on cricket. He scored a total of 61,760 first-class runs at an average of 50.70 including 199 centuries. Neither the aggregate of runs he scored in first-class cricket (Frank Woolley is the nearest with 58,959) nor the centuries he achieved (with Patsy Hendren next on 170) has ever been surpassed and with the restricted amount of traditional first-class cricket played nowadays, probably never will be. Indeed, had it not been for two seasons during his qualifying period and seasons lost to the Great War and when suffering from illness, he would have scored countless more runs and centuries. The other feature of his career as it progressed into 'middle age' was that it was not until 1925 at the age of 42 that he exceeded Grace's record of 126 centuries and after that he just kept scoring heavily until his eventual retirement in 1934 at the age of 51. With reference to minor cricket, Hobbs would play much less and so taking this into account, would not have threatened Grace's total aggregate in all cricket. Hobbs also took only 108 first-class wickets. However, this should not detract from the fact that he is also only one of two players to be effectively declared by *Wisden* as 'Cricketer of the Year' twice- in 1909 and 1926 (the latter as a 'Special Portrait'). In 1953, Hobbs, in the opinion of many belatedly, became the first professional cricketer to be knighted. Of course, when he played at the Field in 1903 and 1904, he was regarded as a promising player and his reputation was forged during the years to come. Hobbs scored 21 in 1903 and just 7 in 1904 at the Field. In both matches the Club & Ground side were dismissed for less than a hundred runs and in the latter, when their total was a miserable 66, their lowest in this sequence of matches, the Heathfield club duly won on the first innings by 30 runs. Remarkably however Hobbs remembered the Heathfield club with affection not for his batting but his bowling! In his book *My Cricket Memories* (published in 1924) he recalls that in 1903 he '... *played for Surrey Club & Ground against Heathfield on Wandsworth Common.... and took six wickets for 41 runs in eighteen overs*' and then '*This Heathfield match was evidently a good fixture for me for in the following year, on the same ground, I took five wickets for 15 runs in the first innings, and four for 27 in the second, including the hat trick*'. Perhaps giving away his professional status he continued, '*There is still an idea in some quarters that any bowler taking three wickets with three successive balls is given a hat. I have never yet seen a hat given on such an occasion, but I have seen one passed round for the lucky bowler, with gratifying results*'. It must have been with a sense of pride that the

Heathfield club watched as Hobbs's career developed and to relate about the day on which the club beat the Surrey Club & Ground – Hobbs and all!

Apart from Hobbs, other well-known international players have visited the Field with the Surrey Club & Ground side, notably Tom Richardson (who played with Charles Mills in the 1890 Club & Ground match), Herbert Strudwick (1900) and Andy Sandham (1912) at a time when they were all striving to prove themselves. Regarding Sandham, his rise to play for England was gradual. It could be argued that the Great War stifled his progress as he did not play Test cricket until he was 31, debuting against the 1921 Australian tourists. However perhaps his most remarkable achievement was the record 325 he made against the West Indies at Kingston in a timeless Test match in April 1930 by which time he was almost forty and which, owing to a relatively minor injury he received in a motor cycle accident shortly afterwards, proved to be his final Test match. He was therefore the very first Test triple- centurion and indeed is still the oldest player to have scored a triple century in a Test match. As regards to the match itself, this was drawn after nine days when, presumably, England had to get the boat back home! He is also one of the select number of players to have scored a hundred first-class hundred's in his career reaching this milestone against Hampshire at May's Bounty in Basingstoke in 1935. He continued to play first-class cricket until the age of 47 and after the Second World War returned as Surrey's coach and was delighted to have played a part in Surrey's seven successive Championship wins during the 1950s. He was less successful against Heathfield in 1912, however, being run out for just four.

Apart from the professionals, the Club & Ground sides contained a number of keen amateurs. Apart from the usual sprinkling of Captains and Majors with links to the military, other amateurs were distinguished by their initials in front of their names whereas for the professionals only surnames were given, or in the case of brothers, initials were included after their names in brackets. Some of the amateurs, however, were distinctly quirky. A couple of examples are mentioned below.

Having also played with the MCC, the Hon S.R. Beresford in 1908 scored 10 against Heathfield in the Club & Ground match. However, his full name was the Honourable Seton Robert de la Poer Horsley-Beresford so it is easy to see why all of this did not make its way into the scorebook! Described as an 'Old Etonian playboy', he was the third son of the third Baron Decies whose seat was located in County Waterford, Ireland. He seemed to live his personal life in the fast lane, and scandal was never far behind. An article suggests that after leaving Cambridge University he spent the next ten years of his life attending social gatherings, playing cricket (we know that!), shooting pigeons and living well, if not lavishly, despite having no noticeable source of income. Shooting pigeons was more than a pastime, as in the same year that he played in the above match against Heathfield, he represented Great Britain at trap shooting in the Olympics! Previously, he was apparently a war correspondent for eight months reporting on the Boer War in South Africa and although it seems that his expenses were consistently more than he earned, it is quite possible that much of it was lost on gaming, or hosting his regiment's officers' mess bar. He claimed to have met Cecil Rhodes, but this account is disputed. In the eight months he was in South Africa it appears that he never filed a single story with the Central News Agency. His first marriage ended when his wife divorced him citing grounds of cruelty and adultery around the same time that he was playing cricket with the Surrey Club & Ground at the Field- not to say that the Heathfield club had anything to do with his difficulties! During his life, he was sued in relation to substantial debts three times and declared bankrupt twice. On the first occasion in 1901, having returned home from his time reporting on the Boer War, he declared his debts to be £5,089 (almost £650,000 at today's money), mostly incurred through gambling. Having moved to America, he temporarily returned and remarried in 1915 at Kensington, before again returning to New York to carry on with his business interests. It transpired that his new wife was a proficient ice skater and in 1918 she won the US Ladies' Figure Skating Championship. The year before, he was successfully sued in New York for a sum totalling over $2 million in today's value, predominantly through running up debts on the New York Stock Exchange, but remarkably it seems the debt was quietly settled in the background. Perhaps his biggest claim to fame was a publication in 1923 entitled *The Future at Monte Carlo*, the book that inspired Norman Leigh to renew his efforts to break the bank at the Casino Municipale in Nice, as recounted in his story *Thirteen against the Bank* which discussed ways to beat the system of betting on the casinos in that town. Beresford's book described the system of playing the tables and its advice was described by one critic as 'complete tosh', and dismissed Beresford's claim of 'using (the system) successfully over the thirty years prior to publication' suggesting that the book's contents should be taken with 'a mountain of salt'. Given Beresford's record, this would seem to have been a fair criticism! In May 1925 a bankruptcy order was made against him in the High Court of London and during the follow-up hearing to appoint an administrator it was revealed that he had left the country (apparently, 'done a runner') and was living in reduced circumstances on the French Riviera at Cap d'Ail just two miles from Monte Carlo where three years later with rumours of further debts accumulating, he died. His dilapidated grave nearby in France is in a closed cemetery unused since 1965. He never did 'Break the Bank of Monte Carlo'. In 1915 shortly before his marriage, he lost his place in the line of succession to the baronetcy to his nephew. It appears that his wife did not follow him to France but remarried only nine months after he had passed away. At the very least you could say he had an eventful life and did not die wondering……! As a footnote the marriage of his mother in 1860 (Dowager, Lady Catherine Decies) to the third Baron Decies must have caused quite a stir at the time, as she would have been no older than 16 when she married the Baron no less than 33 years her senior. She outlived her husband by 48 years and six of her nine children (including Beresford of course), dying in 1941 at the age of 97.

Another player included in the Club & Ground side of 1910 as an amateur and perhaps a man of greater substance was Count V.C. Hollender who scored 11 against Heathfield. Given that Count is predominantly a European title, he was the son of Count Maximillian Hollender and Rose Beufus who were descended from Prussian Jewish emigres. He apparently knew a thing or two about dogs, specifically Bull Terriers, and at various times during his life he was Secretary of the Bull Terrier Club, a member of the Kennel Club, a breeder and a fearless judge. There is a picture of such an animal that was exhibited and indeed won a Certificate at the Metropolitan & Essex Championship Show in 1932 organised under the Count's auspices. Before the Great War, probably around the time of the match with Heathfield, the Count related the following incident *'Mr and Mrs Bennett had gone to a party, leaving the children in the charge of the maids. A man forced his way into the house, one of the maids loosed a dog, a bullmastiff, who held the man from nine o'clock in the evening until Mr and Mrs Bennett returned in the early morning'*. A good guard-dog (the article concluded) acts when it needs to act and should never bark at day or launch itself at fences in mock fury. He was obviously a man who valued his own security and knew the value of a good dog! He must have led a varied life as in 1927 he was interviewed in the Caribbean by the *Kingston Gleaner* about Boxing, Cricket and Jamaica. In 1930 he wrote an article in appreciation of Bull Terriers describing them as 'a model of what a dog should be' and 'the gladiator of the canine race'. In 1935 the Staffordshire Bull Terrier which he had championed along with H.N. Beilby achieved recognition from the Kennel Club. In 1938, by then Major Count V.C. Hollender, broadcasted a programme on 'The Care of Dogs' and in 1952 he edited a widely acclaimed book on Bull Terriers, which apparently is still available today from all good bookshops! He served in three wars (probably the Boer War was the first) and was mentioned in despatches during the Second World War after he had become a pilot officer at the age of 63, when most people would have been considered too old to be involved in the conflict.

It is quite clear with one seemingly being a privileged waster and compulsive gambler whose title and family connections allowed him to indulge in a champagne lifestyle, and the other being a dog lover and military man, that these two gentlemen had other things on their mind apart from cricket and although the former actually appeared in two first-class matches for Middlesex in May 1909 (at the age of almost 41 years old), scoring 22 runs at an average of 7.33, probably playing on the strength of exaggerating his capabilities, he predictably made little impact on the game of as a whole. The latter, Count V.C. Hollender on the other hand, really enjoyed his cricket. Entitled *Cricket in the Dark, Sporting Life* reports a match at Lord's on 30 September 1911, apparently the last day of the season there, between the Count's side and one organised by W.H. Bacon. The Count's side ran out winners by two wickets chasing 189 to win in near darkness. Obviously, he was a man of influence to be able to use Lord's for such a match. He attracted several well-known county players and cricketers for the purpose. He opened the batting for his side and made 20 of the required runs. You could almost say that he made his batting count! This match was not a one off as his side's matches would occasionally be reported in local papers. Whilst this is not suggesting that these two examples were in any way typical of all the amateur players of the time, it gives an insight into the social mobility of those with the resources (dubiously in the case of the former) to do so. However, both Beresford and Hollender, the latter the 'Cricketing Count', could point to the fact that they were part of a winning side at the Field, unlike Hobbs in 1904! As they say - that's cricket.

As the intervening years went by the bowls and tennis sections steadily grew in strength and numbers. In 1904, apparently, the club were the first to host the Canadian bowls side on their visit to these shores. Lawn Tennis was still played on rather an informal basis. One tennis fixture stands out, however-a match in 1905 against Old Grammarians! As if to reinforce this unlikely pairing, there is clear evidence that the Old Grammarians enjoyed their lawn tennis and according to records at the time could put out quite a decent team. They used to play Battersea Grammar School on an annual basis at lawn tennis 'locally', so it would have been possible that some of these matches might have been played at the Field at the Heathfield club, although perhaps more likely in Battersea Park. However, things were not all they seemed to be, as also in 1905, the Heathfield club reported that 'T.T. Fitchie, the Scottish international would again play for the club'. However, he was an international footballer not cricketer, whose main claim to fame was having been signed a record five times by (Woolwich) Arsenal. Given his peripatetic lifestyle, it must have come as some surprise to the Heathfield club that he was available for two seasons in succession!

The strength of the Heathfield club's connections to local Trading Associations as discussed previously was apparent again when on 19 July 1906 the club permitted the Carpets and Furnishing Trades (Wholesale) Associations to play at the Field to compete for a cup. Apart from the afternoon cricket match, a band was engaged to liven up the proceedings and the inevitable *al fresco* concert was arranged in the evening. In September a midweek athletics event was staged at the Field, being the third annual meeting of the Balham & Tooting Traders Association in aid of Bolingbroke Hospital, at which around 3,000 people were present.

Given that the matches at the Heathfield club attracted substantial interest and crowds, perhaps it was no surprise that the odd spectator would try to take advantage of the situation on match days. In 1907, Edwin Steer, a labourer, was remanded in gaol and then convicted of stealing a variety of articles from the pavilion of the Heathfield club. Apparently, the pavilion had been burgled at least four times in a twelve-month period prior to the court hearing. Given so many burglaries, the club had been refused insurance to cover the risk. Perhaps he was eventually caught red handed? The court sentenced Steer to six weeks' imprisonment.

In the meantime, cricket continued. Wicketkeeper batsman E.G. Read collected 137 against Townley Park in 1908. Alan Marchal topped that with 139 against Croydon Amateurs and according to *Cricket,* in 1910, Charles Mills, by now described as the 'old Surrey and South African cricketer', took no fewer than 49 wickets during cricket week! Unsurprisingly Mills was at it again in 1911 taking 100 wickets in the season, apparently a record haul for the club. The 1912 season was probably the most successful in the club's history. The 1st XI lost only four matches all season (having also won 11 and drawn 10). At the end of the season H. Weaver topped the batting averages with a highest score of 128*, followed closely by E.G. Read, whilst, perhaps inevitably, Charles Mills took 93 wickets followed by F. Swancott with 64 wickets. However, an extraordinary report in *Cricket* catches the eye, contributed by their roving reporter called the 'Chiel' who went to Battersea Park to watch the match between Battersea A and Heathfield A and reported that *'With a crowd of over 4,000 all seats outside the enclosure were occupied'.* Heathfield A's total of 190 had been overtaken by Battersea A's total by 28 runs at the call of time, but given that this was only effectively a 2nd XI match, it is very revealing, given that today, if lucky, one might get only four spectators watching a 1st XI match let alone a 2nd XI match! So just how large were the crowds at Heathfield? One estimate says hundreds but it probably was far more for some matches (the London County cricket matches for instance and the chance to see Grace bat) and perhaps into the thousands given the field's proximity to Wandsworth Common station. The income this would have generated was probably quite considerable. The lofty ideals of amateurism on which the club was founded had, in all probability, largely been forgotten by then.

However, the larger clubs were not immune to criticism. In 1910, the sports journalist E.A.C. Thomson who played for Heathfield at the time, at the request of a number of clubs, was the driving force behind and secretary of The Club Cricketer's Charity Fund throughout its existence, being a loosely tied association of elite cricket clubs. Socially, cricket was changing and although it was a reasonably short-lived organisation the membership was open to all clubs playing in and around London. There was no need to question Thomson's credentials. *Wisden* informs us that *'He was the grandson of John William Thomson, who planned the Crystal Palace grounds and reorganised Kew Gardens'.* A picture of the Heathfield side was included in the Charity's yearbook in 1914. The aim of the Charity Fund was *'to provide financial support or annual grants to hospitals and support for the London Playing Fields Association injured or disabled cricketers (from member clubs only) and other charities in the London area'.* Unfortunately, following an abortive attempt to involve junior clubs it became clear that, however well intentioned, the organisation would be highly exclusive in its social make up. Whilst the ideals of the Charity ultimately faltered, it brought clubs together into a more coherent grouping for the first time, for good or bad. On 15 March 1915, the Fund was reformed and the London Club Cricket Conference (later renamed the Club Cricket Conference) was born. Unlike its predecessor, it was not established as a charity but initially to keep clubs going through the war. E.A.C. Thomson was also the secretary of this organisation until his passing in 1941, by which time it had grown into the largest club cricket organisation in the world. The Heathfield club would surely have been one of the thirty-five clubs at its inception. Along the way Thomson assisted in founding the National Playing Fields Association in 1925 and for two years acted as honorary secretary of the Open Spaces Bill Committee. He also played association football, hockey (editing *Hockey World*), where his coaching book is still regarded as a landmark publication today, lawn tennis, bowls, (the latter two possibly with Heathfield), golf, and found time for athletics, cycle racing and boxing. Just to think about all these sports together is exhausting! He was clearly an all-round sports player and a leading administrator trying to do his best for the game he loved.

Meanwhile matters were changing at the Field. When Harlequins had taken up residency for the winter months, the Heathfield club could take advantage of renting the ground out to them. The

The Field and its environs 1868

The original home of Heathfield Cricket Club on Wandsworth Common prior to 1880, taken around 1900. The wall to the gardens of Heathfield Cottages is on the right hand side of the picture. (Courtesy, Patrick Loobey Collection, Wandsworth Libraries & Heritage Services)

An Early Heathfield Team

The Field probably around 1900. (Courtesy, Patrick Loobey Collection, Wandsworth Libraries & Heritage Services

Heathfield Cricket Club and Dan Leno's XI (known as the Dainties) Charity Match for Bolingbroke Hospital 4 July 1900. (Courtesy Royal Photographic Society Collection, Victoria and Albert Museum London)

View towards the Surrey Tavern and the Field from Trinity Road circa 1905. The visitors tent can clearly be seen on the Field to the right of the picture. (Courtesy Wandsworth Libraries & Heritage Service)

FIRST ELEVEN FIXTURES.

DATE.	OPPONENTS.	GROUND.	Oppnts	SCORES. Club.	Indiv.
April 21	Next Sixteen	Home			
,, 28	Clinton	Home			
May 5	Sutton ... ...s	Home			
,, 12	Hampton Wick	Hampton Wick ...			
,, 19	Battersea .. ..s	Home			
,, 26	Mitcham (day)	Mitcham			
June 2	Thames Ditton	Thames Ditton ...			
,, 4	Surrey C. and G. (day)	Home			
,, 9	Catford	Catford			
,, 16	Townley Park..	Dulwich			
,, 23	Addiscombe	Addiscombe			
,, 30	Sutton	Sutton			
July 7	Battersea	Battersea			
,, 12	*Garden Party*	Home			
,, 14	Townley Park...	Home			
,, 21	Boston Park	Brentford			
,, 28					
,, 30	(day)	Home			
,, 31	Banstead ... ,,	Home			
August 1	Gnats ... ... ,, } Cricket Week.	Home			
,, 2	East Molesey ... ,,	Home			
,, 3	,,	Home			
,, 4	Catford...	Home			
,, 6	Mitcham	Home			
,, 11	Hampton Wick	Home			
,, 18	Boston Park	Brentford			
,, 25	Thames Ditton	Home			
Sept. 1	Brixton	Home			
,, 8	East Molesey (day)	Molesey			
,, 15	Albermarle	Home			

Day Matches, 11.30 a.m.   *Half-day Matches, 2.30 p.m*

The 1900 season

Heathfield Fixture List 1900

Anyone for tennis?

Anyone for Tennis? Ladies of the Heathfield club enjoy a break between matches at the Field.

Charles Mills (South Africa & Surrey CCC). Also Heathfield Cricket Club 1899-1917

Charles Gwilt, Clerk to the School Governors 1890 – 1932 & Heathfield club Tennis Secretary 1913-1922.

Daily Graphic sketch of Harlequins v Richmond 1903

HARLEQUIN F.C. 1902–3. *Standing:* F. H. B. Champain, A. C. T. Veasey, H. Tomkinson, W. Martin, W. A. Smith (pres.), D. Linton, J. V. Nesbitt, R. Hutchison. *Seated:* E. W. Dillon, V. H. Cartwright, C. E. L. Hammond (capt.), R. C. Hayward, R. H. Fox. *In front:* F. W. Bewsher, A. D. Stoop, T. Creswell.

Harlequin FC 1902-3

Cricket Practice at the Field 1918. The outfield looks rather questionable!

THE FIELD

THE HEATHFIELD COMPOUND FROM 1914
(and post 1924 alterations)

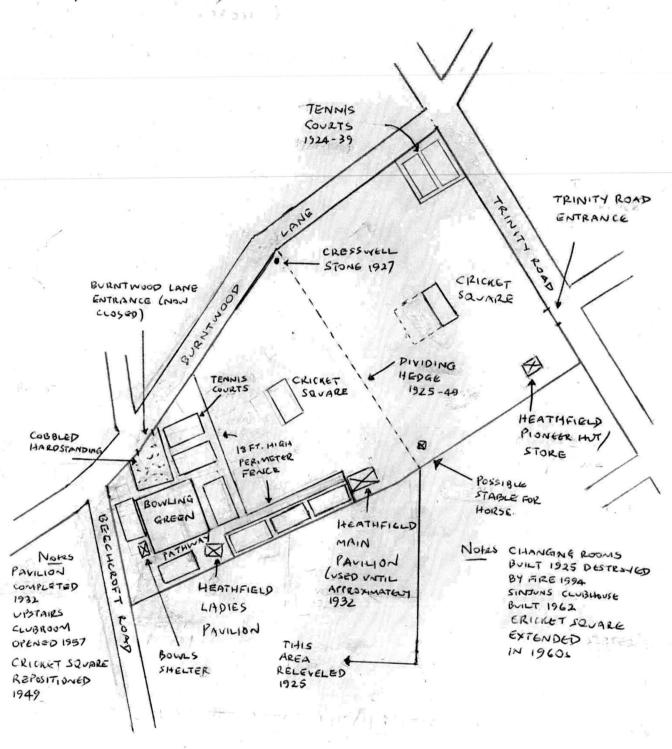

TENNIS COURTS 1924-39

TRINITY ROAD ENTRANCE

CRESSWELL STONE 1927

CRICKET SQUARE

BURNTWOOD LANE ENTRANCE (NOW CLOSED)

LANE

BURNTWOOD

TRINITY ROAD

DIVIDING HEDGE 1925-49

TENNIS COURTS

CRICKET SQUARE

HEATHFIELD PIONEER HUT / STORE

COBBLED HARDSTANDING

18 FT. HIGH PERIMETER FENCE

BOWLING GREEN

PATHWAY

POSSIBLE STABLE FOR HORSE.

HEATHFIELD MAIN PAVILION (USED UNTIL APPROXIMATELY 1932)

BEECHCROFT ROAD

Notes PAVILION COMPLETED 1932 UPSTAIRS CLUBROOM OPENED 1957

CRICKET SQUARE REPOSITIONED 1949

HEATHFIELD LADIES PAVILION

BOWLS SHELTER

THIS AREA RELEVELED 1925

Notes CHANGING ROOMS BUILT 1925 DESTROYED BY FIRE 1994 SINJUNS CLUBHOUSE BUILT 1962 CRICKET SQUARE EXTENDED IN 1960s

The possible layout of the Heathfield compound after the 1913/14 alterations

downside might have required the second square to be effectively renovated after the rugby had finished. Although uncommon, successful examples of renovating a square in this way are known; Epsom College (on one of their junior squares) being an example. When the Harlequins left in 1909, to be replaced by London Welsh Athletic Club, the Heathfield Club were put in a difficult position when in 1911 the ageing owner of the field, John Mills Thorne, conveyed the field to the rugby club for a sum of £3,800 as we know. This meant, at a stroke, that the roles of the occupants at the field were reversed, and the Heathfield Club would now become the rugby club's tenants. The Heathfield Club did eventually agree amended terms (in 1912) with London Welsh and the original lease of 1899 which they had agreed with the previous owner continued. However, the Heathfield Club would continue to employ the groundsman as part of the agreement. The local press expressed relief that a deal had been done. The club were safe at least for another seven years, but on terms that were certainly less favourable than before. Nevertheless, 1912 was a successful season for the bowls section of the club as they were selected with fifteen other clubs out of an entry of 70 applicants to represent the Southern Counties against the Midland Counties in their annual match.

1913 was a busy year with the Heathfield club continuing to run four elevens. The club had a close association with Balham Wanderers who were allowed to use the Field for practice on a weekly basis and also Highfield School. Bellefield (or was it Bellevue, the minute book conflicts?) Cricket Club were allowed, for a small charge, to use the Improved full-length nets with overhead netting for the purpose. However, the season had its problems. Concerns about the horse surfaced, as the vet had examined the bay mare which had been offered to the club and reported that 'she was too small for the work and would not last long pulling the heavy roller'. Another horse had been offered at a price of £12 and the club decided that it would fulfil requirements. Whilst later records, after the Heathfield's club departure, do not specifically record the continued use of horses for such work on the ground, it is likely that this practice continued until the Second World War at least. It is quite possible, in later years, that a horse could have been kept if not at the Field, but at the *Surrey Tavern* across the road, which, of course, was an old coaching inn.

Heathfield at that time did not tour, continuing to prefer a cricket week instead, but H. Weaver guested on Balham Wanderers week-long tour of Kent taking overall 17-139 with his bowling. The cricket week was another success with *Cricket* noting that for the Surrey Club & Ground match, narrowly won by the county, with the normal tent having been erected, there was almost a Festival feeling at the Heathfield Ground. In fact, perhaps, a 'run festival' might have been more correct, because just two days after the aforesaid match the Heathfield club racked up a massive 450-7 (dec) against Mr A.E. Henderson's XI, which is thought to be an all-time 'ground record score' at the Field. Ernie Read, continued to have a vintage season with the bat as a hard hitting 154 in Heathfield's total of 302-4 declared against Boston Park demonstrated, although the latter batted out time for a draw. After taking part in Heathfield's cricket week, Read toured the following week with Brixton and capped it off with another 'ton' for them against White House Cricket Club the following Saturday. His reputation in club cricket was such that he skippered the South London team in the Final of the Inter London Trophy at the Oval on 2 September in aid of the Club Cricketers' Charity Fund, where the South were narrowly beaten by North London by two wickets.

Perhaps as a harbinger of things to come, a letter had been received from the solicitor of London Welsh RFC, the landlords, telling the club they had been approached in regards to using the Field for aviation purposes. The Heathfield secretary had seen the solicitors but until there were more details, he could not take any further action. On the sporting front things were changing too. Owing to the increase in tennis and bowls membership, gone were the days when the tennis courts were used as part of the outfield on match days, as the area had already been sectioned off previously for the purpose by then. The club also considered raising the stop netting to 18 feet, to prevent balls from sailing into Mr Henniker's garden in Brodrick Road, or being lost in the process. These matters coincided with reorganising the Field in the closed season, which was done with the permission of their landlords, London Welsh. The provision of a new full size 'square' bowling green, doubling the size of the previous, was agreed and its relocation would enable the existing eight tennis courts to be reorientated and re-laid on the area vacated. All these adjustments would lead to a further reduction of the cricket outfield, including the provision of similar 18ft stop netting to protect the tennis players from any big hits from the cricket matches when both were in play. So, from fifteen years previously, when at times three cricket matches were played on the Field simultaneously with the tennis courts occasionally being used as part of the outfield, even two matches of cricket at the same time on the Field would now be a bit of a squeeze. Plans, however, to install hard tennis courts for use on a Sunday were, it seems, quietly dropped. By the time that spring had arrived in 1914, and with credit to the club, all the intended improvements had been carried out during the winter apart from a new path on the south side of the new bowling green for access which was subsequently completed, and the repositioning of the bowls shelter to the south west corner of the green.

The 1914 cricket season started eventfully when in April, members of the Amalgamated Society of Cricket Ball Makers, representing about half of the three hundred workforce making cricket balls, including those from Readers and Dukes, went on strike for better pay. Alarmed at the prospect of this disrupting the nation's favourite summer pastime, extraordinarily, the Press threw its support behind the strikers and concerns that a supply issue might derail the season were averted. Normal service was resumed at the Heathfield club with E.G. Read, A Cherry and T. Brewer registered centuries whilst the Press had obviously given up calculating how old the evergreen Charles Mills was, by just saying that he 'played for Surrey ever so many years ago' as he took 5-51 against Mitcham! General committee meetings were often held at the *Surrey Tavern*, and it was reported that an 1888 cricket photograph which was missing from the pavilion had turned up there, and that the club should ask for its return. Despite the tensions across the Channel with Germany threatening the neutrality of Belgium, the cricket 'carnival week' went ahead in the last week of July and was described as the most successful in the club's history with an al fresco concert organised as usual. The Club & Ground match on July 29 was the high point of the week with Heathfield running up an impressive 327-9 (dec) led by E.G. Read (94) and then bowling the county side out for 198, with Charles Mills bagging 5-76 against his former colleagues, to record the club's first success since the Hobbs match of 1904. Unfortunately, the season was about to be derailed not by the lack of cricket balls, but by something else that was to cast a shadow over the world for the next four years.

The following week, Germany invaded Belgium and War was declared on 4 August. As club members were called up to fight, the last reported Heathfield match (Heathfield A v Wycombe House) appeared to have been played at the Field on 22 August. Although some clubs played on into September (indeed the South London Cricket Association which organised league cricket continued throughout the War), the 'Golden Age' of cricket was coming to a close. By the end of the War, not that the club knew it then, changed circumstances would have profound implications for their future at the Field by the time the conflict had finished.

During the Great War and after

By the start of the Great War, the Field was slowly losing its country atmosphere. Despite the passing of John Mills Thorne, the former owner, the Great War delayed the sale of Burntwood Lodge, together with neighbouring Collamore, although they were both demolished shortly afterwards. Today, the only clues that the properties existed are Collamore Avenue, and a footpath barely 100 yards long that runs from Burntwood Lane to Sandgate Lane nearby, and follows the line of the driveway to both former properties. Burntwood Grange, built in 1832 was actually larger than Burntwood Lodge, was renowned for its wonderful gardens and conservatory so much so that it was featured in a book *The Parks, Gardens of London and its Suburbs* by Edward Kemp a prominent landscape gardener during Victorian times. It was the last of the original manor houses to go around 1940, although by then much of its extensive grounds had already been given over to development. In its time it was owned by a young stockbroker Harmon Grisewood who was apparently responsible for its opulence. By 1882 Burntwood Grange was the property of the Holloway family. As Holloway Brothers Ltd the company were responsible for building the Admiralty Buildings on Horse Guards Parade, the Old Bailey, and the fountains in Trafalgar Square, not to mention several landmark bridges across the Thames, such as Chelsea, Wandsworth and Hampton Court and various housing projects including Crawley New Town and, partially, the new Magdalen estate, which was situated next to Burntwood Grange. The company were also responsible in the 1890s for completing Battersea public library and baths and also Battersea Polytechnic. Remarkably both Henry Holloway who was also a prominent Liberal politician was knighted in 1917 for advising the government on the Great War housing crises, and his son Henry Thomas Holloway was knighted in 1945 for his wartime services. The latter was President of the Federation of Civil Engineering Contractors from 1940-46. Although two of Henry Holloway's sons born at Burntwood Grange played first-class cricket for Sussex, there is no evidence that they actually played cricket at the Field. However, one of them, Bernard Holloway, known as 'Babe' (1888-1915), also played lacrosse for England, and was a gifted rugby player. As skipper of Old Leysians RFC, who used to play on the ground now occupied by Battersea Ironsides Sports Club, he invariably played at the Field against London Welsh RFC in the local derby matches between the two sides that were keenly contested and supported both home and away. Sadly, Bernard was killed in action in France during the Great War and a memorial to him can be found in St Mary Magdalene Church opposite the Field. His younger brother, Norman Holloway (1889-1964), played no fewer than 102 first-class matches for Sussex and also recreationally with the Free Foresters, in a career that straddled the Great War. Both brothers apparently did not take any role in the building and civil engineering company, which as Holloway White Allom went into administration in 2011.

At the Field, as the cricketers were called up, the club grappled with the new reality. The 1914 cricket season came to a full stop, and on what would have been the final scheduled match at the Field on 12 September the ground was given over for drilling purposes. By the following May training was underway as a 'bridge' was constructed at the Field under the supervision of the Wandsworth 'A' company commander, P.S. Doherty, and just to prove it was sound the whole battalion marched over it when completed. Perhaps more ominously, trench digging was taking place in Magdalen Park. At the request of the club the army agreed to refrain from using horses on the Field in order to prevent unnecessary damage. By then the club had amalgamated with the Balham Rifle Club to form the Balham and Wandsworth Defence League. It was also agreed that sheep should be allowed on to the Field immediately after the close of the cricket season presumably to keep the grass in check, although how that was reconciled with drilling activities on the Field was uncertain. This might seem to have been an unusual solution to winter ground maintenance, but sheep grazed apparently on Wandsworth Common certainly until 1921 when the last shepherd retired. Whilst accepting the current situation, the Heathfield club intended to continue with the usual winter programme of whist drives and dances, but to be guided by any circumstances which may arise owing to the crisis through which the country is now passing. The former of these produced the sum of £8 which was forwarded to the Belgian Minister. As to the missing photograph of the 1888 cricket side located in the *Surrey Tavern*, this issue was left over, and probably forgotten! In late January 1915, the news came through that the Heathfield Club had suffered its first of at least seven casualties the club would endure during the Great War, when the Cricket Secretary George Aitchison, a member of the club for many years, had been killed in action. It was confirmation, if ever it was needed, that the war which some had hoped would be over by Christmas, was not going away. Suddenly this conflict on a foreign field had become much closer. Amongst the others lost during the conflict in 1917 was A. D. Cherry described by the club as 'one of the most popular and promising cricketers in London' and in a report after his unbeaten 113 against Boston Park in the weeks leading up to the War it was reported that he was '...*such a promising young player, and should be valuable to his county Dorsetshire'*.

In April 1915 at a meeting at Charterhouse Hall in London, which included such clubs as Heathfield, Honor Oak, Spencer and Malden Wanderers amongst its number, it was resolved to carry on playing cricket as long as they could. For the next four years, a limited number of cricket matches were played and some had more of a military flavour as witnessed when the Field was used by the Scots Guards, for instance. A cricket match and entertainment was arranged in conjunction with the Wandsworth Volunteer Training Corps, who used the Field for training and drilling purposes. Two thousand tickets were sold and an amount of over £46 was raised in aid of the Red Cross Society. The Bowls club also remained active, and in July 1915, at the Norwood Bowling Club, won the pairs event, which had been organised by the Surrey County Bowling Association, beating Vauxhall Park, in front of a crowd of about 250 spectators, by 26–20.

The war hit the Heathfield club particularly hard. They were still obliged to pay London Welsh for the rental of the Field. A side was 'bolted' together predominantly out of senior players too old to serve and others in essential services who were needed to stay at home and occasionally soldiers at home on leave. Sometimes, depending on availability, a second eleven was also raised. Paradoxically, the war helped two players who were stalwarts of the club, to prolong their club cricket careers throughout the war, both of whom were the senior side of forty years old when the conflict started. Charles Mills, mentioned earlier in this book continued to take wickets, including a seven-wicket haul in a 2nd XI match in a victory over Dulwich Hamlet in 1917. By the end of the war and his likely retirement from club cricket he had turned fifty and, for those readers in the know, would have been a tremendous asset for Surrey Over 50s had they operated in those days. Another, Ernie Read, in 1915, scored a magnificent 142 in a total of 245-1(dec) although Clapham Ramblers at 131-6 hung on for a draw. He was a hard hitting and heavy scorer of runs at club level. Described by the club as '*the outstanding personality of the team, one of the widest known, best liked and honestly feared cricketers throughout London, either with bat in front or with gloves behind the wicket'*, he was born in Portsmouth and played the occasional first-class match with Hampshire and then Sussex between 1903 and 1906 before joining the Heathfield club. Owing to medical advice he was forced to give up playing cricket for the 1920 season and sadly died the following year aged just 47.

Given the changed circumstances, the club struggled to keep going. The ground staff of three which were employed all year long were reduced to a rump. The club could only afford to employ a groundsman on a seasonal basis plus some voluntary help when required. Although the men's tennis section was effectively closed, this was to a degree offset by the increase in women's membership, and although the bowls section was also hit, there remained sustained interest in it as part of the club and indeed the Bowls Club was accepted into a reorganised structure for 1915. There was even, for a time, a croquet lawn on the cricket outfield, although this was soon transferred to one of the tennis courts which was being used less frequently. Manor House School whose buildings still exist, which operated as a boarding school on Clapham Common North Side between 1876 and 1938 were granted use of the Field on Wednesdays during May, June and July. Whist drives as mentioned earlier were to become a regular fundraising event during the conflict and continued under the superintendence of the club's Chairman E.R. Robinson and almost £14 was raised for a Fund to provide Christmas Dinners for Wounded Soldiers. The Wandsworth Training Corps, used what was known as the Pioneer Shed (adjacent to Trinity Road) for the storage of various items and helped with routine maintenance of the facilities. Additionally, the Main (or Central) Pavilion as it was known, was linked to the former by a new gas main presumably to provide heating and lighting when required. Given that the Corps had been largely formed from Heathfield club members, perhaps there was a degree of self-interest in this act of generosity, but nevertheless the club was keen to do its bit for the war effort and formed the backbone of the Corps in the Wandsworth and Balham area. The continuing help of the ladies in preparing teas was noted. Towards the end of the year the club were considering insuring the Field against aircraft, presumably against it being used as an emergency landing area or possibly for other associated security reasons.

By 1916, to underline the club's support for the emergency services, a photograph shows the Ambulance Service parading at the Field – although looking at their uniforms, they could easily have been mistaken for the Army! With the absence of rugby, both Battersea Polytechnic, and Sir Walter St John's School (the latter more frequently) were, despite some initial resistance, able to hire football pitches and in the case of the latter, cricket pitches on Thursday and Friday evenings for practice, and Saturday mornings from May until July for the sum of £25. In May the *South London Press* declared that '*Club Games (were) at a standstill*'. This was not strictly true, but perhaps less sport was reported as the press was more concerned with the conflict in Europe. However, if there was ever proof that cricket can be a great leveller, on 24 June, the club recorded a score at the Field of 421-8 (dec) to run out winners against Catford by 357 runs. Suffice to say, Catford won the return match later in the season! On 24 July the Field was used for tennis by the South London Schoolgirls Lawn Tennis Association and for the South London Schools Athletics Championships. Events included races over 100 yds, 220 yds, 440 yds and 880 yds with additional competitions for the Long Jump and High Jump. Another competition quite popular in those days was the Throwing of a Cricket Ball, with a winning distance of 59 yds recorded, probably, by a young cricketer! However, such scenes of activity were rare in reality. With the groundsman relieved of his duties for the winter months the ground was closed for the season on 30 September. As a reminder of the ongoing conflict, two Belgian gentlemen who were refugees, applied for membership of the tennis section although it is not certain whether they paid the annual membership fee to play. Again, later, three further Belgian refugees were, after much debate refused membership of the Bowls section as the club did not wish to admit anyone on 'half subs' for fear of introducing a dangerous precedent.

Interestingly, as a precursor of changes ahead, the Field and Pavilion were being used during the winter by Sir Walter St John's School for football purposes. Whilst the London Welsh RFC were still the landlords, Heathfield's groundsman was undertaking work on behalf of the school to erect goalposts and maintain the ground. The use of the Field for football and drilling purposes all took its toll on the cricket outfield and further increased the work that the Heathfield groundsman had to undertake. Eventually a settlement was agreed, but this all added to the other difficulties that the Heathfield club were having with their absentee landlords who were not present on the ground owing to the suspension of rugby during the war.

At the start of 1917, the Local Authority contemplated taking the Field for allotments. The club had already allowed limited use of the Field for growing cucumbers and marrows, whether this was for club members or the war effort in general is unclear, but this separate notification was considered a serious enough threat. In the event this came to nothing just as the earlier request via London Welsh to allow the authorities to possibly use the ground for aviation purposes had a few years previously. The continued use of the Field by Manor House and Highfield Schools in the summer was granted, and the Field was again used by South London Schools. The following season the club again played a limited number of matches and were most successful against the Service Sides. The bowls section also reported that although 1918 was abnormally wet and rain had frequently stopped play, 'Forty members were playing using five rinks' and canvas sheets had been purchased to protect the same from the elements. However, by the end of the conflict, although the tennis and bowls sections had roughly held their own, numerically, overall, membership was down.

Many sports fields perished during the Great War, with some taken for development in the secondary phase of the prolific expansion of London shortly afterwards, and some, if not developed, were never returned to their original use. With the Armistice not signed off until 1919 and with the ongoing influenza epidemic, some clubs did not really get going again until 1920. Other sides were casualties. Perhaps the most notable local club to fail was Upper Tooting Cricket Club in Beechcroft Road, although there is evidence they had played through the early part of the War. A new club called Upper Tooting Athletic surfaced for a time, but it was unlikely they had use of the ground anymore. The club did not register itself with the newly formed Club Cricket Conference and by 1926, its ground in Beechcroft Road was being used for the construction of Bec Grammar School. A later development would see that school merge with Hillcroft. It is now the site of Ernest Bevin College (formerly School) and the original school has been demolished and given over to housing. David Davis the politician, Art Malik the actor and Bob Hiller, now Harlequins' President were Bec Old Boys, whilst Sadiq Khan, the current Mayor of London, who apparently scored a fifty for the school at the Field, and professional snooker players Tony Meo and Jimmy White – the latter probably the most gifted snooker player never to win the World Snooker Championship, were former pupils at Ernest Bevin School.

Change was in the air. In November 1917 the Heathfield committee explained to a Special Committee Meeting that negotiations between a syndicate and the landlords (London Welsh Athletic Club) were ongoing and asked if the club was willing to pay an increased rental for the remaining two years of its lease. This was agreed, but by the next meeting on 1 February 1918 it was clear that the syndicate's efforts to secure the Field had failed. Other potential buyers appeared who, however, were more friendly to the Heathfield club, and as late as 1 March a proposition was agreed that a Sub Committee be appointed and be empowered to draw up counter-proposals and negotiate matters to a completion. However, it was too late. Owing to Samuel Cresswell's deposit in December 1917 (discussed in the next Chapter), the purchase of the Field was duly completed on 25 March 1918. Beyond this date, negotiations on the terms of a new lease were now subsequently in progress with the governors of the Sir Walter St John's Schools Trust.

The realities of the situation were now beginning to become apparent. On 30 April 1918 the Ground Committee of the club was attended for the first time by J.G. Taylor, Headmaster of Sir Walter St John's School representing the School authorities. It was decided that during the summer that the School 1st XI were to use the visitors changing facility in the main pavilion and that the remainder of the players could use the pioneer shed and the tent when erected. As regards to the lease there was however a hitch or maybe a misunderstanding insofar that the Heathfield club had assumed that they could use the Field until 1926-perhaps this was because the existing lease they had still had two years left to run. Negotiations with the Trust dragged on. Matters came to a head in March 1919 when the Heathfield club wrote to the Clerk of the Trust, Charles Gwilt, giving an ultimatum that if matters were not settled by 25 March 1919 (a year after the Trust had purchased the field) then the club 'will not be able to afford any facilities for the Schools' use after that date'. Although it is perhaps difficult to understand why the Heathfield club, as tenants, could dictate to their new landlords on this matter, this may have been because the groundsman was still employed by the Heathfield club and not the Schools', given the difficulties the school were having with the authorities. The ultimatum, however, did galvanise the Schools Trustees into action but it would take almost another two months to formally agree terms, with a rent of £130 per year agreed for the summer season, to allow the Heathfield club to remain at the Field until 4 October 1924. All this must have been uncomfortable for Charles Gwilt at the time because, apart for his involvement with the Trust, he was also Secretary of Heathfield's tennis section, a post he eventually relinquished in 1922.

To a degree, the new lease was an unsatisfactory settlement for the Heathfield club as it only postponed the inevitable. Previous owners of the Field either were content to allow the club to run their summer sports programme as they wished or, in the case of London Welsh for example, only needed to have use of a ground during winter. Despite an effort a couple of years later to try to agree a further lease extension beyond 1924, it was clear that the Sir Walter St John's School Trust were not disposed to countenance this idea. Indeed, there was a suggestion from the Trust to remove the Heathfield club earlier from the Field. During the last few years, the Heathfield club would effectively have to share their lease with their new landlords.

Despite a complaint by the club to the Governors of the Trust about the poor state of the Field after the football season, attributed, as the Heathfield club said, to the boys persisting in playing after the groundsman had declared it unfit (a perennial problem over the years!), the Heathfield club fully resumed its cricket section in 1919, again running four sides and by all accounts had a most successful season. It is likely in part that this was owing to more than fifty Service members who had been retained on the Membership Roll during the war and were now returning. The club's results were regularly reported in the *South London Press,* and familiar opponents resurfaced with notable wins over Beddington, Polytechnic and Cyphers whilst matches with Mitcham and Honor Oak were drawn. Against new opponents Old Whitgiftians, the club ran up a total of 290-6(dec) with both Purver and Swift scoring centuries and then bowling the Old Boys out for 204. In other developments, the main committee opened a separate fund to help reconstruct the finances of the club which had suffered such a battering during the War. This was named the 'Heathfield Ground Improvements Guarantors Society 1919' and its aim was to provide effectively a guarantee for the expense of relaying the bowling green with Cumberland turf and other ground improvements. As a result, the bowling green was obviously the envy of many. In 1921, a record attendance watched the club stage the finals of the Surrey County Bowling Association Championship and both in 1922 and 1923 the club staged the finals of the EBA County Bowls Championship won by Surrey in the latter year by 129-109 over the Kent side. The tennis section ran its first tournaments since 1914 with A Haythornthwaite and Miss D Phillips winning the Gentlemen's and Ladies Challenge Cups respectively. The club was thriving. Over all sections the number of members by September numbered a record 320. The ground staff were restored and a grateful club reinstated their benefit. The good times were back, but for how long?

The 1920 season saw the reintroduction of the cricket week with not one but two concerts arranged on the Tuesday and Saturday evenings. The season was a resounding success and the cricket section had to turn away players as they had more than enough to fill four sides. The club also thanked 'friends' who had officiated as umpires (no official qualifications were required in those days) and A.T. Purver for his constant services as scorer to the 1st XI during the season. A large number of spectators had watched Saturday afternoon and holiday matches, and the club noted that the admission charge had proved a valuable source of revenue. In addition, the introduction of a tour to

Sussex proved successful which was undertaken immediately following the cricket week. It must have been quite an event as members of the bowls section accompanied the team. There were wins over Lancing Old Boys, Cuckfield, and Horsham, a draw with Bognor but defeats at the hands of Haywards Heath and Worthing. In the latter the club suffered a 'double' defeat at Worthing as whilst the cricketers were being defeated, the bowls section were going down to their counterparts at Homefield Park by 46-30. Overall, the 1st XI played 26 times winning 13, drawing 6 and losing 7 matches and the 2nd XI had a similar record. The greatest success of the year was undoubtedly the young player H.F. Gilbert, who scored the highest number of runs, including an unbeaten century, and took 85 wickets at a cost of 14.20 apiece. He was selected to play a few matches with Surrey Second Eleven. Another player, T.G. Purver, was also selected to play for Surrey v Middlesex in the London Conference Matches. The almost annual ritual about hiring or selling the horse at the end of the summer ran into difficulties. Eventually, it seems, a home was found for the beast at the Raynes Park Golf Course for the winter. It is a sign of the times, but nowadays the vexed question is often 'Who is going to do the teas!' and nothing to do with a horse or trying to obtain suitable horse boots to enable the animal to pull the mower or roller around a cricket field!

In 1921 the tennis and bowls section purchased a 90ft Army hut from the Guards' Depot on Wimbledon Common and this was used both as a bowls pavilion and then for teas for the tennis section. The 'Hut' as it was known, was also used for club meetings in the closed season. Also, the tennis section retained the Streatham Hall Tennis Cup, over fourteen other clubs, prevailing over Dulwich Park in the final at the Belmont Club, Streatham High Road in front of 400 spectators. Mr J.R. McFarlane and Miss D Phillips were their "star" players. This success carried over into the Hurlingham Lawn Tennis Tournament in 1922 where Heathfield players continued to impress and show promise. All sections continued to run at full capacity. The cricket club also contemplated running a regular Thursday team. Honor Oak were considered to be the best side in South London at the time and the Heathfield club (in 1921) played them twice. Although in the first match the club suffered a heavy defeat, they achieved a respectable draw in the return fixture. However, Heathfield had the better exchanges at second third and fourth eleven levels, underlying their strength in depth. The matches with the Surrey Club & Ground side resumed in 1921 with a close high scoring draw. However, perhaps the 1921 cricket tour to Sussex was not quite the success of the inaugural adventure the year before, as both matches reported in the local press against Cuckfield and Worthing ended in defeat.

Despite the loss of their star batsman, H.E. Glibbery, who had joined the Heathfield club after the War to Lloyds Bank, the club looked forward to the 1922 season. All four elevens played Honor Oak again with honours even and, with additions to the list, of teams the calibre of Dulwich, Purley and Epsom, the club still enjoyed playing a high standard of club cricket. There was one sad moment, however, when it was reported that a Mr Benjamin Young, a solicitor's clerk of Fullerton Road, whilst watching cricket at the Field, had collapsed and died whilst lighting a cigarette. A verdict of 'death from natural causes' was returned at the inquest. Fortunately, this remains, apparently, the only known incidence of a fatality recorded at the Field for anyone playing or watching sport during its history.

The 1923 season opened on 28 April with a trio of victories for the sides against Highgate, Holloway Ash and Old Wilsonians and three weeks later Banstead were destroyed by 157 runs (196-5(dec) to 39). Given the postponed match in 1924, the club would play what would prove to be its final match against the Surrey Club & Ground side at the Field which the weather curtailed with the club on 159-5 at the close. The limited reporting of results suggested a less successful season overall with many matches drawn, but there were also good wins over Lensbury and in the return match with

Highgate. The other innovation was a Sunday match against Lyon's 1st XI on 1 July, presumably away from home. Whilst the result of the match has not been recorded, we do know that H. Faircloth, bowling against Heathfield, took his one hundredth wicket of the season in that match. It was not until the following year that the council passed a regulation permitting Sunday play on council grounds, although in practice it would be some seasons before Sunday play for club cricketers would be accepted as a norm rather than an exception. The 1923 batting averages were headed by Ralph Davis, with A. Perry and J.K. Frost both scoring unbeaten centuries.

The Final Fling

According to the Heathfield centenary booklet, in early 1923 the landlords (that is the Schools' Trustees) had stated that *'an extension of the lease could not be granted for the 1924 season'*. This was noted by the press and *The Sportsman* ran an article on 14 August 1923 to the effect that the Heathfield club were to *'lose their ground'* at the end of the season. Interestingly, Frank T. Smallwood's recollection (as a member of the School staff from 1911 until 1955 and author of the Sir Walter St John's School History) in a letter to Bill Ellery (later Editor of *The Gazette*) in 1973, is at best ambiguous on the subject by stating that *'..... in 1923 the lease [to the Heathfield club that is] was running out and we did not renew it'*. However, in what must have been a late reprieve, an agreement to permit one final season must have been taken probably in the autumn to prevent the cricketers from drifting away to other clubs. Perhaps the reason for the change of mind was partly to do with the legality of the decision, as the Schools' Trustees had already previously agreed that the lease with the Heathfield club would not expire until October 1924 and anyway, despite the inconvenience, they perhaps thought an additional season's rent would be useful to close out the debt on the Field, which was actually not discharged until June 1924. There could possibly have been another reason, as perhaps a deal was struck between the Heathfield club and the Trustees for the former to install two further tennis courts on the corner of Burntwood Lane and Trinity Road in consideration of an additional season at the Field. This idea had been discounted by the Trustees a couple of years earlier, but it was known that the pupils and school staff used the tennis courts and the two additional courts were indeed left in situ after the Heathfield club had left. The Trust, maybe, also took a pragmatic view, and possibly they were also aware of the Heathfield club's efforts to secure a new ground nearby and did not want to place the future of the club in jeopardy at a crucial phase of their negotiations. The extra season did give the club continuity and in particular provided their 124 tennis members (equally divided between men and women) the opportunity of staying with the club whilst the new ground was made ready. The bowls club, buoyed by the installation of their new Cumberland turf bowling green, were also thriving and were competing in the London & Southern Counties Bowling Association competitions at the time with their results regularly published in the local press, although it seems that in 1924 most of their matches were played away from home.

It must have been quite a surreal situation. The Heathfield club would have known without doubt that 1924 was to be their final season at the Field and yet the cricket section was still running three if not four elevens on a Saturday afternoon. The club still enjoyed a strong fixture list including matches against such sides as HAC, Lloyds Bank, Barclays Bank, Shepherds Bush and Honor Oak. A final cricket week was arranged, for which the Heathfield club were famous by now, and the week was scheduled to commence on 28 July with a match against a strong Surrey Club & Ground side. However, 1924 was a wet season. Although St Swithin's Day (July 15) was sunny, rain was then recorded in London on thirty of the next forty days, and on the day of the scheduled match with the

Surrey Club & Ground the temperature only reached a chilly maximum of 15.7 C in London as heavy rain swept across the country. It would ruin the club's final cricket week at the Field. The last scheduled Heathfield club match at the field was on 11 September against a West Indian XI, but like many other matches the result was not recorded. The following Saturday (13 September) Heathfield played out a tense draw in between the showers, in the somewhat unfamiliar surroundings of North London CC at Crouch End, landing up at close of play on 106-8 just three runs short of victory having dismissed their opponents for 108. For North London CC this was their last match of the season, but invariably for the club it was, save perhaps for an internal club match the following weekend, to have been the very last game of cricket the Heathfield club would ever play. However, almost certainly, the very last cricket match played under the auspices of the Heathfield club was to be one of the most memorable since the Field had been used for sport.

The South Africans at the Field

History records that the 1924 South African tourists were not regarded as one of their strongest sides. The generally damp conditions made it difficult for them to adapt and in the first Test facing an England total of 438 they were shot out for 30 in only 12.3 overs. This remains in terms of balls faced the shortest innings in Test match history, and also in terms of runs equalled a similar score of 30 also by South Africa at Port Elizabeth against England in the 1895/96 series – only New Zealand (26 all out) have ever fared worse in a Test Match. Following on 408 runs behind the South Africans went on to score 390 in their second innings, thereby losing the match by an innings and 18 runs. In the five Test series they lost by three matches to nil, whilst the other two Test matches, ruined by the weather, were drawn. After their last official tour match at Scarborough, they travelled south to catch the boat home from Southampton to South Africa, but not before stopping off to play at the Field on Wednesday 17 September in a Charity Match. The fact that this match was actually played at all was discovered by chance as a result of an entry in a 1951 publication by A.C.L. Bennett entitled 'The Weekend Cricketer' which suggested that the Field had staged a match in the early 1920s involving the South Africans. Details and the scorecard of the match itself against the London Clubs were only reported in the *Wandsworth Borough News*.

The choice of the beneficiaries for this game were interesting. Bolingbroke Hospital was one, but the others were connected with the licensed drinks trade, namely the Licensed Victuallers' School and their Benevolent Institution. At the time the school had recently moved (in 1922) from Kennington to Slough. Founded in 1803, the school was set up to help children of deceased or distressed publicans. Current monarchs since William IV, have been patrons of the school. In 1989 the school moved to Ascot where it exists today educating around 900 pupils. In recognition of its links to the past, three of the four School houses- namely Bell's, Courage and Whitbread are named after well-known brands. Former pupils include Simon Cowell – who needs no introduction, and Tracy Ullman the actress and comedian.

And so, to the match itself. Of the eleven that represented South Africa that day, eight were tourists, all with Test experience. Of the twelve, including the skipper, that faced the South Africans for the London Clubs it seems only four (possibly five) including the skipper had any first-class experience as the rest were just decent club players including, probably, three from the Heathfield Club. Their Captain on the day was M.C. Bird (or to use his full name Morice Carlos Bird) who had skippered Surrey briefly before the Great War and was the only Test player in the side having played ten times for England between 1910 and 1914, remarkably, all in South Africa. Aged 36 at the time he had given up playing first-class cricket shortly after the war. Another was (Herbert) Alan Peach who had played against the Heathfield Club for the Surrey Club & Ground side in 1912 and 1914. The Great War had delayed his first-class debut, and sometime later, as Surrey coach between 1935 and 1939, he was credited with discovering the Bedser twins. Interestingly the scorecard also lists 'F. Bullock'. Research has failed to prove that the player was actually 'Burn' Bullock, but despite a probable error in copying his initial from the scoresheet it was undoubtedly the player that gave his name to the pub formerly known as the *King's Head* overlooking Mitcham Cricket Green. The pub was the setting for the formation of the Association of Cricket Umpires in 1953. Sadly, with the pub closed, the building has been occupied for several years by squatters.

About 2,000 people were there to witness the match, and although the London Clubs batted first, and dismissed at lunchtime for 161, this would seem to have been a reasonably satisfactory, but inadequate score, considering the quality of the opposition. The players were entertained at the *Surrey Tavern* who were no doubt also supporting the match. Afterwards, perhaps having received too much 'lunch', the South Africans were bowled out for a meagre 55 – to lose by 106 runs! They only batted ten, as M.J. Susskind was listed as "Absent" but was this because he was injured during fielding, or simply did not turn up for the match, or spent too much time enjoying an extended lunch interval in the *Surrey Tavern*? We do not know. Although this was in effect an exhibition match, it was nevertheless, a victory very much against the odds which members of the London Clubs team could relate to future generations as 'The day we beat the South African Tourists'. Shades of a similar victory by Ireland over the West Indies in 1969 at Sion Mills when the latter were dismissed for 25 runs spring to mind. At the conclusion of the match the draw for an autographed bat was held with perhaps, appropriately, A. Perry, Secretary of the Heathfield Club, being successful. On his suggestion he generously put the bat up for auction and it was bought by Mr. W.R. Crisp a Trustee of the Licensed Victuallers' School for £11- almost £700 in today's money!

In conclusion, it is not known precisely why the Field was selected for such a match. Maybe it was intended as a swansong because it was known that the Heathfield Club was closing as a cricket club after fifty years or possibly because in the past both George Lohmann (as assistant coach to the South Africans Tourists in 1901) and Charles Mills (the ex-Heathfield club player, who had toured with the 1894 South Africans) had strong connections not only with the Field but also with the tourists. In any event, it would have been a fine 'send-off' for club cricket at the Field and certainly of local interest as witnessed by the attendance. Poignantly, however, this match, would have been the last time that the Heathfield club would have a connection with cricket, and their indigo, blue and white flag (they would certainly have had one) which fluttered above the pavilion for perhaps almost forty years, would be lowered for the final time.

At the end of the 1924 season the players dispersed. Although, apparently, the Heathfield club had not played the Spencer club nearby since the 1890s, a young Guy Tarrant, would, with others, such as Ralph Davis and Harold Dwyer, move there at the start of the 1925 season. Guy Tarrant would establish himself as one of Spencer's most outstanding cricketers and would be their first player to be capped by the Club Cricket Conference in 1930.

With the schools now in full control of the Field for the next twenty-five years at least, the Field would remain 'dry' and any post-match entertainment by the Old Boys' sides would initially have only taken place at the *Surrey Tavern* until the school authorities relented to allow independent club facilities. However, as mentioned earlier, as if by confirmation, the *South London Press* reported in May 1925, *'Spencer appear likely to be stronger than ever. Several of the old Heathfield members have joined…'*. That season the Spencer club ran five Saturday elevens, and become the most prominent side in the area, something that, in many ways, remains the same until the present day.

The Heathfield era was over.

Aftermath

After overcoming some difficulties surrounding a 'no intoxicating liquors' clause, terms regarding the lease, of the new ground were agreed between the owner and the new Heathfield club set up for the purpose. As part of the negotiations in relinquishing the Field, according to the minute book, the Heathfield club, presumably on behalf of the new company that had assumed responsibility for the new ground in Lyford Road, made a request to the Trust to transfer the Cumberland turf laid on the Bowling Green to Lyford Road-a novel request, their solicitor thought, but through the Governors of the Schools', and in consideration of £100, agreed in return that *'the turf could be removed together with the huts, mower, rollers, seats, loose plants and other material'* provided that the main and ladies' pavilions were left for the schools to do what they wished with them. The removal of the bowling green turf was probably carried out as late as December 1924. Perhaps at the end there was some disappointment that the cricket section had to be cut adrift to save the bowling and tennis sections given that the club was originally set up purely as a cricket club. Perhaps the cricket club members had hoped, even after the late reprieve at the end of 1923, that a further agreement might be made for the cricket club only to continue at the Field beyond 1924? As we know that did not transpire.

Although the end of Heathfield's tenure at the Field was inevitable, given the circumstances, sadly, it was the best solution for both parties, but it did mean the closure of an influential and talented club that had contributed so much to club cricket in London. In hindsight, had the Heathfield Cricket Club negotiated purchasing the ground from the London County Council between 1890 and 1898 before it had gone to auction, they might have still been playing at the Field today. In the end, by the time that London Welsh had purchased the Field from John Mills Thorne in 1911 almost, from behind their backs, the club's future at the Field was no longer in their own hands. The club were then hit by a 'perfect storm' at the time of the Great War when they were at their most vulnerable and the opportunity to purchase the Field, even then, slipped away. Paradoxically at the end the club had become a victim of its own success having effectively outgrown the Field as a centre for all their sporting activities. Sports clubs that today provide two cricket squares, proper tennis facilities and a bowls green would need to occupy an area significantly larger than the size of the Field to sufficiently satisfy the requirements of their membership. In a sense, faced with the higher demand and cost of land in an expanding post war London, the club took the only realistic option open to them and cut their losses. Their prize was, of course, that they would now have, minus the cricket, a new purpose made ground, with a new pavilion, enhanced and expanded tennis (including hardcourt) facilities, and an improved bowling green at Lyford Road.

The Heathfield club carried on at the Field almost until the end, holding their last committee meeting there on 24 September 1924 just seven days after the match with the South Africans. Future meetings were generally held at *The Surrey Tavern* until the new ground at Lyford Road was ready. However, for the Heathfield club going forward, they had achieved something almost impossible by today's standards. When a club loses their main ground, this almost always leads to the complete closure of a club. The Heathfield club, to their credit managed to adapt and reinvent themselves on their bowls and lawn tennis sections alone. The original Heathfield club it seems was effectively wound up and in order to protect the interests of the new club in Lyford Road which was still under construction, the Heathfield Club Ltd, a new limited company was incorporated on 13 July 1924 with Its first registered office actually being 'The Heathfield Ground, Trinity Road, Wandsworth Common', a name that had become synonymous with the Field by that time. This remained as the registered office until contracts were exchanged on the new ground around 6 October 1924, when the registered office was transferred to Lyford Road. Regarding the new ground, nowadays accessed from Sandgate Lane (which name had replaced the section of Lyford Road from the bowls club to Burntwood Lane), the Hard Tennis Courts opened on 28 March, with the grass tennis courts and the bowls green following on 1 May 1925. By 1929 the bowls green was good enough to be used for a Surrey v Berkshire match. The tennis section was subsequently wound up in 1967 when the owners of the ground Holloway Properties Ltd sold part of the ground for redevelopment, but the bowls green remains to this day. The club now owns the freehold of the land remaining, and today it is known as the Heathfield Bowls Club.

The Schools Take Over (1918-1945)

We shall go on to the end…we shall defend our island, whatever the cost may be… we shall never surrender.

Sir Winston Churchill (1874-1965)

The Purchase of the Field

During 1917, the School Governors heard that the freehold of the playing field owned by the London Welsh Athletic Club on the corner of Trinity Road and Burntwood Lane was about to come onto the market. Accounts suggested that this situation was forced upon the Trustees of the London Welsh club who were facing a fourth season without rugby. When approached by the Governors, the London County Council showed little interest to assist in acquiring the field; maybe like other organisations during the Great War they were also facing difficult times themselves. However, as Sir Walter St John's School had intermittently hired the Field since 1915, the Trustees were anxious not to lose the opportunity of purchasing it or otherwise losing the use of it to another buyer. Although the original idea was initially to secure the Field for Sir Walter St John's School only, as it was that school and not Battersea Grammar School that had been using it from time to time during the past couple of years, the Governors decided that the two schools should share its use if they were successful. Later that year, it became known that other possible purchasers were showing interest, so one of the Governors, Alderman Samuel Cresswell, deposited £300 of his own money to secure an option on the Field. He then offered the Field to the School Trustees. Cresswell's decisive action and deposit was a masterstroke at the time. The country was still at war, and any private clubs at the time, including the Heathfield club, would not be in a situation to make such a purchase. Apparently for some time afterwards there was an undercurrent of ill feeling from institutions such as Battersea Polytechnic, who had been a possible buyer, but Cresswell's audacious and selfless move had won the day.

Since 1875, the two schools that were jointly part of the Schools' Trust, Sir Walter St John's School and Battersea Grammar School had been on different sites. The latter had been seriously affected in terms of area by the encroachment of the South Western Railway Co who had compulsorily purchased various sections of the school's land owing to the development of Clapham Junction station which had left the school seeking alternative accommodation anyway, let alone a playing field, which both schools lacked. Before the purchase, various grounds had been used including Earlsfield, Battersea Park, Clapham Common and Gorringe Park for Saturday football, so logistically a private ground nearby, for the schools' exclusive use would be an asset to both. In order to raise the total cost of £4,643 which covered the price and incidentals, it was agreed that the Governors would raise £1,500 and the balance would be met by taking over existing mortgages or later by a bank loan. The two Schools were asked to raise £500 each, the Governors voted £150 from Trust Funds and a further £543 was collected from various donors which included an additional contribution from Samuel Cresswell and companies such as the Morgan Crucible, a well-known Battersea company. In the event Sir Walter St John's School (Sinjuns) raised £550 but Battersea Grammar School managed only £100 at this stage, although, together with assurances that the latter school was to be fully involved in this venture, their contribution was subsequently made good. The purchase of the Field was completed on Lady Day 25 March 1918, although the repayment of the loan created by the purchase was not discharged until 27 June 1924.

It should be noted that Samuel Cresswell, as the conveyance records, purchased the Field 'on behalf of Sir Walter St John's Schools Foundation' and quaintly perhaps, it mentions that the Field was in Wandsworth, Surrey which of course was the case when originally purchased by Henry McKellar in 1852, effectively transferring to London in 1889 as the result of the Local Government Act. It was not until the early 1960s, after the death of Samuel Cresswell's wife, that the situation regarding the conveyance was regularised (as Samuel Cresswell's initial deposit had been on behalf of the Trust) and as a result the ownership of the Field was acknowledged to reside firmly with the Sir Walter St John's School Trust.

An article in the School Magazine for March 1918 gave an insight into how the Sir Walter St John's School would make its contribution towards the purchase price of the Field. It stated that the Field *'was over eight acres in area and would provide three football and six cricket pitches and an excellent bowling green and eight tennis courts'*. It then went on to mention that the late Dr W.G. Grace had made a century on the Heathfield Ground, now the property of the Schools. This match has been mentioned earlier in this book but had Grace been caught at slip on five, then this sales pitch would have fallen rather flat! In that sense the dropped catch was the most important blunder by a fielder in the history of the game at the Field! In return, to encourage boys and parents, the Governors decided to present every boy now in the school who raised a guinea or more towards the fund with a permanent Life Membership Ticket which would confer the right to free admission at all times to the Field; *'We should like to see 300 Life Tickets issued here'* so the article finished. This tactic seemed to work. There was no mention at the time of the Heathfield club's continuing involvement with the Field and the fact that the Heathfield club still charged an entrance fee to watch cricket. Perhaps the Life Membership Ticket was one way of ensuring pupils the right to watch cricket at the Field the schools now owned free of charge? However, one of the reasons that the schools agreed to granting Heathfield a new lease at the time was that in reality, with a rent of £130 per annum for the summer season, it would bring in much needed revenue to help pay off the debt. Subsequent to the Great War, London grew rapidly and available land was invariably sold for development at a price that would have been prohibitive for the Schools.

Although the Field is situated outside Battersea in which both Schools were originally located at the time of the purchase, the proximity of the old borough of Battersea to Wandsworth can be appreciated by looking directly down Nottingham Road opposite the Trinity Road entrance to the Field where the original division, bounded by Wiseton Road and Nottingham Road is no more than 100 yards away. Many Inner London schools, even today, have no adjacent or nearby playing fields they can call their own. Although some of the references to Spencer's past influence are obvious, such as Spencer Park and the cricket club named after him, some are less so, by reference to the three roads situated wholly within McKellar's Triangle. Althorp Road is named after Spencer's country estate in Northamptonshire. However, Nottingham Road and Wiseton Road previously mentioned, have perhaps a more indirect historical connection. Wiseton is a small village in northern Nottinghamshire. The Wiseton estate was another of the Spencer family acquisitions. Wiseton Hall was owned, after inheriting from his wife Esther Acklom who died in 1818, by the third Earl Spencer until his death in 1845, when the estate was sold. Sometime later after it became the property of the Laycock family, coincidentally, Harry Elliott who played at the Field in a charity match in 1937 was once employed briefly in 1913, as a groom at Wiseton Hall. Apart from playing four Test matches Harry Elliott played first-class cricket for Derbyshire from 1920 until 1947. In that final season at the age of 55 he was recalled by Derbyshire to assist them in dealing with an injury crisis and played alongside his nephew, Charlie Elliott who is better known as umpiring in 42 Test matches between 1957 and 1974. Harry Elliott was also an umpire officiating in seven Tests between 1950 and 1953.

In early 1922, the London County Council discovered the action of the Governors in granting £150 to the Playing Field Fund. As the Council was making a large annual deficiency grant to the Trust each year, the payment into that Fund had really come out of Council funds which they had never authorised, approved, or even blessed the purchase. With reference to this incident the Council surcharged the Governors with £150, the legal expenses of the purchase, of which the schools were expected to pay half. Since the Field's purchase in 1918 it was clear that 'There were three in this marriage' namely the Heathfield club, that would play on Saturday afternoons from around 2.30pm, and both schools. It must have been a nightmare to organise fixtures particularly on Saturdays during the summer term with matches probably being played in the mornings by both Schools at times, and there is evidence that alternative grounds were having to be accessed to carry out the growing commitment both schools were making to summer sports such as cricket. The Governors acknowledged this, and reassured Battersea Grammar School that they would have exclusive use of half the ground once it was fully paid for. Their four acres would certainly have been an improvement on the three-quarters of an acre of land they had left at St. John's Hill. The relief at both schools in finally securing and controlling the Field for their own purposes was palpable. The termination of the Heathfield club's lease was briefly mentioned in Battersea Grammar School's Magazine in the autumn of 1924 and only confirmed what was known already as it stated that *'It is with the greatest regret that we displace the Heathfield Club, but it was quite impossible for two Schools, well over 1,100 boys, to manage otherwise.'* The school also confirmed that the ground near Earlsfield station which had been used for the past five years as a second ground, thanks to Alderman Cresswell, was to be taken over by the Parks Department and the School hoped to continue use of the same going forward. However, in reality it was probably soon afterwards subsumed into the final extension of Wandsworth Cemetery in Magdalen Road.

The departure of the Heathfield club in October 1924, effectively brought to an end the use of the Field for the purposes of club cricket for the time being, and, with the exception of the Second World War, the schools were now fully in charge. Additionally, Sunday use of the Field, perhaps more by accident than design, was not permitted until around 1950. However, upon examination of cricket club fixture lists, playing Sunday club cricket did not become in any way normal until around the start of the 1930s. With both the Old Boys clubs however, all Sunday matches would be played away initially and although disrupted by the Second World War, with Battersea Grammar School now at Streatham, Saturday cricket at the Field throughout the season was only possible for Old Grammarians CC. In the meantime, Old Sinjuns CC would have to wait until the early 1970s, when school cricket was in decline, to assume full use of the Field for cricket purposes on Saturdays and therefore throughout the weekends.

School Sports: The Early Years.

Before the purchase of the Field in 1918, both Schools had to make use of what was available elsewhere for cricket and football. The very first mention of a cricket match appears in the *South London Press* on 21 June 1876, where, in a match played at Battersea (probably in the Park) between Sir Walter St John's Upper School (soon to be known as Battersea Grammar School), and Albany House (Battersea) resulted in a narrow win for the School (49-40) by nine runs. Indeed, both cricket and football were well established at Battersea Grammar School by the turn of the century. In 1903/04 for instance, the School football side won all sixteen matches before Christmas eventually playing 29 matches losing only two (one against Old Grammarians by 2-1) with an extraordinary tally of 251 goals for and only 37 against. In the following season they were almost as successful and a ridiculous 24-0 defeat of Mercers School seems to have been the high-water mark of their achievements. As with all schools, form can be quite variable from year to year and by 1909/10 they suffered a truly dreadful year culminating with a 25-0 defeat at the hands of Latymer Upper School and unbelievably a couple of years later a 28-0 defeat (no it's not a misprint) against Strand School! Occasional cricket and football matches were played with the sister school, Sir Walter St John's School, with, on balance, Battersea Grammar School having the better of the exchanges coming up to the Great War.

At Sir Walter St John's School, cricket was played before 1892 as in that year there was a mention of the School re-establishing cricket, and matches were played against Malden College, Stormont Cricket Club and Highfield School. For a time from 1899 the use of Burntwood Playing Fields was secured on Wednesday afternoons. Beyond that in 1909 pitches were used in Magdalen Road for the purpose – probably at the same ground that Battersea Grammar School also used. L.L. Beale became the first bowler to take all ten wickets in a match against Wandsworth Technical Institute in 1904. Also, 1892 was the year of the first recorded football match and victory against Highfield School. During that season twenty-two matches were played and opponents soon included Battersea Grammar School, Battersea Polytechnic and Emanuel School. In 1911 the first football match between the School and the Old Boys resulted in a 1-1 draw. The Field had been used occasionally under hire during Great War both in 1916 and 1917. It should be remembered that the country was still at war as witnessed by a report of a cricket match against Battersea Polytechnic at Dulwich which read *'Never before has the commencement of a match been delayed by an air raid. Never before has the booming of a gun not more than ten yards behind the pavilion rendered a cricket field a dangerous place of existence. In consequence of the advent of hostile aeroplanes, one member, after seeking shelter from falling shrapnel, forgot to return, but thanks to our obliging umpire we were able to play a full team'*. In 1918 following the purchase of the Field, the first School cricket match was played barely a month after its purchase, appropriately between Sir Walter St John's School and Battersea Grammar School which resulted in a victory for the former in a low scoring match (49-23). Indeed, the School cricket team distinguished itself by winning every match including the Old Boys twice (although both were unofficial matches before the formation of the club), a first in its history on both counts. One of the reasons for Sir Walter St John's School's success was the extraordinary and superb bowling of P.G. Blackwell during this period. He represented the 1st XI in no fewer than six seasons (1917-22) and in that time he, took at least 214 wickets in 54 matches and on 26 occasions he took five wickets or more in an innings, records, now that the school is closed, that will never be beaten! Even the air raid mentioned above in 1917 did not disturb the young Blackwell, as he took 6-11 in that match, as the School ran out victors by fifteen runs. In 1919 he was described as *'the best bowler the School has had for years'*. He delivered *'very fast spin from the leg'* and bowled left-handed. A comparison in style to a degree of the famous England cricketer Derek Underwood many years later cannot be denied. He was certainly just as 'Deadly!' His best analysis was 9-16 in a match against Rutlish School which remarkably the school lost, although in 1921 he took 8-7 against the County Secondary School Battersea who were dismissed for just 25. A 1918 report from the School versus Masters match, presumably at the Field, sums up his capabilities with the ball. *'Hopes rose when Mr Carr made a hit….. but soon one of Blackwell's "specials" laid him low'*. Admittedly the pitches were invariably not so true in those days as they would be in later years, and although this should not detract from his achievements, it might explain why he took so many wickets. Blackwell was a talented all-round sportsman, captaining both the cricket and football teams at the School.

The Field Divided

When the newly formed Upper School of Sir Walter St. John's School (to be shortly renamed Battersea Grammar School) was located subsequent to the purchase of St. John's Lodge in 1875, the concept was to create a School that was explicitly of higher status than the Sir Walter St John's Middle School in Battersea High Street, in terms of fees, age of admission, and qualification of the staff. However, by 1883, Emanuel School, much to the concern of the Trustees, had relocated to a site a short distance away on the edge of Wandsworth Common, and secondly in the 1890s the Battersea Polytechnic, South Western Polytechnic and Wandsworth Technical School all opened secondary day schools for boys, all charging modest fees. With the nearest of schools outside the Clapham Junction area in South London being Wilson's School at Camberwell, the new School was the most unfavourably sited of all, in terms of numbers and falling income. This became even more pronounced over time with the compulsory purchases by the railway to expand Clapham Junction station and its environs, as noted elsewhere in this chapter. In the meantime, William Taylor, headmaster of the Middle School in Battersea High Street persevered, dropping the word from its name and preparing the boys for various public examinations. In a sense, arguably, it could be said, it was against this backdrop, that both schools had effectively become rivals rather than one subservient to the other, that was a potential cause of the difficulties in purchasing the Field and its subsequent division.

The Field was certainly an improvement on the situation the Schools had faced before in hiring facilities for sport but with both Schools together educating more than a thousand pupils, there had been doubts that its eight acres was still not large enough to fully support both. Nevertheless 'half a loaf was better than none', but in order to be equitable, the two Head Masters agreed to divide the Field into two four-acre plots so each School could have exclusive use of its own half and be responsible for its upkeep and maintenance. This finally resulted in a plan showing the exact division of the field signed off by Mr J.G. Taylor on behalf of Sinjuns and Mr H.R. Ellis on behalf of Battersea Grammar, which was agreed by the latter on 1 April 1924. Was this foolish? The Trust must have acquiesced on the physical division of the Field, because the plan only shows the exact division of the Field but not how it should be marked on the ground itself. During 1925, apparently, a hedge was planted to signify this division although School Trustee Meetings seem not to mention it being discussed at the time. Curiously when today the division of the Field is mentioned, many doubted that it really existed. However, a 1937 picture of the Sir Walter St John's School Cricket 1st XI, clearly proved the hedge's existence as it was curiously used as the background for the picture rather than having the backdrop of the School's Trinity Road changing rooms behind them as you would have expected. The hedge partially impaired the view to the Burntwood Lane pavilion and it could be deduced that it was around six feet high! It would have certainly restricted the extent to which both parts of the Field could be properly coordinated. Perhaps the photographer at the time was trying to make a point.

Like any other hedge, wall or fence in history it helped foster the idea that Grammarians were somehow different from Sinjuns. It also had implications for draining the whole of the Field which had increasingly become an issue during the winter months even as far back as when the rugby clubs had used the ground before the Great War. The only advantage was that two separate pavilions were built rather than one and this would prove ultimately to have been fortuitous in the most extraordinary of circumstances, and would eventually bring the Old Boys sports clubs together. Although not specifically shown on the 1924 plan, the vehicular entrance from Burntwood Lane would have been retained during this time servicing Battersea Grammar School's part of the field and probably not closed until the removal of the hedge shortly after the war when the field was consolidated again into one playing surface. For the meantime, however, it made for some intense rivalry between the Schools on the sports field and it would be fair to say that both Schools played each other at sport only occasionally, until after the Second World War had passed.

With the Heathfield club gone both Schools set about arranging their separate ends of the Field. The Sinjuns portion adjoining Trinity Road assumed the most urgency as perhaps the Pioneer Hut at the Trinity Road end of the ground had gone by then, and even if it had not, it was only a storage facility used among other things to store the tent that the Heathfield club had used during their cricket season. There is a pencil mark on the original signed plan of the partition which shows, perhaps, the intended rough position of the new changing rooms at Sinjuns' end of the ground. In the event, the Head Master of Sinjuns, Mr J.G. Taylor quickly pressed ahead to build a new changing facility during 1925. This was pretty basic, and consisted of two changing rooms with toilets to each and a loggia in front perhaps for seating. This facility was further extended in 1931 to include a further two changing rooms, with a communal plunge bath (later converted into a central bank of showers) either side of a central reception area with a basic kitchen facility at the back to serve lunches and teas. This was also used by the Old Grammarians to provide refreshment for their cricket opposition before the upgrading of their pavilion after the Second World War. There was also a small referees'/ umpires' room with an individual shower – what luxury! The Battersea Grammar School's four acres of the ground was actually about 10% larger but because of the Field's tapering shape to Burntwood Lane, logistically, this area was less user friendly, although the partition had left both the central and ladies pavilion formerly used by the Heathfield club, in Battersea Grammar School's sector. Additionally, it also included the bowling green and tennis courts, and works had to be carried out on the whole area to create a level playing field (quite literally!). Although records show that the Field renovations carried out during 1925 were completed by the following year, because cricket was still played on that part of the Field, it was not until 1927 that it was formally opened. Trust records suggest that the opening ceremony was originally pencilled in to be performed, around 13 June by, rather strangely, the Duke of Sutherland. However, it seems, with the Duke unavailable for the revised date, it still turned out to be a notable event, combining it with a Staff versus School cricket match after tea, which finished in a draw. So it was on 25 June 1927 that Battersea Grammar School's part of the Field was officially declared open before a large attendance of distinguished visitors, parents of boys and friends of the School by a man with a repetitive name, Mr Samuel Samuel MP for Putney, assisted by the Bishop of Kingston who administered a blessing. In his introduction before the opening, the Headmaster Mr H.R. Ellis outlined the extraordinary efforts that had gone into preparing the ground for the School's exclusive use. Then, in a final act that was to prove controversial, it was the duty of Lieut-Col. K.P. Vaughan-Morgan MP OBE, who was a director of Morgan Crucible, a company that had assisted in the Field's purchase, to unveil a granite commemorative stone tablet in appreciation of Samuel Cresswell's contribution in securing the Field in front of a large crowd both inside the Field and out in the roadway. The inscription apparently written in letters of imperishable lead, was headed up Battersea Grammar School is still legible today almost a hundred years later aided by some recent renovation. It reads *'In Honour of Alderman Samuel Cresswell JP Mayor of Wandsworth, Through Whose Efforts The Freehold Of This Playing Field Was Acquired for the School June 1927'*. On Sinjuns' side of the hedge, no such stone was erected. Of course, years later when the hedge was removed any passer-by could be excused into thinking that it was Battersea Grammar School alone who secured the whole field for eternity which, of course, was not the case. Sometime after the hedge was removed the stone was apparently attacked by a drunken Old Sinjun with a cricket bat, with the cricket bat presumably coming off worse as a result! Although the cricket nets which had been in place since around 1950 have only recently been removed, the stone still stands there alone hard up against the boundary fence with Burntwood Lane in the quietest area of the Field, almost like a Cold War relic marking the original land border between East and West Germany.

Although some accounts suggest that the foundations to the new projected pavilion had started as far back as 1925, it is likely that the main cricket and ladies pavilion left behind by the Heathfield club was used as temporary changing rooms until perhaps as late as early 1932 when the Burntwood Lane pavilion was essentially completed. It is a substantial and imposing building and certainly a more superior construction to the changing rooms erected at the Sinjuns end of the field. Although much modified, both inside and out, it stands today as a glorious statement of times gone and has borne witness to some remarkable matches that have taken place ever since. The view from the upstairs Clubroom towards Trinity Road in the distance is one of the best on offer in club cricket. Although both clubs regarded each other as the best of friends and the worst of enemies, a thawing of relations gradually took place. As one Old Sinjun remarked some years later after playing in a competition between the two Golf Societies for the first time 'You know, those Old Grammarians aren't that bad after all!'

Whilst the Heathfield club were at the Field, and after its purchase by the Schools' Trust, the boys of both schools were permitted to use the tennis courts from time to time. This seems to have been an informal arrangement probably on behalf of the Heathfield club to try to keep in with their new landlords. However, the usage of the courts was becoming a little more than the Heathfield club would prefer, and in 1920 the club had suggested that two new lawn tennis courts could be laid in the north-east corner of the Field on the corner of Burntwood Lane with Trinity Road for exclusive use of the Schools. Although the Trustees apparently originally turned down this request, the two tennis courts in this area were indeed constructed and remained in place for use by the masters and boys of Sir Walter St John's School. In 1929 it is recorded that the *'Boys beat the Masters & Friends at cricket and the Masters & Friends beat the Boys at tennis'*. In 1931 on the occasion of new electricity cables being installed in Burntwood Lane probably for street lighting, a plan quite clearly shows the tennis courts' location in the same area that the Heathfield club had suggested. It is unclear just how long after this date that these courts survived, but it is possible that by the Second World War they had fallen out of use and returned to the outfield.

The Advent of Old Boys' Sports: The Early Days

When the Heathfield club left the field at the end of the 1924 season, it gave an opportunity for both Old Boys' Associations to recruit new players. It was true that some cricketers found their way down to Spencer CC as we know, as did others did not have an association with either school, but it was well known over the years that former pupils of both Sir Walter St John's School and Battersea Grammar School played side by side at the Heathfield club. At that stage Old Sinjuns Cricket Club was still in its infancy, and although Old Grammarians did not officially start as a cricket side until 1926, they did play occasional matches before then.

Founded in 1919 the Old Boys of Sir Walter St John's School (Old Sinjuns) were the first of the two Old Boys clubs to play regular club cricket. Hitherto occasional matches had taken place but often on an annual basis with the School (Past v Present), with the first match being played on 26 July

1911 at Earlsfield with the School being victorious. Despite its foundation, it was not until 1920, that fixtures were played against other cricket clubs with home matches being played at Raynes Park. Eleven matches were played, eight resulted in wins – a good start. The next couple of seasons illustrated that pitches were not over sympathetic to batsmen as the club only exceeded a score of 100 runs in six out of fifty-two attempts, but still won a fair number of those contests! An isolated result in *The Sportsman* in 1923 illustrated this point, as having scored a modest 130 the club bowled Aquarius out for just 28 to win by 102 runs. Before the start of the 1922 season, a very successful concert had been organised at Chelsea Town Hall in the presence of the Headmaster. P.G.H. Fender the Sussex, Surrey and England player whose father Percy R Fender attended the school, addressed the meeting together with Rev F.H. Gillingham (Essex) who in 1927 became BBC's first ball-by-ball commentator. Given the connection with the School through his father, P.G.H. Fender apparently coached the School around this time.

In 1922 the cricket club used the Oakey Wellington ground adjacent to Streatham Park Cemetery. This ground had been recently obtained by the company John Oakey & Sons Ltd who were desirous to enter two elevens in the Business Houses League and Cup. Old Sinjuns it seemed would be their first tenants. However, the upkeep and annual rent of £80 proved too onerous, so at the end of the season and for the next two years, the club was on the road again. Remarkably Oakey as a company still exist, but the ground doesn't.

The expiration of the Heathfield club's lease gave Old Sinjuns more scope. In 1925 they were permitted to use the Field on Saturdays during the school holidays. When Sunday cricket was introduced a few years later the club still played away as no Sunday cricket at the Field was permitted in those days, as we know. However, the Saturday matches did give the club an opportunity to entertain some of their opponents. Laurie Bolt skippered the side for five of the first six seasons. Alf Cox was the first player to take fifty wickets and score a fifty for the club (sadly he died at the comparatively young age of 40 in 1937) and Laurie Bolt himself secured the club's first century in 1924 and a second in the following season. In 1929, a year which saw the beginning of a second eleven, the club held its first cricket supper at *The Horse & Dolphin* just off Leicester Square. In 1932 under the captaincy of Gwil Davies, H.E. Avery became the first player to reach a thousand runs in a season for the club and was considered good enough to play for Surrey II in 1934 and again in 1937 & 1938. By 1935 however, he had transferred his allegiance to Malden Wanderers CC and in that year he was capped by the Club Cricket Conference. 1937 was his most successful season with Surrey II, as he played in most of their matches and scored 315 runs (Highest Score 65*) at an average of 28.64. It is possible that he might have played with the Club Cricket Conference alongside Les Merrett from Old Grammarians. Intriguingly, Avery left the school in March 1925 having only joined at the age of 11 in 1922. There is no record of him ever playing 1st XI School cricket. However, it was clear to see why Avery moved to Malden Wanderers as by 1935 the club's fortunes had dipped to such an extent that it, effectively, had to be relaunched. However, players rallied to the cause, and the 1937 and 1938 seasons were very successful with centuries scored by Todd (twice), R.V. Butler (twice) and Gwil Davies, although in 1938, the School defeated the club!

By the time that war was approaching, the club was travelling further. Extraordinarily 1939 saw the first of a series of matches against Leicester Ivanhoe which would continue for a couple of seasons beyond the war! An early start from Clapham Junction Station was required and a late return (2.00am on Monday morning was not unusual!) With the onset of war and the School evacuated to Godalming, the Field was requisitioned by the Air Ministry. The 1939 cricket report in the Gazette states that '.... *the Club scorebook is as yet untraced. It probably lies hidden at the bottom of a hastily discarded cricket bag and will come to light in better times'.* History does not record if it ever was retrieved, or that the averages were eventually produced in 1945! Although the club was suspended during the second world war, in August 1941 G.A. White took a side to Godalming to play against the School XI. Remarkably the match ended in a tie with both sides being dismissed for 111! It was not until 1946 under the enthusiastic captaincy of Gwil Davies that the club was restarted.

Although founded in 1926 the Old Boys of Battersea Grammar School (Old Grammarians) in similar fashion to their counterparts, also played occasional cricket matches against the School prior to their official foundation as witnessed for instance in a match on 30 June 1910, with the School winning narrowly. In 1925, they actually played two matches against Spencer CC with honours ending even. In 1926, however, they were granted permission to use their part of the Field during the summer holidays. The club's official debut as a club was away to St Barnabas on 24 May 1926 which the club won by 62 runs. On 10 July 1926, the club faced the School at the Field for the first time in front of a crowd of supporters reckoned to be over a thousand strong. This match was also won by Old Grammarians. The next few years was a golden period for the cricket club. In 1928, out of sixteen matches played only one was lost and thereafter the strength of their fixtures played was increased. By 1930, the number of matches played had more than doubled to 35, with the introduction of Sunday matches (all played away) which proved to be an exceptional year with 22 matches won and only five lost. Notable victories were recorded against Croydon (on three occasions), Lensbury (twice) plus wins against Edmonton, Kenton, Chipstead and the RAF.

From 1928, the Old Grammarians Association had use of a Club Room at 61 Battersea Rise not far from the school, and from the following year at the Church Institute in Wiseton Road on Tuesday evenings for the opportunity to play 'bridge, billiards, ping pong and snooker'. The latter venue had been occasionally used some years' previously by the Heathfield club for their Annual General Meetings, and as changing rooms for local teams.

During the 1930s, Old Grammarians were regarded as one of the strongest Old Boys sides in London, and not without some justification. 'Chic' Dorey was regarded as a fine allrounder. In 1930 he scored 914 runs in the season, with a top score of 122, exceeded in 1937 by a score of 149. F. Manning and Les Merrett were to form a formidable opening bowling attack. The latter extraordinarily took over a hundred wickets in no fewer than eight successive seasons from 1930, with a record haul of 128 wickets in the 1937 season, and even the reporters of his annual achievements lost count! In 1935 he took all ten wickets (10-21) against Chipstead – so successful was he, that he was selected to play for the Club Cricket Conference on several occasions during the 1930s. By then although still playing away from home, Sunday cricket was becoming a regular feature. The club went on a Sussex tour over the Whitsun weekend from 1932-1936, going on a week-long tour to Devon in 1937, which would eventually pave the way for future visits once the Second World War was over.

In 1938, Charles L'Archer made his first hundred for the Old Grammarians and he was to feature crucially in the activities of the club after the war. In addition, players such as George Simkins, Jack Durham and Tim Finucane would all make their mark more forcefully once the war was over. Old Grammarians, like Old Sinjuns, suspended playing during the Second World War, recommencing in 1946.

————

Apart from annual matches with the School, and various attempts to organise sport before the Great War, Old Sinjuns AFC started their life in 1920 in the Surrey Junior League. The club used the Field for some home matches but when a second eleven was formed their matches were played somewhat distantly at Vicarage Farm Hounslow. Thereafter matches were played at Manor Road Streatham and then in 1924 at Hampton Court Park. In 1925, the first football club dinner was held at the *Cheshire Cheese* in Fleet Street. By this time the first two elevens were playing in the Old Boys League and in 1932 the 1stXI were promoted to the Premier Division in that league. By 1939 the club were fielding four elevens, but the onset of the war changed all that, and in the 1939/40 season despite the majority of the players dispersing, the club, to their credit, managed to run just the one side. Despite the School having been evacuated, and the constraints of the Second World War, the Governors kindly permitted the Field to be used for the season, given that the Sinjuns end of the ground was still used for sport from time to time. As many clubs had closed down for the war, the club apparently found it a little tedious opposing the Old Thorntonians for a fifth time in the season! Thereafter, it seems, with increasing numbers of players away serving their country, the football club suspended their activities, until the war was over.

––––––––

The account of Old Grammarians Football Club is far more complicated, as it was rugby football that was first recorded as being played by the club! So why could this be? Perhaps, in order to appear different and distinct from their sister school at the bottom of the hill in Battersea High Street, rugby may have been introduced for a time as an experiment to run alongside football as a main winter sport. After all, why otherwise would Old Grammarians play rugby? It must be noted that because all this happened before any annual account of the school's activities were recorded, we can only rely on short reports in local newspapers. Unfortunately, no names were mentioned of try scorers and so on. It could be argued that this could have been an Old Grammarians side from another school, but the entry of a match in the 1887/88 season, against an Eaton Rovers side at Chiswick, dispels this theory as the report states that it was an Old Grammarians side from Battersea that they opposed. The season before suggests the rugby club were quite well established. In the first match of the season on 9 October 1886, the club played out a draw against Bedford Park. Wins followed against the Royal Naval School, Bolingbroke (an Old Grammarians 2nd XV fixture, apparently) and Manor Park with their only defeat against Atlas. The result of a fixture against Upper Tooting went unreported. All these matches were played at 'Wandsworth' quite possibly changing at the School and running across to Wandsworth Common to play. It was known that several rugby clubs used the *Freemason's Hotel* for the same purpose, and that these pitches were probably situated close to where the Wandsworth Cricket Club played in the summer adjacent Bolingbroke Grove. After the Eaton Rovers match, however, Old Grammarians' further exploits on the rugby field are not recorded. It seems that the School in the end stuck with playing Association football as it was called in those days.

Old Grammarians AFC was formed, probably, in 1902 and they had a somewhat more illustrious history than their counterparts at Old Sinjuns. However, they played the School before the turn of the century as an entry in *Sporting Life* dated 6 December 1899 shows. In their first full season (being 1903/04), they were playing regular matches. In 1905, they hired Magdalen Playing Fields to play their soccer (also used by the school at the time for cricket). This must have proved a success because by 1906 they were already running two football sides. In 1910 they actually won their first 'international' match away by 3-1 at the Racing Club de Calais. In 1911 their travels abroad extended as far as Prague! 1912 was an interesting season and a nightmare for all researchers, as not only did they beat the former FA Cup Winners, Clapham Rovers, 3-1 in the first round of an AFA Cup Competition as we know, but a couple of weeks later they also beat Clapham Ramblers! The club were not averse, however, to travelling and like many other clubs also made the long trip to Ipswich Town, an amateur outfit in those days, but suffered a 6-0 reversal. It appears that it was not until the

1919/20 season that the club first commenced league football and for the next few years, they performed extremely well in the Old Boys League. Remarkably in the 1920/21 season a last-minute goal in their match with Old Fullerians at Watford robbed them of the Championship. With 31 points out of 18 matches played (two points for a win in those days) and having scored 55 and only 6 goals conceded it seems impossible how they did not manage to win the league. With their hopes of entering the Southern Amateur League put on hold, the next season saw them playing in a league with only five teams. Worse was to follow in the 1922/23 season when they lost use of the pitch at the Field in unfortunate circumstances. This heralded a period when the club were effectively homeless having to rely on the generosity of others to stage matches. The 1st XI initially played friendly home matches at Old Bancroftians ground at Walthamstow with their reserves only playing in the Old Boys League. By 1924/25 the club were ground sharing with Beckenham Park FC. Unfortunately, with this ground being developed, the club were homeless again after another couple of seasons, and for a time used Malden Wanderers' cricket ground as their base. Although they were back at the Field for a while, this arrangement, for some reason, did not last long either. However, the football club still played a good standard of club football and on 31 December 1927 they were granted a match at Craven Cottage against Fulham 'A' effectively their reserve side. Although that result appears not to have been reported, it was not a happy day for the Fulham football club, as their 1st XI lost 1-0 away at Preston North End on their way to relegation at the end of the season.

With the help of Samuel Cresswell, the use of the William Hughes Memorial Ground at Robin Hood Gate from 1930, which was likely the forerunner of the Richardson Evans Memorial Ground at Roehampton, was made available to Old Grammarians. It gave the club greater stability and the confidence to move forward again as the ground was regarded as one of the better facilities at the time in amateur football. In 1931/32, they were back in the Premier Division of the Old Boys League, and having won the Old Boys League Premier Division in the 1936/37 season (in which Old Sinjuns also competed) the club gained entry to the Southern Olympian League to enhance their footballing ambitions. They played during this period in the Old Boys Cup ("Arthur Dunn" version as distinct from the London Old Boys Cup), and were involved in three Cup Finals during this period, being losing finalists in 1934/35 and 1937/38 to Old Owens and in 1936/37 to Old Stationers. 1936 and 1937 also saw the club on tour in the West Country as football programmes from Minehead FC would confirm. It would take around another forty years before regular Old Grammarians 1st XI football would return to the Field and almost another sixty-five years until amateur football was reorganised so that once again Old Sinjuns and Old Grammarians would compete against each other in a league match, before their amalgamation.

School Inter War Sport

In 1923, H.D. Beevers became the first Sinjun to be invited to play for the South London Public Schools against Surrey Club & Ground at the Oval, an honour that was repeated no less than eleven times between 1926 and 1939 with H.G. Greenfield actually being selected twice in 1934 and 1935. Beevers and possibly Blackwell, mentioned previously, subsequently played club cricket for a time with Battersea Cricket Club, whom the Heathfield club had played before the Great War, preferring the proximity of Battersea Park for playing senior cricket. In 1929, both Max King from Sinjuns together with Les Merrett from Battersea Grammar School played at the Oval, an honour that was to be repeated in 1937 when R.V. (Dickie) Butler from Sinjuns and Jack Durham from Battersea Grammar School were the players. In 1928, when the School 1st XI went undefeated throughout the season, this also saw a successful foray into club cricket by defeating a side representing Battersea Cricket Club by six wickets. From 1929 to 1933 a series of holiday matches were played against various institutions at the Field such as the Inland Revenue and the Ministry of Health in the week after the closure of the School for the summer holidays. Also, in 1933, D.C. King made a century against Wandsworth School and took all ten wickets against Southend Grammar School. In 1935, J.F. Lole's 473 runs were scored at a remarkable average of 78.83 and the only match lost that season was against Spencer CC. In the following year against the same club, the school batted out a draw at the Field despite an unbeaten century from a former pupil, Max King. During the 1937 season R.V. Butler scored 121 against Southend Grammar School, and in 1939 K.R. Godin scored 114 at Southend having the year previously scored 105 against Roehampton CC. Annual matches at Southend Grammar School continued to be played after the school returned to Battersea in 1945. The highest score made by the School was in 1939 at the Field when they registered 263-7 against the Clergy of Southwark who uncharitably batted out for a draw. Then came the War.

Battersea Grammar School started using the Field in 1919. In 1920 (16 July), the School played the Young Players of Surrey at the Oval. Although being dismissed for 110 the opposition lost six wickets before reaching their target, before batting on to make 186. In 1922 difficulties in arranging home matches were still being experienced as the continued use by the Heathfield club (presumably for tennis and bowls) meant the portion of the Field which was available was being overused. 1923 followed a similar pattern, with the school now running four senior elevens, but matches at the Field were still restricted with only two of the ten matches played being held there. 1924 was an excellent year for the School as N.F. Dorey scoring an unbeaten 123 against the Masters.

Although 1926 was more moderate in terms of results the school were running no fewer than five senior sides. In 1927, H.N. Curwen captured 47 wickets at an average of only 10.14 in fifteen matches, and topped that in 1928 by taking 42 wickets at a cost of only 6.69 runs per wicket. 1929 was also another good season with L.G Merrett capturing 49 wickets in form that he would quickly translate into success with the Old Grammarians. In 1933, R.L. Ballard was selected to play for the Public Schools of London at the Oval capturing 3-20. In 1935, the school lost only one of their ten matches played, and the following season was almost as successful.

1936 saw the last time that Battersea Grammar School staged their Sports Day at the Field before moving to Streatham. Pictures from the time, and the account of the day, showed it was quite a lively event and not exclusively track and field events. W.H. White won the Throwing the Cricket Ball competition with a remarkable distance of 95 yards and 3 inches.

By 1937, with Battersea Grammar School at Streatham, and attention now focused elsewhere, their pitch at the Field was described as 'bumpy' and indeed the last scheduled match there was abandoned for that reason. Suddenly, although perhaps understandably, that part of the Field had become less of a priority. On 10 July, the match with the Old Grammarians was the first to be played on the new school ground at Abbotswood Road. Although the Field at Burntwood Lane continued to be used at times after the Second World War for midweek sports at junior levels, and even after removal of the hedge, until Battersea Grammar School's closure in 1977, the School's 1st XI it appears, would only rarely return to the Field for the purpose.

In contrast to many other grammar schools, both Schools only played football in winter, which from the Field's perspective was fortunate, as there was no need to use rugby posts on any part of the ground or compromise on pitches.

The Schools Take Over (1918-1945)

Throughout the inter war period Sir Walter St John's School regularly fielded three if not four football senior sides. In 1925, V.M. Rogers was selected to play for London Public Schools against the Country Public Schools and scored his side's only goal. The high point of the period was in 1929/30 and 1930/31 when only four and six matches were lost respectively out of a total of forty-three played. This coincided with J.J. Tompkins, the future Fulham F.C. player, being part of the squad. Also, R.N. Scott the captain was a proven goal scorer. The best result during this period was a thumping win, 19-2 over Archbishop Tenison's School in 1933/34 with both Greenfield and Long scoring six each. R.V. Butler scored seven against the same school in an 11-3 victory three years later. In 1937/38 Harry (Buster) Merryfield who in later life after a banking career with NatWest, found fame as Uncle Albert in the television comedy *Only Fools & Horses*, played 1st XI football scoring the occasional goal and in cricket he even found the time to record an analysis of 5-25 in the summer of 1938 against Sloane School at the Field. He was also a member of the School boxing team and an Army boxing champion. By contrast, the 1938/39 season was poor. The School suffered a 12-0 defeat to St Olave's School in a year where they only won twice in eighteen attempts. Perhaps, from the football perspective, the war came at the right time for the School to regroup at Godalming.

As for Battersea Grammar School 1st XI football, from 1918/19 the school side were reasonably successful. Mercers School were beaten 16-0 at the Field and 10-2 away in the 1921/22 season and the highest victory was equalled in 1927/28 by defeating Bromley County School. Unfortunately, during that period, from the 1924/25 season and for the following three seasons, the School endured some indifferent years and in the 1926/27 season the school suffered an eye-watering record loss (17-1) against St Marks & St Johns College. Perhaps the most extraordinary result was an 8-8 draw against St Joseph's College in the 1930/31 season- that must have brought the crowds in! By the 1936/37 season, the School 1st XI had moved to their new abode in Abbotswood Road to play their soccer in the shadow of their new school.

During the inter-war period, however, the Field was sometimes used for parades or drills mostly by way of displays or training. Both schools had cadet corps, and, perhaps for good reason in those uncertain times, kept a loose link with the armed forces. Indeed, my uncle (E.C. Fox) was a top shot in the cadet corps at Sir Walter St John's School at the time. However, on 18 July 1932, an event at the Field is recorded which deserves mention, when the Battersea Grammar School cadet corps were involved in an annual inspection by General Sir William Thwaites, who at the time was entering his final year of service as Director General of the Territorial Army. Thwaites was educated at Wellington College and subsequently at Heidelberg before entering the Royal Military Academy at Woolwich. He was a Boer War veteran and, perhaps because of his previous education in Germany and fighting on the western front in the Great War, he was immediately after that conflict, appointed Director of Military Intelligence and later of Operations in the same War Office department. Examining photographs at the time at the Field, he cut a fearsome figure in his full military uniform, and certainly some pictures of the young cadets show them, rather nervously, awaiting his inspection.

Other Matches at The Field

From time to time the Field has been used for other matches with the consent of the Schools' Trustees. On 11 September 1937, the Field staged a Grand Charity Cricket Match in aid of the Mayor of Battersea's Children's Fund. The printed scorecard shows the match was between the Mayor of Battersea's XI and Battersea Cricket Club, one of Heathfield club's 'friendliest of rivals', before the Great War. It shows a list of fifteen players for the Mayor's side. Interestingly the match was played outside the borough of Battersea, and perhaps it is surprising, given the considerable crowds that the Battersea Cricket Club used to draw, that the match was not played in Battersea Park. Maybe the Field was chosen as it was essentially a private ground and admission could be controlled and regulated. In the event a rather disappointing crowd of about 250 spectators watched the match finish in a draw. Included within the Mayor of Battersea's XI were, it appears, at least four veteran former Test players who were likely to have played in the match itself if the printed programme for the match is to be believed (ages in brackets at the time of the match) – namely J. O'Connor (39), H. Elliott (45), A.C. Russell (49), (whom *Wisden* described as the original "Jack" Russell) and W.M. Bradley (62). The latter was well known for attending Lord's and upholding the traditions of the game wearing his MCC tie in the Long Room with his friends. Perhaps his involvement was owing to a conversation there to the effect that would he like a run around in a Charity match just around the corner to where he lived! He is one of only twenty cricketers to have taken a wicket with the first ball he delivered in Test cricket. He died in 1944 at his home in Wandsworth Common. The Battersea side was led by their captain J.S.B. Gentry who was a leading player of his time. Educated at Christ's Hospital Horsham, he played first-class cricket between 1919 and 1925 with Hampshire, Surrey and Essex. He served with the Transportation Section of the Army in India during the Second World War and was awarded an OBE in 1942, a CIE in 1946 for services to port management in Calcutta, and finally a CBE in 1965 for services as managing director of Tees Conservancy which was responsible for port management on that river. Perhaps you could almost say that his ship really did come in!

The match bears all the hallmarks of being arranged through Samuel Cresswell, but this appears not to have been the case. Unfortunately, by then in poor health, he passed away just eight days later aged almost 85.

The vacation of St. John's Lodge

There is no doubt the Battersea Grammar School's move to Streatham in 1936 was a success as it provided all that the school would require until it closed forty years later. When the site at Clapham Junction was vacated, the buildings were subsequently demolished with the proceeds going towards the funding at the new school. The ground so vacated was replaced by an art deco-style building becoming Battersea's only 'supercinema' with a lavish interior and opened as a *Granada* Theatre in November 1937, with a seating capacity of 2,475 and a corner entrance on Plough Lane and St. John's Hill. Indeed, even today, it is not hard to imagine that in its past life, it was a cinema. What has happened since perhaps mirrors society's changing tastes and habits as the years went on. From June 1973 it was converted to house three smaller cinemas increasing the overall capacity to around 4,000, but this closed in July 1980. The Wurlitzer organ was removed in 1982 to the College Claparede in Geneva, Switzerland. The venue was converted back to a single auditorium and became a Bingo Club (firstly with *Granada* and then with *Gala*). This closed in December 1997 when thereafter the building stood empty and unused, although not long afterwards an illegal rave party was held and squatters then occupied the building. Although subsequently abandoned, in 1999 the building was granted Grade II* status. Today apartments extend above the original cinema, whilst in late 2012 the restored auditorium was converted back to its opulent past and today it is known by the interesting name of 'Transformation House', providing conference facilities and a spiritual/religious centre for assisting members of the community to overcome addiction. It could be said, if the founder of the schools, Sir Walter St John, and Samuel Cresswell, who did so much to protect the interests of the schools, were still alive today, they would perhaps approve the use for which the building is now intended, although perhaps not the décor!

The Cresswell Legacy

Apart from the Field, Samuel Cresswell continued his efforts to foster and encourage the well-being of the community by being involved in the Woodfield project which would indirectly, and apparently almost accidentally lead to the relocation of Battersea Grammar School. In 1927 the land that was to eventually become the Woodfield Ground was sold to the London County Council by the Mortimer Estate for £2,250. This was offset again by a donation of £600 by Samuel Cresswell and subsequently the ground complete with a sports pavilion was officially opened in May 1933. At its opening Cresswell declared 'Here in this enclosure our young people will be safe from traffic and molestation of roughs'. Cresswell was accompanied to the opening ceremony by Mr H.R. Ellis the Headmaster of Battersea Grammar School and whilst there, the latter noticed a piece of land over the fence also formerly owned by the Mortimer Estate and it struck him as being ideally suitable for a school. The site in Abbotswood Road was around eight acres in size (similar to the Field) but surrounded by Common with no prospect of being enclosed by a railway or being readily developed. Initially the Trust were divided on the proposed move of the School from Battersea to Streatham. Both Headmasters advised the Trust that each school should now have their own Trust, but Cresswell and others were not persuaded. In the end, with the vote tied, the Chairman of the Trustees used his casting vote to preserve the status quo. So, even though Battersea Grammar School was to move to Streatham, the Trust and Governors would keep its control over both schools. Matters moved quickly and the School buildings took only nine months to erect. Cresswell apparently took a specific interest in its construction. The new school was ready by September 1936. The added bonus was that the plans for Battersea Grammar School had incorporated a playing field of their own and the School even used Woodfield from time to time as an overspill option for the School's own playing fields when required.

The Woodfield ground still exists today. Although as a field it was not large enough to accommodate much more than one full sized football pitch, it is now used as an open space. The pavilion has been completely modernised and refurbished and was reopened as a community centre in June 2019. For anyone passing by 16A Abbotswood Road, and the footpath that leads down to the ground, it would not go amiss to discover this further project that Samuel Cresswell helped along its way. It is an oasis of peace and can also be accessed from Tooting Bec Common.

Samuel Cresswell was a remarkable man and well ahead of his time. He made an impact, not only as described in this book, but also on the area in which he served. Born in Derbyshire in 1852, he came to Wandsworth in 1878. A year later he was appointed headmaster of All Saints' School Wandsworth, a position he held until his retirement from teaching in 1896. Not to be content in taking it easy, in 1900 alone, he became a School Trustee, became a member of the Wandsworth Board of Works, was elected to the first Wandsworth Borough Council and also, owing to his recognised aptitude for public work, to the London School Board, continuously serving on all until his demise. He also held many other official positions, including those of chairman of St. Michael's School, Southfields, the West Hill group of Council Schools, the Swaffield Road group, Elliott Central School, the Royal Patriotic School and governor of Whitelands College, and these were only some of his interests! He was also, interestingly, a life vice-president of the National Playing Fields Association and so would have known E.A.C. Thomson, sometime player at the Heathfield club, through that connection.

Apart from the Field, Cresswell secured playing fields for both St. Michael's School and Elliott Central School. During his time as an Alderman, he was also largely responsible for securing Wandsworth Park in Putney Bridge Road for public use next to the River Thames, even after the London County Council had originally approved plans to develop the area. He was primarily responsible for the laying out of King George's Park and was passionate about child welfare and the betterment of young people. Proving his diversity as mayor, during his year in office, the Wandsworth Technical Institute was completed and opened. He also organised a vigorous and successful campaign in securing cheaper electricity for the borough of Wandsworth. He was also a devout churchman, and acted as organist at St Ann's Church Wandsworth for some time. He was also a Trustee of the National Temperance League.

With his links to the School, he was a Freemason of several Lodges included Old Sinjins Lodge, which despite its contrary spelling, is still active today, but is no longer restricted to those associated with the defunct schools. His death in 1937 made headlines in the *Wandsworth Borough News* and tributes to him carried over several pages. Amongst the large number of attendees at his funeral at Wandsworth Parish Church, the School's Trustees were represented by their Chairman, W.B Hards.

Whilst the above list, extraordinary as it is, is not exhaustive, he was obviously a good communicator. Possessing a love of music, he was probably the first Mayor to render a song in public during his mayoralty. On one occasion during a gathering of blind people in Tooting, he sang *Clementine* and another song to the audience, both of which were vigorously applauded.

In total his legacy, as witnessed by the Field, and so many other acts of concern and kindness towards others, has stood the test of time. His local contribution to Wandsworth was remarkable and, to a degree, it is surprising that he was not honoured at a higher level for his services to local affairs. He was a politician who really cared for his community. His wife Marie survived him, dying in 1961 at the age of 95. They are buried together in the Magdalen Road Cemetery in Wandsworth.

Evacuation and Occupation

In September 1938 with tensions rising in Europe, parents' meetings were held in the Gymnasium and the Great Hall at Sir Walter St John's School in Battersea regarding contingency planning for the possible evacuation of the school. A few days later the Prime Minister Neville Chamberlain announced his forthcoming visit to Munich and the crisis passed temporarily. The following month a four-day long Board of Education Inspection was undertaken. With the Field still divided (although Battersea Grammar School had by now removed to Streatham) the need for more playing field space was emphasised. Shortly afterwards one of the Governors Sir Douglas Robinson, tried hard but unsuccessfully to secure part of the Middlesex Asylum's grounds (subsequently renamed Springfield Hospital) in Burntwood Lane for the School's use. Then, subsequent to Germany's invasion of Poland, the news that the whole of the country had been dreading for some time came to fruition when war was declared on 3 September 1939. Unlike the start of the Great War, Sir Walter St. John's School was evacuated at short notice and sent off to Godalming. Indeed, the general evacuation of most schools from London was not uncommon. However, in the initial evacuation barely three fifths of the boys at the School travelled there. Others followed in the next few days but some remained in London, and others drifted back to London as the war dragged on although in the autumn of 1944 the numbers returning were checked by the use of VI and V2 rockets against the capital. In April 1940 the Council opened twelve emergency secondary schools, one of them on the premises of

Henry Thornton School. Forty-one pupils made their way there, and others were received at Sloane School.

The boys at Godalming, were taken to Godalming County School and initially billeted nearby. Eventually classes started on the first Monday in October. This is where most of the teaching was done although initially it was quite a 'squash' and classes had to be shared with the local schoolboys and girls. Others were taken to Charterhouse and billeted there. Charterhouse showed great friendliness from the start in making their unintentional visitors welcome by providing classroom, laboratory and playing-field facilities and this continued throughout the whole six years of the school's stay. Even today, there are records of the school's time there in the Godalming Museum and certainly after the war, the school's presence was remembered generally with affection. Although the School had use of playing field facilities at Charterhouse, their home ground would be Holloway Hill Recreation ground (today the home of Godalming CC) throughout the six years' period of their stay.

As for School sports during the evacuation, the cricket 1st XI for instance, found themselves new opponents in clubs such as Godalming, Farncombe, Horsell and Witley apart from competing against schools such as Charterhouse, RGS Guildford and King Edward's School playing a total of 75 matches, winning 43, drawing 11 and losing 21. J.M. Wilson took a record 64 wickets in 1941 and then beat his own record the following season by taking 65 wickets. By 1945, the bowling of George Coker and David Demeza was leaving its mark as both featured prominently in the dismissal on 30 June of Guildford & District Sea Cadet Corps for just 3 runs (surely the lowest ever total posted against a school or club side representing Sir Walter St John's School), and on 17 July, as Godalming County School were bundled out for only 13.

In terms of results, the School 1st XI football side fared even better, playing a total of 98 matches winning 69 drawing 10 and losing only 19. Indeed, in 1942/43 they won 20 of their 22 matches losing only one with a tally of 102 goals for and only 28 against. During their time at Godalming, they recorded overwhelming victories against Farnham Grammar School (15-0) in 1940/41 and in 1943/44, their largest victory of them all (16-0) against the Methodist Boys FC. So, life in the Surrey countryside was not that unpleasant after all! The first football match back at the Field after the war occurred on 17 November 1945 when the 1st XI overwhelmed Archbishop Tenison's School 11-1.

New friendships were made during this period. Dr John Francis Nichols served in the Great War and was awarded the Military Cross during that conflict. Between 1924 and his retirement in 1954 he taught history at Sir Walter St John's School. When evacuated to Godalming with the school, it is recorded as a memory in BBC People's War, that in June 1940 the boys would set off daily to Peperharow Park and there under the guidance and inspirational vocal encouragement of Dr Nichols in typical *Dad's Army* style, the boys would dig trenches to be a second line of defence in the event of a German invasion! Whilst this activity took place at the time of the Allied retreat from Dunkirk, there was a genuine concern about the prospect of an impending German invasion of Southern England-indeed at this time Battersea Grammar School which had been evacuated to Worthing were re-evacuated to Hertford. It seems unlikely that digging trenches in Peperharow Park would have, in any way, been instrumental in turning the conflict in the Allies' favour. Although Dr. Nichols continued to teach at the School when it returned to Battersea in 1945, he was curator of Godalming Museum from 1942 until 1952, and having returned in 1946 to Godalming to make his home, he died there in 1965.

With the main aircraft battery being on Clapham Common and both schools having been evacuated, the Field was requisitioned under the Emergency Powers (Defence) Act of 1939, for use as a barrage balloon site. The Burntwood Lane pavilion together with the area immediately outside bore the brunt of this activity. The tethered balloons, with the top half filled with hydrogen, would be sent up to around 5,000 ft. in an attempt to deter dive bombers and by 1940 London was protected by at least 1,400 balloons and this figure doubled as the conflict wore on. The bombing of London was severe and balloons were unable to prevent the bombing of Balham Underground station in October 1940 in which 68 people died. However, it did to a degree help to prevent the German's ambitions to completely flatten London. Dive bombers were particularly vulnerable to balloons and indeed these tactics were abandoned by the Axis powers during the war because of the risk of hitting the steel cables, which could be unarmed or armed, that connected the balloon to the ground but were strong enough to bring an aircraft down. Against high level bombers however the balloons were less effective to the planes offloading their deadly cargo. Although the cables accounted for apparently as many, if not more Allied planes lost during the war, they were deemed a success and undoubtedly bombing would have been far more severe without them. It was dangerous to be near the balloons, particularly when hit, as a falling cable could cause much damage and potentially kill anyone standing underneath. It was also officially claimed that 231 V1 flying bombs which usually flew at an altitude of around 2,000 ft were destroyed by balloons during the Second World War. With reference to the Field where their cricket club had played twenty years before, the Heathfield club in Lyford Road played *'host to the men that kept the barrage balloon flying across Burntwood Lane'*. It also seems possible that the Field was also used for army drill purposes too. However, whilst the presence of the balloon site possibly explains why the Field escaped a direct hit, it took at least four years to rectify the collateral damage caused by the war. Barrage balloons had also featured in the Great War. It now became clear as to why the authorities had contemplated using the Field 'for aviation purposes' during that conflict when the Heathfield club were still the tenants. Perhaps too, the Field had been used because to the southwest, it has a good view over the Wandle Valley and would have also been an excellent observation point.

There is another interesting matter to raise here. From local maps between 1931 and the start of the Second World War, two brick-built extensions, one on either flank of the Sinjuns changing rooms were constructed. These were connected by a corridor to the main changing rooms but were obviously intended to be quite separate. With both of similar construction and having flat concrete roofs they just seemed out of place in the whole scheme of thing, and both could be easily separated by use of a sturdy door. Indeed, both were almost bunker like in construction with natural light only finding its way into the area through high level and narrow windows, suggesting something of a more sinister use during the war. In peacetime one of these extensions would act as the groundsman's office. It would be demolished after the 1994 fire to improve parking and access, whilst the other similar extension, in part, was used as a supplementary equipment store and overspill changing facilities. This area was, almost affectionally, known as the Dungeons and still survives today.

With Battersea Grammar School's part of the Field being used as a balloon site, the Sinjuns part of the ground nearest to Trinity Road was used from 1940, by the First Aid Services of Wandsworth Borough Council. Activities were organised by members on their off-duty days, but all this was not an easy proposition at the time of the Blitz. Although the Governors of the School would only have had nominal control of that part of the Field by now, the First Aid Services had sole use of the Field for their purposes, which apart from outdoor sports events, including football (and presumably cricket during the summer) and perhaps athletics, was also used for social purposes from time to time. It was noted that not only had the Mayor of Wandsworth given his support, he had also accepted the Presidency of the club, which also drew in other strands of the emergency services. The Chairman of the club was the Medical Officer of Health in Wandsworth and the Vice Chairman was the commandant of the stretcher parties in the borough. The aim was to connect with the community and keep up morale during those difficult times. However, in conjunction with many other local authorities as the war dragged on, Wandsworth was probably also involved in the 'Holidays at Home' programme which from 1942 until 1944, ran a series of mostly sporting events, aimed to keep pupils who stayed behind in London during the conflict active during the summer holidays. With the School away at Godalming, this would have certainly helped to keep the Field in some sort of order during the war. Most of Wandsworth Common was being used for allotments, anti- tank/air defence trenches or later for prefabricated temporary housing for people who had unfortunately lost their homes as a result of enemy action.

From 1943 'Emergency Classes' were established at Emanuel School which itself had been evacuated at the start of the war. Along with pupils from other schools, including Battersea Grammar School who has stayed in London during the war, the classes included around fifty Sinjuns boys. With Emanuel's playing fields adjacent to the school being out of commission owing to bomb damage, the Sinjuns end of the Field was used for soccer and cricket, as aerial reconnaissance pictures at the time confirmed. No first-class cricket was played during the Second World War but if only to illustrate the resilience of Londoners a special cricket match was arranged on the August Bank Holiday weekend in 1942 between combined sides from Middlesex & Essex and Kent & Surrey which attracted around 22,000 spectators to Lord's. Furthermore, on 7 July 1945, just two months after Germany's surrender, a cricket team representing the 'Emanuel Emergency Classes' very much got the better of a School U14 side at the Field that had travelled up from Godalming to play a match. It was proof, however, that after six years away, the School was coming home to Battersea High Street, which they duly did at the start of the new school year in October. When the Emergency Classes were disbanded at the end of the conflict and the pupils were reconciled with their respective schools when they returned, there was apparently some sadness amongst pupils that were to lose contact and new friendships forged with others who had together endured staying at home during the war.

When Battersea Grammar School returned to Streatham from Hertford in May 1945, they found their Abbotswood Road playing field an overgrown wilderness and no home matches were possible during that cricket season. Unfortunately, the bombing of London during the war had inflicted far heavier damage than in the 1914-1918 conflict. Many more grounds were damaged or put out of service or just simply abandoned to be used for future developments and were never returned to their original use. One of those casualties of the Second World War was Battersea Cricket Club's ground in Battersea Park. The club had effectively folded after trenches had been cut across the cricket ground in 1940, to prevent German aircraft using it as a landing strip. Suddenly Dr Nichols's *Dads Army* antics in Peperharow Park made some sense! For a club with an illustrious past, and the venue of the dismissal of Jack Hobbs in his first qualifying match playing for the Surrey Colts, in 1903 without scoring, it was a sad end for Battersea Cricket Club, but the damage which had literally been done to the ground proved fatal to any revival of the club once the conflict was over.

During the Blitz alone from October 1940 until June 1941 over 738 high explosive bombs were dropped on the borough of Wandsworth – that is one bomb for every 11 acres of land. Whilst the Field, all eight acres of it, had survived another threat to its existence, much work would be needed to return it to its former glory.

Lest we forget

Again, the War brought its own consequences. On 25 October 1940 during the Blitz, Charles Gwilt, who was Clerk to the Governors from 1890 until 1933 and also Tennis Secretary at the Heathfield Club from 1913-1922, was killed by enemy action at his home in Wallington. He was 82. During the negotiations between the Trust and the Heathfield club on the lease, and its possible further extension, he would have been in a difficult position to try to please both parties. It should be noted in the end he chose the School Trust's position over that of the Heathfield club.

Jimmy Tompkins was one of the few footballers to have progressed from school football with Sir Walter St John's School to the professional ranks. Whilst still an amateur, his paid employment was as a member of Arsenal's ground staff. During that period the legendary Arsenal Manager, Herbert Chapman, saw him play and was apparently disappointed to learn that Fulham had already signed him, remarking that 'Tompkins was a future international'. Between 1934 and 1939 he made 154 league appearances with Fulham FC, some as captain. Seeing the imminent approach of World War Two he signed on with the Territorial Army. Shortly after D-Day on 10 July 1944, he was required to lead his unit to secure the town of Maltot. Unknown to his commanders, the town was surrounded by German Tiger Tanks which were hidden in woods and depressions which opened fire as he and his unit entered the town. Fifty-six men were killed before the order to withdraw was given. Tompkins was last seen charging a machine gun nest, but his body was never found. It is assumed that he and his comrades had suffered a direct hit from a German tank shell. By the time of his death, he had attained the rank of Major and held a provisional rank of Lieutenant Colonel, a remarkable rise even in the accelerated promotions of wartime. His wife had sadly died from a liver infection only two months before her husband. They had two children, Neil and Jill. As a poignant reminder, his name is not only inscribed on the School war memorial but also on the war memorial at Bayeux. Fulham FC also remember him at their own war memorial. He paid the ultimate sacrifice in the war, along with others that attended the two schools, and so many more throughout the country.

His son, Neil, who also attended the School, was a gifted all-round sportsman. In 1957 he was selected to play for the London Grammar Schools' Fives Team, played cricket for Surrey II and scored a record 44 goals for the School 1st XI in the 1956/57 season. He subsequently represented the RAF at football having joined the service in 1959. He was killed on 3 February 1965 when the Canberra bomber in which he was navigator crashed into a hillside near Osnabruck in Germany, during a low-level exercise in poor visibility.

In honour of all those pupils of Sir Walter St John's School who died during both World Wars, the Sinjuns Association continues to lay a wreath at the annual Remembrance Day service conducted at St Mary's Church in Battersea, where the memorials are now kept. The memorial in honour to those at Battersea Grammar School that lost their lives during both conflicts was relocated to Graveney School sometime after the closure of the former school in 1977.

Sir Walter St John's School Corps parading at the Field 1920 (top)

Sir Walter St John's School Corps parading at the Field 1920 (bottom)

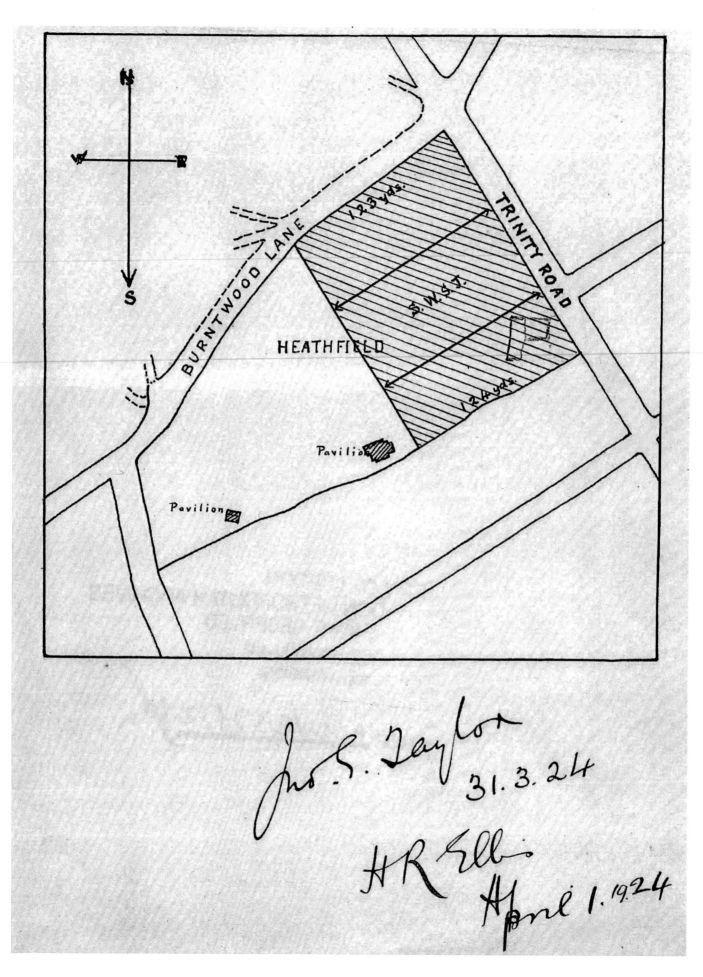

Agreed division of the Field between Sir Walter St John's School and Battersea Grammar School 1924. (Courtesy London Metropolitan Archives)

Battersea Grammar School Football Club 1921

Battersea Grammar School Cricket Club 1921

Old Grammarians Ist XI Cricket Club at Old Boys Day 1927

Prize Giving by General Sir William Thwaites on the occasion of the inspection of Battersea Grammar School Cadet Corps July 1932

Sir Walter St John's School Football First XI 1936 pictured outside Sinjuns Changing Rooms (destroyed by fire in 1994)

Sir Walter St John's School Cricket 1stXI 1937, with the dividing hedge behind.

Official opening of Old Grammarians Upstairs Clubroom in 1957 with Peter May (centre) and   l to r: L.E. Messenger, Syd Turner (Chairman), Charles L'Archer and Walter J. Langford (Headmaster, Battersea Grammar School)

Charles Dixon & Gerry Roff the Staff opening pair v School 1969. The match witnessed the first Staff victory over the School side since 1914.

Old Sinjuns 1stXI Winners of the Area Final of the Surrey Knock Out Competition 1970 (l to r standing) Phil Marshall, Martin Faircloth, Henry Campbell, John Clark, Ron Gambie, Peter Humber, Mick Osmond, Alec McMath (Umpire). (L to r seated) Barry Smith, Viv Landon (captain) Geoff Boothman, Micky Britnell.

A young Viv Landon waiting his turn to bat. Scored over 20,000 runs for Old Sinjuns CC between 1957 and 1990.

Derek Lawrence scored over 20,000 runs and took over 2,000 wkts in club cricket mostly with Old Grammarians CC and Sutton CC and was part of the latter club's Championship winning side in 1991.

Old Sinjuns 1st XI Cricket Club 1978 (l to r standing) John Ware, John Uden, Kevin Sheehan, Henry Campbell, Brian Williams, Viv Landon, Peter Buckett, Graham Jackson (umpire) (l to r seated) Mick Britnell , Brian Dale , Kevin Barry, Jeremy Mills.

Sir Walter St John's School Football action shots from the Field on a muddy day in 1972

6

After The War (1946-1971)

Life was simple before World War II. After that we had systems.

Grace Hopper (1906-92)

Post War changes

It was not until the autumn of 1945 that Sir Walter St John's School returned to Battersea. Sections of the school buildings had been severely damaged, windows had been blown out, and rubble remained almost everywhere. In September 1940, a time delayed bomb had landed in the cupboard adjoining the Headmaster's study and despite attempts to diffuse it, upon detonation it had completely demolished the Headmaster's study, the room above, the boys' lavatory and a stock room! Fortunately, the Butterfield Great Hall (built in 1859) had survived, but it took almost another ten years before the reconstruction works were anything like fully completed.

The Field was more fortunate; bombs had peppered Wandsworth Common during the war and the *Surrey Tavern* had a lucky escape as well, if maps are to be believed. Nearby to the Field, in 1946, the rebuilding of Nos. 8, 10 & 12 Lyminge Gardens, demolished by enemy action was commenced. Although the Sinjuns section of the Field during the war had been used at times for cricket matches and other sports, the changing rooms were in some disarray, and Old Sinjuns were obliged to Gwil Davies for his efforts in restoring the ground whilst also acting as a makeshift assistant groundsman. His contribution was invaluable. However, the damage was somewhat less than that inflicted on the Battersea Grammar School's section of the Field. The Burntwood Lane pavilion according to some reports had been wrecked apparently through misuse by the military and vandalism and was in a sorry state and much work was needed to remove concrete, debris, and to repair the damage to the ground incurred by the barrage balloon site. The considerable refurbishment works were carried out by various Old Grammarians under the guidance of Charles L'Archer. The club also resumed using the Church Institute in Wiseton Road for social evenings and presumably this continued until a proper clubroom was established at the Field.

Whatever the situation, and despite the disarray, the Field had survived again. Unlike Wandsworth Common, it escaped being used for allotments or temporary buildings, the latter remaining in place until the mid-1960's. Perhaps the Field's status as a private ground had something to do with it and that the ground would be used again as a playing field when the schools returned.

With Battersea Grammar School at Streatham, and as the Field was, to a degree, surplus to their requirements, it was realised by the School that the part of the Field administered by them, would be best used by their Old Boys' Association, the Old Grammarians, and the club were effectively given overall control of the Burntwood Lane pavilion to manage things as they wished. Although the damage done by the barrage balloon site was significant, it would certainly be preferable to playing their home cricket matches immediately after the war at Eden Park. Furthermore from 1949 with the Field now being used on Sundays by Old Grammarians, the club were granted a licence to entertain sides when the upstairs clubroom in the Burntwood Lane pavilion came into use from 1956, and alleviated using the *Surrey Tavern* for the purpose.

The end of the war also brought two new Headmasters, firstly Walter Langford to Battersea Grammar School and shortly afterwards, James T Wharton to Sir Walter St John's School, whose appointment brought to an end the 'Taylor Dynasty of Headmasters' which had lasted at Sinjuns since 1873. This acted as a catalyst for change not only between the Schools but also at the Field.

There were other changes as well. On 1 April 1945, under the new Education Act all tuition fees were abolished (save for private lessons in music and the like) and that preparatory forms in secondary schools would be gradually eliminated. Admission to the schools would likely (in most cases) to be by the way of a common entrance examination arranged by the London County Council. In 1946 the Governors of the Trust issued an appeal to secure more funding to secure Voluntary Aided Status for the Schools. However, this ultimately was unsuccessful and after much debate in 1951, the status of both schools under the Trust became that of a Voluntary Controlled School with five members appointed by the Governors of the Trust and ten by the Local Authority. Effectively control had passed from the Governors to the Authority and from this point on, both schools would be regarded effectively as State Schools and not Public Schools. It was at this stage that the word 'Grammar' was added to the Sir Walter St John's School's name - a title that apparently had been approved some forty years before but never officially used, so that the School was now known as 'Sir Walter St John's Grammar School' on equal terms with Battersea Grammar School, which had been known as such virtually since its foundation in 1875.

In the end however, it was effectively another 'Heathfield' moment for both schools insofar that any autonomy the schools enjoyed before 1951 was taken away from them and any thoughts of becoming independent were lost. It is true, that as part of the agreement, the Sir Walter St John's Schools' Trust maintained a financial interest in the buildings in Battersea High Street, as it owned some of the land through its historical ties. Although, at the time, no one could have foreseen the site being sold, it turned into a welcome bonus some forty years later. As regards to the Field, and because of its purchase in 1918, the title effectively remained with the Trust, although, because of the maintenance required to keep the ground in an orderly state, it was regarded more of a liability than an asset by both the Trust and the authorities as the years went on, particularly when both schools were closed. However, from now on the State would dictate terms which would eventually lead to downgrading both schools effectively to Comprehensive status. Although the authorities had originally backed the idea of the two schools continuing, falling school numbers in Inner London would eventually seal the fate of both either by closure or amalgamation.

Reunification of the Field

In 1950, in recognition of their shared founder Sir Walter St John in 1700, both sister Schools celebrated this landmark. With Battersea Grammar School at Streatham using Abbotswood Road and the Old Grammarians Cricket Club only playing home matches at the School (pre-war) during the summer holidays, it would seem that the part of the Field Battersea Grammar School had controlled since effectively 1925 had been underused for the best part of the previous decade owing to the war and renovations required afterwards. However, by 1949 things were on the move, and a reconciliation of the two schools to acknowledge this was planned. A new cricket square was laid and works continued to improve the Burntwood Lane pavilion. The hedge was dug up and for the first time in twenty-five years the Field's full potential could be maximised. This led to the creation of a new full -sized football pitch which ran between Burntwood Lane and the back of the gardens in Brodrick Road which hitherto were not wide enough for senior football. It would also give a more flexible and larger outfield space between both cricket squares being no longer constrained by the hedge. However, whatever realignment or extending of the Grammarians' square was carried out, it could not compensate for the short straight boundary into the back gardens in Brodrick Road and to Burntwood Lane. Consequently, since the merger of the Old Boys cricket clubs in 2006, it is used, predominantly, as a second square for 3rd XI, 4th XI and junior cricket. The outfield area in front of the Burntwood Lane pavilion, which, although only big enough for junior football matches (u12 and u14), was to later become known as 'Monkeys Island' and was also used as a training area and apparently also for those of a lesser sporting ability. At times during the winter this area is floodlit for the purpose. Today, it is rather blandly known by the private schools as 'Area 7'. However, the picket fence enclosure which used to separate the Burntwood Lane pavilion from the playing area enjoyed by Old Grammarians Cricket Club is no more. Two new cricket nets were constructed at right angles to the Burntwood Lane boundary fence adjacent to the Cresswell stone, sitting astride where the hedge had been. One was used by Old Grammarians CC and the other by Old Sinjuns CC and this roughly remained the case up until the merger of the clubs in 2006. Obviously in the past, athletics took more centre stage with the schools, but today the Long Jump approach and pit is rarely used, the 'Shot Put circle' never used, and the High Jump area was covered over some years ago and returned to outfield although apparently the hardstanding still survives underneath. From around 1950, the Field would be looked after by one groundsman and an assistant, so this would also be a benefit in reducing maintenance costs. It really was a 'win-win' situation. With the plans for the new cricket square, there was also provision to make structural alterations to the Burntwood Lane pavilion which were undertaken in conjunction with the London County Council and would eventually lead to the creation of new dressing rooms, showers and kitchen. These works were mostly carried out by club members. This cut out the need to use the Sinjuns changing rooms for teas and washing from zinc baths full of cold water at the end of the match in the Burntwood Lane pavilion. Until the creation of the upstairs clubroom, visiting sides were entertained in a rather bleak room above the *Surrey Tavern*. Hitherto, the Field had only been used on Saturdays because apparently there had been a covenant on the Field that prevented use on Sundays. Questions were asked about the validity of this, particularly when it was discovered, rather extraordinarily, that the condition excluding Sunday play had lapsed apparently around 1924 when the council had decided to relax restrictions on Sunday recreational sport! As a result, Sunday use was granted by the Trust, in consideration of a peppercorn rate of £1 per annum from both the sports clubs.

In 1950 celebrations were enjoyed by both schools and the Field played its part. On 20 July these events came to a climax. Rare film footage shows a carnival atmosphere at the Field. The afternoon cricket match between a Masters and Boys team from both schools was narrowly won by Sinjuns by two wickets and during the interval between innings the large crowd was treated to a gymnastics display by both schools. Later in the day, interestingly, another sport took the stage literally, as the film shows an open-air inter school boxing match. This was no unofficial brawl, but reflected the boxing tradition of both schools which remained intact until the early 1960s. A proper ring had been constructed and, watched by several hundred spectators, two pupils in full boxing gear were gladly pummelling away at each other. Sinjuns whose pedigree at boxing was second to none both sides of the war in providing Great Britain (amateur) champions on no fewer than seven occasions, comfortably beat Grammarians by 6 bouts to 3. It should be said however, that earlier in the year Battersea Grammar School had beaten Sinjuns at football by 1-0, and also comfortably won the inter- school cricket match by 69 runs, so perhaps, overall, honours were even.

During 1954/55 the upstairs roof space in the Burntwood Lane pavilion again under the guidance of Charles L'Archer and others, was converted into a clubroom and in 1957, it was officially opened by English cricket legend Peter May, so Old Grammarians could entertain visiting sides at their leisure.

As a tribute to Charles L'Archer's efforts some years later the Old Grammarians Cricket Club magazine, *Occasional Glances,* printed a somewhat cryptic appreciation.

O'Genesis-The First and Last Epistle of Charles The Apostle to the Grammarians

I. In the beginning L'Archer created the Grammarians and Burntwood Lane.

2. And Burntwood Lane was without benches or boundary boards, and darkness was upon those fielding in the deep and the spirit of gin moved upon the face of the Clubhouse.

3. And L'Archer said let there be light, and there was bitter.

4. And L'Archer saw the light that it was bottled, and L'Archer divided the light from the brown.

5. And L'Archer called the light Worthington and the brown he called Watneys and a bar rota was posted on the first day.

6. And L'Archer said let there be a wicket in the middle of the firmament and let it divide cricketers from the rest of the members.

7. And L'Archer made the wicket and divided the spinners who were below the fast bowlers from the all-rounders who were above suspicion: and the wicket was slow.

8. And L'Archer called the wicket "mine" and they all agreed on the second day.

9. And L'Archer said let the Grammarians gather together and let the dry sherry appear, and the wicket remained slow.

10. And L'Archer called the dry sherry Bristol Cream and the gathering together of the waters he called rain and L'Archer saw play abandoned.

11. And L'Archer said let the groundsman bring forth grass and good wickets and I will yield all the runs and wickets, and L'Archer saw that it was so.

12. And the wicket brought forth grass and Charles topped the averages, and the scorer saw that it was good.

13. And the bar was crowded on the third day.

14. And L'Archer said let there be dancing, fruit machines, and a pie-warmer.

15. And keep those footballers off the square.

16. And L'Archer made two elevens. He ruled the greater and somebody else the lesser- he also had a car!

17. And L'Archer often set his leg trap to take catches in the firmament.

18. And as a rule they played all day and were in the bar all night.

19. And few went to work on the fourth day.

20. And L'Archer said let the pigeons and fowl fly carefully over the firmament.

21. And L'Archer created great whales (yes, it's true) and the rain brought forth solo and abundance, and L'Archer knew that he was good.

22. And L'Archer blessed them saying be fruitful and multiply and fill the waters in the seas and let the fowl multiply in the earth.

23. And (not surprisingly) nobody turned up on the fifth day.

24. On the sixth day L'Archer rested.

For those of you who know the Laws of Cricket, for 'wicket' please read 'pitch'. Perhaps also our preferences for alcoholic beverages have changed since those days!

Old Sinjuns, by contrast, whilst Sunday-use of the ground had been granted, were still constrained by only being able to use their part of the Field during the summer holidays on Saturdays as it was still used for school cricket during term time. Additionally, without an equivalent clubhouse at that stage, the club had to resort to continuing to use the *Surrey Tavern* to entertain visiting sides. However, during 1962, Old Grammarians generously shared their bar facilities as a focal point for players returning from away matches as both clubs had very limited use of the ground that summer owing to the installation of an extensive new drainage system and the laying of a new electricity mains cable.

The issue of draining the Field properly went back many years. Even reports from the rugby years had talked about puddles and quagmires and a good number of matches in severe winters were cancelled as a result. At least this was an attempt to tame the London Clay that lurked underneath, and was probably the first radical attempt to do so since then. Various further attempts to improve the drainage have been tried, but these have only had a limited success because most of the playing surface adjacent to the crossroads of Trinity Road and Burntwood Lane lies below the level of the road. As *The Gazette* recorded, the whole experience came as a dreadful shock. '*All last summer the playing field was a dreary sight. Rolls of electric cable, weird machines and all sorts of pipes, a workman's hut, and a churned-up track from Trinity to Beechcroft Road gave an air of unreality to the field. Strange criss-cross trenches appeared, one even touching a corner of the square and gum-booted strangers stalked the outfield. One eventually became a little ashamed of it and preferred not to look. As a result of this drain and cable laying, we became almost a wandering side, abandoning the majority of our home fixtures and relying upon the hospitality of our long- standing opponents for our weekend pleasure. To them we give our thanks'*. It was not until around mid- August that the field was available for use again. If all this seems familiar today, fast forward sixty years!

Another product of this work, it seems, was the introduction of a high perimeter chain link fence to the gardens in Brodrick Road. This had the effect of 'squaring the field off' as the line between the gardens with the Field, although finally established around 1865 when the housing to Brodrick Road was constructed, was not completely straight. The upshot was the creation of a strip of land owned by the Trust which although entirely falling within the Field's domain, varies from around three metres at the Trinity Road end to less than a metre at the Beechcroft Road end of the Field but is unusable for sport. Whilst it is certainly not the most attractive part of the Field, and at the former end, the gardens are somewhat above the general level of the Field, it was obviously a cost-effective measure to prevent the need for a proper retaining wall and to provide an effective barrier as far as possible to prevent cricket balls from being hit into the gardens – although some still do find their way over the fence from the square adjacent to the Burntwood Lane pavilion!

Whilst the drainage may have helped matters somewhat, it had little time to prove itself as in late December 1962 what was described as 'The Big Freeze" set in. Beyond the School match with the Old Boys on Boxing Day there was no football for almost three months as next day heavy snow set in and blizzards swept the country cutting off vast areas of the country for days on end. Two feet of snow, reportedly fell in London. Overall, it was the coldest winter since 1740 (as if anyone could remember that far back). The sea froze around coasts and on parts of the Thames, and upstream in Oxford, cars could be driven across it. The demolition of the old London Bridge in 1833 had meant that with water flowing more freely the river escaped totally freezing over, although locally it did. The weather finally did relent in early March but the following thaw meant that few grounds were playable even then. In amateur football, although some recreational leagues struggled through, against the 1962/63 season the words 'Emergency Competition' are often entered. The London Old Boys Football League encouraged clubs to play as many matches as possible. Divisional Champions and league placings would be decided on an average basis of matches played against points gained but promotion and relegation for the season were suspended. Even the professional clubs struggled (no underground pitch heating in those days) and the league season was extended by four weeks from the intended finish date of 27 April to clear the backlog of fixtures – often playing twice in a week.

By 1962, Old Sinjuns had been given permission by the School Trustees to build their own pavilion. The plans were drawn up by Len Turner. Most of the labour to do so was undertaken by club members. Whist digging the foundations, Joe Millgate accidentally located the new electricity main, puncturing the high voltage cable (presumably laid the year before) which had been installed underneath that part of the Field emanating from the sub-station built adjacent to Trinity Road within the Field's curtilage. A study at the London Metropolitan Archives shows two plans with a slightly different route for the cable on both! Obviously, the incorrect plan had been consulted. This was no consolation to Joe, but, at first, he almost thought he had struck oil! Fortunately, it was part of the protective casing around the cable he had punctured which subsequently overheated and reportedly blacked out half of Surrey. Joe lived to tell the tale – but only just! As a word of caution the cable is still there today and the curious raised manhole about thirty yards distant from the Sinjuns clubroom is actually a cable route control box which is built in such a way as to prevent it being flooded in wet weather. Eventually, after a couple of years of toil on Boxing Day in 1964 the new clubhouse was opened, and the club were at last able to entertain visiting sides in a similar fashion to Old Grammarians. Additionally, the erection of the clubhouse led to an annual "Barbeque" on a Saturday evening in July and this event continued for around fifteen years from its establishment towards the end of the 1960s. With a disco in the clubroom and a band in the white marquee, some raucous evenings were enjoyed, with the latter serving as a temporary sightscreen for those playing afternoon cricket! Thursday became a regular 'social club' evening, but, perhaps, not without its surprises. An impromptu visit from the constabulary at Tooting Police Station came looking for cricket boxes (no internet in those days) to help provide improvised protective equipment against local riots. It was not known to this day if they were really put to good use! From having no licence to sell alcohol (post 1924) the Field now had two licences to do so- one at Old Sinjuns end of the Field and another at Old Grammarians end. The extension of the clubroom in 1976 was also an opportunity for Old Sinjuns to employ Joe Nelson as their first permanent bar steward.

1965 was a particularly difficult year for the School in Battersea. The deaths of R.V. ('Dicky') Butler and Neil Tompkins are covered elsewhere, but the unexpected and tragic death at home of the Headmaster, Dr W.L. Presswood in April, just before the Easter holidays, was a bitter blow. He had been responsible for bringing Old Sinjuns Football Club back to its spiritual home in 1958 and was a 'Stout member of the Staff Cricket side'. Apparently on the day before his death, he had been supervising a group of pupils practising in the cricket nets in the School playground. Under his guidance the School had grown in stature academically, but he had never lost sight of the importance that sport played in the curriculum. He was sorely missed.

After The War (1946-1971)

Post War School Sports

After the war, with Battersea Grammar School at Streatham, Sir Walter St John's School carried on using their part of the Field. Whilst it was almost inevitable that the high success rate in cricket would be difficult to emulate after returning to Battersea, in 1951 the 1st XI lost only one match out of fifteen. In 1958, Viv Landon scored 110 not out against Westminster City School in what was at the time the highest score made at the Field by a schoolboy. Landon's record is remarkable. He played no fewer than five seasons in the School 1st XI playing in probably a record of 73 matches of which he captained thirty, and in addition took 150 wickets along the way. A talented schoolboy cricketer, it was his batting, that would predominantly feature with Old Sinjuns cricket club in the years to come.

In 1963 the 1st XI played fifteen matches winning eight and only losing three under the captaincy of D.L.O'B. Rowe who scored a record aggregate of 479 runs. A year later Geoff Boothman scored only the ninth century by a 1st XI cricketer since 1910, and Alex Wilson represented the school in a Young London Cricket XI against Denmark.

After the war the Staff v School cricket match was not revived until 1956 and looking at the results since, it was clear to see why. In 1967 Steve Emler took 7-27 in the drawn match with the Old Boys, and in 1968 took 7-20 as the Staff were shot out for 48. He was the School's top wicket taker in both seasons. Although in 1969 results were rather mediocre, the season did start with an overwhelming win against Sloane School by scoring 162-4 and then dismissing them for only 16! However, in July 1969 the almost unthinkable happened when the Staff beat the School for the first time since 1914 by 28 runs. In fairness, this just reflected the reality that the staff were an increasingly youthful side by then. A few could actually play a bit and one of the staff, Mr T Smith played regular club cricket with Weybridge. Nevertheless, the Staff were at the top of their game on that day and the School, for whatever reason, were somewhat subdued. What happened was really the equivalent to an FA Cup shock! History records that in front of the School, well that is about half of the pupils that had bothered to turn up, the Staff carefully mustered 123-9 before tea and almost on the stroke of time bowled the School out for 95. The report concludes that *'Mention must finally be made of the admirable umpiring of the Rev Keith Blackburn and G. Jackson.......... the latter concentrated admirably totally unrecognisable in dark glasses and a sensible white hat'* -well I was only 17 at the time! Although the School avenged that defeat in 1970, winning by the comfortable margin of 100 runs, further contests were much closer.

In 1970, results also included a notable win against Battersea Grammar School (admittedly narrowly by one wicket in a low scoring match) with Micky Hearsum capturing 45 wickets in the season, but hereinafter the gradual decline of school cricket began to set in. The 1972 season saw the Staff beat the School again at the Field, this time by no less than 86 runs. The junior sides however were still reasonably active. A young Stephen Titchener was an outstanding cricketer and in 1971 he scored 104 not out playing, probably, for the U13s against Glyn Grammar School. Unfortunately, some six or seven years later, he was tragically killed in a car accident and his cricketing potential was never fully realised.

No account should be complete without a mention of Battersea Grammar School's 1st XI cricket. Within six years of each other the school produced two players who would go on to play Test cricket, Mike Selvey (last year at school 1967) and David M Smith (1973). Some decent sides visited their ground next to the School in Abbotswood Road. The MCC were regular opponents during this period and in 1971 the school dismissed Ted Dexter the former England Test Player for only two runs. The match was drawn. With the assistance of David Smith in 1973 the school won the *London Schools*

Cricketer Trophy against Ernest Bevin School. David is still involved in cricket. He currently manages Lashings who describe themselves as the 'Harlem Globetrotters of Cricket' and have former international cricket players at their disposal to assist in their corporate entertainment business and draw large crowds wherever they play. David is also President of Mitcham Cricket Club where he played most of his club cricket after leaving school.

After the heady days of the war years, it was unlikely that, with the return to Battersea, that the Sir Walter St John's School 1st XI soccer side would be as successful. However, in 1954, the School beat the Old Boys for the first time in twenty-four years. This was the beginning of an upsurge in football. In 1956, J.D. Robertson and A.H. Hudson were selected to play for the London Grammar Schools' football team as Captain and goalkeeper respectively, the former going on to play for Corinthian Casuals and Tooting & Mitcham FC, and 25 times for the England amateur side, also captaining an AFA Youth XI against an FA Youth XI in 1956. In the following year J.H.C. Miller the School football captain and Neil Tompkins who held the School goal scoring record of 44 goals in the 1956/57 season also represented London Grammar Schools. B.T.S. Swain repeated that honour in 1959. By 1960 the School were turning out three senior elevens in addition to the 'junior age' group sides.

In the 1963/64 season, Peter Smith played in Copenhagen for a Young London soccer side and in the following season Kevin Sheehan and M.J. Rothery played for London Grammar Schools. During the autumn term of 1965, Graham Holder scored seven goals in an 8-0 defeat of Ealing Grammar School, which equalled the record of individual scorers in a school match by R.V. ('Dickie') Butler set in 1936/37.

In April 1968 the First and Second Elevens went on soccer tour to Jersey and this would mark the start of tours to other parts of the country in the years ahead.

Results in the 1969/70 season showed that the School 1st XI had enjoyed one of their best seasons ever, playing 41 winning 28 of these and losing only eight. Amongst the magnificent number of 174 goals scored, Martin Faircloth scored 64 of them-another 1st XI record. This proved to be a high-water mark as far as results went as in the following season, the Staff emulated their cricket counterparts, by beating the School by 2-1, their first victory over the School since 1918!

In 1965 the School was transported by a special train (apparently the first instance of doing so since the evacuation to Godalming) from Clapham Junction to the newly constructed National Sports Centre at Crystal Palace for the annual school sports day. This was very much a one-off event. The trophies were presented by the distinguished Sinjun athlete Peter Driver. Despite the removal of the hedge, annual sports days were normally held away from the Field taking place more often than not at the less inviting Hurlingham Stadium for the purpose. However, by 1973 for the first time, a full-sized athletics grass track was marked out at the Field during the summer term, and the long jump and high jump facilities which had originally fallen into the Battersea Grammar School sector of the ground were improved, although both have since become redundant. All this witnessed a strong improvement in athletics and the school performed creditably at the South London Grammar School Championships at Crystal Palace for several years leading up to its dissolution.

Post War Old Boys Sports

Both sports clubs resumed after the war, but peace came somewhat too late for either club to resume cricket until 1946. The next few years, and into the 1950s, saw both Old Sinjuns and Old Grammarians Cricket Clubs at least re-establish their presence at the Field with increasing support from the schools. What did not change was the continued decline in the number of spectators watching amateur cricket. This was underscored at the Field. When the Heathfield club left in the autumn of 1924, the link with the playing of good club cricket at the Field was broken. Now the schools were in control, there would no longer be a standard charge for entry to the Field. So, beyond the end of the Second World War, onlookers or parents of pupils simply watching their son play, would invariably number in their tens rather than hundreds. Both Old Boys clubs would send around a box for donations from time to time. On sunny days a favoured spot was the bank within the confines of the ground adjoining Trinity Road, with even an opportunity to indulge in an impromptu picnic. However, by the early 1960s even that method of securing additional funds by the cricket clubs had been abandoned.

The reappointment by Old Sinjuns CC of Gwil Davies as skipper was important as it maintained continuity and an important link to where the club had been in 1939. As previously mentioned Gwil's efforts also meant that the School had a playing field to use after its return from Godalming. Although the introduction of National Service restricted new membership, as it did for many clubs at the time, the Club continued to run one Saturday and one Sunday side and was able to use the Field on Sunday as previously explained. This gave the club more scope to entertain visiting sides. In all Gwil Davies skippered the Club from 1929 to 1956 apart from the 1951 season which he spent abroad on business in Madagascar. It was a testament to the commitment Gwil made to the club over almost thirty years, that when he passed away in 1988, some of his ashes were sprinkled over the square according to his wishes. By the time of Gwil's retirement both Owen Cooper (Hampshire) and Mick Britnell (Surrey & Glamorgan) were considered good enough for county trials and in 1957 a young Viv Landon made his debut for Old Sinjuns at the start of what would be a long and productive association with the club. In those days, Stan Morris and Albert Oborne would soften up the opposition batsmen and D.A. 'Tommy' Weston would mop up.

One Old Sinjun remains a legend and skippered the side in 1951 during Gwil Davies's absence. The war years probably robbed R.V. ('Dicky') Butler of the opportunity to play at a higher level. Between 1946 and 1955, save one season when he had a broken wrist, he scored over a thousand runs each season (over 1,500 runs in 1952) with a highest score of 163 not out against Croydon M.Os. He was a prolific and aggressive opening bat, capable of destroying any attack and it is not surprising that at the time he shared the highest unbroken opening partnership of 255 with Owen Cooper. Between 1956 and 1959 he played for and captained Harrogate (having been posted there) in the Yorkshire League. Unfortunately, soon after his return, failing health curtailed his playing career, and he died in 1965 at the young age of 45. During Gwil Davies's captaincy, it was his custom to mark his players' centuries by a gift of a cricketing book individually inscribed and 'Dicky' naturally won a number of these. His obituary records *'His exploits are legion – brilliant catches behind the stumps; scoring 150 before lunch; a scoreboard which at lunchtime read Old Sinjuns 113-1, Butler 105; a catch at mid-off to win the match at Kenley and the success of his plan to get an Old Sinjun who was playing against us caught at fine leg'.* During this period the club relied heavily on his runs, and his wicket was a prized asset for any opposition side, particularly if you could dismiss him for under a century!

With the increasing strength of the side, a glance at the 1959 fixture card reflected changes. The country fixtures such as Kilndown, Outwood and Ifield had gone as had the long and challenging trip to Leicester Ivanhoe some years earlier. However, all day matches (starting at 11.30am) accounted for more than half of the Sunday matches whilst Gidea Park remained the only East London fixture. The 'all day' visits to the Nevill Ground at Tunbridge Wells (a regular outground for Kent County Cricket Club) were eagerly awaited. However, travelling could be problematic (no motorways in those days) and on one occasion, the openers had to bat cautiously to allow time for eight of the team apparently stuck in traffic to turn up. Well, you cannot win the toss with three players on the ground and field first! On another occasion an unexploded bomb was discovered under a bank where the team had been sunbathing only a couple weeks previously. Tunbridge Wells generously granted the club a Wednesday fixture at the Nevill Ground during its 75th Anniversary celebrations in 1994.

With the increase of players owing to the abolition of National Service, a 2nd XI Sunday side was introduced in 1964. Then, in 1965, the Sinjuns Parents' Association donated the sightscreens. With a clubroom to call their own, the Field actually began to look more like a cricket ground and Old Sinjuns were establishing a reputation on the club cricket circuit. In a precursor of things to come the club enjoyed success in a more competitive environment. On three occasions, with the semi-finals and finals being held at the Oval, in 1969, 1970 and 1973, the club just missed out, reaching the quarter finals of the Surrey Knockout Competition (15 eight ball overs per side) in a competition entered by almost one hundred and fifty clubs, going out to Surbiton, Old Emanuel and Beddington respectively. In 1972 the 'Dickie' Butler clock was donated, and for some years it resided on a mini clock tower adjacent and above the entrance to the Clubroom. In the same season, the club had its best run in the Kemp's Cup proceeding to the fourth round (last sixteen) having beaten Woking & Horsell, Roffey and Thornton Heath on the way, going out to a strong Camberley side at the Field which included Jim Standen the ex-Worcestershire cricketer and West Ham goalkeeper amongst their number. The era of well-known sportsmen combining winter and summer sports was coming to an end but before it did, Bob Hiller was another that combined two disciplines. An Oxford University cricket blue, he played international rugby for England and played against Old Sinjuns Cricket Club in 1969 with Bec Old Boys, the school where he had been a pupil and also was a teacher. With his long association with Harlequins (he has been their President since 2002) he was probably not aware at the time of the association the Harlequins club had with the Field during its time there at the start of the twentieth century.

Old Grammarians, once the new square had been laid, ran a much larger cricket club. Seating for 200 spectators had been installed by 1954 and the old dressing rooms were converted into a dining room and in 1955 renovations to the kitchen were undertaken so that visiting sides could be served with teas and lunches for the first time. The new square meant that the club could run two Saturday and two Sunday sides, and sight screens were provided at both ends of the ground, with hang over screens to help maximise the short boundary to the Brodrick Road gardens. In 1949 Charles L'Archer completed the double by scoring 1,363 runs and taking 143 wickets, the latter a club record, followed by 130 wickets in 1950. By then many of the 1st XI matches were all day affairs. This led to a golden period in the club's history. In 1952, Jack Durham was in fine form and over a weekend in June and scored 135 against Oxshott, and on the Sunday, 174 not out against Ickenham. The 1st XI were undefeated at the Field throughout both the 1952 and 1953 seasons, with Jack Durham and A.G. Simkins being selected to play for the Surrey Association of Cricket Clubs during the 1953 season. Notable victories included wins over Richmond, Esher, South Hampstead and Horsham. In 1954 Charles L'Archer took 100 wickets in a season for the 1st XI for the eighth year in succession. John King was selected to play for the Royal Engineers versus the Royal Artillery at Lord's and top scored in both innings for the former, although the match was drawn. In 1959, both J Warren and S Manzoor took over a hundred victims each and both were also selected to play for the Surrey Association of Cricket Clubs against a County XI at the Oval. Additionally, this season saw the introduction of an occasional 3rd XI for the first time. John King scored 1,554 runs for the 1st XI which remains a club record. In 2016 John, having been a lifetime member of Surrey County Cricket Club was presented with an award by Richard Thompson, Chairman of Surrey County Cricket Club, to mark his seventy years' continuous membership of the Club. A newsletter was introduced which ran until 1967. Thereafter, the club produced a magazine called *Occasional Glances,* as we know, which looked at various aspects of Old Grammarians Cricket Club both past and present, often in a satirical manner with some articles penned by The Groaner, which ran for at least the following fifteen years.

During the 1950s, the Old Grammarians enjoyed an annual fixture in Wallington's cricket week. Danny Smith recalls *'I had taken delivery of my Austin Westminster [car] and I was using it proudly on the first day at the match. It must have been well after twelve when we tottered out of Wallington pavilion all of us being very careful not to slam the car doors and wake up all of the neighbours. People were congratulating each other, fond farewells and 'See you next season etc'. I eventually found my keys and fumbled for the lock. Suddenly they fell and 'plop' straight down a drain. I swear within ten seconds flat I was as sober as a judge with ideas running through my mind that didn't bear thinking about.... My verbal expression of disgust reached everyone's ears because all quickly gathered round to find out what had happened. Amongst those listening to my tale of woe was John Harris and before I could finish the story he stripped to the waist and was lifting up the drain cover. 'Don't worry Dan' he said 'I'll find them'. I really couldn't believe my eyes. Here was a chap at almost one in the morning preparing to go head first into a drain. But down he went with me sitting on the kerbside holding his legs, because had he have fallen God knows what would have happened. After what had seemed an age John gave me a kick to indicate he wished to be hauled up and with McCarthy's aid we hoisted him to the surface. Covered in all sorts of rubbish he exclaimed 'It's a bit murky down there, there's been a lot of rain recently. I can't find them yet because I am trying not to stir up the sediment down there which is about six inches deep. If I do, they will sink into it and be lost forever'. We decided therefore to replace the drain cover and determine which slot they had fallen through. This completed John took a deep breath and we again lowered him head first into the drain again. In the meantime, everyone was killing themselves with laughter not because of my or John Harris's predicament but at the queue which was forming of volunteers to follow John into the drain if he failed to find the keys. Most of the queue consisted of some Welsh friends of Mac who had joined us for the evening and had needless to say, enjoyed it to the full. They were in turn stripping to the waist and saying to me 'Don't worry Bach I have got a long thin arm. I'll find them for you Boyo'. At that moment three kicks came from John and up he came more dirty than before but there in the palm of his hand – my car keys. I expressed my thanks to John more than once and also to Mac's friends but if there was ever an example of the motto 'No greater love hath man than he lay down his life for his friends' this was it. I shall be eternally grateful to John Harris and those who were there will never forget it'.* It should be said that after the introduction of the Road Safety Bill in 1966 there was a gradual but significant reduction of the amount and degree of post-match entertainment! The Bill was obviously intended for the good to prevent the problem of drink driving. That, combined with the gathering pace, demographics and demands on people's lives have generally much diminished the importance of the club bar in today's game, which, from a personal view, is to the game's detriment because cricket, being a longer and more social game to play than most, relies far more heavily upon the interaction of the players and characters that are involved, than in some other sports.

By 1961, Old Grammarians were rebuilding after the loss of many experienced players. However, John Warren took well over 100 wickets and as a portent for things to come, schoolboy Derek Lawrence scored 56* against Forest Hill. In the same year (given this match was played on a time basis), a low scoring tie was recorded against Old Mid Whitgiftians. Both sides were not only dismissed for 93 but both faced exactly the same number of legitimate deliveries (35.5 overs each). In 1966 another schoolboy, Mike Selvey, was beginning to make his mark taking 5-20 also against Forest Hill and proved to be too quick against Addison. In 1970, it was reported that Bert Garrard 'in his fifty-first year scored more runs than his years on seven occasions', but pride of place would go to Derek Lawrence for scoring 1,245 runs in the season and together with John King both scored unbeaten centuries at Old Lyonians by the time the declaration came at 266-1. In 1971, Derek Lawrence did the 'double' (1,000 runs and 100 wickets). It is strange that with so much talent at their disposal Old Grammarians, only had limited success in the Surrey Knockout Competition or the Kemp's Cup compared with their rivals at the other end of the Field.

In 1972 with Old Sinjuns now playing league cricket, a joint cricket week was arranged with them. 1973 was the final year before Old Grammarians entered league cricket. Derek Lawrence scored over 1,000 runs for the fourth season in succession.

In another development in 1969, the club largely through the efforts of Don Clarke and Bert Garrard, built a 'first -class' size scorebox and for a few years, having given their old scorebox to Old Sinjuns, the Field was well served. Inevitably, of course the second-hand scorebox at Old Sinjuns end eventually fell apart and the same fate would also befall Old Grammarians scorebox which lasted for another thirty years before going the same way.

By the early 1970s it was clear that change was ahead. Hitherto, whilst both clubs had engaged in Cup competitions, league cricket was about to change everything. To be competitive the policy of drawing players essentially only from Old Boys of the schools would be replaced by extending this to friends and other players who enjoyed the improved facilities the Field had to offer. In truth, this process had already commenced and the start of targetting the wider local community only increased as time went on, as the talent from the schools decreased. This change in recruitment was here to stay but few realised at that stage what the sweeping changes the next twenty years would bring to education not just locally but nationally.

Regarding football, Old Sinjuns re-joined the Old Boys League in 1948 and home matches were continued to be played at Hampton Wick. This was because the school played soccer on Saturday afternoons. However, in 1958 when the School 1st XI switched to morning kick offs the Headmaster at the time, Dr W.L. Presswood, offered the Field as a home ground instead. This was a popular move with the club and brought the school and Old Boys soccer closer together. In the 1970/71 season the club marked a notable success by beating Catford Wanderers 2-1 in the AFA Senior (Surrey) Cup Final replay (after a 5-5 draw) at the Guardian Royal Exchange Sports Ground at East Molesey. To give an idea how things have moved on since then in amateur football terms, the ground on which the match was played no longer exists, and if it was not for the proof that this Cup was won by the club, given the absence of internet records, no one would be the wiser, apart from the fact that I witnessed it all from the touchline, in an April snowstorm! Since the final, Catford Wanderers fortunes have been mixed and this is not untypical in amateur football. From running anything up to seven Saturday sides the club actually closed its doors to adult football in 2000, but this situation was reversed in 2008 and in 2020 the club re-joined the Southern Amateur League that they had left in 1982. They are obviously a side rebuilding after a traumatic episode in their history and we wish them well in their efforts to recover past glories.

Old Grammarians continued to play in the Southern Olympian League after the war, considered to be of a somewhat better standard at the time. Their 1st XI home matches during this period were played mainly at Richardson Evans Memorial Ground Roehampton and then later at Wimbledon Common Extension. However, one match that was played at the Field on 18 October 1960 was the resumption of the match with the School 1st XI. With the England Amateur International Player, Bobby Brown in their ranks, the Old Grammarians ran out 4-2 winners. Indeed, both Bobby Brown and J. (John) Martin, both Old Grammarians, represented the Great Britain Amateur Side at the Rome Olympics in 1960. It was not until the 1970s under the captaincy of Terry Withers that the

Field again was preferred for regular Saturday 1st Xi matches after a break of almost fifty years, and lesser matches which had been played previously at the Field before, were switched elsewhere.

Something in the Air

The late 1960s and early 1970s was recognised as a period of significant social change. Although victorious, the Second World War had almost bankrupted the country. Rationing remained in place and it was not until July 1954 that restrictions were finally lifted on meat and bacon. It was not really until the 1960s however that there was a new confidence within the country to take advantage of the loosening of the ties and austerity which had shackled the country after the War for almost twenty years.

In 1969 David Emerson-Thomas was appointed as head of physical education at Sinjuns. His young and attractive wife, Angel, supported David by making tea for the footballers and spectators on Saturday mornings at the Field. Unusually apart from being a teacher (at another school), Angel from the age of 17 had a hobby as a model which carried on beyond her retirement from teaching, having been principally involved towards the end of her teaching career in the education of deaf children. In 1983 in a blaze of publicity, under the famous obstetrician Dr Patrick Steptoe, she was the first women to give birth to test tube twins in the United Kingdom. David enjoyed his rugby and cricket, although he sadly passed away in 2010, but not before he got a week's work at the Ashes Test Match in Cardiff in 2009, where he was given the members' lounge to steward, meeting players and their families. Angel returned to teaching in New York with David, undertook voluntary work in Nepal, and then in 2019 she helped set up a new EFL (English as a Foreign Language) unit in Nanjing, China at an International Baccalaureate College. Angel continues her modelling work and has undertaken photographic, cat walk and walk on parts in films and commercials working around the globe in such places as the United States, Middle East, Paris and Hong Kong. She has also travelled to Japan, Australia and New Zealand.

In 1972 Bob Broad left the physical education department at Sinjuns and briefly joined the well-known group called 'The Love Affair'. He vowed never to return to teaching! By the mid-1970s he was working with the homeless in London whilst still maintaining his links with the music industry. He then worked in several Inner London boroughs as a teacher and probation officer before becoming a lecturer at the London School of Economics. When last noted, as Prof. Bob Broad, he was a visiting professor at London South Bank University in the Weeks Centre For Social Policy and Research, having been previously a Director of the Children and Families Research Centre at the De Montfort University in Leicester.

The late 1960s and early 1970s also saw the increase in nightclubs, discos and loud music. In 'Hazetheques' managed by former pupil Ed Harrison, the Sinjuns clubroom enjoyed some interesting evenings of entertainment at the Field which culminated with the annual barbeque evening in midsummer after the afternoon cricket match – whoever the opposition might be. Additionally, 'Hazetheques' was for a time, the resident discotheque at *The World's End* pub at the Elephant & Castle and also ran a float at the Battersea Park Easter Parade, sometimes in the most inclement of weather!

Yes, in the words of the song by the group Thunderclap Newman, there definitely was 'Something in the Air'. However, perhaps there was something else 'in the air' too. During the early 1970s – a decade known for its strikes and questionable industrial relations, a teachers' overtime ban came into force which would severely cripple Saturday state school sport and in particular, with the longer time required to play a proper match, cricket. Additionally, a further chain of events was starting that would lead to the end of selective education as we know it, and further downgrading and closure of schools and implications for the Sir Walter St John's Schools' Trust after over 275 years of education.

7

All Change (1972-1996)

Sometimes if you want to see a change for the better, you have to take things into your own hands.

Clint Eastwood (1930-   )

Which League? The early years

Although the commencement of the Surrey Championship in 1968 took almost two years' planning, it was a game changer as far as amateur cricket in Surrey was concerned. It only mirrored the growing dissatisfaction at the way cricket was drifting along in south-east England which had hitherto been the preserve of the Club Cricket Conference to administer and the way it was conducted. There were strong opinions voiced on either side of the divide and strongly rooted opposition in some quarters to league cricket which had existed certainly since the turn of the century in most parts of the country. Essentially, it was all about power, control and influence, but it was only ever going to be a matter of time before the northern idea of league cricket was going to win out. In a sense it had already. The l'Anson League based mostly in west Surrey had existed quite happily since 1901, and indeed most of the clubs involved in the early stages of that competition are still with us today. None were members of the Club Cricket Conference for the sole reason, it seemed, that they were content to play, essentially, village cricket within a tight geographical area and this demonstrated the impotence of the Club Cricket Conference to influence matters on their patch. Whilst the Club Cricket Conference initially tried to rally support against league cricket, as they had hitherto administered cricket over a wide area of south east England, they were ill prepared to manage affairs in individual counties. A revealing letter from Don Clarke, Secretary of the Old Grammarians Cricket Club at the time in response to a circular from the Conference, probably summed up the thoughts of many Conference clubs, for whilst he criticised the approach of those trying to form the Surrey Championship, he thought that on the basis that all friendly matches were played competitively anyway, a league approach to this situation was not a bad idea after all. Once the die had been cast, opposition from the Club Cricket Conference melted away. In a sense it was surprising that it had taken until 1968 for matters to change. However, once the seventeen founder clubs had defied the establishment and started the league, the floodgates were opened. It was the guidance of Raman Subba Row that was crucial in this respect. Although having, as a Test player, been involved in the highest echelons of the game, he nevertheless maintained a keen interest in regular grassroots club cricket and the desire to avoid stagnation of the game at that level.

What followed, within a couple of seasons, was an almighty scramble to join a league which clubs considered suitable for the playing standard enjoyed by them at that time, and also the type of cricket a club wished to play. Because the Surrey Championship involved the stronger clubs in Surrey, they opted for a 'time' or traditional format which they had always played, whilst others thought an 'overs' format or a win/lose situation, was more suited to their requirements. Although most leagues today embrace both formats, that argument is still, to a degree, going on today.

Although Old Sinjuns were quick to embrace the benefits that league cricket could bring, by propelling the club onto a bigger stage, the club were really ill prepared when the change came. The School 1st XI still used the Field on Saturday afternoons and as a result the club only ran one side on Saturdays whilst the stronger fixtures were played on Sunday's, where some were all-day matches and where the club ran two sides. Eventually the club was accepted into the newly formed South

Middlesex/North Surrey Cricket League (later known as the 'SoNo' league) and renamed as the Thameside League from 1977, with only five other clubs out of a league of sixteen having any direct link with Old Sinjuns, and then all but one of these on Sundays. The club, however, took the plunge. In the first season of league cricket, the club continued to run only one side in the league. The first match was at Thames Ditton on 20 May 1972 in which the club disappointingly lost in a low scoring encounter. However, in another, the eventual runners up Kew, were shot out for only 47 on Kew Green by virtue of a John Clark hat-trick (Nos 3, 4, & 5) and Tony Bird's 4-16. Both bowlers were subsequently selected to play for the League Representative XI. During term time all the matches were away so the first home league match at the Field was not until almost the end of July against Richmond Town! Nevertheless, the club had acquitted itself well to finish in fifth position in the table, and had they have been successful against Thames Ditton in their opening match, they would have finished as runners up. Indeed, with a bit more luck, had close results gone their way the club could have actually landed up winning the league in its inaugural season! The champions in that first season were Olinda who included former Surrey spinner Roger Harman amongst their ranks. The club had given an undertaking, effectively, from 1973 to run two Saturday sides and fortunately owing to the decline of school cricket were able to arrange some matches at the Field during the first part of the season and make arrangements if needed for a second ground elsewhere. This was opportune, and the arrangement for playing the 1st XI matches entirely away from the Field at the start of the season continued for another two seasons until 1976 when, with the almost total collapse of Saturday school cricket, a more balanced fixture list could be followed. The fact that two Saturday league sides were now established attracted additional players to the club, and this did not have a significant impact upon Sunday fixtures. The club was now running two sides on both days over the weekend. As an illustration of the increased membership that league cricket brought, in 1951 it is recorded that only twenty- seven players were used for the entire season, but by 1994 – the seventy fifth year of the club's founding, and by now running three Saturday sides, by definition, a minimum of thirty-three players were turning out on Saturdays for league cricket alone. Effectively Old Sinjuns and Old Grammarians had become open clubs. A 1978 picture of the Old Sinjuns 1st XI cricket team taken before the club's match with the Surrey Club & Ground, showed that only five of the eleven players were genuine former pupils at the School.

With Old Grammarians there were no such restrictions on Saturday cricket at the Field, but they were somewhat slower to embrace league cricket until it became clear that they had no choice, if only to prevent good players drifting away. They certainly had the talent to make an impact in league cricket with players such as Derek Lawrence and Bill Hart, both who subsequently represented the league, at their disposal. Although the club had applied to both the South Middlesex/North Surrey Cricket League and the Surrey County Cricket League with a preference for the latter, they were initially put in a difficult position when the former league accepted their membership. However, they soon heard that the Surrey County Cricket League had rejected their application, so in 1974 they entered the same league in which Old Sinjuns already played. From now on, both clubs were inextricably linked through league cricket in the seasons that followed.

The other upshot of league cricket was the need to remain competitive. Up to that point, with a few exceptions, the players involved with both clubs had come from their respective schools. The decline of school cricket meant that the links with the Schools were also loosening and to remain competitive this policy became unsustainable. Before then even the Old Boys Football League had accepted the reality that restricting clubs to 'School only' membership was unrealistic. It took a little while for old habits to die hard but in 1985 Jeremy Mills became the first non Sinjun to become 1st XI cricket captain and conversely in 1997 Peter Lang became the last genuine Old Sinjun to do the same. The same sequence of events would be true at Old Grammarians. With membership now extended to any player who wished to play for the club and the locality of Wandsworth and Tooting being a melting pot as far as cultural affairs were concerned, both clubs were now competing on a 'level playing field' with their opponents.

Cross county cricket leagues were more vulnerable to change and as the seasons went on the influence of the Club Cricket Conference further declined. It took almost another twenty years before other further significant changes would occur to cricket within Surrey involving the two clubs, but in respect of league cricket, there would be no going back.

School Sports. The final years.

In 1974, reversing a previous decline, the School cricket 1st XI had quite a reasonable season losing only two of their eleven matches and Martin Brooks taking 7-10 against Strand GS and 7-14 against Salesian College. They also played out a creditable draw against the Old Sinjuns and the Staff match was also drawn. Although 1975 was a little less successful, the team were only narrowly beaten by Westminster City School (the eventual winners) in the quarter final of the *London Cricketer Trophy*. Martin Brooks also took his final overall tally of 1st XI wickets to ninety-nine. However, from then, with Saturday School cricket effectively jettisoned in 1976, only five 1st XI matches were played, and apart from a tie with Wimbledon College, the other four matches ended in defeat.

With Sir Walter St John's School now having become Comprehensive, it would be easy to blame the School's change of status for the decline, but a teachers' overtime ban had not helped either as it severely restricted all Saturday sports at state schools. The honour of representing the School had also diminished with the increasing demands of the Saturday job market, and the rewards that it brought, was favoured to spending a Saturday afternoon playing cricket, not only at Sinjuns but in many state schools across the land.

However, there were exceptions. in July 1978, Ian Thompson was selected to play at the Oval for London Under 16s against Richmond Cricket Club, winners of the Surrey Cup. He top scored with 47 (including one six that went out of the ground!) in a total of 164, and the match was coincidentally won by the same margin of 47 runs. He won the Man of the Match award and afterwards was approached by coaches from Essex, Kent and Middlesex to come for trials. However, in that season the 1st XI played only six matches with Kamal Alam scoring 205 from four innings which restricted the opportunities of young players with talent to shine, and beyond that coupled, with the discontinuation of the school magazine *The Sinjun*, the records of School cricket fell silent.

As regards Battersea Grammar School, after its closure in 1977 cricket declined and, although the School cricket ground at Abbotswood Road survived for around another ten years under its new occupants, the South West London College, it was eventually lost to cricket when, perhaps predictably, two thirds of the ground was given over to an artificial surface for football and hockey. The annual cricket match between the Old Boys and Battersea Grammar School's successor, Furzedown School was now played at the Field. By 1984 it was recorded that the match with Furzedown School was the only occasion and opportunity on which the School 1st XI had taken to the field, that summer! These matches came to an end after the 1986 season. It was hoped that Furzedown School's subsequent integration with Graveney School would bring a revival but it seems the new school was not overly interested in cricket.

The link with Graveney School, however, is fascinating as it claims to have a link with Sir Walter St John going back as far as September 1668 as previously discussed. Quite what this had to do with Graveney School is uncertain. Not bad for a school that was effectively created in 1986! However, despite tenuous links with Battersea Grammar School, two of the School's five 'houses' (St John's and Battersea) acknowledge the links with the past.

Although the early 1970s were poor years for Sir Walter St John's School soccer, during the 1972/73 season a young Mark Morris scored an amazing 117 goals for the U12s of the 210 scored in total. His exploits carried on through the seasons and although he left school early, and records are a little uncertain, it is quite likely he scored around 375 goals in his school football career. Mark's success carried through to the 1975/76 season when the 1st XI side was described as the finest that the school has ever had. The 1st XI, U15 XI and U12 XI all won the Wandsworth Cup, the U13 XI were losing finalists with the U14 XI reaching the London Schools final. Peter Stebbing was the first pupil to reach the final trial for England Schools U19s. However, neither Stebbing nor Morris, who trained at Chelsea FC, would make it all the way to the professional ranks.

All School soccer sides were performing well and there were eight London or district players in the squad. The best result was against Roan Grammar School (English Schools Champions for the past two years) who were beaten 3-1. In 1978/79 the results were even better, with the 1st XI losing only four of the twenty-three matches played. However, unofficial accounts suggest that a decline set in for similar reasons given for schools' cricket, and the record of Sinjuns sport, was sadly no longer recorded. Although it was hoped after 1986, when the school was closed, that some link might be established with Battersea County School who also used the Battersea High Street buildings as an annex for a further two years, this was not to be, as that school already relied on the artificial playing surfaces now available nearby to their school in Battersea Park Road and demand for the services the Field could provide slowly ebbed away.

However, despite this decline, paradoxically, the School did indirectly produce one player who would make it all the way to the professional game at the highest level, but in the most unconventional of circumstances. James ('Jamie') Lawrence played at the school in its dying days as a Comprehensive School. He played with the Old Sinjuns FC for a while where Johnny Sackett, effectively as their coach, encouraged him to try and play at professional level. However, he slipped into trouble and consequently served two prison sentences, the second at HMP Camp Hill on the Isle of Wight. It was there that he was spotted playing in an inter prison match and in the season before his release, he was allowed to play with Cowes Sports who competed in the Wessex League. He turned professional in 1993 at the age of 23 with Sunderland FC, although he predominantly spent most of his career with Leicester City and Bradford City in the Premiership. He also played twenty-four times for Jamaica. His story is told in his book *From Prison to Premiership*, and let's just say he has had a far more eventful life than most of us! He now runs a football academy with the aim of supporting and developing emerging young elite footballers.

Mention should also be made of Leroy Rosenior who joined Battersea Grammar School before its closure in 1977 and then attended Furzedown School. With the annual cricket matches with Furzedown School having moved to the Field in 1982, he played for the School side in their match with Old Grammarians. He also briefly appeared for Old Grammarians Football Club before turning professional with Fulham. He recalls that the catalyst for his start in professional soccer was a match he played with London Schools at the Richardson Evans ground in Roehampton where he was spotted by a Fulham football scout. Within weeks terms were agreed and he signed up for the club.

He also played for QPR, West Ham and Bristol City and in that time scored a total of 73 goals in 244 appearances. In 1993, having switched allegiance to Sierra Leone, he made a single appearance for their national side. He now works as a pundit and was awarded the MBE in 2018 for his work in tackling discrimination in football and elsewhere in society.

House sports

In 1908, the house system at Sir Walter St John's School was reorganised and reduced from ten sections named after a particular master to six sections or houses. These were to be known as Beauchamp, Bletsoe, Bolingbroke, Grandison, Lydiard and Tregoze. The new titles were taken from the old family names and estates of the St Johns. A house championship table would be published annually and amongst the seven elements that made up the total marks awarded to each house, was football and cricket. In September 1969, the number of houses was reduced to four by combining Lydiard with Tregoze and Grandison with Bletsoe and only two years later reduced to just three houses when Beauchamp was combined with Bolingbroke. In earlier years the house system was taken seriously. Captains for each house were published as were the results of inter house soccer and cricket matches that were played at the Field, but the reduction of the houses just reduced competition, rather than enhancing it.

When the school went Comprehensive, the houses were reorganised again into four houses, namely Beauchamp, Bolingbroke, Grandison and Tregoze, with Bletsoe and Lydiard being dropped. By 1979 soccer was played up to senior level whilst cricket was played from first to fourth year level. When the school closed in 1986 it seems the house system was not adopted in the successor school.

The house system had been adopted at Battersea Grammar School in 1907, so in that sense Sir Walter St John's School followed the former's lead. Looking at the annual house reports in Battersea Grammar School's magazine, their encounters were every bit as competitive. Initially there were only four houses, namely Bolingbroke (the only house name to align with their counterparts), St John's (or 'Sinjins' as noted in some earlier reports, but not to be confused with the Masonic Lodge of the same name), Spencer and Trinity but this was later expanded to six, to include Dawnay and Erskine and this system remained in place until the end. From looking at various school magazines, it would appear that the Battersea Grammar School put far more emphasis and enthusiasm into the house system, and at one stage detailed reports of each houses activities and fortunes were included. From 1936 most of the house activity concerning football or cricket would take place at Streatham rather than the Field.

Colts' Cricket

In 1976, to try to encourage colts cricket as a means towards recruiting young players from the School into Old Sinjuns CC, a colts' team was formed using the School U 15 and U 14 sides as a basis. These were limited overs evening matches and the shortened format on a win/lose basis was possible during the long summer evenings. A year later the club entered a team into a new league, the North East Surrey Colts Cricket League, together with club sides from Mitcham, Roehampton, Spencer, Streatham, Thornton Heath and Wimbledon. Much against the odds the side was reasonably successful finishing as runners up in 1978 and again in 1982. In 1979, Ian Thompson, following his exploits at the Oval the season before, became the only colt ever to score a century in these matches, against Wimbledon. Another decent player before the School closed was Aamer

Shah who spent Saturdays predominantly playing league cricket at Spencer CC. In 1993 the colts side progressed to the quarter finals of the John Charcol Cup beating Spencer on the way until being comfortably beaten by the eventual winners Old Whitgiftians at Croham Road who included David Sales (the future Northamptonshire player) in their team. In 1993 also, the National Cricket Association installed an artificial pitch at the Field at no cost to the club for use by schools and young players, one of only three granted in the county of Surrey during that year. By this time membership of the colts' side had been thrown open to other young players with no association with the school. Among these, were Kevin Molloy, who succeeded Alex Tudor as London Schools captain, Zil Sheikh (who later played for the Surrey Young Cricketers) and Kevin Green all of whom played most of their league cricket on Saturdays at Spencer CC who together with Aamer Shah, mentioned earlier, maintained links with Old Sinjuns CC for Sunday matches.

The last year that the club participated in the colts' league was 1998. The league was eventually incorporated into a wider reorganisation of colts' cricket instigated by the Surrey County Cricket Club. Although colts' cricket at Old Sinjuns then withered, in later years it would, with a reorganisation of the club, spark a revival.

Old Grammarians Colts were operational long before their counterparts, starting an occasional side in 1963. Now playing at the Field, an account, in 1975, tells us that no fewer than ten players have represented the senior sides. Thereafter, to much the same degree they followed the same pattern as Old Sinjuns, although the club did not always compete in the North East Surrey Colts Cricket League. From the records we do have, Old Grammarians Colts finished runners up in the previously mentioned league in 1979 when the side was captained by Steve Batley. In 1981 the side was skippered by Simon Tray. Both went on to serve the Old Grammarians with distinction. Additionally, in those days, a Colts Cricket Week was arranged. Again, other players from this side were encouraged to play some senior cricket. As the end of the century drew near, partially owing to the closure of both schools, colts cricket at Old Grammarians fell away as it did at Old Sinjuns, but again would be revived some years later after the merger of the clubs.

Old Boys Sport

In 1972, both clubs organised a joint cricket week at the Field, and although thereafter these were only arranged sporadically, it was a demonstration of how the two clubs were gradually moving closer together.

For Old Sinjuns although having not entered a 2nd XI into the league until 1973, it outstripped the 1st XI's performances by finishing runners up in their division in 1974 and then champions in 1975. The 2nd XI also finished as runners up again in 1980 and 1983 and champions again in 1985. In all 1st XI matches in 1977 off spinner Kevin Barry snared 132 victims in a season, which is probably still a club record. However, paradoxically, the 1st XI went from going unbeaten in 1978 (although with a record ten draws were to finish eighth) to 1981 when they actually failed to win a match and finished in penultimate position in the league! Some of this decline could be directly attributable to the relaying of both ends of the main square at the finish of the 1980 season which, owing to an extensive build-up of material over the years, resulted in the removal of the 'bowlers' humps' that had developed over time. This work was essential, but given that the renovated section led to the interface between the existing surface and the new being virtually on a length, this would lead to some indifferent pitches during the earlier part of the 1980s whilst the renovations fully bedded in. Indeed, the removal of this material was enough to level the area between the small supplementary cricket table adjacent to the football cross pitch and the main table, so some good came out of these works. This area, just on the other side of the artificial pitch, is still sometimes used today for schools' use and also for net practice using the 'roll on roll off' net.

In 1983, the Old Sinjuns team included a player who was to become a cricket Double International in a loose interpretation of the words. Introduced by Len Wallis, one of a number of Old Sinjuns working in the City, Jon Ravenscroft remembers his time with the club. He went on to skipper Guernsey's cricket side and having married on the Isle of Man also represented them whilst living there. Today having returned to the Channel Islands, he is heavily involved in the organisation and support of Guernsey cricket.

Fortunately, after several mediocre seasons, results picked up and under the captaincy of Peter Wheeler the 1st XI was third in 1987 having lost only two league matches and fourth in 1988 thanks in no small part to the fast bowling of Australian Paul Goldberg who seized 8-35 against Evershed and at Chiswick House engineered a surprise victory by twice bowling out Turnham Green's No. 11 off the last ball of the match - the first having been a no ball! Uniquely the club holds two records in the Thameside League which, now defunct, will never be broken! Firstly, John Ware for the 1st XI in 1978 and secondly Kevin Adamson in 1986 for the 2nd XI achieved 'Super hat tricks' (four wickets in four balls) both against Hook & Southborough and both at the Field! Kevin Sheehan, left hander John Uden, and Brian Williams, who would never give his wicket away cheaply, are all mentioned as making a contribution to the club's success during this time.

The club continued to enter the evening competition in which they had so nearly succeeded on three occasions to getting to the Finals Day at the Oval. In 1975 a young Australian visited the Field with Dulwich to play in that competition and his talent was soon apparent. Less than two years later, David Hookes made his Test debut in the Centenary Test Match against England at Melbourne (the first of 23 Tests he would play for Australia). Dulwich comfortably won the match but the club did dismiss Hookes *c Goodson b Bird* with the former having taken a superb catch down by his ankles to do so and landing up with an oval wedding ring for his efforts! Sadly, Hookes died as a result of a brawl at a hotel in Australia in 2004 at the age of just 48.

Sunday cricket remained strong. The fixtures tell their own story. In 1971 and 1974 both all-day Sunday matches with Blackheath Wanderers were tied. Sunday cricket also had its surprises because around this time, Max Norman brought a friend of his to play at the Field on a one-off basis, who turned out to be Greg Benaud son of Richie Benaud the celebrated Australian Test player and cricket commentator! There were usually around six all day matches, involving clubs such as Bickley Park and Sutton. In 1976 a hastily arranged all-day Conference match with Orpington at the Field went to the wire with Peter Buckett being involved in the first and last action of the match. Having been dismissed by the first delivery of the day, he took the catch to dismiss their final batsman to secure a one run victory! The matches with Orpington continued until 1987 and during that period Steve Bennett often opened their bowling whilst also playing the occasional second eleven match with Kent. Although a useful cricketer, Steve was better known in footballing circles as the seasons went on. He claims that he got into football refereeing almost by accident, but this led him to the pinnacle of that sport, firstly as a Football & Premier League referee between 1995 and 2010, and then taking charge of the League Cup Final between Chelsea and Liverpool in 2005 and the FA Cup Final between Chelsea and Manchester United in 2007 which was the first final to be staged at the new Wembley Stadium. As a FIFA referee between 2001 and compulsory retirement in 2006 at the age of 45, he travelled the world widely and sometimes to the oddest of places. Whilst in 2002 the World Cup Final was being staged in Japan (Brazil winning 2-0 over Germany) he was refereeing what became known as 'The Other Cup Final' in the Himalayas between the two lowest FIFA ranked teams in the world at that time, Bhutan and Monserrat, which was won by the home side 4-0. He also admits to having given Vinny Jones his marching orders in a league match on one occasion, although given the footballer's reputation this was certainly not an exception! Underlining his interest in cricket, upon an invitation from the English Cricket Board Officials Association, he sat as an independent director on the new ACO Board from 2009.

As the years went on the trips to the coast to play Worthing, always played on the August Bank Holiday, and at Eastbourne on The Saffrons, were enjoyed. In 1981, Luke Harding made an impression in the latter fixture literally, as whilst in the process of scoring a quickfire 70, hit a ball for six straight through their committee room's window!

Between 1977 and 1980 a series of all-day matches were played at the Field against a very strong Surrey Club & Ground side. With the past history of the fixtures with the Heathfield club unknown at the time, this was the resumption, at least for four years, of the Club & Ground matches that had ceased 54 years previously. Of the matches, the 1978 result was the closest with the club only two runs short of victory with three wickets in hand with Henry Campbell having taken 4-27 in the Club & Ground's total of 174-5 (dec). In the 1979 match, Old Sinjuns also played out a draw but despite Brian Williams's 5-79 and Mick Britnell's 58 were forty runs short with only one wicket remaining when rain curtailed play for the day. What happened next is etched in the memories of those involved as Duncan Pauline (the former Surrey, Glamorgan and Scotland player) explains. *'We had come off the field at around 5.30pm and had indulged in some drinking and bar games after the match. Eventually Sinjuns suggested that had rain not curtailed the match they would have got the forty or so runs required to win the game. The reply from the Surrey Club & Ground team was 'Oh really'! It was then decided to resume the match (not entirely sure who was present at this stage) at around 10.30pm. Some of the players trained their car headlights onto the ground but this really made little difference as it was still pretty much pitch black. After a few balls there was a "clunk". The batsman facing had somehow hit the ball somewhere into the outfield but no one had a clue where it had gone. The batsmen started running. The fielders got down on their hands and knees and started patting the outfield to see if they could locate the ball but to no avail! Eventually with the batsmen tiring someone had a good idea. One of the fielders went to the changing rooms and got a spare ball and ran one of the batsmen out!'* And so ended the only recorded day/night match at the Field! Needless to say, the Sinjuns view of this was different insofar it was claimed that they did indeed make good all forty runs to win the match. Probably best to make up your own mind about this, but after a long evening in the bar it is anyone's guess who was right! In the final match of this series in 1980, Surrey Club & Ground powered their way to 223-2 (D.B. Pauline 117, A.J. Stewart 78) and Monte Lynch, not famed for his bowling finished up with 9-29 in a comfortable victory! On that day playing with the Club & Ground side was Wayne Pascall, who as a useful all-round bowler and batsman would later join the club. His aggregate of 1,594 runs in 1993 being possibly a club record. Wayne now coaches age group cricket with the Wiltshire Cricket Board and is also currently Director of Cricket with Swindon CC.

Old Sinjuns were also scheduled to play the Club & Ground side in 1981, but owing to extensive works on both ends of the square as mentioned earlier, the club had to withdraw. At Surrey, the Club & Ground fixtures continued for a while, but owing to a reorganisation, the County now has one of the strongest performance programmes in the country. Eventually an Academy side consisting exclusively of young players was established. Owing to the decline of state school cricket, the strength of youth cricket in recent years has been more than compensated by that of public school cricket in the county with home grown players such as Jason Roy, Ollie Pope and Rory Burns making it all the way to the England side and powering Surrey to the County Championship in 2018. Another ex-Surrey schoolboy player, Dominic Sibley who attended Whitgift School, was also part of this reorganisation, but now plays at Warwickshire.

On 1 September 1990 after scoring in excess of 20,000 runs for the club, Viv Landon decided to retire from Old Sinjuns cricket. Viv had contributed over fifty in a successful pursuit of Merton's target in the last league match of the season, so getting his wish to go out at the top. With fellow left handed bat and wicketkeeper Mick Britnell, both had contributed so much to the club over the years especially when league cricket started in 1972, having played for a time at Honor Oak and Barnes respectively. They both decided to commit to playing league cricket with Old Sinjuns. Born only a few days apart from each other in 1940, they had become synonymous with the ethos of the club and well respected within club cricket circles. It was the end of an era.

In 1991, the club staged a benefit match for Monte Lynch. In a 40 over per side match, Monte's side which contained virtually the entire Surrey County XI racked up 296-9. Young Kevin McGuigan will remember the match for a long time however, by claiming three the scalps of Surrey skipper, Ian Greig and David Ward within three deliveries of each other. He subsequently played cricket with East Molesey CC.

On another occasion (1993) after the club had achieved a notable success against Richmond CC in the Bertie Joel Cup at the Field, they were treated to a memorable evening's entertainment in the Clubhouse bar by the incomparable Peter Ray, a renowned amateur cricketer and raconteur in club cricket circles. It was well after midnight by the time he left and the mind boggles as to how much longer he might have stayed had Richmond won the match!

In 1994, the club's seventy-fifth anniversary year, Kevin Molloy at 16, became the youngest player ever to score a thousand runs in the season for the club. He also won the Colts League batting award for the second year running and skippered the North East Surrey Colts League side to a two-wicket victory over the West Surrey Colts Cricket League at Burpham.

With Old Grammarians having entered the league in 1974, there were a number of competitive matches between the two clubs at either end of the Field. By comparison, Old Grammarians 1st XI were somewhat more successful, being runners up in both the 1975 and 1976 seasons, and for the most part, without actually winning the league, their 1st XI would generally finish in the top half. In 1978 a young Mark Wilson played occasional matches with Surrey Second XI before moving on to Wimbledon to further his club cricket career. An exceptional player during this period was Derek Lawrence, scorer of 14,491 runs, capturing 1,306 wickets and 317 catches (1985 figures) before he left the club to join Sutton. There he would go onto score another 4,000 runs and take over 600 wickets for the them. He skippered the Sutton side between 1981 and 1984 and, in 1991, he was part of the Sutton side that won the Surrey Championship. Thereafter he played a few seasons with Chipstead, Coulsdon & Walcountians before retiring from cricket.

Meanwhile, Old Grammarians 2nd XI usually were less successful, finishing bottom of their division in 1977 and in the penultimate position in their league table on three occasions during the early 1980s.

On Sundays, the club also enjoyed a full fixture list but reports on matches tended to concentrate more on the tours to the West Country and matches against the School. There were a series of special matches at the Field and these are noted in the following paragraphs. To pick out a few

Sunday highlights, there were notable wins in 1978 against Parkfield, Old Emanuel and Old Rutlishians and some really close matches in 1979 where two matches were won by one wicket, with the last pair knocking off 26 against Ditchling and the last two 75 against Old Elthamians! The emphasis was on youth with the School side, in some cases, providing most of the players. In 1983 the Sunday 1st XI side went through unbeaten and at times in 1984 no fewer than four Sunday sides were turned out with the club using the former school ground at Abbotswood Road on occasions as a second ground. In 1987 it was recorded that the 'perennial' Alan Milhouse blasted an unbeaten 123 against Ewell Ruxley, and in the following season Richard Brough hit over 600 runs on Sunday alone. In no particular order, Glenn Gershkoff, Mervyn Amos, Keith Tushingham, Simon Tray, Anant Patel were all mentioned as key players.

In 1986, as part of their sixtieth anniversary celebrations, the club organised a cricket week at the Field, but before getting there played Dennis Smith's XI on the Sunday before, which included the former England Test player Graham Roope and several other celebrities, one of whom was actor Brian Jackson better and affectionately known as 'The Man from Del Monte'. The advertisements must have certainly raised the company's profile and fortunes. He normally played cricket for The Stage but on that day batted a bit before umpiring. Much to the amusement of the players whenever he made a decision in the affirmative 'The man from Del Monte says Yes' was heard around the ground! No one apparently found out what happened when 'The Man from Del Monte' said 'No'! So well-known were the adverts, he almost had a cult following, and his fame spread to Northern Ireland rather strangely getting entangled in the troubles. Scrawled on a wall, somewhere in Belfast apparently, was a slogan which claimed 'Ulster Says No, But the Man From Del Monte says Yes'! On the Monday, perhaps inevitably, the opposition were Old Sinjuns. Derek Lawrence was an Old Grammarian of course but coincidentally also taught at Sir Walter St John's School and decided on this occasion to play against his old club. Towards the end of the match with Old Grammarians digging in for a draw, he was a little frustrated at his former club's tactics, although it would seem that the survival of Mike Hodges, a tailend batsman, was perhaps a little bit more down to luck than judgement. At one point Derek's frustration boiled over as he asked Mike 'If I bowl you a piano would you be able to play that?' Eventually Dennis Smith and Glenn Gershkoff blocked out well for the draw but the report of the match remarked that it was *'Definitely a most enjoyable day and one of the most sociable games of the week'*.

1987 was the year for a special match involving David Smith's XI v Old Grammarians at the Field in aid of St George's Hospital Scanner Appeal to raise money for a charity very close to Andy Frost's heart. Andy's young son Jamie, suffering from childhood meningitis, was in urgent need of a brain scan and because St George's Hospital did not have a scanner, he and his son were subjected to a harrowing dash across London to Great Ormond Street Hospital for treatment. As a gesture for all the help St George's gave to Andy to facilitate this process, he undertook to organise a fund-raising event for their appeal. Even the weather played ball as the match was played late in the season beyond the end of the County Championship matches on 27 September. Eventually the appeal raised £6,000 owing to the efforts of the club and others. The fact that David Smith was able to call upon so many of his team mates and colleagues to support him on the day also speaks volumes for the help he gave to make the day such a success. It should be recorded that David's side were actually 9 for 3 at one stage with Simon Tray having disposed of David Ward, and Mervin Amos of Jack Richards and Neal Radford. However, Steve Gritt of Charlton Athletic and Hampshire II, with 124 and David Smith himself with 59 restored some sanity to the proceedings and in the end they narrowly ran out as winners. Andy eventually moved out of his house in Lyminge Gardens selling it to Mark Dyer without realising at the time that Mark was an Old Sinjun and today is a Trustee of the Trinity Fields Trust. Andy's son, now Dr Jamie Frost, having given up a job in the City now teaches mathematics at Tiffin School in Kingston. In December 2020 he won a special 'Covid Hero Award' for his work in developing 'Dr Frost's Maths' a free website that has hundreds of videos enabling teaching to continue to schools around the world during lockdowns and school closures. Its resources have been downloaded over eight million times. A remarkable achievement for someone who failed his 11-plus! He also lectures in various other parts of the world when time permits.

In September 1989, Old Grammarians played another match at the Field as part of David Smith's testimonial year. Details are somewhat lacking, but involved some of the protagonists (on both sides) from the 1987 match.

In soccer, building on their strength in the early 1970s, Old Sinjuns were promoted at the end of the 1974/75 season back into the Old Boys Premier Division for the first time since the Second World War. The following season saw the club lift the London Old Boys Veterans Cup. In 1978/79 the 1st XI finished fifth in the Premier Division and progressed to the final of the London Old Boys Cup for a meeting with Old Grammarians resulting in defeat. Unfortunately, the following season saw them relegated but in 1982/83, back in the Premier Division, the 1st XI attained their highest ever position culminating in a 5-1 defeat of the eventual champions Old Salesians. The following season the 1st XI were third in the Premier Division, another high point. Unfortunately, beyond then, and perhaps understandably, a decline set in. Relegation occurred at the end of the 1987/88 season and a further relegation at the end of the 1989/90 season saw the 1st XI playing in Senior Division 2 for the first time in twenty years. The league having been reorganised meant that the club were promoted from Intermediate Division South at the end of the 1992/93 season. The club also produced a monthly magazine during this period rather dubiously called *The Orifice* which summarised results, reports on matches and other items of interest. In 1981 it was reported that it had died but it was subsequently revived and ran for a few more seasons before dying again in the late 1980s – never to be resuscitated! For several years a Boxing Day football match at the Field was arranged either on an internal club basis or, as the clubs rarely played each other, with rivals Old Grammarians for the Franks Cup. It was an opportunity for club members to meet in the Clubhouse as part of the Christmas festivities.

Old Grammarians, however, now playing at the Field, met with far greater success and were a real force in amateur football particularly throughout the 1970s and 1980s. The list of achievements is notable. In 1975/76 the club won the Old Boys Cup (as distinct from the London Old Boys Cup) with a 4-3 victory against Old Monovians and in 1978/79 they beat neighbours Old Sinjuns 3-0 in the London Old Boys Cup Final played at Leatherhead FC, retaining that trophy the following season with a 3-2 win against Albanian. This was the first of three doubles the club would achieve as in the same season they defeated Old Esthameians 2-1 in the AFA Senior Cup Final at Norbury. In 1981/82 the club won the AFA Senior Cup again by defeating Old Parmiterians 2-1 at New Beckenham after a replay, and then achieved a double by winning the Southern Olympian League for the very first time. In 1986/87 they won both the Southern Olympian Senior League Cup, and the Southern Olympian League again (another double). These successes would mark the apex in the fortunes of the club. Although the 1991/92 season would see the club relegated after fifteen seasons in the top flight, they were promoted again in the following season. The same thing would happen again only for the 1st XI to return to the top division of the Southern Olympian League in 1997/98. However, the club would never again repeat the successes of previous seasons.

Whilst the storm clouds gathered regarding the future of the Field, there was always time for a little light relief. Although the Field has had a number of burglaries over the years, and from that perspective witnessed several visits from the police, the Burntwood Lane pavilion was turned into a temporary film set and used as a location in an instalment of the television police series *The Bill* which regularly used the area for filming. The episode in question was shown in May 1996. You could say that *The Bill* picked up the bill for using the Field on national television! In the following few years, both before and after the lease between the Sir Walter St John's Educational Charity and the Trinity Fields Trust was agreed, various organisations used the Field as a base for or for supporting filming nearby.

Women Cricketers at the Field

The first report of women being involved in cricket at the Field occurred in September 1905 when it was reported that eleven ladies from the Battersea Polytechnic played a match against eleven male relations, and were only defeated by eleven runs. Obviously, symmetry must have been a factor in the result!

Occasional matches were arranged at the Field with women's sides. Almost as a novelty match at the time, in 1971 a Surrey Ladies XI played against an Old Sinjuns Cricket Club side in an evening match which, for various reasons, the players engaged in the match remember well!

The demise of the schools gave the opportunity to provide sport for girls at the Field. Given the Old Grammarians connection, Don and Kathy Clarke's daughter Sarah represented a South East Ladies XI in July 1995 when they took on the Maharashtra U19 Ladies from India in an afternoon friendly match at the Field. Also playing in the match were Amy Terriere and Catherine "C.J." Jones who both represented England at age group level, plus Jenny Wostrack, niece of the legendry West Indian Test player Frank Worrell, who was instrumental in the development of cricket in Inner London and Surrey and was responsible for getting many women players including Sarah Clarke and Ebony Rainford-Brent, now a television commentator, into cricket. Jenny represented Surrey Women for many years and worked at the LCCA/ Cricket4Change centre at Wallington before sadly dying of cancer in 2013, as *Wisden* records.

Having made her full senior debut for Surrey Women in 1999, Sarah Clarke then represented England in six One Day Internationals with her last appearance against India in Pune in 2002. She was one of the first four women cricketers to be capped by Surrey in 2015 shortly before her retirement and made a record 108 appearances for the county club with her leg spin bowling, taking a record 132 wickets in the process, including a hat- trick against Warwickshire and a best of 5-11 against Essex. Including T20s and friendlies, which are not included in the above figures, Sarah played a total of 143 matches for Surrey Women. Apart from the match mentioned above, she also played at the Field on a number of occasions for Old Grammarians. Her brother, Simon, learnt his cricket with their colts' side and played for the senior sides before moving away to Sussex and joining Rottingdean where Sarah was already a member. In 2011 he was part of the Rottingdean side that participated in the Village Cup Final at Lord's.

The change towards the provision of sport at the Field for both genders has continued to grow since those days, and it is true that any further development of the Field along these lines will be needed to accommodate and reflect this change. Although SinjunGrammarians do not run a women's side yet, Tessa Bruyns has, in recent years, turned out occasionally for the 3rd XI. With increased interest the standard and profile of women's cricket has greatly improved in recent years. Expect to see some of that translate onto the pitch at the Field anytime soon.

Reorganisation of Saturday League Cricket

By the end of the 1980s, league cricket in Surrey was about to undergo a realignment. Only minor changes had occurred since the establishment of the Surrey Championship back in 1968 and other leagues had been established in its wake. Although various clubs had since taken the opportunity to move into leagues more suited to their requirements, there was a realisation that without a proper system of promotion and relegation between leagues this would lead to stagnation and a lack of meaningful competition. This would be counterproductive to the aspirations of clubs to better themselves. There was also to be more emphasis put on county-wide structures rather than regional cross county leagues. It was from the Surrey Championship, as the acknowledged leading cricket league in Surrey, that change was needed to overcome this situation. It arrived in the form of Chris Brown who was the son of the late Freddie Brown who played Test cricket for England from 1931 until 1953. Never far from controversy, Chris was not a first-class cricketer but enjoyed the camaraderie of cricket, especially through touring, and would play cricket in most corners of the world. He was very much his own man. Quoting from his obituary in the 2006 edition of the *Club Cricket Conference Yearbook 'To all who knew him, Chris was by turns aggressive, loud, annoying and at times downright cussed but always a good friend and a good man to have on your side in a tight spot. The fact that he was often the reason you were in a tight spot is another story!'* As Chairman of the Surrey Championship, and also a club member at Wimbledon, he was the true instigator of the change towards structured cricket in Surrey. In 1987 the Surrey Championship subsumed the Surrey Cricketers League which at the time was regarded as the second league in the county and promotion and relegation between the resultant two divisions was established. In 1991 the expanded Surrey Championship introduced another division comprising effectively the best of the rest of the clubs throughout Surrey. This was somewhat more of an arbitrary and controversial move as the selection of such sides was at the Surrey Championship's behest. However, the sixty clubs so chosen, given subsequent promotion and relegation, still form the basis of the Surrey Championship today. For clubs such as Old Sinjuns and Old Grammarians who fell outside this monolith an anxious period of assessment followed, as the clubs adjusted to the new reality. The main league affected was the now decimated Surrey County Cricket League which was wound up but, with the considerable advantage of being able to continue with the sponsorship of Fuller's Brewery already in place, a new league arose like a phoenix from the ashes. This attracted clubs from all corners of Surrey and a new league, the Surrey County League, was able to commence seamlessly in 1992. It was to this league that both clubs were admitted. The first season was an unmitigated success. Old Sinjuns, although finishing eighth in the 1st XI league, won the 2nd XI league and were runners up in the newly formed 3rd XI league. Old Grammarians just entered two elevens into the league and although struggling somewhat with their 2nd XI finishing in the penultimate position, survived as there was no promotion or relegation in the inaugural year. However, it should be said that in 1993, Old Grammarians did win the League Cup, an achievement which eluded Old Sinjuns who were runners up in that competition in 1996.

With the introduction of a second 1st XI division (and attendant 2nd XI division) in 1993, promotion and relegation between divisions in the Surrey County League was introduced, but it would not be until the end of the 1998 season together with the financial and moral support of the Surrey Cricket Association, that promotion and relegation (two up and two down) was finally standardised and established with the Surrey Championship. Both leagues still exist today, based on the principles that were established over twenty years ago, and Fuller's Brewery, remarkably, still sponsoring the Surrey County League in what is claimed to be the longest continuous amateur cricket league sponsorship in the country.

Changes to the Trust & Schools

The changes in the status of Sir Walter St John's School, and the closure of Battersea Grammar School in Streatham in 1977 created a good deal of uncertainty. Old Grammarians, linked to the latter, felt the closure keenly. Although Battersea Grammar School had been amalgamated with Rosa Bassett School to create Furzedown Secondary School, the Sir Walter St John's School Trust had no involvement or association with the new school in Welham Road and there were genuine concerns for some years that the club would eventually be expelled from the Field. A move by the Old Grammarians to relocate to Morden for sport was even contemplated at one stage. Although both Old Boys' Associations tried to recruit members from the successor schools to carry on the link, these attempts ultimately failed to have an impact.

In 1976, Sir Walter St John's Grammar School had become Comprehensive owing to its amalgamation with William Blake School. Additionally, with the closure of the Sir Walter St John's Comprehensive School in 1986 and with the buildings finally closing in 1988, the remaining pupils were finally absorbed into Battersea Park School. The Battersea High Street site and the former William Blake School buildings – which had become incorporated into the former as the Comprehensive School in 1976 were sold in 1990. Although the London Residual Body (as the successor to the Inner London Education Authority) had a financial interest in the buildings, so did the Sir Walter St John's Trust which owned parts of the Battersea High Street site outright as confirmed in the 1951 agreement. Eventually a windfall of about £1.8 million passed to the Trust on the proceeds of the sale, yielding with that capital an interest of about £100,000 per annum, in those days of higher returns, that the Trust could potentially use for charitable purposes. Back in 1700, it was never contemplated that the buildings would ever be sold but the Trust was now in a better financial position than ever before in its 290 years' existence. Ironically though, it no longer had any associated schools on which to use its charitable status. Crucially, however, omitted from the sale was the Field because it was still in use, although principally by the Old Grammarians and Old Sinjuns sports sections, but also during the week by a few nearby state schools. The purchaser of the Battersea High Street site was Thomas's London Day Schools, a private body concerned with the provision of education of boys and girls between the ages of four and thirteen. The news was greeted with a mixture of relief and delight. Relief because the buildings, although left empty for two years, had not been subject, by some miracle, to bouts of vandalism or unwanted occupation, and delight that the whole site was to be put to good use for educational purposes for which the buildings had originally been intended. Since the sale, the new owners have enhanced, adapted and improved the school buildings for the benefit of its pupils and today the school is better known for the ongoing education of Prince George and Princess Charlotte.

The Trustees searched for new ways of carrying forward Sir Walter St John's aspirations in the changed circumstances and reached agreement with the Charity Commissioners on the terms of a scheme approved on 28 February 1992 which would provide continued benefit from the assets of the Trust for the education of young people in the area. The agreement included, in addition to the Sir Walter St John's Schools Trust, four other linked charities which were consolidated into a new body to be known henceforth as the Sir Walter St John's Educational Charity. In July 1992 the trustees appointed a part-time administrator to professionally manage the charity's investments. During the first four years the new Charity approved grants amounting to nearly £160,000 for a total of seventy-four projects. With the new Charity in ownership of the Field, the Trustees sought ways of encouraging greater use by the local community in conjunction with local schools without really having any dynamic plan of what to do with it. The Field was regarded, it seemed, as it had been through history, more of a liability than an asset. Arrangements were made to allow the continued use of the Field for training and weekend matches by the football and cricket clubs of the Old Sinjuns and Old Grammarians, but an event was to happen only a couple of years later that was to concentrate minds.

Flaming June!

1994 was the seventy-fifth anniversary of the founding of Old Sinjuns Cricket Club. A special commemorative brochure had been printed. The season marked a high point in the number of matches arranged, as across all elevens, including the colts no fewer than 134 club fixtures were scheduled. The club had organised a whole raft of events including not only the tour (as normal) but also a cricket week to celebrate this event. The fact that the club were celebrating their seventy-fifth anniversary was even mentioned on Test Match Special! One of the commemorative brochures was indeed signed by the Test Match Special team and raffled. By some fluke having won the raffle, I still have that brochure today.

All things were going to plan but in June the unthinkable happened. After an evening match when everyone had left for the night, an electrical fault (so the Fire Brigade thought) caused a fire in the boiler room at the back of the changing rooms. Being predominantly a timber structure, and although it had been only renovated a couple of years previously, with most of the electrics updated, the fire spread rapidly. By the time the blaze had been noticed from the road, the back of the timber building had sustained severe damage and was deemed unusable and unsafe. It also transpired that the building which was around seventy years old was only nominally covered by insurance and to that degree it was effectively a total loss with no provision made for its replacement.

The loss of the changing rooms was catastrophic. It was almost as if the club had lost a close friend. It had witnessed the division of the Field and survived the Blitz but had succumbed to the fire. However, some good came out of this disaster as the club were able to continue with their season as Old Grammarians generously offered use of their pavilion for changing facilities. The legacy of a divided field before the Second World War now proved to be a blessing after all as at least, with four decent sized changing rooms the Burntwood Lane pavilion could service two cricket matches on the Field simultaneously. It also brought the two cricket clubs closer together in what would transpire to be a testing period for the future of both clubs, but ultimately would end in a merger, albeit, ten years later.

Nevertheless, despite the disaster, the club were determined to enjoy themselves and fulfil a series of special matches already arranged. The club had already been asked to host a Surrey U12 match with Essex U12 which did go ahead. The County club were very understanding of the situation and both sides changed in the Burntwood Lane pavilion. The son of Robin Hobbs the ex- Essex and England leg spinner, played for the opposition and the pitch was praised by the County which was a recognition to the outstanding service and work that Steve Irons as groundsman had given to the Field for the past nine years in what was (unbeknown to everyone at that stage) to be his last season at the Field. The cricket week also was completed achieving wins over Turnham Green and Odiham

& Greywell and only losing to a strong league representative side. In proof that ageism was still in fashion, during the week an 'Over 40s' match was arranged with Old Grammarians of a similar vintage, which perhaps predictably ended in a draw.

As for the changing rooms these were eventually completely demolished apart from the 'Dungeons' which were adapted to form two temporary changing rooms, a bank of showers and a toilet. If *Time Team* ever visited the Field, they might find some interesting building materials underneath the tarmacked car park area! The club did return, although using the adapted changing area was never really a satisfactory solution, but ultimately, once the merger occurred some ten years later, the changing facilities would effectively revert to the Burntwood Lane pavilion. Teas, which had been taken in the Sinjuns Clubroom after the fire (whereas before they had been taken immediately outside the changing rooms in the reception area) were transferred to the Burntwood Lane pavilion after the merger. The 'Dungeons' still exist today, but more as a storage facility and sometimes as a shelter in poor weather during the summer months. However, what was clear was that the Sir Walter St John's Educational Charity showed very little drive or enthusiasm to finding a solution to the situation which had been compounded by the fire.

As it appeared that the Charity were ill equipped to administer or maintain the Field from their offices in Battersea Park Road, options about its future were being openly considered. Because of the 1852 covenants, the value of the eight-acre site solely as a playing field, was reasonably nominal and would not make a significant difference to the £1.8 million the Charity had already obtained from the sale of the School. The Charity were also mindful however, that the status quo could not continue as it would prove to be a drain on their resources not only to maintain the ground economically, but also with the need to urgently upgrade all the useable buildings that badly needed refurbishing or replacing. At the same time their objects of providing the Field as a base for the benefit of the local community would likely be compromised if sold to the highest bidder. Predictably, a couple of private schools had already expressed an interest. Politically this was a difficult issue. There were members of the Charity who were also uneasy about the future and with the council showing little interest as far as purchasing the Field was concerned, it was not long before unofficial discussions were taking place between a group of representatives from the sports clubs led by Terry Smith, an Old Grammarian, and Charity members led by Jeffe Jeffers to see if another way forward was possible.

In January 1995, Terry Smith presented a report to the Sir Walter St John's Educational Charity called *The Playing Field – A Plan For The Future*. Amongst the suggestions was a proposal 'to establish a user Company with Charitable status that will be responsible for all financial and administrative matters connected with the Playing Field' and that 'The user company to enter into a lease arrangement to use the Field'. There was also a picture and plan of a proposed new Pavilion. However, it was not all plain sailing as there was opposition from elements within the Sinjuns Association, and also some members of the Charity, who thought the best approach, commercially, would be either to directly involve Thomas's London Day Schools in the purchase of the Field, to go with their previous purchase of the school in Battersea High Street, or if not, despite the limited financial benefits a sale of a sports ground would bring, to sell the ground to the highest bidder. Either way it all added to the uncertainty.

The ramifications of the demise of the Inner London Education Authority, now administered through the London Residual Body, (who had been responsible for the disposal of the School Buildings) soon became apparent as for the 1995 season the groundsman was withdrawn and maintenance of the ground passed back to the council. This was greeted with alarm, and it soon became clear that emergency action was required to secure an acceptable level of maintenance and pitch preparation at the Field. Worse still, the council removed most on-site ground equipment and the council's plan of using just 'mobile' equipment was obviously unsatisfactory as was the method by which they intended to prepare pitches. Suddenly the future of the Field and the sports clubs were now open to question as it never had been before. Decisive measures were required.

The ground equipment was now at the council's Battersea Park depot and, in a move to remedy the situation, both cricket clubs working together decided to buy back the equipment so removed. Fortunately, the opportunity to purchase, at a very reasonable price, similar equipment from the council presented itself, before being put under the auctioneer's hammer. The overall cost was about £6,000 with the two clubs sharing the cost. The price included the roller used at the Field– an absolute 'steal' at £1,000- which although thirty years old- was still in reasonable working order. As proof that 'Old rollers never die' after several upgrades and recons, the roller was eventually replaced after a further twenty years. It was bought by an enthusiastic amateur cricketer, Denham Earl, who completely refurbished it for his club and today it services the pitches at Warlingham CC.

However, by 1996, for the very first time, both clubs had the independent means to prepare its own pitches, and with the council out of the equation, the Sir Walter St John's Educational Charity faced up to their responsibilities and generously gave a one-off allowance to the sports clubs to help contribute to the cost of maintaining the Field for that season. With only limited use of the Field midweek, including colts' cricket, the sports clubs demonstrated that they were able through self-help led by Tony Bird (Old Sinjuns) and Ian Muirhead (Old Grammarians) and a small team of volunteers, to bring back the pitches to an acceptable standard.

Discussions and negotiations continued. On 8 October 1996, the Trinity Fields Trust, with Terry Smith as Chairman, was incorporated as a company without share capital with the equivalent objects as the Sir Walter St John's Educational Charity, in providing funding for educational and training projects, including physical education, for young people within the Boroughs of Wandsworth and Lambeth. The Charity Commissioners duly gave their consent to the scheme, paving the way for the Trinity Fields Trust to lease the Field. In the meantime, the support and backing of several local private schools, all with limited playground facilities for sport and recreation had been obtained, which would potentially add financial security to the enterprise. However, for the whole scheme to fly, it had to receive the backing of the Sir Walter St John's Educational Charity which was certainly not a formality. In the end, it was a close-run thing as the scheme was apparently passed by a single vote but nonetheless a lease had been secured for twenty-five years until 2021.

Now that both the lease and the ground maintenance issues were resolved, the challenge was for the Trinity Fields Trust to follow through on its commitments.

Old Grammarians AFC. AFA Senior Cup Winners 1980. (l to r: Back Row: P. Philpott, P. Rowley,   S. Lee, D. Boynton, R. Hards, R. Hill, S. Kiy. I to r: Front Row D. Petch, I Davies, T. Withers, D. Ludford, P. Hill)

D.M. Smith's XI v Old Grammarians. St Georges Hospital Scanner Appeal Match in 1987 (l to r standing) Ian Muirhead, Don Clarke, Mick Meyer, Simon Tray, Glenn Gershkoff, Keith Tushingham, Alan Millhouse, Tony Gardiner, Mervin Amos, Tony Fretwell, Gary Wilson, Greg Purnell, Andy Frost, Alec Stewart, Trevor Jesty, Steve Gritt, Dennis Smith. (I to r seated) Steve Thompson, Mark Feltham, Ian Greig, Nick Phipps, David Smith, Jack Richards, David Ward, Tony Trick, Neal Radford,

Old Sinjuns Over 40s v Old Grammarians Over 40s at the Field in 1994, with Micky Britnell batting, Derek Lawrence at slip, Micky Francis keeping (having flown from America to take part in the match) and Mick Meech in an unfamiliar role as the umpire at square leg.

View from the automatic weather station on top of Sinjuns Clubroom during Andrew Crawford's time at the Field 2014

Inside Burntwood Lane Pavilion. View from upstairs clubroom 2000

Private schools using the Field during summer 2011

Winter evening training at the under floodlights

Evening midweek corporate cricket at the Field 2017

New covers for the second pitch 2018. Provided with help from the Surrey Cricket Foundation

An Old Grammarians Tour Group at Sidbury 2018 l to r: Joe Purnell, Dave Boynton, Mervyn Amos, Dave Petch, Neil Oakford.

Woodfield. Another ground supported by Samuel Cresswell. Pavilion refurbishment 2019.

View from the boundary towards Burntwood Lane

Dramatic Skies over the Field 2019

Sarfraz Nawaz with SinjunGrammarians C.C. at the End of Season Get Together 2019

Drainage problems at the Field Autumn 2020

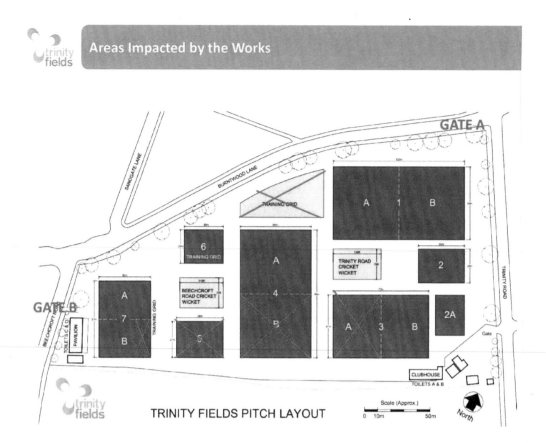

Areas under repair showing current layout of the Field 2021

Tractors, Sightscreens and Covers! Repair works get underway 2021

8

A New Start (1997- 2019)

Start by doing what's necessary, then do what's possible, and suddenly you are doing the impossible.

Francis of Assisi (1182-1226)

Trinity Fields Trust Improvements

When the Trinity Fields Trust took over at the Field, there were pressing needs to materially improve conditions but, initially, resources were stretched. For the next three years, from 1997, Tony Bird (with Ian Muirhead as assistant on the Old Grammarians square) continued to maintain the Field in an enthusiastic if not rather eccentric manner, but this was only ever going to be a temporary measure until the finances became stronger. Logistically, there was much organisation and planning to do, and regular meetings were held with the private schools, Finton House, Hornsby House, Northcote Lodge and Thomas's London Day Schools, (known rather grandly as The Consortium) to agree who should use which parts of the Field and when. Additionally, the usage would be shared with state schools in order to fulfil the Trust's objects.

There were also to be changes in the relationship with the Old Sinjuns and Old Grammarians Sports Club. The peppercorn rent established in 1949 was effectively replaced with a more commercially realistic charge for the use of the facilities at the Field, and the Trust was keen to foster the link between junior sport and the two Old Boys Sports Clubs which was to be made easier once the amalgamation took place in the autumn of 2005.

The Trust ambitiously launched into upgrading the Field. With a contribution from both Old Grammarians and the new Trust to the tune of around £90,000, the Burntwood Lane pavilion was completely refurbished and the ageing roof was retiled together with the clock tower. The two upstairs rooflights looking over the ground were adapted so that players could sit outside and watch the match from an elevated position. The timber floors in the changing rooms which had become hazardous and uneven over the years were pulled up and replaced with a sensible non slip flooring throughout. The showers were upgraded and the antiquated kitchen modernised so that the provision of lunches and teas could be managed easier in accordance with current legislation. The electrics were completely upgraded and a new boiler system was also installed. Perhaps almost as important, access to the ladies and gents' toilets was improved to enable direct access internally rather than have to venture into the wind and rain in the winter (or summer) for the purpose. The renovated upstairs clubroom is now a popular place to congregate after a cricket match. The plaque outside the Burntwood Lane pavilion proudly proclaimed its reopening on 1 July 1999 by Alex Tudor who played as a colt at the Field with Spencer CC. Unfortunately, despite what the plaque says, Alex was unable to perform this task, as he had been a late call up into the England squad for the first Test Match against New Zealand commencing on that day at Edgbaston! The record shows that having been picked for his bowling, he only had modest success with the ball, but as a 'night watchman' in England's second innings made an unbeaten 99, to help win the match by seven wickets. This is the highest innings by an England night watchman, surpassing 98 made by Harold Larwood at Sydney in the 1932-33 'Bodyline' Test series. Despite Tudor's efforts and understandably winning the 'Man of the Match' award, it was his only Test appearance that summer and New Zealand won the four-match series by two matches to one to record only their second series win in

England, with their third series win in England being in 2021. As for Alex Tudor, he played a total of ten Tests for England, but would never again get anyway near hitting a Test century for his country.

In 2000, the Trust employed John Doe, effectively as their first full time groundsman. In the spring an extensive upgrade to the drainage system was undertaken. However, the Council refused to agree to a new drainage outfall into Beechcroft Road given that the existing drains already discharged into an outfall under Burntwood Lane. As the discharge of water from the Field during wet weather would have been identical either way, this seemed like a strange decision but it was, perhaps, due to controlling the discharge into the Beechcroft Road sewer rather than Burntwood Lane that could have been a factor. Unfortunately, the water from the new drainage system would need to be pumped into the original outfall rather than letting gravity take its own course, all adding to the cost. The football season finished early so the Field could be stripped bare of turf in readiness for the works and, save for the cricket squares which provided an oasis of green, the Field looked an extraordinary site amongst a barren wilderness and a confusion of plastic pipes and fittings. Some doubted whether the Field would ever stage a cricket match again but remarkably, almost against the odds, once the outfield had been levelled and re-laid cricket resumed although initially you needed to be a lottery winner to guess how the ball might react running across the outfield whilst the new system bedded in. It was some seasons before the scars of the drainage installation were completely absent. The following winter was extremely wet and although some doubted that the upgrade was worth the investment, further works on the outfield, making it more permeable, improved matters.

As the ultimate irony, in the spring of 2006, an irrigation system was introduced throughout the outfield. The Field was one of the first amateur sports grounds to receive such a system and this work was to disrupt the outfield again. The new drainage system could now be tested by turning on the sprinklers at night. So far there have been no incidents or any major malfunctions in the system and no players getting soaked unintentionally during matches! With hot and dry summers becoming more common, leading to uneven and parched outfields, it was always a pleasure playing on a green and level surface, when other outfields were brown or yellow. A new large timber shed housing the tanks and controls was constructed to replace the previous one next to the Burntwood Lane pavilion which had seen better days. That shed was fondly remembered by Old Grammarians as housing the props and other items used by the Old Grammarians Dramatic Society who as the 'Upstagers' used to present and produce a variety of plays and musicals in various locations, but more notably at the Arts Centre in Falmouth ('The Falmouth Week') and at the *Secombe Theatre* in Sutton. On one occasion passers-by in Burntwood Lane would have been amazed to have seen cricketers in their whites and ladies in their bonnets at the Field on a cold winter's day in November. It was the 'Upstagers' organising a photoshoot ahead of their latest production of *Outside Edge* that was to be staged at Seely Hall Tooting later that month. The Dramatic Society was very much an integral part of Old Grammarians life. Indeed, as Old Grammarians Dramatic Club, its existence can be traced back until at least December 1887, when a performance was given in the large hall at Battersea Grammar School. The latest reincarnation ran for almost forty years headed by Don and Kathy Clarke but on 13 September 2003 a farewell dinner brought down the curtain on its activities. It made the few attempts at similar entertainment in the Sinjuns Clubroom look distinctly amateurish!

The other issue which was addressed was the renewal of perimeter fencing not only to the gardens of Brodrick Road but also the extension of fencing along the interface with Burntwood Lane to prevent balls sailing out of the ground on the shortest boundary and into the path of unsuspecting pedestrians or cars. This has largely improved matters and today balls being hit out of the ground particularly towards roads or pavements are thankfully fewer and further between.

A New Start (1997- 2019)

The Decline of Sunday Cricket

Since the establishment of league cricket some twenty-five years previously, Sunday friendly cricket had carried on in much the same format as before. There was still the interesting match here and there as witnessed by the appearance at the Field of David Cook – better known as David Essex in an early season match with Long Ditton CC. He was instrumental to that club winning the match, and it must be said that with the weather being cold on that early day in May a headline on any report of the match could easily have read 'Only a Winter's Tale!' However, times were changing, and so were the players. In the case of Old Sinjuns the number of all-day 1st XI cricket matches had declined from eight in 1980 to just one by 1996. The club had also effectively given up on running a regular Sunday 3rd XI cricket side by 1994. In 1997 competitive Sunday league cricket, was beginning to manifest itself. These were 45 overs per side matches played on a win/lose basis and both Old Sinjuns and Old Grammarians entered the Old Boys Sunday League as a result. Despite the name, there was really no ethos involved in setting up the league as all clubs were now effectively open but as South West London had its fair share of Old Boys sides there was a realisation that Sunday cricket needed in some way to be co-ordinated and a local competition between like-minded sides seemed at least to be a good, if only, temporary solution. The matches only involved one eleven in the league, although in the case of Old Sinjuns five of the seven matches played would be shadowed at 2nd XI level, but 1997 would also the last season in which Old Sinjuns regularly ran two Sunday XIs. Old Grammarians soldiered on until the end of the 2000 season, when they too admitted defeat. Just like School cricket before them in the 1970s, there were too many distractions for players to play Sundays and the time of the two-day weekend cricketer playing both Saturday and Sunday was already a thing of the past. The sudden collapse of Sunday cricket, perhaps, was to be expected as clubs would, from now on, be more accurately judged by the strength of their Saturday league sides and the competitive environment that league cricket brought to the game.

A young player who spent his entire club cricket career at Old Sinjuns, was Amol Rajan, who as a journalist has made an impact at the BBC, firstly as their Media Editor and now combining that role as one of the presenters on the *Today* programme on Radio 4. He was very willing, and at 18 years old, the youngest Sunday 1st XI skipper, in 2002, to take on the responsibility of organising the side, during his gap year working for the diplomatic service. Those involved in the infamous cricket match at Old Whitgiftians in the rain, which was more akin to playing water polo, will vouch for Amol's enthusiasm! Amol alludes to his time at the club in his book called *Twirlymen* about the history of spin bowling. He was known to all at the club, affectionately, as 'Mushy' after Mushtaq Ahmed the Pakistani leg-break bowler but even Amol would concede that this was where the similarity ended. Working with the BBC restricts the amount of cricket he can play to almost zero, but in a televised charity match representing Radio Five Live in 2018 their side beat a *Test Match Special* side much against the odds. It is true this was a charity event so little really serious cricket was played, but when Phil Tufnell hit a slow full toss hard to extra cover, where Amol promptly caught it, the picture of Phil's face at the time confirmed that he had not expected that outcome!

However, in the years before the merger, not only was the quantity of Sunday cricket in sharp decline, so was the quality.

Old Boys Sports prior to 2006

With more of an emphasis on league cricket, the two clubs had varying fortunes during this period. Although both clubs played in the Surrey County League, with a promotion link to the Surrey Championship established, there was an added incentive in trying to do well.

Old Sinjuns 1stXI however, were the first to suffer relegation within the Surrey County League in 1999. Unfortunately, the side skippered by Paul Weston was so severely depleted by a combination of unavailability and injuries that most weeks the 1st XI team resembled a 2ndXI as they plunged from a respectable sixth to nineteenth position. The other consequence of this was having to withdraw the 3rd XI from the league, being unable to fulfil fixtures.

The end of the 1999 season also saw the end of Old Sinjuns as a club after eighty years in existence. To a degree this was only a technical change as the club simply dropped the 'Old' to be known as 'Sinjuns', in an attempt to try to broaden the club's appeal given that the school connected with the name had closed in 1986!

In 2000, under new skipper Sibbi Sheikh, the renamed club regained their first division status by finishing runners up in Division Two. The following year the fixture card shows that the club had a brief flirtation with Old Castletonians CC who used the Field for Sunday fixtures on a few occasions. In 2002, the 2nd XI achieved promotion to the Surrey Championship for the first time by finishing runners up under the captaincy of Matt Drury, and whilst the following season the 1st XI struggled again, the 2nd XI consolidated their position within the Surrey Championship. In 2004 with the 1st XI finishing half way in the Surrey County League Division One, the division in the Surrey Championship in which the 2nd XI played was split into two. As a result, the 2nd XI now skippered by Alun Watkins, effectively helped themselves to another promotion by finishing in the top half of that division and found themselves in Division 4 of the 2nd XI League in the Surrey Championship for the 2005 season and remarkably finished as Champions of Division 4 at the end of that season.

However, a fundamental change was coming as amalgamation of the two clubs beckoned. On 25 September 2005 the club played its last match under the name of 'Sinjuns'. Club cricket on Sundays in September used to be carried on deep into the month, always playing away from home, weather permitting. It was perhaps appropriate, if not ironic, that a genuine Old Sinjun Mark Boome brought down the curtain on eighty-six years of history with the winning hit, a boundary four, in a narrow three wicket victory at North Holmwood.

Regarding Old Grammarians, events almost uncannily followed a similar pattern to Old Sinjuns. The 1st XI remained in Division One of the Surrey County League until in 2002 they were relegated. Having retrieved their position for the 2004 season, the club were unfortunate not to be promoted to the Surrey Championship. Playing in the final match at the Field, in a match where a positive result for either Old Grammarians or Effingham would have seen the victors promoted, the match was drawn when Effingham finished 132-9 chasing 182, allowing Carshalton & Croydon Gas to squeeze home as runners up. In 2005 the club again finished strongly in third position. In both seasons the side was skippered by New Zealander Steve Baker. The 2nd XI having been promoted back into Division One (2nd XIs) for the 1997 season remained there throughout this period. The club ran a 3rd XI in the league and finished runners up in some seasons before 3rd XI promotion and relegation was established with the Surrey Championship. In 2003 Old Grammarians 3rd XI finished third and then spent the last two seasons before the amalgamation in mid table.

On the football front, at Old Sinjuns for the 1996/97 season, David Demeza was made President of the London Old Boys League. His playing career spanned 42 years. David in his later playing days played in the lower elevens and was famous for calling 'Demeza' to claim a ball nearby. On one occasion at the Field, having done so, the referee (certainly 'old school' and hard of hearing) blew his whistle for an infringement on the basis that by law you are required to call a name to claim the ball. When David questioned why the referee had blown up, he replied 'You called "Me sir"' David protested. 'No, I called Demeza, that's my name'! Believe me, this is a true story. I was keeping behind David at the time and a very tricky free kick resulted.

With the honour bestowed on David, Old Sinjuns Football Club were on the rise again and by the 1997/98 season after successive promotions the 1st XI found their way back into Senior Division 2. After avoiding relegation as a result of a technicality in 1998/99, they were promoted into Senior League One for the 2000/2001 season, by which time, like the cricket club, the football club had changed their name to Sinjuns.

Regarding Old Grammarians, they started this period in the top division of the Southern Olympic League, and maintained that position throughout until the end of the 2001/2002 season when reorganisation of amateur football took place.

The merger of the Southern Olympian League with the London Old Boys League to form The Amateur Football Alliance was one of the largest reorganisations that amateur football had ever seen. This league, based around London and the Home Counties, contained no fewer than 33 divisions overall, and was believed to be the biggest adult football league in Europe. This meant for the first time in sixty-five years' teams from Sinjuns and Old Grammarians might be able to play each other at football on a regular basis which indeed they did, with Old Sinjuns finding themselves in Senior 5 South alongside Old Grammarians Reserves. Although in 2002/2003, there must have been considerable uncertainty if sides had been placed in the correct leagues on playing strength, Sinjuns 1st XI settled into Senior 5 South by finishing fourth in the table. By now the club only ran three Saturday XIs and a Veterans' side – a far cry from those heady days in the 1970s when no fewer than six Saturday XIs turned out. Next season as the divisions settled down the 1st XI had effectively been promoted and were now playing in Intermediate South (how does that work?). However, in the final year as an independent club in 2004/05, the 1st XI finished in a relegation place in Intermediate South, as did the Reserves in Division 3 South. Playing on Sunday, the Veterans won Division 2 of the Morden & District Vets League! Overall, however, the football club's final season as Sinjuns had ended on a disappointing note.

In the 2002/2003 season, after the reorganisation of the leagues, Old Grammarians 1st XI played in Senior Division Two. They also won, in the last year as an independent club, the AFA Veterans Cup in 2004/2005. When the merger came the AFA, it appears. decided to maintain the 1st XI status of the merged club in the same division that Old Grammarians had held previously.

A Sporting Merger

After several years of informal discussions and meetings the inevitable happened at the start of the 2005/2006 when Sinjuns and Old Grammarians merged both their cricket and football sections. When the merger of the sports clubs came it was probably the right time to do so. It was a logical and a pragmatic solution in the increasingly competitive environment of not only amateur club cricket but also football. To a degree this made perfect sense. Both played on the same Field and both could comfortably trace their origins back to the same source. This was not an exception - in fact it was fast becoming a trend. Clubs in similar positions such as Alleyns and Old Alleynians for instance had already taken the plunge and others were to follow. Additionally, there was pressure not only from the Trinity Fields Trust, as this would make it easier for an administrative approach in dealing with the cricket and football sections (two sections rather than four), but also apparently from the Amateur Football Combination who thought, and probably rightly so, that with Old Boy sides now being 'open' clubs, the need for 'Old' to be prefixed against any club's name was in most cases unnecessary and archaic. The other perhaps most important reason was that a larger club would be better able to withstand fluctuations in membership year on year. The new club was to be known as SinjunGrammarians for cricket purposes whilst the footballers apparently preferred Sinjuns Grammarians, both being a rather clumsy and uninspiring compromise on all fronts. It is perhaps ironic that with effectively no link to the defunct schools the crest was maintained as part of its livery and is still used today on cricket and football shirts. The ongoing continuation of the name may not last until the expiration of the current lease in 2067 in the event that the clubs do so, but it is notable that at present there is no rush to change.

On the football side, the merger in principle had been agreed in the spring of 2005. This was important so that the Amateur Football Alliance could be advised of the clubs' intentions. The other proviso in the first season, as agreed between the clubs, was that Old Grammarians would effectively be the 1st XI (on merit) and that the Sinjuns Clubroom bar would be used for after match hospitality. With Sinjuns' three Saturday league sides and Old Grammarians' six, this had, at the time, created potentially the largest football club in South London. However, this situation was short lived. Many Old Grammarian footballers found that the move to effectively close the upstairs bar in the Burntwood Lane pavilion during the football season was an anathema, considering the club were using the changing rooms below. Although the combined side secured promotion from Senior Two as Champions at the first attempt, other sides were less successful. Ultimately this led to an unsettling effect on the overall membership, and a negative impact on the merged club. Before the end of the first season Mike Naylor stood down as Chairman to be replaced by Laurie Dempsey although the latter was involved with Mick Lang with the football colts. The club entered two sides U13s and U14s in local competitions. The former side did exceptionally well. In the 2005/6, Surrey Cup they made it through to the quarter finals only to be beaten by a strong Tooting & Mitcham side. Also, the Veterans won the AFA Closed Veterans Cup. It was just that the senior sides in between came up short!

In the case of cricket at the time of the merger, Sinjuns (founded in 1919) had two Saturday sides playing league cricket and Old Grammarians (founded in 1926) had three. The amalgamation came at the start of the 2006 season. Both clubs ran a Sunday side. As Simon Baker the Old Grammarians skipper was a proven, effective and organised leader of the club's 1st XI it was decided that he would skipper the side in the Surrey County League whilst Alun Watkins was to run the 2nd XI which now played in Surrey Championship Division 3. Matt Mee, from Old Grammarians, would skipper the 3rd XI and Tahir Akhtar would skipper a new 4th XI in the separate Surrey Cricket League Division 5. The Secretary of the merged club for the first year was to be Sam Loxton from Sinjuns. His grandfather, also Sam Loxton, toured England with Bradman's 'Invincibles' in 1948, and became the only Australian cricket tourists to have gone through the entire summer unbeaten. Although theoretically the new club could have run five elevens on Saturday, one side was sensibly dropped on the basis that finding a third ground for the side would pose significant problems for the club and would logistically prove too much of a challenge. it was a decision that proved to be correct over time. Provided fixtures could be co-ordinated properly, the Field could accommodate all the home club fixtures there. On Sundays only one side would be run under the captaincy of Brian Williams, and the combined club remained members of the Old Boys Cricket League until that league disbanded in 2011.

In a summary as Old Grammarians put it after the merger, 'The newly formed club is now to all intents and purposes a private members' club'. The idea or pretence of being anything else with the schools closed was a commonsense and pragmatic approach going forward, and coping with new challenges together.

SinjunGrammarians Sports

The amalgamation of the two clubs had a negative impact on the football club as detailed above. As time went on, the number of sides being put out into the field every Saturday continued to fall as players drifted away. So also did the quality of the sides as the results testified. At the start of the 2019/20 season the football club accepted the inevitable and moved back into the upgraded and superior confines of the upstairs clubroom of the Burntwood Lane pavilion for after match hospitality. The cricket club had always used the Burntwood Lane pavilion, all of it, during the summer, since the merger. The Sinjuns clubroom is now effectively unused all season, but will remain in place until future plans are agreed. Although the social evenings of the 1960s and 1970s are no longer, the cricket club supports company private lettings during the summer by providing food and bar facilities.

In terms of SinjunGrammarians Cricket Club, the first year of its existence in 2006 under Simon Baker was a resounding success. Both the 1st XI and the 3rd XI were promoted as Champions of their respective divisions and entered the Surrey Championship for the first time. 2007 was a year of consolidation but the 2nd XI finished third in Division 3 (2nd XI) of the Surrey Championship which proved to be a high point of their success. The 4th XI after just one season in the Surrey Cricket League, joined the Surrey Championship in their inaugural year as part of the new 4th XI competition. In 2008 although the 1st XI won Division 5 of the Surrey Championship, the 2nd XI were relegated from Division 3. In 2009, the split format of overs and time matches reached the lower divisions of the 1st XI and 2nd XIs of the Surrey Championship with the 3rd XI still playing all time matches were promoted from Division 2 of the 3rd XI league, but the following year (2010) there was a reversal of fortunes. At the end of the 2011 season, the 1st XI were relegated to Division 5 of the Surrey Championship having won only one match all season and although the 2nd XI were again promoted to Division 3 of their competition, the club were set to enter a difficult period. This was highlighted in the following season when the 1st XI were only reprieved from relegation by a reorganisation of the league.

In 2012 with overs matches having been introduced a few seasons earlier, forbidding declarations, this meant that some results were a forgone conclusion before the side batting second had started their innings. The differences between the two forms of cricket are quite fundamental as overs matches are based effectively on restricting runs, whilst time matches rely more heavily on taking wickets to bowl sides out, to get a result. In a 2nd XI match against Warlingham CC at the Field on 11 August 2012, the 2nd XI scored 430-8 in their allotted 50 overs. This is the highest single innings score for a league match at the Field, although twenty runs short of the all-time record set 99 years previously in a friendly match by the Heathfield club. Needless to say, the club won the match by 274 runs. However, the following season (2013) made for some grim results as the 1st XIs reprieve in the Surrey Championship came to nothing when, again having won only one match again in the season, they were relegated back into the Surrey County League from where they had come at the end of the 2006 season. The 2nd XI also suffered relegation from Division 3 of their competition. The only scant consolation was that the 4th XI gained promotion to the Premier Division of that competition for the first time.

The next few seasons with the 1st XI back in the Surrey County League were to be a challenge. However, having at one stage flirted with a further relegation, in 2019, as Champions of the Surrey County League the previous season saw the 1st XI returned to Division 5 of the Surrey Championship. Although the 2019 season also saw the 2nd XI back in Division 5 of their competition (having been unluckily relegated at the end of the 2018 season) they had throughout the existence of the new club always competed in the Surrey Championship, and with the reorganisation of the 3rd XI and 4th XI leagues it was still an achievement that the club still ran, comfortably, four Saturday league sides, when other clubs had faltered or folded during a period which had seen enormous changes in amateur cricket. The club also enjoyed limited success in the 'Surrey Slam' a new evening competition started in 2018, with odd and unfathomable modifications to the Laws of Cricket and generally run on a T20 basis. It is a credit that under the Chairman, Asim Hafeez, the club has found some stability. Pakistani Test cricket legend, Sarfraz Nawaz, was guest of honour at the 2019 end of season prize-giving, and he actually turns up from time to time for nets to assist the younger players with their cricket!

On Sundays all-day cricket is long gone, and in recent years, with the Surrey All Stars programme, Sunday mornings at the Field are given over to the colts. The club still retains a Sunday side to a lesser or greater degree based on availability.

With the desire to play some competitive cricket but for reasons unfathomable to any impartial observer, the club was accepted into the National Village Cup competition in 2017 and played away at Rowledge and then the following season played Blackheath (the Surrey variety) at the Field. It would have been debatable by 1918, let alone by 2018 that Wandsworth was a village-or indeed that even the mythical village of SinjunGrammarians could have ever possibly existed! An early exit on both occasions saved both the club and the organisers any further embarrassment!

The Field was now looking its best on match days with new sightscreens and the introduction of roll on, roll off covers for both the main pitch (in 2014) provided by the Trinity Fields Trust, and the second pitch (in 2016) provided by the ECB in connection with their 'Get The Game On' programme nationwide. Even the outfield, which for so many years was something of a lottery to fielders was looking good. Additionally, the main cricket field is encircled with a boundary rope. Specifically, during the summer, the cricket club also have roll on roll off nets which give them an opportunity to use turf practice pitches on the square. Other improvements planned are the purchase of a bowling machine and an electronic scoreboard. All this adds to the perception that the Field is a serious cricket ground as W.G. Grace would vouch for.

Independent from SinjunGrammarians CC, continuing under the name of Old Grammarians, two or three friendly matches were played during each season from the date of the merger relying on a mixture of, by now, mature players from the defunct Battersea Grammar School, and their siblings. In 2018, to celebrate one hundred years since the purchase of the Field, a Sunday match was arranged against a SinjunGrammarians side resulting in a narrow if somewhat controversial defeat for the 'visitors'. In September 2019, a final Old Grammarians match was played at Warlingham. Although, it was yet another 'Heathfield club' moment, insofar that this really was the end, it was finished off in the bar afterwards as all good cricket matches should.

Regarding the football club, to say the least, the last few years have been challenging times. Indeed, from running nine senior sides in 2005/06 after the amalgamation, this shrunk alarmingly to just three sides by the 2018/19 season. Also, the club no longer runs Veterans' football. However, there has been a revival in the last couple of seasons. A 4th XI was reintroduced in the 2019/20 season and a 5th XI at the start of the 2020/21 season. Although the pandemic delayed the season just finished, owing to an internal reorganisation of the league, the 1st XI were promoted from the Intermediate South Division into Senior Division Two South. With a continuing resurgence in cases, a further nationwide lockdown was introduced in January 2021. This again put the soccer season on hold, and although another relaxation again permitted a resumption to amateur football at the end of March it took to early June to complete the league programme. The league is undecided on promotion and relegation issues in what has been a disrupted season, but with all the club's sides finishing in mid-table little change for the 2021/22 can be expected. The delay gave Sinjuns Grammarians FC the opportunity to play regular league matches in unfamiliar places. It is not every Saturday that you get the opportunity to play at a proper football stadium such as the Meadowbank Football Ground, home of Dorking Wanderers and the Surrey FA, but it was good to see that the authorities realised that many regular grounds would not be available and acted accordingly.

Revival of the Colts

Although the running of the Colts cricket section at both clubs had fallen away, there were various attempts to resurrect colts' cricket by way of coaching and participating in matches. In 2002 under the management of Kevin Molloy as many as forty young players attended Wednesday evening coaching and they reached the semi-finals of a competition in Beckenham beating some notable sides on the way. When the two cricket clubs merged in 2006, Laurie Dempsey carried on with colts' cricket and in that season the club entered a Sunday side in an Under 13 League. However, within a couple of years attempts to develop colts' cricket had stalled. The Trinity Fields Trust was anxious (as indeed was the club) to ensure that a colts' section was revived not least because it continues to be a central plank of the strategy in managing the Field and serving the local community, but also vital to the club's future existence. The problem was finding and maintaining a team of club volunteers to do so.

The most recent reincarnation occurred in 2013, and progress under the management of Dan Roberts in conjunction with Dave Petch has been rapid as it has been impressive. From an initial uptake of ten juniors, which grew to about forty-five in the second year, steady growth since has meant that the junior section consists today of around 200 juniors and whilst these are predominantly boys, girls also take part on an equal basis.

Although Wandsworth together with Lambeth has an extensive catchment area, the problem is trying to accommodate the needs and enthusiasm of younger players to play cricket compromised by the acute lack of local facilities. Colts cricket through the Surrey All Stars programme is far more coordinated and organised than it ever has been. Indeed, it could be argued that it has almost been too successful in its aims. All local cricket clubs are running at full capacity in this respect, and trying to balance these requirements and keep focussed on the overall strategy can be problematical in providing competitive cricket rather than just being a training platform or a glorified kindergarten for those of lesser ability, which would be counterproductive to the development of cricket. At SinjunGrammarians in Dan Roberts words, '*The approach to coaching is to make cricket as accessible and unintimidating as possible ensuring high participation and activity, so anyone can turn up with any knowledge of the game and be hitting a ball in no time. There is also a preference to encourage participation from state school pupils. The club operates a 'pay as you play' model to remove as many barriers as possible. The latest objective is to develop an academy which concentrates on the pathway from junior to adult cricket for eventually, both genders. This is particularly important for state school kids that do not have school cricket at the weekend and benefit from learning by playing rather than a formal cricket education. This involves an approach aligned with adult nets and the gradual introduction to adult league cricket. The timing of this depends on the ability of junior players as some are more adult-ready than others at a young age. It also has some welfare issues that we need to guarantee, but it is a real measure of success for us to involve both the juniors and adults in membership of a wider club. Our aim as well is to increase not just the number of juniors, but also to preserve diversity across the junior section and produce 'club cricketers for life' from as many backgrounds as possible, so that in the event that a junior in adult life moves to a new area, the first thing they do is to look up their local club and join them. That is success in our eyes. To develop a love for the game and the ability to contribute to a team no matter what talent the individual is blessed with.'*

The Field is particularly busy on Sunday mornings during the summer. The club have five qualified coaches amongst their membership, together with assistants who although not fully qualified are experienced and with DBS and first aid qualifications. It really goes without saying, but the existence of a colts' section is pivotal to the well-being and continuation of the cricket club in the years ahead. However, with such a demand, certainly in SinjunGrammarians case, the importance is not to lose sight of the overall object, which is also tailored to the needs of the club, and aims to help younger players to continue their interest in cricket into adulthood.

The Threat from Below

A more recent and new threat to the Field's survival surfaced as a result of the proposed route of the Crossrail 2 project from Wimbledon to Broxbourne under central London. When the original plans were issued, they showed the line of the tunnel passing directly under the Field with 'an Area of Surface Interest' located on the corner of Trinity Road and Burntwood Lane. In conjunction with a further 'Area of Surface Interest' located on Wandsworth Common close to the Skylark Café. The number of comments or more precisely objections, to the two areas accounted for 3,728 out of the total of 3,875 for the entire length of the project across London! Areas of Surface Interest are effectively ventilation shafts which also provide an escape route in the case of an emergency between stations and are required at approximately every mile along the route between stations which exceed this distance. Requiring a permanent structure in such a location with access to the surface, as would have been the case, would totally and permanently have compromised the playing area of the Field even after completion quite apart for the four years to construct the shaft and attendant infrastructure. In a report issued in March 2015 by the Department of Transport detailing the 'Government's Response to the Consultation on Upgrading the Safeguarding from Crossrail 2' it concluded that *'Given the impacts of the Area of Surface Interest on Trinity Fields and the availability of sporting facilities for children in the area, the Area of Surface Interest has been removed from this site'*. It seems that opposition both locally and by other organisations concerned with sport has paid off. For instance, Surrey County Cricket Club objected to the plans on the basis that *'...any loss of use of the playing fields as having a detrimental effect on the local community.'* That view was also echoed by other organisations such as the London Football Association, the London Playing Fields Foundation, Sport England and of course, the Trinity Fields Trust. The removal, also, of the Area of Surface Interest from Wandsworth Common has been accepted although the report did conclude that *'... the location will be determined after further consultation in the area'*. Apparently, owing to since discovered potential geological and engineering problems in the Tooting Broadway area, a revised realignment of the tunnels now takes the preferred route through Balham station. This realignment also indicates (on interactive maps) that the underground tunnel(s) will no longer pass underneath the Field irrespective which option is eventually chosen. The Area of Surface Interest formerly intended for the Field is now to be situated further down Burntwood Lane at a point where the two options intersect, in the event that the project is ever constructed.

Although the future of Crossrail 2 is still being debated and is likely to be unresolved until well after publication of this book, it is perhaps a demonstration of the determination of local residents and organisations to preserve the local environment which they cherish, and to uphold and preserve the principles established by the Wandsworth Common Act of 1871 and, from the Field's view, the 1852 covenant agreed between Earl Spencer and Henry McKellar.

Recent Arrangements

The period since 1997 has changed the method by which the Field is used and some of the sports upon it. As it is used principally by primary schools the wear and tear on the ground is perhaps less than it would be if used by senior school sides, and both football and cricket pitches can be temporarily adapted to suit the types of sport played in relation to the age and requirements of the participants. Five a side football is played, and girls' cricket has supplanted rounders as a summer sport. Also, as seen from recent aerial pictures, a junior rugby pitch occupies what used to be the small football pitch outside Sinjuns clubroom. From September 2021, the Field will be used primarily during the week by Finton House and Hornsby House Schools who supported the Trust's acquisition of a new fifty-year lease in 2017. Both schools are similar insofar that they are both administered by an educational trust and cater for boys and girls between the ages of 4-11. Finton House was founded in 1987 and moved to their current premises in Trinity Road in the following year. The school caters for around 340 pupils and in 2017 established an Old Fintonians Association for former pupils. Hornsby House are based out of Hearnville Road in Balham and with a capacity of 440 pupils, was established in 1988. Both schools run a house system to encourage competition. However, although inter school matches are played, these are centred more upon developing the pupils' aptitude to sport rather than being over-competitive. Annual sports days are also held and a grass running track appears on occasions around the outfield of the Field. This flexibility helps to cater for other outdoor activities beyond conventional summer and winter sports. There is also an annual firework display which helps funding, and the crowds of juniors and parents who watch this spectacle, rival those who used to watch leading rugby matches at the Field all those years ago! This is no mere display. In 2011 an account by a nearby resident, records that '...*the fireworks are so ostentatiously expensive they can be seen and heard by everyone living within a half a mile radius. Our neighbours actually throw an annual party and all their friends come around and see the whole thing for free beside a nice warm brazier in the comfort of their front garden.*' It is no secret that the organisation and enterprise that the private schools bring helps to contribute towards the aspirations of the Trinity Fields Trust towards making the Field a leading sports venue in an area where such facilities are altogether at a premium. The Field is also used by state schools and the Trust effectively subsidises the use of this time to fulfil their charitable obligations, as state funding for the using of outside school grounds by state schools for such purposes, is nominal.

Apart from SinjunGrammarians using the ground on Sundays principally for friendly cricket, between 2013 and until and including their sixtieth anniversary in 2015, the well-known wandering side Carnegie used the ground on occasional Sundays. For a time, they also used the Sunday morning colts' sessions to engage in coaching sessions. Another organisation, Clapham Chasers, the running and triathlon club, use the Burntwood Lane pavilion as a starting and finishing point of their runs on Monday and Wednesday evenings, organising a mixture of social and hill runs. With social runs of about five miles duration around the area mostly encompassing Wandsworth and Clapham

Commons, it is similar to the same excursions made from the *Surrey Tavern* that past sports clubs enjoyed over a hundred years ago.

Regarding soccer, apart from Sinjuns Grammarians FC on Saturdays, for some years Balham Blazers, a youth side, have used the Field on Sunday mornings during the winter. The Blazers were a feeder club for Balham FC and have now been amalgamated with their senior counterparts. Although they still hold local recruitment and trials within the Balham Area, the senior club as a result of their transfer to the Premier Division of the Southern Counties East League now groundshares with AFC Croydon Athletic at Mayfield Stadium in Thornton Heath which has a modest capacity of 1,500. The club were winners of the London Senior Cup in 2018.

The Trinity Fields Trust actively supports the charitable aims of its foundation. Various local charities are frequently using the facilities for their outdoor activities in particular through the summer months. Summer camps are planned during the school holidays to support local youngsters. In another demonstration of its commitment the Trinity Fields Trust is actively involved in supporting initiatives with the local community. As mentioned, other users include local state schools including, during the winter, an annual primary school football competition. Girls' football is also enjoyed. Coordinating bookings can be quite complicated in what is quite a busy schedule. The private schools use the ground for a variety of sports and also for junior cricket. On the commercial side, the Field is also heavily used during the long summer evenings for company cricket matches when not required by the beneficiaries. On Sunday afternoon the Field is used by the Trust for other various clubs when not required by SinjunGrammarians cricket, for a mixture of friendly and sometimes more competitive league cricket.

Looking Back & Moving Forward

To understand where we are today, we need to consider the past. The area of Wandsworth and Lambeth in which the Trinity Fields Trust dispenses its charitable aims might seem curious. After all, when the Field was purchased, both schools were situated in Battersea which at the time was run as an independent borough. However, with its purchase, and the Field in Wandsworth, when Battersea Grammar School moved away to Streatham in 1936, this hardly changed the position as the new school although no longer situated in Battersea was now situated in the metropolitan Borough of Wandsworth as was the Field. What changed the dynamics were the local government changes introduced with the creation of the, now defunct, Greater London Council in 1965. However, before we get there, we have to go back even further to 1888, when the London County Council was created. This was part of a nationwide reorganisation and effectively for the first time it officially recognised London as a separate identity. The other matter it addressed was to tidy up various anomalies. For instance, bizarrely, Penge had been hitherto administered as a detached area of the parish of Battersea, but in 1888 it was excluded from the London County Council area entirely and included within Surrey, eventually transferring to Kent in 1900. In 1965, with the creation of the Greater London Council, Penge took its place within the London Borough of Bromley. In 1888, the new Metropolitan Borough of Wandsworth was the largest of all the newly created metropolitan boroughs but did not include Battersea. When the Greater London Council was created, although the newly formed London Borough of Wandsworth acquired Battersea, Streatham was transferred to the London Borough of Lambeth, together, of course, with Battersea Grammar School which is situated in Abbotswood Road. As the School Trust administered both schools and with Battersea now subsumed within Wandsworth, the School Trust had little alternative but to expand their loyalties in 1965 to include Lambeth. The inclusion of both Wandsworth and Lambeth within the Sir

Walter St John's Educational Charity and, subsequently the Trinity Field Trust's objects, broadened the area so covered. The catchment area in terms of population is around 700,000 almost equally divided between the two boroughs, and with the Oval being the only recognised cricket ground in the London Borough of Lambeth the Field is uniquely placed as an Inner London ground for any aspiring young cricketers looking for a game in south west London.

With regard to players, there is little doubt that far more are locally based now than in the days of the Old Boys sides, who relied on their schools for membership. However, it is to the credit of the current football and cricket clubs, with varying degrees of success, to have been able to adapt to the reality of the situation and continue in partnership with the Trinity Fields Trust to support local sport.

In recent years, the Trinity Fields Trust has concentrated on improving the Field's facilities for its users. This has already been a costly exercise and more needs to be done in an ongoing process that will completely transform and reorganise the dynamics of the Field but still protect traditional summer and winter sports. These developments will ensure full compliance with current standards and requirements with particular reference to gender and people with disabilities.

The original lease granted by the Sir Walter St John's Educational Charity at the end of 1996 for twenty-five years was never going to be long enough to attract sufficient investment to fully upgrade the Field. In 2017, four years ahead of schedule, this was remedied and a new fifty years' lease was agreed between Trinity Field Trust and the Charity which gave sufficient time for the plans for the Field to materialise which it so desperately needs. This lease was supported by Finton House and Hornsby House, two of the original schools within the Consortium. These arrangements will also make a meaningful contribution to the financial activities of the Sir Walter St John's Educational Charity, as it continues to carry out its charitable aims within Wandsworth and Lambeth effectively independent of the Trinity Fields Trust. At an event held in the upstairs clubroom of the Burntwood Lane pavilion to celebrate the agreement of the new lease, it was clear there was more than enough support for the Trust to carry through appropriate changes through sport to aid the beneficiaries of the Trinity Fields Trust, and provide improved facilities for all concerned.

9

Through the Looking Glass (2020-

Tomorrow will be a good day.

Captain Sir Tom Moore (1920-2021)

2020 - Coronavirus comes to Town

I was getting towards the end of my research into this book when the country was hit by one of the gravest worldwide public health emergencies since the Spanish Flu pandemic of 1918/19. Fatalities from this pandemic a century ago were put at 228,000 in the United Kingdom alone on a population roughly two thirds of the size it is today. Fortunately, the Spanish Flu pandemic eventually subsided of its own accord. Sadly, only time will tell if the casualties of COVID-19 will surpass the epidemic of a century ago, but globally the implications and ramifications of the virus will continue for some time yet, like an unwanted guest at the 'table' of life, long after this book is published. No one is exempt.

The 2019/2020 football season had been exceptionally wet and many sides were behind with their fixtures. However, the pandemic was to truncate the season less than two months after the first outbreak had been diagnosed.

'Lockdown' in the United Kingdom was effectively declared on 20 March 2020, when all pubs, clubs, restaurants, gyms, libraries and schools were forced to close by midnight, and any non- essential travelling was prohibited. Full lockdown was implemented from 23 March. The result was that for the first time in its history the Field was unable to stage sport. In effect the country was put on a wartime footing until the pandemic had passed. 20 March also coincided with Dame Vera Lynn's 103rd birthday, and older readers of this book will remember her wartime song, *We'll meet Again*. However, according to social distancing maybe, but not closer than two metres apart! As the song continues *...some sunny day'*; hopefully that will be true in the future, for there is nothing more enjoyable than playing cricket on a field somewhere in pleasant weather during those long summer months without having to worry whether your fellow players are transmitting something you do not want.

With the virus spreading like wildfire, normal life turned into the surreal. 'Social Distancing' and 'Self-Isolation' became the new terms to grapple with and gatherings of more than three were banned. As a cartoon in the *Sunday Telegraph* put it: *We shall keep off the beaches, We shall vacate the landing grounds, We shall be absent in the fields, And in the streets, We shall steer well clear, Of the hills.* Perhaps at the time cricket grounds should have also been included in the cartoon, although it was unclear just what the implications would be for recreational sport. In a situation which was unprecedented in peacetime, and in a bid to slow the spread of the virus, emergency legislation was introduced. However, the fine weather tested people's patience. On 23 May, police were brought in to disperse a large number of picnickers and sunbathers on Wandsworth Common next to Bellevue Road estimated to be well over a thousand. It was just a demonstration that the Common has retained its popularity with the masses originally noted almost a hundred and fifty years previously – even if social distancing regulations were being flouted as a result. As the lockdown gradually eased, perhaps perversely, face coverings became mandatory on public transport and then in shops. They almost became a fashion accessory!

Initially cricket clubs hoped that the excitement generated by England's World Cup victory in 2019 would lead to a 'spike' of interest in the game at club level, but the only 'spike' seemed to be caused by the virus. The ramifications for club cricket would be potentially devastating, particularly for a season which is little more than four months long anyway. Even the Spanish Flu epidemic, mentioned earlier, although disrupting club cricket, did not lead effectively to a ban on recreational sport. However, just to rub salt into the wound, immediately after the lockdown commenced the weather dramatically improved! April and May turned out to be warm and dry and both months together were- in London at least- the sunniest on record, which would have been ideal for early season cricket matches which can be notorious for the uncertain weather. Ironically, almost farcically, one to one net practice was allowed by the government from the end of May – but no organised matches! A further gradual relaxation was introduced to permit socially distancing groups of six training to enjoy some limited practice. The Field reopened but only to cater for the limited amount of exercise permitted as regulations dictated.

During June various sports were allowed out of lockdown. However, for the first time in history, a cricket ball was, according to the government, rather erroneously, labelled as 'a vector for the disease' (as distinct from a basketball or tennis ball) and the idea that a normal maximum of fifteen people on a cricket field at any one time was just too dangerous to contemplate, rang hollow considering the massive crowds that invaded resorts such as Bournemouth to take the opportunity of fine and warm weather. As a result, and in the view of many, this unnecessarily delayed the commencement to a season which had been blighted from the start. Additionally, although it is not thought that a cricket match has been directly responsible for spreading the virus at all, 'sanitisation breaks' were introduced after every six overs or twenty minutes (the latter requirement was relaxed for the 2021 season) whatever came the sooner.

Eventually 'adapted' (or 'socially distanced') cricket was allowed to proceed on 11 July 2020. The Field was no exception. A whole new batch of terminology entered cricket lore, complete with sanitisation breaks, mentioned above, and other such oddities as 'batting lines' (which were dropped for the 2021 season) to keep social distancing, on the field of play. There were challenges as well for every club to ensure that the protocols required for social distancing were maintained and local lockdowns threatened to disrupt the hard won right to stage cricket matches at all. Players and umpires needed to come ready changed as changing rooms were effectively shut save for welfare purposes–and there were no teas! An umpire was spotted at the Field wearing a face covering, because although it seemed the worst of the virus had passed, it was a stark reminder of the risks still present by transmission. However, perhaps appropriately, after this enforced period of inaction, the first side to visit the Field to play SinjunGrammarians in a hastily arranged friendly on 11 July was Spencer CC who had, approximately, 130 years previously, played Heathfield, at a time when both clubs would have still been finding their feet in club cricket.

In an echo of the 1914 cricket ball strike the major suppliers had little alternative but to close their factories until the start of August as many of their staff were furloughed. Some council and private grounds were closed altogether, although many, belatedly, did reopen. Regarding any competitive cricket in 2020, this commenced on 25 July when the Surrey Championship combined with the Surrey County League, devised a programme of Group matches of 40 overs per side running until 5 September. Although no promotion or relegation was involved the programme of over 950 matches cobbled together at the last moment when cricket was finally allowed to start, was by far the largest programme attempted anywhere in the country. Typically, in the first round of matches almost all were lost owing to the poor weather! However, as the weather relented, and using this period to their advantage, SinjunGrammarians entered all four sides into the Competition and indeed, overall, showed an improvement on their expected final placings based on the 2019 season's results. Hammad Amir Malik scored back-to-back centuries against Kingstonian at the Field and away at Long Ditton and the club finished runners up in their group. Having moved on his talents will be missed in 2021. Given that this was effectively a Holiday Competition, as foreign holidays were out of the question, this event was a better success than anyone could have envisaged. SinjunGrammarians also competed again in the Surrey Slam competition which was crammed into the later part of the season and again showing an improvement winning their "mini" league containing Spencer, Alleyns and Streatham & Marlborough, before a somewhat disappointing exit in the last sixteen on a dark September evening. Colts' cricket resumed and carried on through August given that many children would be staying at home with their parents. Friendly matches at senior level carried on deep into September. A further lockdown was introduced in November 2020. It goes without saying that the annual firework display at the Field, which attracts local interest and strong support from the schools, was also a casualty.

With the cessation of cricket as a main sport in many state schools, more responsibility has been placed on clubs to take up the challenge and help preserve cricket for future generations. It is hoped that the success of the colts' section will help in the overall development of the club in the future. Although in 2020 the pandemic scuppered plans to run competitive sides within the overall colts' programme, the 2021 season has exceeded expectations with the U12 side running away with the title at the top of their division. The U13 side although eliminated early from the Cup competition, play evening friendly matches and the hope is to extend these fixtures in the coming seasons to cater for the needs of an expanding colts section. These fixtures with other like-minded clubs have added a new direction and purpose given that before the colts had previously only organised matches between themselves. Hopefully eventually, this will give all age groups from U8 to U17 the opportunity to play some form of organised cricket on a regional basis to supplement the training and coaching given.

Apart from Saturday league cricket, the club continues to run a mixture of friendly and competitive matches on Sunday afternoons to give an opportunity to those who might not be able to play on Saturdays and also to perhaps a few aspiring colts to give them an idea of competitive adult cricket. However, challenging times lay ahead, and it will not be until the 2022 season when the full impact of the pandemic will become apparent and cricket returns, hopefully, to normal, to assess the full impact of two cricket seasons living under the shadow of COVID 19. Once again, with foreign holidays to most parts of the world being discouraged, the usual exodus of players on holiday in July is not likely to happen during the 2021 season.

Another area of discussion was instigated by the Sussex League when it revealed that their clubs had voted to abolish cricket teas! The subject was debated in the press and on the satirical programme *Have I Got News For You.* An article in *The Times* reminded the readers that in Hugh de Selincourt's 1924 novel (who was born in Wandsworth Lodge as we know) he described the tea interval and the sundry sandwiches, cakes and, of course tea, as the outstanding feature of the village game. It might be since then that the urbanisation of Britain has perhaps diminished the number of village clubs, but not the desire to drop what most people regard as something traditional and quintessentially British with a reminder that the tea interval has been around almost as long as the game of cricket itself. The Sussex League subsequently retreated from their position, but it is still proof that unexpected events can potentially have unexpected consequences. For the 2021 season the Surrey Championship quietly abandoned teas for the whole season, giving clubs the option to provide them when restrictions eased. Although some clubs are doing their best to provide lunches and teas where possible, the situation remains patchy particularly at the lower levels of the league and particularly on third grounds where only limited facilities can be provided.

At the time of writing, whilst it is thought that the country is in the grip of a third wave, the only hope is that the vaccination programme will outpace the virus and its variants to soften any impact and eventually bring a better future. The speed at which vaccines to combat the virus have been developed as the only realistic way to protect populations against the threat of even more widespread infection, effectively makes this by far the largest clinical trial the world has ever seen. The signs are encouraging but unlike the Spanish Flu epidemic a century ago, it appears that the virus is here to stay with the hope that future outbreaks and variants can be managed and contained.

Plans for the Future

The renewal of the lease in 2017, gave the Trinity Fields Trust some certainty and confidence to plan ahead for a total upgrade and modernisation of the Field to more easily cater for sport across the genders. There had been a possibility that the Beechcroft Road cricket square nearest to the Burntwood Lane pavilion might be lost in favour of an artificial and floodlit playing surface more suited to football. The Trust have decided not to pursue this option, partly owing to opposition from the local community, but also because natural turf offers more flexibility for the provision of other sports and provides sufficient revenue to enable the Trust to fulfil its charitable aims. Additionally, the artificial surface of the static cricket nets has been removed to be replaced by mobile net facilities using prepared strips on the cricket squares instead.

Going forward, the current thinking, apparently, is for the facilities at the Trinity Road end of the Field to be totally rebuilt to comply with current ECB requirements on approximately the same footprint as existed before, together with an office facility for the Trust to aid with administration. This will totally replace the assorted miscellaneous collection of ageing or temporary buildings at that end of the Field including those which survived the fire of 1994. Once completed, at the other end of the Field, the Burntwood Lane pavilion, now ninety years old and somewhat 'user unfriendly' when it comes to accessibility, may possibly be demolished in favour of a small artificial surface for sports such as netball or tennis, whilst retaining the two cricket squares and outfields in approximately the same areas as present. Additionally, these plans will also cater for the reorganisation of other facilities in the longer term, to fully unlock the potential of the whole ground. Also, some resetting of existing facilities will occur, with the cross pitch, perhaps, becoming the main football pitch, in preference to the current pitch that runs parallel with Burntwood Lane. The reorganisation of the Field together with a new facility under one roof would sweep away the last vestiges, save the Cresswell stone, of the division of the ground almost a century ago. Assuming the demolition of the Burntwood Lane pavilion, at some stage, the Field will then be left with one address rather than two!

A major setback to the overall plans are the extensive works being currently undertaken to level and repair the areas most damaged by poor drainage, and to a lesser extent, essential maintenance of the irrigation systems. The interface between the Field and the fence with the Brodrick Road gardens which causes major waterlogging, is one of the major concerns as is the previous overuse of the Field. A report revealed that test pits showed in some areas building rubble underneath perhaps from 'bombed out buildings post war' and the possibility is that some undulations are from settling of landfill from such material such as rotted down wood. So just what was used to level the Field after the barrage balloon site was removed at the end of the Second World War? Works to improve matters were attempted at the start of 2020, but, unfortunately, if anything, this made things worse, and by autumn the Field was inundated. The drainage of the Field has been an intermittent problem for over a century since the rugby years and widespread drainage works were carried out in 1962 and 2000. The installation of secondary drainage and the use of sand banding and seeding during the 2021 summer should mitigate this, but the Field faces significant disruption for the first time in almost sixty years until the problem has been fully resolved. All kinds of machinery will appear on the outfield. It is hoped that the works will be completed by the start of September 2021. However, in order to give time for the works to settle, restrictions are likely to be kept in place throughout the winter to enable the Field to fully recover. For SinjunGrammarians cricket club this means that the Beechcroft Road square will be out of operation all season and the main Trinity Road square from July onwards. It is no exaggeration to compare the area under repair to the "quagmires" of old, particularly after rain! Visits are being made to unfamiliar grounds such as the Kings House School Sports Ground in Chiswick, St James's School in Ashford and St Georges College in Weybridge to play 'home' league matches in order to meet the club's obligations. For a club that is used to playing on the same home ground year on year this is unsettling, and judging by current results, a period of rebuilding will be necessary once matters return to normal. Additionally, from the Trust's perspective, it is more likely that winter use will need to be carefully monitored in the future. The repairs will also have serious implications for Sinjuns Grammarians FC as having been unable to use the Field to any degree during the 2020/21 season, the prospects are no brighter for the forthcoming 2021/22 season in having to play most if not all of their matches away from home. During the works, entry to the Field will be restricted and the infrequently used pedestrian gate in Burntwood Lane close to the crossroads with Trinity Road, apparently called the 'Marmalade Bear Gate' after the nursery that uses it, will be the main point of entry at that end of the Field. The positioning of this gate is interesting. It is possible, in times gone by, that this might have been the access point to the two tennis courts that previously occupied that area of the Field in the 1920s and 1930s. Another pedestrian gate in Burntwood Lane near to the Cresswell stone will remain closed and has not been used for some time.

There is considerable pressure on existing resources. Remarkably, with the glorious exception of the Oval, the home of Surrey cricket, the adjoining London Borough of Lambeth does not have a single club cricket ground within its boundaries. Whilst Wandsworth is somewhat better off, the combined catchment area with Lambeth is around 700,000. There is little doubt that demand will be unrelenting, and the Field can only provide a fraction of the requirement. What the remedy might be is not a subject for this book, nor is the shape of recreational sport and amateur cricket when the current lease expires in 2067.

Anyone familiar with the present ground, in several years' time will not recognise the new facilities, and perhaps the Field in general. However, it can be taken that what replaces the existing will be much more in keeping and appropriate for the current crop of young amateur sportsmen and sportswomen using the ground in the future. There will also be a need and a continued emphasis on providing sport for juniors and the Field will also play its part in their development. There will be challenges ahead, particularly if the drainage continues to be an issue. Hopefully, with improvements to the drainage and the construction of new facilities to look forward to, in the whole scheme of things, it can truly be said that at least 'Tomorrow will be a good day'!

-10-

Extras

Groundsman

One important person not included in this book so far is the groundsman at the Field without whose efforts would have detracted from the experience of using it. When the Heathfield Cricket Club first rented the Field in 1883, it had already been a playing field for six years. Unfortunately, the identity of any groundsman is unknown, although with Clapham Rovers being tenants and a leading amateur club in those days, coupled with being a ground very much in demand, it is likely that there was a groundsman to keep it in order even if only in a rudimentary sense. However, if a report from the Heathfield Cricket Club from 1900 is to be believed, when E. Martin parted company with them it was noted that he had been at the Field for upwards of fifteen years. Whether Martin had formally applied for the post back in 1891 on the basis that he was already working there is not known, but in March of that year, the London County Council, who were owners of the Field by then, had advertised for a groundsman *'for three to four months for a cricket club near Wandsworth Common'*. His replacement was E. Collett who was praised for his pitch when W.G. Grace famously made a century at the Field in 1902. Collett a report said *'comes from the Parks with the highest of credentials'*, which, given the Parks was and still is the home of Oxford University cricket is almost as good as it gets regarding already having first-class experience in preparing pitches. His appointment coincided with the complete upgrade of the Field to include lawn tennis and bowls, and the arrival of the Harlequins in September 1901. Indeed, the Field needed a first-class groundsman to be in attendance all year long given the high standard of amateur sport being played there. There was no doubt, owing to the agreement that the Heathfield Cricket Club had made, that he would have been directly paid by them. Although Collett was only at the Field for four years, it is evident from reports and scores that the pitch was viewed in the highest regard, and that at a time when pitches generally went uncovered come rain or shine, preparation was key. The press also viewed the general changes to the Field favourably. In other words, Collett was brought in to do a job and by all accounts was successful.

From 1904, it is likely that another Martin was involved as groundsman at the Field for the next seven years. It was quite possible that perhaps he was a son or relation of E. Martin, but in reality, we really do not know. The minute books suggest that F. Martin could have been involved from 1904 until 1910, and then again from 1916. What we do know is that from 1916 until 1918 his daughter, Matilda, was employed as an assistant groundsman and after the Great War his son may also have assisted with the ground. There is a possibility that after the Heathfield club left the Field in 1924, F. Martin was retained by Sir Walter St John's School to look after their section of the Field. An Old Sinjun writing about his experiences from the 1930s remembers, *'I never pass the Field, or I suppose to think of it, without remembering Toothy Martin, the groundsman. Toothy, so called because of a sad deficiency of what are colloquially called 'choppers' was rather a fearsome character, gangling and thin, with a petulant, weather-beaten face and a distrust of all small boys- indeed a state of hostility usually reigned in the pavilion when the lower school were about'* It is likely that the pavilion referred to was actually the Sinjuns changing rooms that were destroyed in the 1994 fire. With the introduction of the hedge in 1925, 'Mr Heather' would possibly have been in charge of the Battersea Grammar School's section of the Field as his name is occasionally mentioned in connection with the preparation of pitches. When the hedge was removed around 1949, the need for two permanent groundsmen became unnecessary, but like today, others were employed to assist. The appointment of a groundsman from 1951, given the schools were now in state control, was probably transferred from the Schools to the Council.

Moving on to the 1950s, and Mr Lewis was the groundsman. Some of the older members still remember his contribution with affection and credit him with the improvement of the square and pitches after the War years. He apparently, literally, got down on his hands and knees from time to time to remove weeds from the square. He only left when he was offered a house to go with the job at what was then called the Private Banks Ground at Catford Bridge (now owned by St Dunstan's College). Perhaps his attention to detail was rewarded, because in 1959 that ground staged a Second Eleven Match between Kent and Worcestershire.

During the 1960s, Tom White was now groundsman. By this time the London County Council were responsible for the maintenance of the ground until ILEA assumed their responsibilities in 1967. Apparently, Tom's reason for going was also 'a house' and for his remaining years until his retirement, he was groundsman at what is known today as the Thomas Wall Park at Rosehill in Sutton. A small memorial to Tom was erected in his honour and appreciation of the work he did on the ground, containing a flower bed, but sadly the memorial no longer exists today.

Various other groundsmen came and went. Mick Meech was groundsman twice (1972-74 & 2005-12) and during his first time at the Field, played cricket with Old Sinjuns there. Steve Irons was the last of the Inner London Education Authority's (ILEA) appointed groundsmen. However, the winding up of ILEA in 1990 had implications, and another organisation, the London Residual Body was created in its stead to dispose of its assets on their behalf. With both the schools already closed and the Field not used to its full capacity it was no surprise that Wandsworth Council outsourced these services to independent contractors, along with other grounds under their control. Rather than being involved in these new arrangements, Steve Irons sensibly accepted a position as groundsman at Spencer Cricket Club where he still works today.

The next couple of years were a struggle as it soon become clear that the service being provided by the independent contractor, did not meet with the cricket clubs' requirements or expectations as explained earlier in this book. By 1997, however, the maintenance of the Field fully rested with the Trinity Fields Trust.

In more recent times, Andrew Crawford was Grounds Manager for a couple of years and was credited with improving both the outfield and the pitches and the introduction of an automatic weather station, which was attached to the roof of the Sinjuns Clubroom to monitor conditions at the Field when he was not present at weekends. He played a good standard of cricket, and in his time was a groundsman at Oxford University Sports Department, Radley College and Bloxham School. At the time of his sudden death in 2017, aged just 40, he was heavily involved in Oxfordshire cricket, and in particular with Stonesfield Cricket Club as their Chairman, groundsman, player and youth cricket coach. He also had connections with Oxford United Football Club. James Watson represented the Trust at his funeral at Bladon Parish Church.

Jason Gill followed Andrew as groundsman in 2014 and applied his golf club knowledge to the outfield. In a sense the outfield became more like a huge golf green, but the players appreciated the evenness and overall appearance achieved. In 2019, he took up a post at Claremont Fan School at Esher. Tony Reely replaced him and continued to improve the pitches, but tried a radical approach towards solving the drainage problems by ripping up large areas of the outfield. Owing to health reasons and travelling from North London, he moved on in February 2021.

As a footnote, in 1988, a young Australian, Tony Hemming played with Old Sinjuns for a season whilst he was temporarily on the ground staff at the Oval to learn more about pitch preparation in English conditions. Apparently, he was trusted in preparing the last county pitch of that season for Surrey CCC. He was an assistant groundsman at the MCG (Melbourne Cricket Ground) where he subsequently became head groundsman. A chance meeting with Rodney Marsh, however, whilst he was playing cricket socially with Sharjah CC in the UAE, changed the direction of his career, and led to a further challenge, and his involvement from 2007 at The Dubai Sports City complex with a brief to take over turf management across all sports. Working in such an extreme climate must have been challenging indeed, but it was evidently a success as Pakistan made it their home ground for the playing of Test matches after the terrorist attack on the Sri Lankan Test team in 2009. By any definition, Tony is now a world class groundsman. In 2017 he returned to Australia and is currently Arena Manager at the OPTUS Stadium in Perth, where Australia plays a Test match during their summer and various One Day and T20 internationals. With a 65,000 capacity it is also used for the Australian Big Bash competition.

In April 2021, the Trinity Fields Trust appointed Nurette Stanford as its first General Manager who will be involved in the administration of the Field and the coordination of its users and beneficiaries. Her role will also include raising the profile of the Field and working in conjunction with the ground staff to ensure that the quality of the surfaces are maintained to the highest standards.

Meteorological Events

Although the abandonment of the final match played at the Field by London Welsh RFC in 1914 are well documented elsewhere, the earliest recorded meteorological event at the Field occurred in the Clapham Rovers rugby match with Blackheath on 17 December 1881 when it was noted that as there was such a heavy gale that it was almost impossible to keep the goalposts upright, and both sides resolved to settle the result by tries only. It must have been difficult to play in such conditions because Blackheath won the match by scoring the only try.

In 1976 the protracted drought combined with a hot summer accounted for three trees on the bank adjacent to the bus stop in Trinity Road. Apart from an attempt to plant low level bushes, the trees were eventually replaced and today form an acceptable backdrop to that area. The outfield irrigation system now ensures that the yellowing of the outfield in dry and hot summers is invariably a thing of the past.

Playing cricket in the snow is unusual but on one occasion (probably on 27 April 1985) it actually coincided with the opening cricket match at the Field in a match involving Old Sinjuns and Carshalton. Playing for the opposition on that day, Richard Thompson, now Chairman of Surrey County Cricket Club, recalls that it 'was the coldest day on which I ever played cricket'. Whilst the cricketers persevered, the footballers came back from playing their final match of the season and sensibly preferred to watch the cricket from the bar! Higher up on the North Downs (at Banstead CC for instance) there was a real covering of snow and play had to be abandoned. The latest report (in terms of the time of year) of the 'white stuff' falling at the Field, accompanied a general report in the *South London Press* when on 12 May 1923 *'Blizzards of snow and hail followed by drenching rain stopped practically every cricket match'*.

The infamous hurricane of October 1987 accounted for three mature close to the crossroads by the *Surrey Tavern*. One tree toppled over and crashed through the boundary fence blocking off Trinity Road completely and even putting the *Surrey Tavern* opposite in peril. It took most of the following day to remove all the debris from Trinity Road and a little longer to repair and secure the wire mesh fence. One advantage was that there was no need to get permission to cut back the lower branches of the trees from the council which had been partially obstructing the proper taking of corners on the adjacent soccer pitch as the hurricane had done its work for them!

There have been far more incidents of flood rather than drought over the years. On some occasions great sheets of water have covered the Field. With the prevailing wind from the south-west, invariably if Wimbledon disappears behind a cloud there is rain on the way- or is there? Umpiring at the ground one day a storm moving up the Wandle valley towards the Field, decided it would spare us. Heavy rain could actually be observed falling beyond the ground in Burntwood Lane. Play was not interrupted but both Battersea Ironsides and Spencer endured long delays as a result. With any rain supposedly there has to be a demarcation between areas of wet and dry, and the Field, fortunately, was on the dry side of the line on that particular day,

The winter months, of course, see more extreme weather. The Field did not avoid the cold and icy weather of the infamous 1962/63 winter mentioned elsewhere in this book. On one occasion winter came early, and speaking from personal experience, playing football under a covering of snow at the Field on the last Saturday of November in the 1970s, springs to mind.

Umpires & Scorers

Unlike football, where all referees at 1st XI standard are independently appointed, both clubs, as the Heathfield club did as well, had to rely on club appointments at cricket over the years whether it be retired players or an enthusiastic non-player to carry out umpiring duties. At Old Sinjuns this task was carried out from the club's earliest days by Alf Deering until his death in 1947. Claude Holt, a former club player, continued in this role after the War. Alec McMath umpired during the 1960s and 1970s umpiring the club's first league match in 1972 away to Thames Ditton. Graham Jackson was also an enthusiastic umpire at the Field before umpiring appointments took him elsewhere. Those early days saw the continuation of umpires coats, often supplied by the club which unfortunately saw them get increasingly dirtier and in a state of disrepair as the season continued!

One of the umpiring characters during the late 1970s and early 1980s was Henry Webb whose son Richard Webb attended the school. Henry, not that you would think it, was the brother of Rita Webb the overweight actress who appeared in many bawdy films and television series such as *Up the Chastity Belt*, *Up Pompey* and *The Best of Benny Hill*. He enjoyed umpiring and was very knowledgeable when it came to cricket; you could certainly have some profound discussions with him about famous cricketers. He lost an arm during the Second World War and was also an actor himself, albeit predominantly in minor roles. He complained that opportunities for one armed actors were limited and once said that he was only considered useful in war films as an extra for scrambling out of shell craters immediately after an explosion to imply to the watching audience that the soldier shown on film had just lost an arm as the result of the incident! No one would ever consider him as being biased as you were just as likely to get a poor decision out of Henry as were the opposition players. One incident, however, sticks in the mind, as there was a confident appeal from behind the stumps for an LBW. Henry gave the batsman out but it was clear to most of the players that the ball had first hit the batsman's bat on its way to the pad. Viv Landon, always the gentleman and captain on that day at Old Sinjuns, given that the batsman was now, reluctantly, walking back towards the pavilion, had a quiet word with Henry, 'Can we bring the batsman back please, because we think he actually hit it'. Henry agreed and the batsman was recalled. A couple of overs later and there was another appeal for LBW against the same batsman. 'You're out this time' Henry declared as he raised his finger! Ill health restricted his appearances in later years before he emigrated to Tasmania with his wife to be close to his son Richard who had emigrated there previously. Henry died there in 1990 at the age of 84. It is not recorded if he ever umpired in Tasmania!

Old Grammarians umpires in the 1960s included Bert Stanley, Ken Dobson, Syd Turner and Freddie Horwood. All were mentioned in connection with their help in umpiring over many years. Unfortunately, in 1965 Bert Stanley received a blow from a cricket ball which fractured his leg and forced his retirement after almost twenty years of umpiring. From about this period firstly Stan Bland (1960s and 1970s) and then Ray Legg umpired many matches, the latter almost until his death in 2001. Dave Petch has been a willing umpire not only with Old Grammarians but also with the merged club since 2006. Also, since the merger, Barrington Hall (not to be confused with a National Trust property somewhere in England!) and 'Sunny' McGill have also stood with the club on various occasions. Today, shorter umpires' jackets are preferred and, many officials, if not fully qualified do their best to look the part.

Scorers were unfortunately harder to find, although the Heathfield club had a scorer in the latter part of their existence. Both clubs were not short of ideas as to how to obtain one. In 1965 at the age of 13, Don Latuske affectionately remembers his time as a scorer. He was asked at school by Ken Dobson who umpired with Old Grammarians, about scoring with the club's 1stXI. He was uncertain what to wear on the first occasion but arrived by bus at the Sinjuns end before walking the length of the ground towards the pavilion in his uniform complete with school cap! The first person he met was Derek Lawrence whose reaction set the scene for the rest of his education. Following that first match he was allowed to drink some shandy which soon turned into beer following many jug top-ups. On one occasion, delivered safely back at home in a slightly befuddled state, he virtually fell inside the house when his mother opened the door. She complained to him saying she would talk to Ken about those people who had allowed him to get into such a state, not realising that Ken had been at the forefront of it all! In later years Jenny Darsley and Kathy Clarke at Old Grammarians scored for the club for many years before moving away to Dorset and Sussex respectively. At Old Sinjuns, Eileen, Henry Campbell's girlfriend used to keep an immaculate scorebook for the 1st XI, and the during the 1990s Adrian Fuller (nicknamed 'Statto') did the same. Adrian's job as an actuary took him away from London, but he still scores cricket matches with Clifton Alliance Cricket Club, a side that plays in the Yorkshire Premier League North and he keeps in touch with his London friends. However nowadays technology with the introduction of the Duckworth Lewis system to determine the result of rain affected matches in league cricket has meant that an application can be used for such purposes and live scoring is possible on the 'play-cricket' website. The standard scorer's accessories include a laptop backpack! The old traditional method of scoring, whilst used less frequently, still has its uses, particularly in the event of a failure of the technology. It is safer for both systems to be used side by side in the event, of course, that both clubs have a scorer.

Lunches & Teas

Cricket has uniquely been associated with its teas, usually between innings. No other sport has such an event so woven into the fabric of the game. When all-day matches were played this required quite a degree of organisation – so much so, that it was almost a requirement at one stage for the skippers appointed to have a strategy over providing both lunches and teas when required, let alone being involved in running a match. At one stage up until the early 1950s teas were organised at the Sinjuns end of the ground for both clubs within the communal area between both sets of changing rooms. Subsequently, with the Burntwood Lane pavilion upgraded this was no longer necessary. Tea at the Sinjuns end of the ground was increasingly organised in Sinjuns clubroom. With the destruction of the changing rooms at the Trinity Road end, and subsequent to the merger, teas are now taken by all sides in the Burntwood Lane pavilion or 'al fresco' depending on the weather, on the covered hardstanding immediately outside the changing rooms.

Lunches actually require far more organisation. All day matches are very much on the decline and can no longer be staged at the Field on Sundays during the first part of the season owing to Colts cricket in the morning. Most clubs quite sensibly arrange for salads or sandwiches to keep any hot food to a minimum. However, from a personal perspective, perhaps, one of the best lunches ever experienced as an umpire was the '24 Hour Slow-Cooked Beef' served up at the Hurlingham Club restaurant, which although apparently discontinued, almost beats the cricket as the main event of the day.

Big Hits

In cricket, there has always been something of a romance about 'Big Hits'- indeed, some are intertwined in cricket folklore, such as a ball that disappeared over the pavilion at Lord's. Ian Botham had a reputation for hitting balls a long way and in more recent times so does Ben Stokes. Whether the latest bats and the advances in technology make that easier or not is, of course, debatable.

Hits out of the ground have been included in match reports from time to time from well over a century ago, and the Field is no exception, witnessed by the Heathfield club appointing a person to go and retrieve balls hit into the Brodrick Road gardens from time to time. Some hits have landed clubs up in court either to retrieve a ball, as we have seen earlier in this book, or owing to a disgruntled neighbour.

The Field contains two squares. The outfield and square nearest to the Burntwood Lane pavilion, now known as the Beechcroft Road cricket square, originally used solely by Old Grammarians, is by far the smaller. Indeed, special local regulations were drafted during the 1980s to inform visiting sides, should there be any doubt. *'A four shall be scored when the ball crosses the boundary square of the wicket or when it clears the ground having been hit straight. The boundary for a straight hit four will be the fence, except where the run up to the jumping pit takes precedence. In the above instance a six will still have to clear the ground, this means that there will be a dead ball area between the run up and the fence'.* Confused? It is easy to see why these instructions were effectively ignored. The boundary fence is now taller on the road side with Burntwood Lane, so hits out of the confines of the ground are less common in that direction, but unlike then the boundary runs inside the fence and is not the fence itself. When batting from the road end it is also not unusual to hit a ball directly into one of the Brodrick Road gardens.

The playing area of the main square at the Trinity Road end is used for all senior league matches on Saturdays and is much larger. Brian Dale, once removed a few slates from the now demolished Sinjuns changing rooms, and the ball plunged through the roof never to be seen again. Henry Campbell apparently struck a ball across Trinity Road which entered an open window on one of the properties above the shops disturbing one of the occupants who was just settling down to watch television. However, hits out of the ground into Burntwood Lane and beyond are less common, although, famously, schoolboy Bob Doe once cleared the fence in this area. It is not always a recognised batsman that might hit a ball a long way. Although described as a tail ender during his first-class career, Hugh Wilson playing for the Surrey Club & Ground (probably in 1978) hit a ball directly onto Wandsworth Common beyond-an estimated carry in excess of 100 yards. Perhaps the most remarkable big hit happened off the very first ball of a match, when 'Dicky' Butler, never a batsman to hang around, clouted a ball over the now demolished changing rooms, hitting the "A" in "Daren's Bread" (on the former word apparently!) on the baker's wall some distance behind. And that was before he had got his eye in!

Stories about a ball actually hitting the bell of St Mary Magdalene church opposite the Field however seem just too far-fetched to be true.

Sometimes big hits have unforeseen consequences. Although certainly rare, it is not unusual for the odd unsuspecting car to be hit waiting patiently at the traffic lights on the corner of Trinity Road and Burntwood Lane.

Before the boundary fence was extended to the Brodrick Road gardens, balls found their way over the short boundary far more easily. During the early days of the schools' ownership at the Field, apparently, a teacher struck up a relationship with one of the occupants of the houses whilst retrieving cricket balls from time to time. They, apparently, eventually married in what you could truly call a real 'cricket ball romance'.

The Cricket Tours

Although cricket weeks at the Field were a feature for the Heathfield club, for both Old Sinjuns and Old Grammarians they were only arranged sporadically. However, both clubs were well known for their annual cricket tours, just like the rugby clubs all those years previously, and the Heathfield club's foray into Sussex in the early 1920s. A cricket tour was a popular way of getting away from it all for a few days, or even longer. They were a good method of bonding players from the same club together particularly in larger clubs where players might normally play for different elevens on a Saturday. By using specific examples, the account below gives an idea as to the different ways that both clubs organised and enjoyed their tours.

Apart from a joint venture with the Economicals CC touring the Canterbury area in 1961 and 1962 under the rather contrived name of Sinecs, Old Sinjuns CC toured from 1976 until 1994. The idea of a tour was conceived by Graham Cox in a Chinese restaurant adjacent to Wandsworth Police Station after a day's cricket. Inspiration can occur in some strange places, but nevertheless it would set in motion a series of tours that would keep the club busy for almost the next twenty years. Usually held in the first half of July and loosely covering an area in or around Gloucestershire and South East Wales, the first tour coincided with the driest and one of the hottest summers in living memory, although unfortunately the match with Usk on the Tuesday was rained off! Having actually got to the ground, in the rain, it was interesting to note that the distant Welsh Hills were biscuit coloured rather than the traditional green. The day before, the very first tour match in 1976 was played at Wootton Bassett, (not 'Royal' in those days) and featured an innings of 96 by Kevin Barry (still the highest score recorded on tour), unusually batting up the order, before being given out LBW (controversially he thought). Cirencester, Bristol Optimists and on the way back Basingstoke on the May's Bounty ground, (at that time used by Hampshire CCC as a county out ground), were the remaining fixtures, the latter being the scene of Sandham's hundredth century all those years previously. The matches at Basingstoke were always tough but in 1977 there was a rare victory there by one wicket off the very last ball of the match. Beyond 1983 an extra night on tour, meant a mad scramble back up the M4 to play the afternoon Saturday League matches.

The tour headquarters for the first tour was the *Cross Hands Hotel* in Old Sodbury which was considered to be far too sober and traditional for the club's liking. The following year upon a recommendation the headquarters moved to Chepstow's answer to *Fawlty Towers* and some good times and long evenings were enjoyed there. In August 2020 the hotel in question was mentioned in *The Times* in connection with the differing lockdown measures employed between Wales and England. Pictures of it seem to suggest it has hardly changed! The advantage of this location was that it was also ideally placed for players to enjoy a round of golf at the nearby St Pierre Golf & Country Club in the morning before heading off to cricket in the afternoon. It was also close to Bristol, just over the Severn Bridge, where a chance encounter with Steve Kember, the professional footballer, at the Platform One club was fondly remembered both by him and Tony Bird who had some years earlier (probably in 1972) given the former a badly bruised big toe when Steve had tried to keep out a yorker at Thornton Heath's ground in a Kemp's Cup Match there. 'Try explaining that to the Chelsea manager when you turn up for training!', Tony had apparently told Steve at the time!

The traditional opening match from 1977 would be at Cirencester in the picturesque and quiet surroundings of the Park. Given that the tour was always a midweek affair, it would start at Viv Landon's house in Claygate on Monday morning for an early breakfast and the obligatory bucks fizz by the pool. A fine was imposed for any player failing to meet at the rendezvous just outside Cirencester by noon and there were, on some occasions, some anxious moments for latecomers trying to get there by the required time as they drove madly down the M4! Cirencester has strong connections with W.G. Grace. He played once on the ground during his time with Gloucestershire, and as if to underline the connection in 1989, another Grace-a 'distant relative' he said, of the great man, actually played for Cirencester against the club, a match which Old Sinjuns won by 21 runs.

As the years went on other cricket venues were introduced, included Abergavenny (used by Glamorgan CCC at the time), and Panteg where some members of the touring party will never forget playing snooker (or was it 'flooker') after the match which shared its headquarters with Panteg House and the local working men's club. Halfway through the game, and on the vacant snooker table, two players and a referee appeared - this was obviously a serious match with all the traditions of the game in that part of Wales. At an opportune moment we decided to quietly leave the arena. As we did so an elderly spectator critically observed our efforts, 'I've never seen snooker played like that before, Boyo'. he uttered! Other locations included Bath, where on one occasion in our Association blazers, we were apparently confused for a touring jazz band as we strolled around the town. In fine weather, hot air balloons would be observed floating above the town. Their ground at North Parade is in a marvellous setting in which to play cricket adjacent to the River Avon. However, perhaps Malmesbury brings back some of the most interesting memories, such as the arrival of 'Lord Burton of Sinjun' and his batman Cliff Martin, who made an impression apparently on three lady American tourists. Their side against us invariably included Richard Cooper the ex-Somerset and Wiltshire player. Described as having a similar stature to Colin Milburn, with the build of a typical village blacksmith, he just hit fours and sixes almost at will - no need to run! Sadly, during his second spell as Wiltshire captain at the young age of 44 he passed away, but he will always be remembered fondly as an opponent who just enjoyed life. Their ground at The Worthy's is on top of a hill and on one occasion both sides were subjected to a quite extraordinary and frightening thunderstorm with an accompanying power cut just after having ceased playing and having escaped to the sanctuary of the changing rooms. Apart from Richard Cooper, another Minor County player for Wiltshire, Jeremy Newman, also played with Malmesbury in the tour matches and is apparently still connected with the club. The family owned the local abattoir and in January 1998, Malmesbury was the centre of international media attention when two pigs, just after having being delivered by truck to the Newman's slaughterhouse and about five minutes from meeting their end, escaped by squeezing through a fence and swimming across the River Avon into nearby gardens. It took over a week to recapture the young porkers, having been finally located in a thicket on Tetbury Hill just outside the town, and six years later a full comedic account of the story was recalled by the BBC. The pair were nicknamed Butch and Sundance after the American Outlaws. The escape coincided with queries about the enhanced performances of the Chinese swimming team. A comparison was drawn. 'So, the pigs escaped from the abattoir's thugs. They swam the River Avon like the Chinese Team on drugs!' However, such was the media attention, that the Tamworth Two as they were also known, were saved and transported to the Rare Breeds Centre in Ashford Kent, to see out their days where they became an ongoing attraction until the end. If we can draw any conclusion from this episode, it is that pigs can certainly swim, but they cannot fly!

Unfortunately, on tour the club were not always lucky with the weather. In 1987 the Wednesday match at Stinchcombe had been called off the evening before owing to heavy rain. Someone suggested an alternative. The Nat West match between Gloucestershire and Warwickshire was taking place at Bristol. Next morning in uncertain weather, around a dozen of the touring party, decked out in Association blazers, set out to the match hoping the weather would hold. What happened next is almost written in Old Sinjuns folklore, as just before lunchtime there was an announcement on the loudspeaker 'Would all members of the Old Sinjuns touring party please proceed to the pavilion for lunch'. It transpired that Mick Britnell with his Surrey connections had managed to persuade Gloucestershire County Cricket Club to allow the party into the pavilion dining room. The weather held and a good day was had by all. When the party arrived back at the hotel to tell the others of their day, one of the younger members, Simon Wilkinson, enquired 'Who was that person I was talking to?'. The answer was M.J.K. Smith, the former Warwickshire and England cricket captain! Fortunately, the weather had improved by Friday, and on the final tour match of the week, Brian Hugh-Jones took 7-10 as Cam were dismissed 22 runs short of a modest total of 127. This was the best bowling performance of all on any tour.

In later years the club settled at the rather grandly named *Royal Gloucestershire Hussars Hotel* (today called the *George Inn* rather sedately) in the hamlet of Frocester within the shadow of the Cotswolds and virtually opposite the village cricket ground, now a leading club in that area. The quiet and idyllic surroundings were invariably compromised by long and raucous hours at the bar extending well beyond midnight. By then the club tour drink was a screwdriver- a double vodka and orange, so one can only imagine what a Phillips and a Posidriv were, which were invariably drunk during most of the week! Accompanied with it was a tour song to the tune of Song Sung Blue by Neil Diamond with lyrics adapted by Nick Knight. The first two lines were, 'Screw-dri-vers, everybody loves one; Screw-dri-vers 'cos we are Old Sinjuns!'. The rest of the words just got lost in an alcoholic haze! There were exceptions, Peter Lang just drank rum and coke all week. For those who fancied an evening out the night clubs of Cheltenham were not far away. Thursday night was the fancy dress evening – even the locals joined in the fun! Inevitably, one player dressed up as a member of the opposite sex. On one occasion, earlier in the week, (helmets with faceguards had not really taken off by then) he had top edged a ball into his cheek attempting a hook shot. The resultant black eye gave some authenticity to his outfit on that Thursday evening.

The final tour in 1994 also coincided with the 75th Anniversary Celebrations and a cricket week in early August. In retrospect the club always struggled to make an impression on a very strong fixture list but played on some of the best grounds in the area, and after that an ageing squad admitted defeat. It had been almost twenty years of bedlam, but fondly remembered and certainly not forgotten.

If the Old Sinjuns tours were epic, they were almost a cameo compared to the Old Grammarians CC tours which were absolutely legendary. The history goes back pre-war when the club started touring in 1932 over a bank holiday weekend to Sussex, and then as a precursor to what was to come, a week-long tour to Devon in 1937.

After the war the tours to Devon resumed in 1949 and ran until 1953. They were then resurrected in 1959 with the assistance of four Old Sinjuns in the squad of twelve, namely Owen Cooper, Albert Oborne, Viv Landon and Mick Britnell, before the Devon tour was revived yet again in 1965, with help from three Old Sinjun players, with matches against South Devon and Exeter amongst others. This time the tours ran unbroken until 1996 always in the Devon area. In 1966 the tour was extended to include an all-day match at Sidmouth, and with the help of a fifty from another Old Sinjun guest player, Mike Osmond, and with a young Mike Selvey amongst the wickets, the club emphatically beat the home side by 75 runs. In 1969, Mick Britnell recorded the highest score ever on these tours (136* at Dawlish). He is actually recorded as finishing top of Old Grammarians averages that season on the strength of his tour exploits – despite being a regular player at Old Sinjuns! Travel arrangements were different to those enjoyed by Old Sinjuns as Alan Millhouse records: *We started by travelling from Burntwood Lane with a supply of booze travelling to all of the games by coach with our great old coach driver Steve. We then graduated to four years of rail journeys, meeting at Paddington. A coach for the Paignton fixture seemed a little luxurious (only three miles) and so we now travel by car and use the coach for the longer journeys.* What Alan did not say was that in later years the journey to Torquay, the tour headquarters, would involve a madcap journey after the league match on Saturday evening often arriving in the small hours of the morning in readiness for the first match on the Sunday! In 1970 the tour report stated that *..more attention this year was paid to the cricket than the other local diversions.* Perhaps the club were more disciplined on tour than their counterparts, although judging by some of the reports that was probably unlikely! By now the tours were six matches long (Monday to Saturday) and had settled into the weekend around the late August Bank Holiday weekend. On the 1975 tour, Don Clarke took his 1,000th wicket for the club at Tiverton. In 1976, the year of the drought, Ray Gowan scored 103 at Plymstock. The last match of the tour was due to be played at Tiverton Town's ground but owing to the drought the ground was utterly unplayable and the match was switched to Blundell's School. Ironically on that day the weather broke and in cooler damper conditions the rains came shortly before tea, but relented long enough for Old Grammarians to defeat Tiverton Town by 35 runs. With the government having appointed a Minister for the Drought, It then rained incessantly throughout the autumn!

The Old Grammarians also liked their evening entertainment. The *Blue Angel* was a night club near Paignton station which the team visited after the match there. The waitress service involved one young lady constantly employed managing the large round of drinks for the party – sounds to me just like the painting the Forth Rail Bridge – once the drinks are distributed for the first round it is time to start ordering again! Alan again reports: In the disco lights, the tumblers of gin and tonic looked positively Alkaseltzerish.' (with reference to the dictionary no such word exists, but perhaps older readers of this account will understand!)

As with Old Sinjuns a fines system was enforced. It was absolutely allowed to juggle with a ball three times before catching it, as that automatically incurred three fines! (well, it did on Old Sinjuns tours). Alan Millhouse again: *... at a South Devon game on their old ground in 1969, OGs were fielding and a square drive went past Peter Finucane's left hand at cover. The grass was close cut and sloped away slightly at the boundary. Peter gave chase, no mean sprinter, but was always a yard or so behind the ball as it accelerated away towards the boundary. Pete did not see the one-foot high wire fence until* *the ball was collected by it. Pete travelling at a brisk pace, chose to leap the fence. He disappeared hands aloft, legs astride, screaming. By chance the day's fine collector was strolling that edge of the boundary as Pete re-appeared, complaining that he hadn't been informed of the muddy stream that the fence was protecting. He was soaking wet, covered in mud and green slime. He was fined: For leaving the field of play; wearing dirty boots; wearing dirty trousers; for his foul language; for taking a dive; and for giving a poor impersonation of a steeplechaser, a hurdler and a diver!* Memories of touring are made of incidents like this!

As mentioned, in 1981, the Devon tour was extended to no less than eight days in length. By 1983 the report says that the tour was almost an unbelievable ten days long (very unlikely – just think that someone had lost count midway through the week!) and that by 1984 it was admitted that, unlike Old Sinjuns, and having been evident for a few years, the tour was no longer a stag affair. 1985 saw the first time that the club returned from a tour without a win, but Don Clarke (v Paignton) and Glenn Gershkoff (v Plymstock) both managed five wicket hauls. In 1988 it was back to winning ways with Whitchurch and Tiverton being the victims and Richard Brough scored a ton to no avail in the defeat at South Devon. By now so familiar was the club with that part of England, that Old Grammarians actually became affiliated to the Devon Cricket Association, probably the only London club to do so!

By 1990 the tour had become a two- centre affair staying in Plymouth for the first six nights and then at Sutton Barton Country Club near Axminster for the last night. In 1992, because of the league reorganisation, the tour was cut to six fixtures starting on a Sunday and finishing on the first Friday in September. In 1995 owing to the shortage of players the last two fixtures at Bovey Tracey and Whitchurch had to be cancelled. Although the 1996 tour made something of a revival and three of the five matches were won, with the victory at Bovey Tracey being the first against that club for many years, it proved to be the last hurrah and after that further tours were suspended.

The stories and fables told in the reports on the Old Grammarians website proved that the club's tours were indeed the cornerstone of their season, but, like their counterparts, Old Sinjuns, age eventually caught up with most of the participants. What was quite clear upon reading the Old Grammarians reports was the old adage of 'What goes on tour, stays on tour' which did not, it seems, apply to them! Perhaps it was no coincidence that Old Sinjuns and Old Grammarians tours finished about the same time. Far fewer club tours seem to be organised nowadays. Some of this must be put down to the development of technology. When both tours started mobile phones, for general use, had not been invented. Phoning home from a call box or using the hotel phone was a fineable offence. By the time the tours ended the mobile phone, however cumbersome, was beginning to take over our lives. Inevitably this led to the general use of what we know today as the internet. The idea today, that anyone can spend an entire week playing cricket away in isolation, without reference to either, apart perhaps from a daily newspaper, would be beyond any younger player's comprehension! Yes, those were the days!

Soccer tours were also run sparodically over the years, principally by both Old Sinjuns and Old Grammarians AFCs and some even go back further than the cricket tours. Tour matches were even arranged abroad. The reports again reflect life on tour and not all to do with football!

However, that was not quite the end. A 'Last of the Summer Wine' version reappeared in 2004 principally consisting of seasoned players with help from their offspring to help run around the outfield to strengthen the fielding, under the name of Old Grammarians. This tour originated before the merger of the clubs a couple of years later. The first year was confined to a single match in Worcestershire but then eventually migrated back to the West Country, with the tour headquarters in Exeter from where three matches were arranged – a limited overs match on the Friday evening, followed by two regular matches on the Saturday and Sunday. Although these tours were only intended to be a temporary diversion, they lasted well beyond expectations. Glenn Gershkoff was the principal architect and organiser. Eventually the matches were cut back to the weekend, with Sidbury and Cheriton Fitzpaine providing the opposition. Sadly, Glenn passed away in 2017, so the tour missed a year, but in 2018 it resurfaced again with the same opposition but this time under the enthusiastic leadership of Dave Boynton. Having made a promise to Glenn a few years earlier, I attended the tour as the umpire. By then it seems evenings were more leisurely with a pre-tour drink at the *White Hart* and a meal in Exeter on the Friday evening. Next day someone enquired 'Did anyone go clubbing it yesterday evening?' to which the reply was 'No didn't bother!' The matches were less taxing but still competitive. Fortunately, we chose a couple of hot and dry days on which to play the matches. The last tour took place in 2019.

As a footnote, few clubs toured London. None of the clubs mentioned above made a visit in the reverse direction, perhaps preferring the open countryside to the hustle and bustle of the City. However, Briton Ferry Town CC from Wales visited Old Sinjuns during the 1980s and in 1987 Old Grammarians played out a tense draw with Merrion CC, visitors from Dublin, Ireland. Happily, both clubs survive to this day, with the latter claiming to be the largest and most diverse cricket club in Ireland.

In tandem with cricket tours, cricket weeks have also become less common as well, and with fewer spectators watching matches over the years, have become less of an attraction, with clubs restricting themselves to the occasional impromptu barbeque after matches. Times have changed, and so has society and cricket.

Close of Play

Lord, if I should die today, Make it please before the close of play.

Sir John Major (1943 -   )

Club & Ground

The Wandsworth Common Act did not prevent the improvements to Trinity Road occurring around a century later. Indeed, as early as 1938 an Act of Parliament had been passed to enable the road taking a long slither of common on the immediate south-west side of Trinity Road converting it to a dual carriageway opposite the prison and beyond to Wandsworth Bridge. However, the Second World War intervened and this improvement was not completed until 1970. In compensation minor adjustments were made to incorporate adjacent areas into Wandsworth Common including the playground behind the Heathfield Cottages and a strip of land running north alongside Trinity Road from the *County Arms*. Additionally, the section of Marcilly Road running across the Common was removed and returned to the Common in much the same way. Satellite pictures still show the row of trees that used to line the road. The original plans were for a flyover to be constructed to Wandsworth Bridge but this was abandoned as were the plans for a dual carriageway to be constructed further south towards the A24 at Tooting Bec, which would have potentially impacted on the Field. So, to this day, the dual carriageway section of Trinity Road from Wandsworth Bridge finishes abruptly at the *County Arms*, but not before reducing the Common, locally known as 'Heathfield' beyond Windmill Road on its way towards Wandsworth Bridge.

There has long been a discussion within the Sinjuns Association regarding the name of the Field. In one respect, the school's historian Frank Smallwood was right insofar as the Heathfield Cricket Club had taken its name from the site of the original ground at Heathfield on Wandsworth Common. A Stanford map from 1864 shows the area in question to be distinct from the normal common and the 1865 Whitbread map of London names it as such, and confirms Heathfield as a district within Wandsworth Common itself, to be unsurprisingly linked to the Heathfield Cottages (better known today as 1-6 Heathfield Gardens) at the northern end of Heathfield Road. Some of these properties were built before 1825 and it was from the detached cottage next to the Common itself that Mrs Nixon had complained about cricketers playing too close to her house in 1880. The brick wall to the flank of her property which separates the garden from the Common running parallel to Trinity Road still exists today, and before the whole area was landscaped a wicket was painted on that wall to provide casual games of cricket for all and sundry! In reality the Heathfield ground was really too public to become a viable cricket ground although it possibly survived, in one form or another, until the Great War. For a time, after the cricket square had disappeared, the two football pitches occupied the area but with the dualling of Trinity Road and the planting of trees along it once the works were completed, only a portion of what was the original ground is left. As we know, in 1883 when the Heathfield club moved, taking their adopted name with them, to what is now known as Trinity Fields, the Field was soon identified with the Heathfield club that played there from 1883, so that Bonner's Field, Heathfield and Sir Walter St John's Playing Field amongst others are all former names of Trinity Fields. Although Smallwood flatly denied in a letter to the local authority that Bonner's Field and Heathfield are one and the same place, this really ignores the reality of the situation. It is a bit like saying that Clapham Junction is not part of Battersea! In a sense, posthumously, Frank Smallwood has got his wish, as he would be glad to know by way of confirmation that the Heathfield Cricket Club took its name from the site of the original ground, as

165

he stated all along, although he might still disapprove that the location of the current Heathfield Bowls Club in Sandgate Lane is still somewhat distant from the original district of Heathfield.

And what about the Field? It would be folly to think that since it became a playing field probably almost a hundred and fifty years ago, that it has changed little over the years. Because of its need to adapt through the special requirements of the clubs and its owners, that have used the ground for all kinds of sport, the actual layout of the field has changed over the years, and conceivably could change again in the future. What we see today, however, uses the whole of its eight acres almost to capacity, to suit its current needs. After all, who would have thought that, firstly the high-profile Heathfield club, one of the most influential and leading clubs in London, would expire, and secondly that the two Schools who effectively bought the Field through Cresswell's efforts in 1918 and divided it between 1925 and 1949, would expire also. The Field's survival since 1852 in some quarters has been described as a miracle. Regarding the vistas, the view to the southwest, which is partially blotted out by the Burntwood Lane pavilion, has remained the same since the 1930s when it was constructed. The spire of St. Mary's Church which often features in panoramic views in the BBC's coverage of the Wimbledon Lawn Tennis Championships, is still quite clearly visible from the upstairs clubroom. Once the church view starts to disappear, owing to advancing rain, it is most likely that cricket matches at the ground will shortly be disrupted. On two of the remaining three sides, including the perimeter to the Brodrick Road gardens, apart from the disappearance of the Dutch elms, and the erection of the higher perimeter fence, and across Trinity Road, to St Mary Magdalene's church, the views remain reasonably similar. The view across and beyond Burntwood Lane however has been lost. A 1900 photograph from the Field shows a very different perspective across the Common to distant houses in Routh Road. It was then still heathland, but over the years the area, previously home to the Scope, has changed completely. Nature today has reclaimed the area thanks in part to a replanting scheme, so the heathland and gorse are gone. The 'Cinder Patch', where apparently members of the Chelsea Football Club such as 'Chopper' Harris, Peter Osgood, Alan Hudson and Peter Bonetti used to train on occasions, has become overgrown and forgotten, and the area has become a natural wilderness. Whilst we can comfort ourselves that this is still protected common land, the original view around 1900 gives, at least to me, a far more agreeable depiction of this area, with an almost countryside setting. However, time marches on and things change. Apparently, all is not well in the Scope. A recent report tells us that it is home apparently, as in other areas of Britain, to the Giant Hogweed, regarded as one of Britain's most dangerous and evasive plants, introduced from the Caucasus in the early 19th Century. An article in *The Times* in May 2020 describes the plant as a *... beast (that) has purple blotches and coarse hairs on its stems* and *in most places where you see it in summer, it is enormous.* A mature plant can grow to a height of around 4 metres and the huge leaves can be up to 1.50 metres wide. Contact with its sap in summer can cause very painful burns, scarring and even blindness. So be careful what you find in the undergrowth! Apparently Japanese Knotweed had been a problem in the area of 'no man's land' between the Broderick Road gardens and the Field. Burntwood Lane is no longer a lane, but a busy thoroughfare between Wimbledon and Clapham, and Trinity Road likewise between Tooting and Wandsworth. Additionally, the view across Wandsworth Common beyond the *Surrey Tavern* is more restricted, as it was possible to view the very top of the Post Office Tower (the highest building in the UK from 1964 until 1980) across London in the early days shortly after its construction, but no more. Perhaps conversely, we should actually celebrate that the gradual encroachment of trees and undergrowth has obliterated that view today. One thing we should remember, however, is that nothing remains the same forever. Perhaps we should reflect and draw upon the inspiration of people like Samuel Cresswell as one of those people that saw a way to make a difference and did.

A Personal View

For whatever reasons, Earl Spencer's introduction of the covenant in 1852 as a pre- condition for its purchase set the Field on an interesting and perhaps unintended journey. When John Bonner in 1877, so it seems, acted as a catalyst to convert the Field into a sports ground, he started an unstoppable chain of events to take us to where we are today. In the intervening years since, it has been host to some of the greatest and influential players ever seen in sport, such as cricketers of the calibre of George Lohmann, W.G. Grace, Jack Hobbs and more recently Alec Stewart, plus Adrian Stoop from Rugby Union. Yet perhaps, paradoxically, the purchase of the Field in 1918 meant that, in a sense, the elitism continued, as use of the Field was effectively restricted to the school's use – notwithstanding that it was desperately needed for the well-being of the pupils at the time. It was not until 1996 that it could be said that the Field is now, in a sense, much more closely linked to the local community than it has ever been. Much has been written about the social divide in other documents, and the distinction and division between clubs with private facilities and council-run grounds still exists today. If circumstances had been different the Field could have developed in a completely different way. It could still, in fact, have been the home of London Welsh RFC or the Heathfield Club or both if Samuel Cresswell had not taken an interest in 1918. On the other hand, by now, it might not have even been a playing field.

The uncomfortable truth was that E.A.C. Thomson who played for the Heathfield club, and from its foundation until his death in 1941 was Secretary of what was known as the London Club Cricket Conference in its early days, actively sought to protect the ethos of friendly cricket, opposing change, and abhorred the idea of competitive league cricket so much so, that the Conference actively sought to exclude any club from their organisation that contemplated competing in league cricket. Before that, as Secretary since at least 1895 of the South London Association of Cricket Clubs, described as the largest cricket association in the South of England at that time, his whole life was spent predominantly in cricket administration. He was also involved at the highest level in working with others to advise the government on the resumption of recreational cricket after the Great War.

There is some suggestion that by the start of the nineteenth century (early days indeed) that cricket was predominantly on the retreat in the north and was really only common as a summer sport in southern England centred on Kent, Surrey and Sussex. The game did stage a revival in the north of England however, and even Scotland (they must have been a hardy bunch of souls north of the border!) as the century wore on, so perhaps there was an underlying resentment against northern cricket being somewhat different. We think of league cricket as being a northern invention. However, the newspapers carried fixtures and scores from the South London League and the Battersea Churches Association matches on Wandsworth Common. Amongst others the London Business Houses League was active for member companies to promote cricket as a form of recreation amongst their staff, whilst at the other end of the scale, the interestingly named Red Triangle League probably promoted cricket for more run of the mill cricket sides in nearby Middlesex. There was even a Thursday league for sides with a midweek eleven. The *South London Press* also extensively reported league cricket results. The I'Anson League which still exists on the boundaries of Surrey, Sussex and Hampshire, and founded in 1901, claims to be the oldest continuous village cricket league in the world. The Lambeth Cricket Association which in 1902 was running league cricket for 43 clubs over six divisions in South London, and the Clapham & Battersea Cricket League which was founded as early as 1897 (under its original name of the Clapham Common Cricket League) and running league cricket for a similar number of sides, was certainly still operational as late as 1934 and probably ran until the Second World War. One of the league's Vice-

Presidents was none other than Jack Hobbs! Looking at the League's yearbook for 1930, it extended from grounds as far afield as Blackheath to Hampton Court Park. These were only examples of the number of clubs playing league cricket at the time in and around South London alone. All these leagues had been established well before the Club Cricket Conference came into being. Given all of this it is remarkable to think that the Club Cricket Conference was able to hold back the idea of League cricket amongst elite clubs for so long. For the record, cricket is still played on the Wandsworth Common Extension, but organised matches are now confined to three smallish cricket tables and an artificial cricket pitch. A new public footpath now separates these pitches from a softball pitch next to the railway and behind the tennis courts, which used to accommodate a further cricket square.

In the autumn of 1920, the South London League was actively discussing the possibility of introducing a 'private grounds' division to strengthen their cricket league which like most others was based around smaller clubs playing on council pitches. This idea came to nothing and it was not until the formation of the Surrey Championship in 1968 almost fifty years later, as previously discussed in this book, that the Club Cricket Conference's monopoly, not without some initial resistance, was broken, in a move that was to empower other clubs in southern England with the same ideals. League and friendly cricket can run side by side, although the latter may be played, sometimes, in a more relaxed manner without the rigid structure of any league-generated special regulations, or promotion and relegation. In my fifty years' experience as an umpire, friendly matches are often still played as keenly as any league fixture. Indeed, many clubs often use friendly matches as a tool to blood younger and potentially try out new club members for the future of their clubs. Things have changed since then at the Conference; indeed today, as the Club Cricket Conference Ltd, the organisation is now a Charity, actively supporting all formats of cricket.

We have celebrated in this book players that have excelled and rightly so. Most of them were batsmen, however, but for a minute let's consider the bowlers. The late David Morgan of Cheam collected no fewer than 1,325 1st XI wickets in the Surrey Championship- a tally that is unlikely to be broken any time soon. However, even he admitted that regarding batting in his club career, he did not score the equivalent number of runs to match the number of wickets he had taken! In perhaps a less extreme way, an Old Sinjun who was an effective bowler predominantly in 2nd XI friendly cricket, and who still occasionally plays village cricket in Hampshire, and also gives up his time to coach colts, could claim that distinction as well, as *Play-Cricket* confirms that fact! In terms of batting, both nowadays would be known as ferrets insofar that they would follow the rabbits to the crease. I would even go as far as to call them pest controllers as they would follow the ferrets! However, the essence is for the game of cricket to be enjoyed and open to all whatever one's prospective talents.

Unfortunately, it seems, the authorities, in terms of cricket, have virtually forgotten that a draw is still a fair result, and, with a few exceptions, timed matches are invariably becoming more a thing of the past. At the professional level, Test Matches once regarded as the pinnacle of the sport are now under real threat. It is really sad that some Sunday skippers simply have no idea how to play a timed match or indeed when to declare an innings closed! What is wrong with a draw? Football still recognises it as a fair result. If not, to my mind, it damages the fabric of the game we love. Limited over matches have also been adopted widely in league cricket and, in protest, the recreational game has lost administrators because of this, which is unfortunate. Having umpired an overs match where the first side have scored 301-9 off 50 overs and the second side have commenced their reply with 12-6, with only a loss to look forward to, even an optimist would surely agree that the best course of action would be to concede the match there and then, and have a couple of extra hours in the bar, perhaps even watching cricket on the television rather than playing on to an inevitable conclusion- but that is only if the teams choose to stay on after the match! Such one-sided matches, particularly if your side is on the wrong end of a result which is effectively known sometime before its conclusion, can surely potentially drive players away from the game and can only decrease participation. There are exceptions of course, but over matches infrequently lead to close finishes, and the principle of saving runs rather than taking wickets to win matches is foreign to the way our forefathers intended. It is really an easy way out if you do not have the strength in bowling to dismiss a side. Indeed, in essence, it is a different game! Perhaps the only benefit, and this is really equivalent to a two-edged sword, is that because batsmen tend to play the game more aggressively nowadays, this translates into timed matches, where the art of building an innings has largely been lost. The only reason that there is a debate about reducing Tests from five to four days is because the number of draws has declined in recent decades and the pace of matches invariably quicker. You can be sure that if Test matches are reduced in length, then the spare days will not be used for more timed matches! To me, cricket is like a good wine to be enjoyed and appreciated at leisure, not like some fast food take away outlets offering instant results to quickly satisfy one's hunger! Cricket has obviously had to adapt commercially to survive at the professional level. If Monty Panesar is to be believed India relies on the Indian Premier League, which plays the shortened T20 format of the game for a third of its economy. With statistics such as that, it is no wonder that the shortened overs format now holds sway. It would be interesting to know what members of the Heathfield Cricket Club would have thought of such an idea. Overs cricket has its place, but it is unfortunate that economics and time restraints have taken over as the predominant form of the game from traditional cricket. It is not for this book to enter the debate or whether this is symptomatic of the changes in social history or lifestyle. I will leave it to others to form their own opinion.

However, when the Field was purchased in 1918, the Heathfield club were hit by a perfect storm when, through the ravages of the Great War, they were most vulnerable. By the time they perished it would be fair to say that the lofty ideals to remain a truly amateur club had been seriously compromised or even forgotten. Given also what we know about the rugby clubs even pre-1914 and the financial guarantees they would require to travel to other parts of the country, it is surprising that it took so long for rugby union to accept the inevitable and turn professional – although there are still financial caps on what a club can reasonably pay to its players today as witnessed by the swingeing penalties imposed on clubs such as Durham (cricket) and Saracens (rugby union) in an effort to keep some sort of level playing field on the competition. The irony is, that despite all their power and influence, the Heathfield club were brought down by a Trust whose School was originally set up in 1700 for the 'Education of Twenty Free Scholars of Battersea'.

The other paradox also is that before the general availability of the motor car, sides used to travel considerably greater distances by train to play matches. Early morning meetings meant that rugby teams such as Bath, Neath, and even Devonport Albion could travel to the Field for an afternoon match and be back home by midnight (or shortly afterwards). The same was true in the opposite direction and not just by the rugby clubs – as witnessed in the case of Old Sinjuns CC who thought nothing of travelling as far as Leicester to play against the Ivanhoe club. Today, paradoxically, the emphasis is on short or local journeys. So, in that respect, despite the use of the internet and so on, although we have become more upwardly mobile, we have become more insular and parochial in our outlook. Today most of club cricket is concentrated into an afternoon, or less if playing the T20 format. All-day fixtures particularly on Sundays are fast diminishing and have disappeared entirely from most clubs' fixture lists. Personally, I think that detracts from the game rather than enhances it. The idea that 'Cricket is not just a game but more a way of life' seems to have got lost somewhere along the way. Life now runs at a far quicker pace and the decreasing involvement of the adult population in amateur sport is to be discouraged, and not just in cricket, is being abandoned for other pursuits that take less time, and are, perhaps, certainly from a cricketers' point of view, more superficial.

The other matter is that cricket is perhaps more vulnerable to change and this is maybe because of the comparative expense to play the game compared to other sports and the fact it relies on a far greater interaction between team players. From the social point of view, as previously noted, the Road Safety Act of 1967 eventually had a profound effect, as it brought a standard set of regulations into force, rightly so, against driving under the influence of alcohol. At first, it seems, matters were taken more gently. Certainly, in the early days, with the Association blazer on the hook above the back seat, and with your cricket gear on the back of your car, you might have even escaped with a warning from a policeman and directed to park your car on the side of the road and walk or take a taxi home. Not nowadays, and whilst, of course, such behaviour outside the realms of the law is considered reckless and rightly cannot be condoned, this single act of legislation has certainly curtailed sides staying on after the match and most are away within half an hour of the finish of a match if not before. To be a properly functioning cricket club today, it needs to be run as a small business. Managing to make good bar profits is a struggle without a proper membership base and maintaining a good square and outfield costs increasingly large sums of money. Cricket does and always will unfairly depend on volunteers to keep clubs going. Although it is true today that there is more financial assistance available to clubs in providing new or replacement equipment, times are never easy. The result is many clubs struggle to survive, and this has led to closure and the loss of playing fields and grounds that used once to be the hub of the local community. The connection of cricket with pub or church teams linked to either are also today very much a thing of the past, together with the lack of spectators that today bother to turn up and watch club matches. One man and a dog is more the norm today, and the dog is probably only there because its owner chooses to exercise it around a cricket ground! It is perhaps remarkable however, that as of 2021, Fuller's Brewery still sponsors the Surrey County League which it has done so since 1987, but generally in these challenging times direct sponsorship of amateur sport appears to be somewhat in decline.

Then and Now

The closeness of the Field to Wandsworth Common station was crucial to its success in the early days of its existence. The 2.14pm train from Victoria to Wandsworth Common station was often given as the one to catch, but unless it was a 'special' to get the crowds to the Field (hardly likely) it would surely have taken longer than seven minutes advertised, particularly if stopping at Clapham Junction. Today, of course, the 2.14pm train does not exist. The nearest comparison is the 14.06 or 14.30 (note the twenty-four-hour clock), and for no apparent reason the former at eleven minutes, takes a minute less than the latter to arrive. The station at Wandsworth Common today, given the general massive increase in motor vehicles and other forms of transport, is little more than a side station invariably ignored by the faster suburban trains on their way to East or West Croydon or further afield to Sutton, Epsom or even Horsham. Other earlier adverts said that it takes only three minutes to walk from the station to the Field, which would be alright provided you were on a cross country run! Of course, in those days the station was situated in almost open countryside, whilst today very few people indeed ever use the station to get to the Field by rail.

The other matter is the times that matches used to start. These were generally around 3pm even in winter so during the months of November through to January matches would often finish in the dark. Reports of rugby matches consisting of only twenty minutes each way were not particularly uncommon and in some extreme circumstances matches never happened at all if any team was unduly delayed. It would get pretty dark during the cricket season in September as British Summer Time was not introduced until 1916. There is perhaps an important point to make here. The amateur clubs who played at the Field before the Great War were keen to get spectators into the ground to watch matches and provide a vital source of income. Only occasionally would an estimated number of spectators be given in reports, but where reported it would often amount to something perhaps like a couple of thousand or perhaps more for a special match-about the same number that would today (in normal times) attend a Forest Green Rovers football fixture in League Two at the New Lawn! Most people who watched these matches had to work on Saturday mornings so it was right to emphasise the accessibility of the Field to local transport. Today, of course, the idea of paying to watch a local cricket or football match has gone and the emphasis is more on welcoming and involving the local community. Besides that, there are still many other ways to balance the books.

There was also a matter of getting your team together for a match. Before the Great War, with telephones at a premium, it almost was a status symbol if you had one. Team lists would be published regularly in the sports newspapers. There were numerous times when sides turned up short to play a match and made up the numbers by enlisting bystanders or spectators. Yes, the matches were friendlies, but they were still competitive. The newspapers presumably were also the way to find out if you had been dropped for a particular match! Nevertheless, sides travelled impressive distances to play matches as we know, witnessed by the Heathfield Cricket Club's annual visits to Bexhill in the 1880s and the London Welsh's visits to Northampton and Bedford for instance. Nowadays we are far less adventurous in travelling to matches, and it almost requires a passport to go further than Woking!

Other pursuits may have loosened the grip on the more traditional summer and winter team sports. There just seems to be a kind of social disconnect, and for many people to properly engage in cricket is far too demanding on their spare time. Try explaining to a foreigner that a cricket (Test) match can last for up to five days-and even then, it could result in a draw! Cricket has even been cited as a reason for divorce! Perhaps we should not be that surprised that today we live in a divided land. It just seems that looking back to, say only fifty years ago, it just used to be more fun!

At present, however, there is an opportunity through the Trinity Fields Trust, who maintain the Field, and whose charitable objects reflect those of the Sir Walter St John's Educational Charity, to provide and upgrade the facilities at the Field which it so desperately needs for the benefit of the local community it serves, and by doing so, to try to and help bring people together. It is my hope that this aspiration will succeed.

And Finally….

If you, as a reader, have stayed with me through this historic and social adventure, this really is the end of the book. It is a sad fact that because of the Field's longevity, by definition most individuals who have played at the Field, some at the highest level, are no longer with us. It is important going forward to remember them, as without their involvement and commitment there would have been no history. Additionally, throughout this account there have been so many other individuals and organisations that have had an involvement in the making of the Field it is today. So, who were the heroes and who were the villains, perhaps some were both? I will let you decide.

I would also, in a general sense, like to dedicate this account to the many thousands of cricket volunteers who, particularly at local level, give up their time through their love of the sport and keep the flame burning bright, even during the most difficult and challenging of times. Your involvement is as vital today as it ever has been. If you can persuade your wife, husband or partner, if not already involved, to think not 'Why are you going out to Cricket?', but 'When are you going out to Cricket?', then, you are more than halfway there!

Appendices

A. Field Timeline

B. Clapham Rovers & The FA Cup

C. Casuals Matches at the Field

D. Harlequins matches at the Field

E.   London Welsh RFC matches at the Field

F.   London Irish RFC matches at the Field

G   Heathfield CC matches – Selected Results

H. Scorecard Heathfield v Heron 1876

I.   Scorecard Heathfield v London County 1902

J. Scorecard Heathfield v Mr A.E. Henderson's XI 1913

K. Scorecard London Clubs v South Africans 1924

L. Scorecard Old Grammarians v D.M. Smith's XI 1987

M. Scorecard SinjunGrammarians 2nd XI v Warlingham 2nd XI 2012

N. Matches against Surrey Representative XIs at the Field

O. international Sportsman at the Field

P. Old Sinjuns Cricket Club Captains (1920-2005)

Q. Old Grammarians Cricket Club Captains (1926-2005)

R. SinjunGrammarians Cricket Club Captains (2006-2021)

S. Old Boys Football History Notes

T. List of Groundsmen at the Field

Appendix A

Field Timeline

1832

First shown on maps

1852 (20 September)

Henry McKellar of Wandsworth Lodge buys a piece of land, part of Wandsworth Common from Earl Spencer for £180, subject to the condition /covenant that the land shall not be built upon. The land in question is enclosed, and effectively becomes a field.

1862 (5 October)

Henry McKellar dies and leaves his estate to his wife Ann McKellar.

1863

Wandsworth Lodge is sold by Ann McKellar but it appears that she probably retains ultimate ownership of the Field.

1871

The field is not included in the 1871 Wandsworth Common Act.

1877

Advertised as Lot 2 to be let on a short agreement but that the land could not be built upon. Likely that John Bonner, landlord at the *Surrey Tavern*, agreed terms with a view to using it as a playing field.

Clapham Rovers commence using the Field in the autumn. Possible use for cricket thereafter.

1883

Heathfield Cricket Club commence renting the Field.

1886 (15 May)

Ann McKellar dies and the Field reverts to Lord Spencer.

1890 (30 December)

Earl Spencer conveys the Field to London County Council for five shillings on condition that the Council agrees to the 1852 covenants originally agreed with McKellar.

1898 (11 August)

The London County Council conveys the Field upon auction to John Mills Thorne owner of the Nine Elms Brewery and Burntwood Lodge. 1852 covenants to apply. Heathfield Cricket Club subsequently agree terms, to manage the Field on a year round basis.

1911 (2 June)

John Mills Thorne conveys the Field to the London Welsh Athletic Club for a sum of £3,800 subject to the 1852 covenants as before.

1918 (25 March) The London Welsh Athletic Club conveys the Field to Samuel Cresswell who declares the property is held for the benefit of the Sir Walter St John's School Foundation (effectively the Trust) for the sum of £4,643, subject to the 1852 covenants as before.

1924 (4 October) Heathfield club vacates the Field on expiration of their lease.

1992 (28 February) Without a school to administer, The Walter St John's Schools Trust is effectively wound up. Ownership of the Field is passed with the approval of the Charity Commissioners to the Sir Walter St. John's Educational Charity.

1996

The management and maintenance of the Field is taken over by the Trinity Fields Trust by way of a lease agreement with Sir Walter St John's Educational Charity, initially for a period of 25 years.

2017 (August)

The Trinity Fields Trust in negotiations with The Sir Walter St John's Educational Charity agrees to a new lease on revised terms for a further 50 years.

Notes

Battersea Grammar School closed in 1977

Sir Walter St John's Grammar School closed in 1986

Appendices

Appendix B

Clapham Rovers and the FA Cup (since arriving at the Field)

Season	Round	Opponents	Played at	Result F	A	Notes
1877/78						
Oct 27	First Round	Grantham	Grantham	2	0	
Dec 20	Second Round	Swifts	Kennington Oval	4	0	
Feb 2	Third Round	Oxford University	Kennington Oval	2	3	Att 700
1878/79						
	First Round	Finchley	Walkover			
Dec 7	Second Round	Forest School	Kennington Oval	10	1	
Feb 1	Third Round	Cambridge University	Kennington Oval	1	0	
Mar 8	Fourth Round	Swifts	Kennington Oval	8	1	
	Semi Final	Bye				
Mar 29	Final	Old Etonians	Kennington Oval	0	1	Runners Up Att 2,000+
1879/80						
Nov 8	First Round	Romford	Romford	7	0	Played away rather than home
Dec 20	Second Round	South Norwood	**The Field**	4	1	
Jan 17	Third Round	Pilgrims	Kennington Oval	7	0	
Feb 14	Fourth Round	Hendon	Kennington Oval	2	0	
Feb 21	Fifth Round	Old Etonians	Kennington Oval	1	0	
	Semi Final	Bye				
Apr 10	Final	Oxford University	Kennington Oval	1	0	Winners Att 6,000
1880/81						
Nov 13	First Round	Finchley	**The Field**	15	0	
	Second Round	Bye				
Jan 8	Third Round	Swifts	Kennington Oval	2	1	
Feb 12	Fourth Round	Upton Park	Kennington Oval	5	4	
Mar 19	Fifth Round	Old Carthusians	Kennington Oval	1	3	aet (1-1 after 90 mins) Att 1,600
1881/82						
Nov 5	First Round	Old Etonians	Kennington Oval	2	2	
Nov 19	First Round	Old Etonians	Kennington Oval	0	1	Replay
1882/83						
Nov 4	First Round	Kildare	Shepherds Bush	3	0	Played away rather than home
Dec 2	Second Round	Hanover United	**The Field**	7	1	
Jan 6	Third Round	Windsor Home Park	Windsor	3	0	Played away rather than home
	Fourth Round	Bye				
Feb 2	Fifth Round	Old Carthusians	Kennington Oval	3	5	
1883/84						
	First Round	Kildare	walkover			
Dec 1	Second Round	Rochester	**The Field**	7	0	
Dec 23	Third Round	Swifts	**The Field**	1	2	
1884/85						
Nov 8	First Round	Hendon	**The Field**	3	3	Played on adjacent pitch to Casuals v South Reading match
Nov 22	First Round	Hendon	Hendon	0	6	Replay
1885/86						
Oct 31	First Round	1st Surrey Rifles	Camberwell	12	0	Played away rather than home
	Second Round	Bye				
	Third Round	South Reading	Disqualified			Unable to travel and play before deadline of 31 December
1886/87						
Oct 30	First Round	Old Brightonians	East Sheen	0	6	Played away rather than home

Appendix C

Casuals Matches at the Field

Season		Result		Notes
1883/84	Opponents	F	A	
Nov 8	St. Thomas's Hospital	2	3	
Nov 12	East Sheen	1	4	
Dec 20	Guy's Hospital	2	2	
Jan 5	Upton Park	2	3	
Feb 7	St. Thomas's Hospital	2	3	
Feb 16	Burgess Hill	1	4	
Mar 1	Old Westminsters	1	3	
Apr 5	JG Ferns XI	0	2	
1884/85				
Oct 18	Old Westminsters	3	4	
Nov 8	South Reading*	1	4	FA Cup First Round
Nov 29	Somerset	2	2	
Dec 18	Guy's Hospital	2	0	
Dec 20	Old Brightonians	0	5	
Dec 22	East Sheen	1	0	
Dec 26	Mr Perez XI +	0	2	
Dec 27	Wimbledon#	7	1	Also match at Derby Co.
Jan 3	Barnes #	2	2	
Jan 10	Reigate Priory	0	5	
Jan 22	Guy's Hospital	5	3	
Jan 31	Barnes	1	2	
Mar 14	Old Brightonians	0	8	
unknown	Oxford University #	2	1	
1885/86				
Oct 15	St. Thomas's Hospital	5	0	
Oct 24	Old Etonians	0	4	
Nov 7	Tottenham Hotspur	8	0	London Senior Cup Round 2
Nov 14	Old Westminsters	3	2	
Dec 9	Lyndhurst	1	1	
Dec 16	St Bartholomew's Hospital	1	3	
Dec 17	Guys Hospital +	1	3	
Dec 19	Clapham Rovers	1	3	
Dec 21	Condors	7	0	
Dec 22	East Sheen	5	1	
Dec 26	Wimbledon	5	2	Also match at Derby Co.
Dec 31	H.T. Grandrigs Team	5	2	
Jan 2	Old Brightonians #	4	4	
Jan 4	Condors	10	4	
Jan 30	Barnes	4	4	
Feb 20	Clapham Rovers	3	4	
Mar 13	Old Malvernians	0	1	

Notes

1st XI matches only.
Unless where specified as Cup matches, all others were designated as Friendlies.
* According to the FA Cup draw, South Reading should have been at home. However, match recorded as being played at the Field.
+ Played as a 12 a side match
# Home matches but location not given (Assumed at the Field)
 Matches with Clapham Rovers played on the Field

Courtesy of Rob Cavallini

Appendices

Appendix D

Harlequins matches at the Field

Season		Result		Attendance
1901/02	Opponents	F	A	
Oct 5	Richmond	5	12	
Oct 26	London Scottish	0	10	
Nov 2	London Irish	0	8	1,000+
Nov 9	Marlborough Nomads	6	8	
Nov 23	St Bartholomew's Hospital	8	0	
Nov 30	Rosslyn Park	21	6	
Dec 14	Old Leysians	19	3	
Jan 4	Old Alleynians	13	0	
Jan 18	Old Merchant Taylors	6	5	
Mar 1	Kensington	6	11	
Mar 8	Guy's Hospital	11	3	
Mar 15	Lennox	8	0	
1902/03				
Sep 27	Old Merchant Taylors	16	16	1,000
Oct 11	Royal Indian Engineering College	8	11	
Oct 29	Royal School of Mines	12	3	
Nov 8	Marlborough Nomads	21	6	
Nov 12	Catford Bridge	8	0	
Nov 15	Oxford University	14	5	
Nov 22	St Bartholomew's Hospital	30	0	
Dec 20	Old Alleynians	0	29	
Jan 10	Blackheath	0	0	2,000+
Feb 7	London Welsh	0	3	
Feb 21	Kensington	0	11	
1903/04				
Oct 3	Richmond	3	6	
Oct 10	London Irish	14	8	
Oct 24	Lennox	10	8	
Nov 7	Marlborough Nomads	11	3	
Nov 28	Rosslyn Park	3	3	
Dec 19	London Welsh	0	14	
Dec 26	Kensington	15	11	
Jan 9	Blackheath	3	9	
Jan 16	Old Merchant Taylors	3	9	
Feb 27	Old Alleynians	5	8	
1904/05				
Sep 24	Old Merchant Taylors	3	15	
Oct 1	Richmond	3	3	
Nov 5	Marlborough Nomads	17	14	
Nov 9	Hampstead Wanderers	3	8	
Nov 12	Oxford University	3	27	
Nov 19	Old Alleynians	6	10	
Dec 3	London Scottish	5	6	
Dec 10	Royal Indian Engineering College	0	18	
Dec 31	Old Alleynians	5	13	
Feb 4	Leicester	0	9	
Feb 11	University College School Old Boys	15	3	
Feb 18	Guy's Hospital	13	14	
Mar 11	Lennox	3	0	

A History of Trinity Fields

1905/06

Date	Opponent			
Oct 7	Richmond	3	18	
Oct 14	London Scottish	12	16	
Oct 21	Lennox	19	0	
Oct 28	Marlborough Nomads	9	16	
Nov 4	United Services Portsmouth	16	6	
Nov 8	Hampstead Wanderers	13	9	
Nov 18	Old Alleynians	42	5	
Nov 25	Rosslyn Park	9	15	
Dec 9	London Welsh	3	8	
Dec 16	Blackheath	6	13	
Dec 23	Old Merchistonians	0	21	
Dec 26	Surbiton	17	10	
Jan 6	University College School Old Boys	20	8	
Mar 10	Northampton	3	18	

1906/07

Date	Opponent			
Sep 29	Old Merchant Taylors	19	3	
Oct 6	Richmond	35	9	
Oct 27	Marlborough Nomads	39	10	
Nov 3	Cambridge University	11	0	2,500
Nov 7	Hampstead Wanderers	23	9	
Nov 17	Devonport Albion	0	6	
Nov 24	Rosslyn Park	3	9	
Dec 15	Lennox	29	0	
Feb 2	United Services Portsmouth	30	14	
Mar 9	Old Alleynians	33	3	

1907/08

Date	Opponent			
Oct 5	Richmond	42	0	
Oct 12	London Scottish	13	3	2,000
Oct 19	Bath	49	8	
Nov 16	Rosslyn Park	16	3	2,000
Nov 23	Old Alleynians	32	3	
Nov 30	London Irish	31	0	
Dec 7	Marlborough Nomads	23	8	1,000
Dec 21	Blackheath	11	0	
Dec 26	Surbiton	31	3	
Dec 28	Old Merchistonians	21	13	
Feb 15	United Services Portsmouth	3	18	
Feb 29	London Hospital	3	20	
Mar 28	Old Merchant Taylors	17	13	3,000+

1908/09

Date	Opponent			
Sep 26	Old Merchant Taylors	53	5	
Oct 24	United Services Portsmouth	6	16	1,000
Oct 31	Cambridge University	5	22	3,000
Nov 7	Oxford University	8	28	5,000
Nov 21	Rosslyn Park	36	3	3,000
Dec 5	Marlborough Nomads	35	0	
Dec 26	Surbiton*	74	3	
Jan 23	London Scottish	8	5	
Jan 30	Blackheath	30	8	
Feb 20	Richmond	11	0	

Notes

All matches were friendlies

* Club Record Win

Twelve matches won in a row in the 1908/09 season between 21 November and 20 February (home and away). A club record that stood until 2005/06 season

Courtesy of Nick Cross

Appendix E

London Welsh RFC matches at the Field

Season	Opponents	Result F	A	Attendance
1909/10				
Sep 18	Glamorgan	6	3	4,000
Sep 25	Catford Bridge	9	5	1,000
Oct 2	Bristol	8	5	2,000
Oct 9	Old Whitgiftians	13	3	1,200
Oct 16	United Services	0	3	1,000
Oct 23	Middlesex Hospital	22	3	
Nov 6	Blackheath	9	9	4,000
Nov 13	Guy's Hospital	3	7	
Nov 27	London Irish	16	3	
Dec 18	Richmond	10	6	
Jan 8	Leicester	6	16	
Mar 5	Rosslyn Park	12	9	
Mar 19	Neath	8	6	4,000
1910/11				
Sep 17	Streatham	26	0	
Sep 24	Catford	16	0	
Oct 1	Torquay Athletic	0	0	
Oct 8	Bath	3	0	
Oct 26	St. Thomas's Hospital	13	0	
Oct 29	Old Merchant Taylors	3	3	
Nov 19	Northampton	0	11	
Dec 10	United Services	11	5	
Jan 7	Leicester	8	9	
Jan 21	Old Whitgiftians	24	5	
Feb 4	Oxford University	3	8	3,000
Feb 11	Guy's Hospital	8	3	
Feb 18	Cheltenham	13	0	
Mar 11	Blackheath	3	0	2,000
Mar 18	Ealing	17	14	
1911/12				
Sep 23	Catford Bridge	9	0	
Sep 30	Gloucester	0	13	
Oct 7	Pontypool	10	12	
Oct 14	United Services	8	11	
Oct 21	Bristol	0	9	
Oct 25	St. Thomas's Hospital	3	9	
Nov 11	Guy's Hospital	5	19	
Nov 15	Ealing	31	0	
Nov 18	Maoris	13	0	
Nov 25	Bedford	3	5	
Dec 2	Blackheath	15	5	
Dec 16	Richmond	5	0	
Dec 27	Upper Clapton	26	0	
Dec 30	London Irish	0	6	
Jan 13	Rosslyn Park	12	3	
Feb 17	Cheltenham	0	3	
Feb 21	Cambridge University	5	44	
Mar 2	London Hospital	13	5	
Mar 16	Old Whitgiftians	16	3	

A History of Trinity Fields

1912/13

Sep 21	Catford Bridge	11	8
Oct 5	Old Whitgiftians	8	16
Oct 12	United Services	12	11
Oct 19	Ealing	34	3
Oct 26	Old Merchant Taylors	0	33
Nov 2	London Irish	22	3
Nov 9	Guy's Hospital	11	3
Nov 16	Middlesex Hospital	29	11
Jan 11	Bedford	5	6
Jan 25	London Irish	9	6
Feb 8	Guy's Hospital	3	3
Feb 15	Cheltenham	0	6
Feb 22	Streatham	6	3
Mar 8	Blackheath	5	8

1913/14

Sep 20	Catford Bridge	31	15
Sep 27	Ealing	20	6
Oct 11	London Irish	5	8
Nov 1	Northampton	8	13
Nov 8	Guy's Hospital	5	13
Nov 22	Old Leysians	11	11
Dec 6	Blackheath	3	28
Dec 13	Richmond	0	18
Jan 10	Bedford	9	0
Feb 28	London Hospital	11	5
Mar 14	Rosslyn Park (match abandoned)	0	0

Match played in conjuction with London Irish

1913

Nov 12	London Celts v Middlesex	3	0

2nd XV matches not included

Appendices

Appendix F

London Irish RFC matches at the Field

Season	Opponents	F	A	Attendance
1912/13				
Nov 23	Royal Engineers	5	4	
Dec 21	London Welsh II	5	20	
Jan 18	United Services	15	3	
1913/14				
Sept 27	Civil Service	10	8	
Oct 4	Old Leysians	5	14	
Oct 11	London Welsh	8	5	
Oct 18	United Services	14	3	1,500
Oct 25	London Hospital	8	5	
Nov 29	Old Alleynians	11	0	
Dec 20	UCS Old Boys	27	5	
Jan 31	Old Merchant Taylors	3	5	
Feb 7	Bedford	3	0	
Feb 21	London Scottish	15	3	

Matches run in groundshare arrangement with London Welsh RFC

Appendix G

Heathfield C.C. Matches – Selected Results

Like many other clubs the reporting of Heathfield Cricket Club matches and results was somewhat patchy in the local press together with end of season batting and bowling averages. The below is a summary of various matches which have their own significance, one way or another. Although there are results going back as far as 1867 and scorecards too, as the club maintains that it was founded in 1875, none of those results is included here as examples.

Where a match was 'Won on first innings', this meant, that if applicable or by agreement the side batting second continued batting on after attaining the side batting first's total until 'time' had been called, or being dismissed. If not, the side batting second was declared the winner by the number of runs in excess of the side batting first it had reached when 'time' together with the number of wickets to fall at the end of play.

1876

26 August   Heathfield 89 Heron 71   Heathfield won by 18 runs

Earliest known scorecard since the foundation of the club in 1875. Played on Wandsworth Common, but probably on the original Heathfield ground.

1882

10 June   Aeolian 42 Heathfield 62   Heathfield won on first innings by 20 runs

A good win over a well-established club. Heathfield included a Rev J.H. Hodgson in their side, the only known reference to a vicar playing for the club who was dismissed without scoring. It has to be assumed that both sides agreed not to play a second innings to pursue a further result

7 August   Bexhill 97 & 86 Heathfield 82 & 24-5   Bexhill won by 15 runs

Part of a series of matches that Heathfield played against Bexhill on the south coast during the 1880s. Sufficient time existed to play a second innings. At close of play, Heathfield were a long way short of a winning target of 102 runs, so lost the match by being dismissed 15 runs short of their opponents score on the first innings.

1884

14 June   Heathfield 99 Kew 33   Heathfield won by 66 runs

Played at the Field – invariably known as Wandsworth Common by the Club in those days. Another good win against an established club.

28 June   Heathfield 139 Spencer 69   Heathfield won by 70 runs

Played at the Field with Heathfield achieving the double over Spencer having won the first match on 31 May by six wickets

26 July   Alleyns 66 Heathfield 70-1   Heathfield won by 9 wkts

Played at the Field. Alleyns are still active today and play SinjunGrammarians CC in League Cricket. Once Alleyns total was achieved apparently the two sides called it a day.

Appendices

1885

27 June   Heathfield 92 Thames Ditton 53   Heathfield won by 39 runs

A comfortable win at Giggs Hill Green against established opposition in a season which probably brought the best series of results for the club so far.

17,18 & 19 August   Heathfield 186 Private Banks 110   Heathfield won by 76 runs

Played at Catford Bridge over three evenings. Avenged a defeat suffered by the club in a similar format earlier in the season also at the Private Banks ground.

1887

2 July   Heathfield 167 Hampton Wick 107-3   Match Drawn

First recorded match played by Heathfield in Bushy Park.

1888

9 June   Heathfield 235 (A.F.W. Humm 103) Honor Oak 80-2   Match Drawn

Away to Honor Oak. First reported ton by a Heathfield player

30 June   Heathfield 69 Malden Wanderers 40   Heathfield won by 29 runs

A victory in a low scoring match at Malden Wanderers

21 July   Heathfield 60 East Molesey 21   Heathfield won by 39 runs

A second win of the season at East Molesey during the season. One of the lowest aggregate of runs- just 81 runs in total for the loss of 20 wkts!

1889

22 June   Heathfield 173-5 (dec) Dulwich 107-4   Match Drawn

A sound result against an established club. Probably first example of declaring an innings closed in a match involving Heathfield after the change in the Cricket Law to permit the same. The return match at Heathfield on 14 September saw O. Jones score 104 for Dulwich.

1890

14 August   Surrey C & G 71 & 257-5 Heathfield 17

         Surrey C &G won on first innings by 54 runs

Played at the Field. Not the best day for the club having bowled out Surrey Club & Ground relatively cheaply. Possibly the lowest score recorded by the Heathfield Cricket Club. Surrey Club & Ground however must have enjoyed their day as they resumed regular visits to the Field from 1895. Charles Mills, a future influential Heathfield member played for the Club & Ground in this match.

1891

20 June   Ibis 174 Heathfield 76   Ibis won by 98 runs

Played at the Field. A heavy defeat.

A History of Trinity Fields

1893

3 June   Heathfield 219 -2 (dec) (M. Humm 101*) Spencer 105

                     Heathfield won by 114 runs

Another Humm gets a ton. An overwhelming victory for the Club.

1897

19 June   Heathfield 297-5 (dec) (F. Morel 104*) Honor Oak 170-3   Match Drawn

An improvement on the loss of the first fixture played at the Field earlier in the season. Ton for Morel against a side reckoned at the time to be the strongest in South London.

1902

29 July   London County Cricket Club 264-3 (dec) Heathfield 188-4   Match Drawn

See separate scorecard. Played at the Field. The match in which WG Grace scored 137*. Part of a sequence of matches played by the club with London County. London County Cricket Club were regarded as a first-class County between 1900-1904.

1904

23 May   Heathfield 96 & 127 Surrey C & G 66 & 31-1

                  Heathfield won on first innings by 30 runs.

Having batted first at the Field, Heathfield then shot out the opposition, including Jack Hobbs, for a mere 66, the Club & Ground's lowest innings total in the series of matches with the club. Heathfield winning by 30 runs.

18 June   Mitcham 104 & 157-6 (dec) Heathfield 145-9 (dec) & 85-1

                Heathfield won on first innings by 41 runs & 1 wkt

Played on Mitcham Green in the very first year of Mitcham's new pavilion! Mitcham presumably declared their second innings in an attempt to win the match, having trailed on first innings in this all day match.

25 June   Heathfield 163-8 (dec) Ealing 53   Heathfield won by 110 runs

Played at the Field. A convincing win against a well-known club

1905

24 April   Ashford 75 & 37 Heathfield 132   Heathfield won by an innings and 20 runs

Played at the Field, A reasonably rare result of a win by an innings. Heathfield batted second and still had time to dismiss Ashford twice.

1906

11 August   Heathfield 69 Mitcham 409-7 Mitcham won on first innings by 340 runs & 3 wkts

An embarrassing loss on Mitcham Green in what was an indifferent season. Probably the club's heaviest defeat.

1912

22 June   Heathfield A 190 Battersea A 218 Battersea A won on first innings by 28 runs

Played at Battersea Park in front of a reported crowd of over 4,000. Not bad for a 2nd XI match!

Appendices

1913

1 August   Heathfield 450-7 (dec) Mr A.E. Henderson's XI 148   Heathfield won by 302 runs

A ground record innings score at the Field, with W.E, Fuller leading the way with 109. H.W. Weaver, E.G. Read and F.W. Jackson all scored half centuries. Weaver (again), Mills and Hawkins combined to share the wickets between them to record a resounding win.

1914

29 July   Heathfield 327-9 (dec) Surrey Club & Ground 198   Heathfield won by 129 runs

First win by the club for ten years in a Cricket Week victory against Surrey Club & Ground at the Field. Charles Mills took five wickets, against his former county of twenty- five years ago!

22 August   Wycombe House 206-9 (dec) Heathfield A 112-8   Match Drawn

Last reported match at the Field in the 1914 season, after war was declared on 4 August 1914.

1915

31 July   Heathfield 245-1 (dec) Clapham Ramblers 131-6   Match Drawn

At the Field. Some fine hitting by Ernie Read (142) and H.W. Weaver, secured a formidable total, but the visitors played out time.

1916

24 June   Heathfield 421-8 (dec) Catford 64   Heathfield won by 357 runs

The margin of victory is the largest at the Field. Another century for wicketkeeper/ batsman Ernie Read (131). Others also joined in the fun! Catford won the return match later in the season!

15 July   Heathfield 215 Third Scots Guards 120   Heathfield won by 95 runs

One of the matches during the war with a "military" flavour, although not all these matches ended in victory!

1920

6 August   Heathfield 159 Horsham 132   Heathfield won by 27 runs

A good win on the club's first visit to Horsham on tour against one of the stronger Sussex clubs. Lost heavily the following year

1923

1 July   Lyons v Heathfield

Result not reported but played away from the Field. First Sunday match to be played by the Club.

1924

13 September   North London 108 Heathfield 106-8   Match Drawn

Last reported match that the club played, away at Crouch End. Finished in a tense draw after rain interruptions.

Appendix H

HEATHFIELD CC v HERON CC

Scorecard of a match played at Wandsworth Common on Saturday 26 August 1876

First known documented scorecard after the 1875 establishment

Heathfield CC
Only Innings

		How Out	
1	Mason	b Powell	17
2	Barlow	c E. Smith b Powell	15
3	Hance	b Powell	22
4	Larkins	b Powell	0
5	Hicks	b Baker	6
6	Stutfield	b Baker	14
7	Wakeman	c C.Sherring b Kinns	6
8	Muny	c Patten b Powell	4
9	Pullen	b Baker	0
10	Watson	not out	0
11	Herring	run out	0
	Extras		5
		All out	**89**

Heron CC
Only Innings

		How Out	
1	King	b Mason	2
2	Patten	b Hance	0
3	Powell	b Hance	7
4	Baker	run out	1
5	Kinns	c Mason b Hance	11
6	C. Sherring	run out	0
7	F. Smith	c Larkins b Barlow	6
8	F. Sherring	b Hance	1
9	E. Smith	not out	12
10	H. Smith	st Hicks b Mason	2
11	Ethrington	c Barlow b Larkins	0
	Extras		29
		All out	**71**

RESULT : HEATHFIELD CC WON BY 18 RUNS

Courtesy of South London Press

Appendices

Appendix I

HEATHFIELD CC v LONDON COUNTY CC

Scorecard of a match played on the Field between Heathfield CC and London County CC on Tuesday 29 July 1902

London County Cricket Club
Only Innings

		How Out	
1	W.G. Grace	not out	137
2	R. Haywood	c Fuller b J.C. Adams	32
3	Woolven	b J.C. Adams	1
4	W.L. Murdoch	LBW b Paice	60
5	H. Murch	not out	30
	Extras		4
		3 wkts (dec)	**264**

Did Not Bat
C. Wood
W. Smith
E. Ford
Covell
J. Campbell
R. Kenward

Heathfield Cricket Club
Only Innings

		How Out	
1	C. Mills	b Kenward	23
2	J.C. Adams	b Kenward	57
3	F. Morel	b Kenward	82
4	W. Fuller	b Kenward	0
5	G Adams	not out	18
6	T. Brewer	not out	2
	Extras		6
		4 wkts	**188**

Did Not Bat
W. Paice
E. Hyem
P.Baxter
J. Wasp
Ream

RESULT: MATCH DRAWN

Courtesy of South London Press

189

Appendix J

HEATHFIELD CC v MR. A. E. HENDERSON'S XI

Record of match played at the Field on 1 August 1913

Heathfield total believed to be a ground record score

Heathfield C.C
Only Innings

		How Out	
1	W.E, Fuller	b Davis	109
2	H.W. Weaver	c Abbott b Henderson	81
3	M.A.Jackson	b Davis	33
4	G. Swift	run out	21
5	R.J.J. Gunner	c sub b Blogg	13
6	E.G. Read	b Henderson	52
7	M.S.McFarlane	run out	0
8	C.N.Hawkins	not out	47
9	F.W.Jackson	not out	53
	Extras		41
		7 wkts (dec)	**450**

Did Not Bat
C. Mills
F.M. Swancott

Mr. A.E. Henderson's XI
Only Innings

All out   148

RESULT: HEATHFIELD CC WON BY 302 RUNS

Courtesy of Sporting Life

Appendix K

LONDON CLUBS v SOUTH AFRICANS

Scorecard of a match played at the Field between the London Clubs and South Africans on Wednesday 17th September 1924

London Clubs
Only Innings

		How Out	
1	W.T. Cook	lbw b Nupen	34
2	W.G. Tarrant	b Carter	15
3	C .Shaw Baker	b Nupen	38
4	A. Jeacocke	lbw b Carter	14
5	A. Peach	c Nourse b Nupen	0
6	A. Perry	c Saggers b Meintjes	7
7	F. Bullock	run out	12
8	E.J. Sullivan	b Meintjes	0
9	A.W. Randall	c Hearne b Nourse	24
10	B.E.Shales	c & b Nourse	4
11	T. Knight	not out	2
12	M.C.Bird	st Hearne b Carter	0
	Extras		11
		All out	**161**

Bowling

Meintjes	2 for 38
Hearne	0 for 21
Nupen	3 for 41
Carter	3 for 43
Nourse	2 for 7

South Africans
Only Innings

		How Out	
1	J.M.M. Commaille	b Peach	15
2	G.A.L. Hearne	c Sullivan b Peach	2
3	T. Herbert	st Knight b Randall	9
4	E.P. Nupen	c Bird b Shaw Baker	11
5	T. Meintjes	b Randall	8
6	C.P. Carter	c Jeacocke b Shaw Baker	0
7	S.J. Pegler	st Knight b Shaw Baker	0
8	J.A. Saggers	run out	6
9	A.D. Nourse	c & b Randall	2
10	Ritz	not out	0
11	M.J. Susskind	Absent	0
	Extras		2
		All out	**55**

Bowling

Shales	0 for 2
Peach	2 for 19
Randall	3 for 15
Shaw Baker	3 for 17

LONDON CLUBS WON BY 106 RUNS

Attendance 2,000

Courtesy of Wandsworth Borough News

Appendix L

OLD GRAMMARIANS CC v D.M. SMITH'S XI

Scorecard of a match played at the Field between Old Grammarians CC and D.M. Smith's XI on 27 September 1987

D.M. Smith's XI
Only Innings

		How Out		
1	David Ward	c & b Tray		1
2	Jack Richards	b Amos		1
3	Neal Radford	c Gershkoff b Amos		0
4	Steve Gritt	b Gershkoff		124
5	Alec Stewart	b Gardiner		5
6	David Smith	st Tushingham b Gershkoff		59
7	Trevor Jesty	c Phipps b Gardiner		21
8	Steve Thompson	b Wilson		10
9	Tony Trick	b Wilson		7
10	Mark Feltham	not out		12
11	Ian Greig	not out		1
	Extras			21
	40 overs	9 wkts (innings closed)		**262**

Old Grammarians Cricket Club
Only Innings

		How Out		
1	Andy Frost	b Feltham		0
2	Greg Purnell	b Thompson		1
3	Keith Tushingham	c Ward b Greig		61
4	Nick Phipps	c Thompson b Greig		27
5	Simon Tray	b Radford		55
6	Alan Millhouse	b Radford		13
7	Mervin Amos	c Feltham b Stewart		2
8	Mick Meyer	b Thompson		18
9	Tony Gardiner	b Radford		9
10	Gary Wilson	b Ward		16
11	Tony Fretwell	not out		32
12	Glenn Gershkoff	not out		2
	Extras			19
	40 overs		10 wkts	**255**

Toss. By arrangement, D.M Smith's XI batted first

Twelve to bat. Eleven to field

RESULT: D.M.SMITH'S XI WON BY 7 RUNS

Appendix M

SINJUNGRAMMARIANS CC 2nd XI v WARLINGHAM CC 2ndXI

Innings of a 2nd XI match played at the field between SinjunGrammarians CC 2nd XI v Warlingham CC 2nd XI on Saturday 11th August 2012

Highest known league cricket innings score recorded at the Field

SinjunGrammarians won the toss and batted

SinjunGramarians 2ndXI

		How Out	
1	Raza Khan	c Fuller b Khalique	107
2	Gaurang Vyas	b Aleem	36
3	Zeeshan Chaudhry	b J.C. Adams	86
4	Kash Malik	c & b Mirza	9
5	Zohaib Sheikh	c Bashir b Hussain	89
6	Asim Hafeez	st Sherwani b Fuller	31
7	Nadeem Malik	b Khan	2
8	Faheem Abbas	b Hussain	19
9	Sakib Shafi	not out	0
10	Adil Lateef	not out	3
	Extras		48
	50 overs	8 wkts (innings closed)	**430**

Did Not Bat
Dharmesh Vaghela

Warlingham 2ndXI

30.5 overs		All Out	156

RESULT: SINJUNGRAMMARIANS CC 2nd XI WON BY 274 RUNS

Courtesy of Play-Cricket

Appendix N

Matches against Surrey Representative XIs (all played at the Field)

v Heathfield CC

1890 Surrey Club & Ground 71 & 257-5 Heathfield 17 Surrey C & G won on first inns by 54 runs

1895 Heathfield 160; Surrey Club & Ground 152   Heathfield won by 8 runs

1896 Surrey Club & Ground 87 & 107-4(dec); Heathfield 111 & 48-2 Heathfield won on first inns by 24 runs

1897 Surrey Colts 103 & 102; Heathfield 78 & 13-1 Surrey Colts won on first inns by 25 runs

1900 Heathfield 80 & 70-3; Surrey Club & Ground 179 Surrey C & G won on first inns by 99 runs

1901 Surrey Club & Ground 194 & 62-1; Heathfield 127 Surrey C & G won on first inns by 67 runs

1902 Surrey Club & Ground 90; Heathfield 94   Heathfield won on first inns by 4 runs

1903 Heathfield 84 & 75-6; Surrey Club & Ground 87   Surrey C & G won on first inns by 3 runs

1904 Heathfield 96 & 127; Surrey Club & Ground 66 & 31-1 Heathfield won on first inns by 30 runs

1905 Surrey Club & Ground 106 & 29-1; Heathfield 69 Surrey C & G won on first inns by 37 runs

1906 Heathfield 184; Surrey Club & Ground 212-6 Surrey C & G won on first inns by 28 runs & 4 wkts.

1907 Surrey Club & Ground 200; Heathfield 84 Surrey C & G won on first inns by 116 runs

1908 Heathfield 155; Surrey Club & Ground 255 Surrey C & G won on first inns by 100 runs

1909 Surrey Club & Ground 123-3   Match Abandoned as a Draw

1910 Heathfield 114 & 79-3; Surrey Club & Ground 182 Surrey C & G won on first inns by 68 runs

1911 Surrey Club & Ground 328-9(dec); Heathfield 192 Surrey C & G won on first inns by 136 runs

1912 Surrey Club & Ground 259; Heathfield 162-9 Match Drawn

1913 Heathfield 190: Surrey Club & Ground 200 Surrey C & G won on first inns by 10 runs

1914 Heathfield 327-9 (dec); Surrey Club & Ground 198 Heathfield won by 129 runs

1921* Surrey Club & Ground 254: Heathfield 243-9 Match Drawn

1922* Heathfield 144; Surrey Club & Ground 161-4 Surrey C & G won on first inns by 17 runs & 6 wkts.

1923 Heathfield 159-5 Match Abandoned as a Draw

*Probably played at the Field, but record states 'Upper Tooting'.

v Old Sinjuns CC

1977 Surrey Club & Ground 235-6 (dec); Old Sinjuns 113   Surrey C & G won by 122 runs

1978 Surrey Club & Ground 174-5 (dec); Old Sinjuns 173-7   Match Drawn

1979 Surrey Club & Ground 248-8 (dec); Old Sinjuns 208-9   Match Drawn (rain)

1980 Surrey Club & Ground 223-2 (dec); Old Sinjuns 137 Surrey Club & Ground won by 85 runs

Courtesy of Surrey County Cricket Club Yearbooks

Appendix O

International Sportsmen at the Field

Cricketers (Test players only)

The most famous of all cricketers, W.G. Grace, played several times at the Field representing London County Cricket Club against the Heathfield Club. Indeed, on 29 July 1902 when W.G. Grace (at the age of 54) made a century at the Field (137*) there were no less than seven players in that eleven with first class cricket experience. In total Grace played 22 Test matches for England between 1880 and 1899. Apart from Grace, although not exhaustive, the following Test players are known to have played at the Field. Country represented, if not England, in brackets, dates, and caps awarded. This list is not exhaustive, but is based upon known information.

Ashfaq Ahmed (Pakistan) *(1993 ; 1 Test)*

Morice Bird *(1910-1914 ; 10 Tests)*

Walter Bradley *(1899; 2 Tests)*

Cyril Browne (West Indies) *(1928 – 1929 ; 4 Tests)*

Michael Carberry *(2009-2013 ; 6 Tests)*

Claude Carter (South Africa) *(1912-1924; 10 Tests)*

J.M.M 'Mick' Commaille (South Africa) *(1909-1927; 12 Tests)*

Ross Edwards (Australia) *(1972-1975 ; 20 Tests)*

Harry Elliott *(1927-1933 ; 4 Tests)*

George Hearne (South Africa) *(1922-1924 ; 3 Tests)*

(Sir) Jack Hobbs *(1907-1930 ; 61 Tests) CY 1909, 1926*

David Hookes (Australia) *(1976-1985 ; 23 Tests)*

Ian Greig *(1982 ; 2 Tests)*

Walter Lees *(1905 ; 5 Tests) CY 1906*

Douglas Meintjes (South Africa) *(1922 ; 2 Tests)*

Charles Mills+ (South Africa) *(1891 ; 1 Test)*

W.L. 'Billy' Murdoch (Australia)* *(1877-1892; 19 Tests)*

Ali Naqvi (Pakistan) (1997 ; 5 Tests)

A.W. 'Dave' Nourse (South Africa) *(1902-1924; 45 Tests)*

E.P. 'Buster' Nupen (South Africa) *(1921-1935 ; 17 Tests)*

Jack O'Connor *(1929 ; 4 Tests)*

Sidney Pegler (South Africa) *(1909-1924 ; 16 Tests)*

Ray Price (Zimbabwe) *(1999-2012 ; 22 Tests)*

A.C. 'Jack' Russell *(1920-22 ; 10 Tests)* CY 1923

Neal Radford *(1986-1987 ; 3 Tests)*

C.J. 'Jack' Richards *(1986-1988 ; 8 Tests)*

Tom Richardson *(1893-1897 ; 14 Tests)* CY 1897

Graham Roope *(1973-1978 ; 21 Tests)*

Andy Sandham *(1921-1929 ; 14 Tests)* CY 1923

Mike Selvey *(1976 ; 3 Tests)*

David M Smith *(1985 ; 2 Tests)*

Alec Stewart *(1989 -2003 ; 133 Tests)* CY 1993

Micky Stewart *(1962 - 1963 ; 8 Tests)* CY 1958

Herbert Strudwick *(1909-1926 ; 28 Tests)* CY 1912

Manfred Susskind (South Africa) *(1924 ; 5 tests)*

Alex Tudor *(1998 -2002 ;10 tests)*

*Played in the match with WG Grace in 1902. Also played for England in the only test of the 1891/1892 tour to South Africa.

+ Charles Mills played for Heathfield from around 1898 until 1917 and also in the 1902 match against London County Cricket Club. Although he played one Test match in 1891 for South Africa and toured with the 1894 South Africans in which no Test match was played, he was born and died in England.

CY =*Wisden* Cricketer of the Year and date.

Rugby Players

The following players are known to have played at the Field, but the list is not exhaustive, but is based on reports. Country represented, if not England, in brackets, dates, and caps awarded.

Willie Arnold (Wales) (1903; 1 cap)

John Birkett (1906-1912; 21 caps)

Reginald Birkett (1871; 1 cap)

C.C. Bryden (1875-1877; 2 caps)

Henry Bryden (1874; 1 cap)

Vincent Cartwright (1903-1906 ; 14 caps)

John Daniell (1899-1904 ; 7 caps)

Rev J Alban Davies (Wales) (1913-1914; 7 caps)

Ted Dillon (1904-1905; 4 caps)

Nigel Fletcher (1901-1903; 4 caps)

'Reggie' Gibbs (Wales) (1906-1911; 16 caps)

Arthur Harding+ (Wales) (1902-1908; 20 caps)

Bob Hiller* (1968 -1972; 19 caps)

John 'Jack' Jenkins # (Wales) (1909; 1 cap)

Thomas Kelly (1906-1908 ; 12 caps)

Douglas 'Daniel' Lambert (1907-1911 ;7 caps)

Clem Lewis (Wales) (1912-1923 ; 11 caps)

Roy MacGregor (Scotland) (1909 ;1 cap)

'Hop' Maddocks (Wales) (1906-1910 ; 6 caps)

Percy Nicholson (Ireland) (1900 ; 3 caps)

Ronnie Paulton (1909-1914 ; 17 caps)

John Raphael ~ (1905-1906 ; 4 caps)

Shirley Reynolds (1900-1901; 4 caps)

James 'Jimmy' Ross (Scotland) (1901-1903 ; 5 caps)

Herbert Sibree (1908-1909 ; 3 caps)

Adrian Stoop (1905-1912 ; 15 caps)

F.M. 'Tim' Stoop (1910 -1913 ; 4 caps)

Percy Stout (1898 – 1899 ; 5 caps)

Bert Winfield (Wales) (1903-1908 ; 15 caps)

*Played cricket against Old Sinjuns CC for Bec Old Boys.

+ Also Great Britain (Lions) 1904 & 1908 3 caps to Australia & New Zealand

~Also Great Britain (Lions) 1910 1 cap to Argentina

Rugby League Cap

Footballers

The following players are known to have played at the Field but the list is not exhaustive and is based on known information. Country represented, if not England in brackets when, and "caps" awarded.

Norman Bailey (1878 -1887; 19 caps)

Reginald Birkett (1879; 1 cap)

Bobby Brown* (1959-1961; 14 caps)

Walter Buchanan (1876; 1 cap)

Edgar Field (1876-1881; 2 caps)

Thomas Fitchie ~ (Scotland) (1905-1907;4 caps)

Richard Greaves (1875; 1 cap)

Tony Kay (1963; 1 cap)

James ('Jamie') Lawrence (Jamaica) (2000-2004; 24 caps)

Robert Ogilvie (1874;1 cap)

James Prinsep (1880 : 1 cap)

Leroy Rosenior (Sierra Leone) (1993; 1 cap)

John Robertson+ (1962-1969;25 caps)

Francis Sparks (1879-1880; 3 caps)

*Also three caps for Great Britain at 1960 Olympics

+ Also seven caps for Great Britain – including five caps at Olympics

~Played cricket with Heathfield CC

Amateur Internationals in Italics

Appendices

Appendix P

Old Sinjuns Cricket Club Captains

1920-21 & 1923-25	L.G. Bolt
1922	B.C. Jones
1926	G.A. Pepper
1927	F.G. Collins
1928	F.G. Thorn
1929-39,1946-50 & 1952-56	G.O. Davies
1951	R.V. Butler
1957-61	O.C.W. Cooper
1962,1966-73,1977 &1983	V.J. Landon
1963-65	J. McIntyre
1974-76	M.C. Britnell
1978- 80	B.S. Dale
1981-82	K.J. Sheehan
1984	M.J. Faircloth
1985	J.I. Mills
1986-89	P.K. Wheeler
1990-92	R.F. Brighton
1991	Z. Mohamed
1993-96	B.T. Williams
1997	P. Lang
1998-99	P. Weston
2000-02	S. Sheikh
2003	K. Molloy
2004-05	N. Raja

Appendix Q

Old Grammarians Cricket Club Captains

1926 -29	G.A. Harding
1930 -31	P.C. Smith
1932- 39 & 1947-55	L.G. Merrett
1946	F.S. Manning
1956	J.S. King
1957-58	L.H. Hockin
1959-60 &1963-65	D. Smith
1961-62	A.B. Palmer
1966-69 &1973-76	D.J. Lawrence
1970-71 &1981	A. Millhouse
1972	H.S. Garrard
1977	C.R. Hicks
1978-80	T. Withers
1982-85	G. Gershkoff
1986-89 & 1991	N. Phipps
1990	D. Ludford
1992; 1995;1998-99	S. Batley
1993-94:1996-97;2000-01 ;2003	S. Wilson
2002	A. Rehman
2004-05	S. Baker

Appendix R

SinjunGrammarians Cricket Club Captains

2006-07	Steve Baker
2008-10	Simon Wild
2011	Andrew Stocks
2012-13	Shaf Malik
2014	Ross De Gannes
2015	Ahmed Khan
2016	Kash Malik
2017-20	Abu Bakr Malik
2021-	Zohaib Sheikh

Appendix S

Old Boys Football History Notes

Old Sinjuns

(Originally the Former Pupils of Sir Walter St John's Grammar School. Closed 1986)

Established 1920.

1920 Elected to Surrey Junior League.

1923 Elected to Old Boys' League.

1971 Winners AFA (Surrey) Senior Cup.

1976 Winners London Old Boys Veterans Cup.

2002 Elected to the Amateur Football Alliance after reorganisation of leagues.

2005 Merged with Old Grammarians AFC.

International Players to have represented the club: James (Jamie) Lawrence (Jamaica)

Old Grammarians

(Originally the Former Pupils of Battersea Grammar School. Closed 1977).

Established 1902

1912 Defeated Clapham Rovers (FA Cup Winners in 1879/80).

1919 Elected to Old Boys' League.

1937 Winners Old Boys League. Elected to Southern Olympian League.

1976 Winners Old Boys Cup (Arthur Dunn).

1979 Winners London Old Boys Cup (Old Sinjuns were Runners Up).

1980 Winners London Old Boys Cup. Winners AFA Senior Cup.

1982 Winners Southern Olympian League. Winners AFA Senior Cup.

1987 Winners Southern Olympian League. Winners Southern Olympian League Cup.

2002 Elected to the Amateur Football Alliance after reorganisation of leagues.

2005 Winners AFA Veterans Cup Winners. Merged with Old Sinjuns.

International Players to have represented the club: Leroy Rosenior (Sierra Leone)

Appendices

Appendix T

List of Groundsmen at the Field

Year		Year		Year	
1878	Unknown	1926	F. Martin	1974	Mick Meech
1879	Unknown	1927	F. Martin	1975	Ivor Fry
1880	Unknown	1928	F. Martin	1976	Ivor Fry
1881	Unknown	1929	F. Martin	1977	Peter Horne
1882	Unknown	1930	F. Martin	1978	Peter Horne
1883	Unknown	1931	F. Martin	1979	Peter Horne
1884	E. Martin	1932	F. Martin	1980	Peter Montgomery
1885	E. Martin	1933	F. Martin	1981	Peter Montgomery
1886	E. Martin	1934	F. Martin	1982	Peter Montgomery
1887	E. Martin	1935	F. Martin	1983	Peter Montgomery
1888	E. Martin	1936	F. Martin	1984	Richard Bacon
1889	E. Martin	1937	F. Martin	1985	Richard Bacon
1890	E. Martin	1938	F. Martin	1986	Steve Irons
1891	E. Martin	1939	F. Martin	1987	Steve Irons
1892	E. Martin	1940	Council	1988	Steve Irons
1893	E. Martin	1941	Council	1989	Steve Irons
1894	E. Martin	1942	Council	1990	Steve Irons
1895	E. Martin	1943	Council	1991	Steve Irons
1896	E. Martin	1944	Council	1992	Steve Irons
1897	E. Martin	1945	Council	1993	Steve Irons
1898	E. Martin	1946	SWSJ School	1994	Steve Irons
1899	E. Martin	1947	SWSJ School	1995	Council sub contracted
1900	E. Collett	1948	SWSJ School	1996	Tony Bird
1901	E. Collett	1949	SWSJ School	1997	Tony Bird
1902	E. Collett	1950	SWSJ School	1998	Tony Bird
1903	E. Collett	1951	Council	1999	Tony Bird
1904	F. Martin	1952	Council	2000	John Doe
1905	F. Martin	1953	Lewis	2001	John Doe
1906	F. Martin	1954	Lewis	2002	John Doe
1907	F. Martin	1955	Lewis	2003	John Doe
1908	F. Martin	1956	Lewis	2004	John Doe
1909	F. Martin	1957	Lewis	2005	Mick Meech
1910	F. Martin	1958	Council	2006	Mick Meech
1911	Shepherd	1959	Council	2007	Mick Meech
1912	Shepherd	1960	Council	2008	Mick Meech
1913	Shepherd	1961	Council	2009	Mick Meech
1914	Littlewood	1962	Council	2010	Mick Meech
1915	Littlewood	1963	Tom White	2011	Mick Meech
1916	F. Martin	1964	Tom White	2012	Mick Meech
1917	F. Martin	1965	Tom White	2013	Andrew Crawford
1918	F. Martin	1966	Tom White	2014	Andrew Crawford
1919	F. Martin	1967	Tom White	2015	Jason Gill
1920	F. Martin	1968	Tom White	2016	Jason Gill
1921	F. Martin	1969	Tom White	2017	Jason Gill
1922	F. Martin	1970	Tom White	2018	Jason Gill
1923	F. Martin	1971	Don Abbott	2019	Jason Gill
1924	F. Martin	1972	Mick Meech	2020	Tony Reely
1925	F. Martin	1973	Mick Meech	2021	Tony Reely

All groundsmen incumbent as at 1 January each year

Notes   Prior to 1924 Groundsman appointed by the Heathfield club
1925-1939 & 1946-1949 Appointed by the School at SWSJ end
1926-1939 and possibly 1946-50, A. Heather groundsman at BGS end of ground
1940-1945 Council likely to have maintained the Field during WW2
1939-1945 Battersea Grammar End of field used as barrage balloon site
1951-1967 Groundsman appointed by the London County Council
From 1967 until 1995 Groundsman appointmented by ILEA
Cricket Club Appointment in 1996.
Groundsman appointed by Trinity Fields Trust since 1997

Acknowledgements

There are many people and organisations I would like to thank in the production of this book if not specifically mentioned in it. Firstly, I would like to mention Roy McNamara who was responsible for the editing and the additional material contained in the publication of *A History of Sir Walter St John's School Battersea 1700-1986* by Frank T. Smallwood. Roy's advice and guidance in the early stages including directing me to files I should access at the London Metropolitan Archives was invaluable. Also, to Mark Dyer, Captain of the Heathfield Bowls Club, for allowing me to rummage through information in their store and giving me permission to take away long forgotten minute books for my research, which helped me understand the basics of the Field's sporting history during the Heathfield cricket club's years. Also, I would like to thank archivist Peter Camden and Martin Faircloth at Sinjuns for their assistance, and the considerable amount of information on the Old Grammarians website which proved to be such a valuable source of information during the lockdown, together with their magazine editor Simon Hooberman. Then there were visits to Godalming Museum, the Archives at Twickenham Rugby Stadium to research the Stoop family papers, and the Surrey County Cricket Club Library at the Oval. Don Shelley and the Club Cricket Conference also need a mention here. It was during this process, if I had not realised before, that this book would be far more than an extended pamphlet! A subscription to the British Library Newspaper Archives also paid dividends. Most of my visits were to the Wandsworth Heritage Archives at Battersea Library, and I thank Emma Anthony and Sofia Akram for putting up with me there, and to the Association of Cricket Statisticians and Historians for their advice and access to the *Cricket* magazine which was published between 1882 and 1914.

Thanks also to all those individuals who gave up their time. Steve Kersley at Spencer CC helped in my understanding of how, logistically, things might have worked in the early days. Local historian Philip Boys, whose knowledge of the area knows no bounds and together with the Wandsworth Historical Society and the Friends of Wandsworth Common who are planning events to celebrate the 150th Anniversary of the Wandsworth Common Act. I was invited to the launch of their book, *The Wandsworth Common Story* which was released in May 2021. Others include Nick Cross and Rob Cavallini for their permission to publish historical results for the Harlequins and the Casuals respectively from their own publications, and also to Rob Dale from the 'Historic Don' for his help and suggestions, and to the Trinity Fields Trust (particularly Virginia Priest and Sarah Parsons) for understanding and realising the importance and historical significance of the Field in the early days of amateur sport, which is now under the Trust's care.

I must also thank BBC's Amol Rajan for taking time to write the Foreword to this book given his obvious affinity for the Field on which he played his cricket. Thanks also goes to Chris Evans for his technical assistance with the cover design and pictures, Andy Collier for his advice in self-publishing this book and Roger Packham for his suggestions, support and proof reading and for correcting my elementary English, reminding me that I cannot qualify the word 'unique'. Finally, to Roger Severn at Aquatint Ltd and his staff for their enthusiasm and tolerance in getting this book across the line for me.

If I have missed anyone in the background who should be mentioned here, they know who they are. I thank them for their interest and for putting me on the right course.

Graham R Jackson   June 2021

Bibliography

Further to the publications mentioned in the Acknowledgements, I also used selected information from the following books as a basis of my research. My thanks to all the publications below for providing me with the inspiration and information to make this book into what it is today.

50 Years of Football 1884-1934 – Sir Frederick Wall

A Brief History of the Woodfield Estate and Woodfield Recreation Ground

A Casual Affair – A History of the Casuals Football Club – Rob Cavallini

Britain's Lost Cricket Grounds – Chris Arnot

County Cricket: Sundry Extras- David Jeater

Cricket at the Crystal Palace- Brian Pearce

Cricket Match Report North London v Heathfield – Hornsey Historical Society

Dragon in Exile – The Centenary History of London Welsh RFC. – Paul Beken & Stephen Jones

Harlequins. The First 150 Years – Nick Cross

Heathfield Club Minute Book 1913-1920

Heathfield Club Ltd Minute Book 1924-1933

Heathfield Club Tennis Section Minute Book 1920-1929

Kim Simmonds Family Genealogy

My Cricket Memories – J.B. Hobbs

Nunquam Dormio, 150 Years of Harlequins – Brendan Gallagher

Old Sinjuns Cricket Club 75th Anniversary Commemorative Brochure

Survey of London 2013 (Draft) – English Heritage

The First Hundred Years of the Heathfield Club – Bill Cormack

The Wisden Book of Cricketers Lives – Benny Green

The Wandsworth Common Story- The Friends of Wandsworth Common

UK–21's Degenerate Gamblers Pages

Wisden

Picture Credits

My thanks to all those who have contributed pictures and illustrations for inclusion within this book. I have ackowledged the sources of such pictures where known, but special mention is due to the Old Grammarians Association for freely making their website available for the purpose. As the Author, all reasonable efforts have been made to contact copyright holders for permission and apologies are made for any omissions or errors in the form of credits given, Corrections may be made to future printings.